Microsoft® SharePoint® Designer 2010

Step by Step

Penelope Coventry

Microsoft

Microsoft® SharePoint® Designer 2010

Step by Step

Penelope Coventry

ISBN: 978-0-7356-2733-8

2 3 4 5 6 7 8 9 10 11 TG 6 5 4 3 2 1

Printed and bound in Canada.

Microsoft Press titles may be purchased for educational, business or sales promotional use. Online editions are also available for most titles (*http://my.safaribooksonline.com*). For more information, contact our corporate/institutional sales department: (800) 998-9938 or *corporate@oreilly.com*. Visit our website at *microsoftpress.oreilly.com*. Send comments to *mspinput@ microsoft.com*.

Microsoft, Microsoft Press, ActiveX, Excel, FrontPage, Internet Explorer, PowerPoint, SharePoint, Webdings, Windows, and Windows 7 are either registered trademarks or trademarks of Microsoft Corporation in the United States and/or other countries. Other product and company names mentioned herein may be the trademarks of their respective owners.

Unless otherwise noted, the example companies, organizations, products, domain names, e-mail addresses, logos, people, places, and events depicted herein are fictitious, and no association with any real company, organization, product, domain name, e-mail address, logo, person, place, or event is intended or should be inferred.

This book expresses the author's views and opinions. The information contained in this book is provided without any express, statutory, or implied warranties. Neither the author, O'Reilly Media, Inc., Microsoft Corporation, nor their respective resellers or distributors, will be held liable for any damages caused or alleged to be caused either directly or indirectly by such information.

Acquisitions and Development Editors: Juliana Aldous and Kenyon Brown
Production Editor: Rachel Monaghan
Copy Editor: John Pierce
Technical Reviewers: Sara Windhorst and Marlene Lanphier
Proofreader: Nancy Sixsmith
Indexer: Ginny Munroe
Cover Designer: Karen Montgomery
Compositor: Nellie McKesson
Illustrator: Robert Romano

[2011-08-05]

This book is dedicated to the memory of my goddaughter, Nia Kate Griffiths, who died at the age of 21. She suffered from cystic fibrosis, and although she was relatively fit all her life, the last four years were tough on her. No matter how ill she was or the number of visits to the hospital she had to endure, she was always a happy person and a treasure to know.

She will be missed.

Contents

Part 1   Getting Started with Microsoft SharePoint Designer 2010

What do you think of this book? We want to hear from you!

Microsoft is interested in hearing your feedback so we can continually improve our books and learning resources for you. To participate in a brief online survey, please visit:

microsoft.com/learning/booksurvey

Part 2 Working with Information

What do you think of this book? We want to hear from you!

Microsoft is interested in hearing your feedback so we can continually improve our books and learning resources
for you. To participate in a brief online survey, please visit:

microsoft.com/learning/booksurvey

Acknowledgments

I want to thank my husband for his continued support while I wrote yet another book. I don't know why I write books. This one should have been easier; however, they are never easy and place a considerable amount of strain on my personal and professional life. Yet again, I ignored my husband and my dog, Poppy, but they still love me and are pleased to see me in those odd moments when I leave my computer. I don't understand why I'm so lucky to have both of them in my life.

I'd like to thank Kenyon Brown (O'Reilly Media Senior Content Development Editor), Rachel Monaghan (O'Reilly Media Senior Production Editor), John Pierce (copy editor), Sara Windhorst (technical reviewer), Marlene Lanphier (technical reviewer), and all the other people who kept me on track and provided such excellent suggestions.

I would like to include a special thanks to my contributing authors, Nikander and Margriet Buggeman, Heather Waterman, and Nikki Ashington, whose knowledge added greatly to this book.

Lastly, I would like to thank the members of the SharePoint User Group U.K. and my fellow SharePoint MVPs. I am truly honored to be part of this unique community, and I have learned much from their blog posts, presentations, books, and discussions.

Thank you all!

—Penny Coventry

Is This the Right SharePoint Book for You?

This book is about Microsoft® SharePoint® Designer 2010, but before you buy it, please read the following guidelines to learn why you should or should not be using this book.

Note SharePoint Designer 2010 is not a Web authoring tool. If you want to learn how to create Web pages on non-SharePoint Web sites, use a different product such as Microsoft Expression Web.

Buy This Book

This book is for you if:

- You have access to Microsoft SharePoint 2010, either Microsoft SharePoint Foundation 2010, Microsoft SharePoint Server 2010, or both products in your organization.

- You want to create and manage SharePoint sites and perform other tasks, such as creating and modifying Web pages and workflows for SharePoint sites.

- You do not know how to program and have little or no experience using SharePoint Designer.

Do Not Buy This Book

This book is NOT right for you if:

- You use Microsoft FrontPage 2003 to build or amend non-SharePoint sites.

- You're an instructor and use FrontPage 2003 to teach Web page authoring on non-SharePoint sites.

- You're looking for a general introduction to SharePoint.

- You do not have access to SharePoint 2010 in your organization, school, etc.

- You use SharePoint Designer 2007 to build sites based on Windows SharePoint Services 3.0 or Microsoft Office SharePoint Server 2007.

- You want to upgrade to SharePoint Designer 2010 to modify those sites.

Important SharePoint Designer 2010 connects only to SharePoint 2010 sites.

Introduction

Welcome to *Microsoft® SharePoint® Designer 2010 Step by Step*. SharePoint Designer 2010 is a free, powerful tool that together with Microsoft products such as Microsoft InfoPath 2010 Designer and Microsoft Visio 2010 plays a key role in building solutions with Microsoft SharePoint Foundation 2010 and Microsoft SharePoint Server 2010.

- SharePoint Foundation is a free download that provides a collection of services that you can use to build sites. It is also a platform on which you can build applications. SharePoint Server is such an application, and all the features in SharePoint Foundation are available to SharePoint Server. SharePoint Server comes in a number of editions, all of which you can use with SharePoint Designer.

- SharePoint Server 2010 is used for intranet scenarios, in which either the Enterprise or Standard client-access license edition can be used.

- SharePoint 2010 for Internet Sites is available in the Enterprise or Standard edition. These editions can be used to build extranet Web sites.

- FAST Search Server 2010 for SharePoint is used to design enterprise search solutions.

- Office 365 brings together the 2010 editions of SharePoint Online, Exchange Online, Lync Online, and Office desktop software as a cloud serivce.

Don't be put off by its name. SharePoint Designer is not aimed just at Web designers. Everyone who has had some training with SharePoint Designer should be able to use it, but it is not necessarily a tool that everyone should use. Some solutions you can develop quickly as no-code solutions; others may take time, and you might need to modify the underlying client-side code. For some users, the experimental and investigative aspects of developing a solution with SharePoint Designer might be new, frustrating, and initially unfriendly compared with tools they might be used to.

This book gives you a fundamental understanding of how SharePoint Designer works with the SharePoint platform. It helps you understand the consequences of performing tasks with SharePoint Designer and gives you the skills and understanding for how to best build and modify your solutions to meet your business requirements.

How to Access Your Online Edition Hosted by Safari

The voucher bound in to the back of this book gives you access to an online edition of the book. (You can also download the online edition of the book to your own computer; see the next section.)

To access your online edition, do the following:

1. Locate your voucher inside the back cover, and scratch off the metallic foil to reveal your access code.

2. Go to *http://microsoftpress.oreilly.com/safarienabled*.

3. Enter your 24-character access code in the Coupon Code field under Step 1:

(Please note that the access code in this image is for illustration purposes only.)

4. Click the CONFIRM COUPON button.

   A message will appear to let you know that the code was entered correctly. If the code was not entered correctly, you will be prompted to re-enter the code.

5. In this step, you'll be asked whether you're a new or existing user of Safari Books Online. Proceed either with Step 5A or Step 5B.

   5A. If you already have a Safari account, click the EXISTING USER – SIGN IN button under Step 2.

Step ❷

5B. If you are a new user, click the NEW USER – FREE ACCOUNT button under Step 2.

○ You'll be taken to the "Register a New Account" page.

○ This will require filling out a registration form and accepting an End User Agreement.

○ When complete, click the CONTINUE button.

6. On the Coupon Confirmation page, click the My Safari button.

7. On the My Safari page, look at the Bookshelf area and click the title of the book you want to access.

How to Download the Online Edition to Your Computer

In addition to reading the online edition of this book, you can also download it to your computer. First, follow the steps in the preceding section. After Step 7, do the following:

1. On the page that appears after Step 7 in the previous section, click the Extras tab.

2. Find "Download the complete PDF of this book," and click the book title:

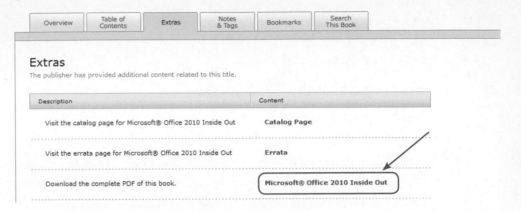

A new browser window or tab will open, followed by the File Download dialog box:

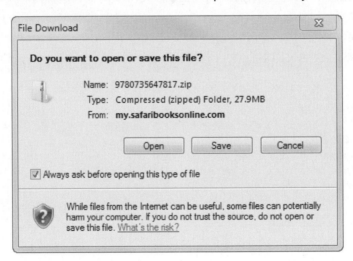

3. Click Save.

4. Choose Desktop and click Save.

5. Locate the .zip file on your desktop. Right-click the file, click Extract All, and then follow the instructions.

Note If you have a problem with your voucher or access code, please contact *mspbooksupport@oreilly.com*, or call 800-889-8969, where you'll reach O'Reilly Media, distributor of Microsoft Press books.

Using the Practice Files

Before you can complete the exercises in this book, you need to copy the book's practice files to your computer. These practice files can be downloaded from the book's detail page, which is located at:

www.oreilly.com/catalog/9780735627338/

Display the detail page in your Web browser, and then follow the instructions for downloading the files.

By using the practice files, you won't waste time creating your own sample files and sites—instead, you can jump right in and concentrate on learning how to get the most out of SharePoint Designer 2010.

To complete the exercises, you need a copy of Microsoft SharePoint Designer 2010 installed on your computer and access to a SharePoint site. The SharePoint site can be created using Microsoft SharePoint Foundation 2010. However, to complete all the exercises, Microsoft SharePoint Server 2010 is required.

Tip In many of the chapters, you will use the default SharePoint sites, lists, and libraries, so those chapters do not include any practice files. For other chapters, you need to use a site created from the solution file SPDSBSPracticeSite_Starter.wsp, which is the only solution file for this book. You need to create a site using this solution file only once. You can then use that site to complete all exercises for all chapters that require the solution file site. If you want to, you can also use the solution file site for exercises in other chapters, except for those exercises that require a publishing site.

Important You must have access to a working SharePoint site before using this book. SharePoint Foundation 2010 and SharePoint Designer 2010 can be downloaded from Microsoft's download Web site at no cost.

What's on the Web?

The following table lists the practice files and site solution that are supplied on the book's Web site for each chapter.

Chapter	Files and WSP Files
Chapter 1, "Exploring SharePoint Designer"	None
Chapter 2, "Working with SharePoint Sites"	None

Chapter 3, "Working with Lists and Libraries"	WideWorldImportsSaleData.xlsx WideWorldImportersExpenses.docx b_NewAnn16x16.gif b_NewAnn32x32.png b_NewTask16x16.png
Chapter 4, "Creating and Modifying Web Pages"	SilverlightSPDSBS.xap
Chapter 5, "Working with Data Views"	Use solution file site SPDSBSPracticeSite_Starter.wsp sale.png SPDSBSC05.xsl.txt
Chapter 6, "Working with Data Sources"	Use solution file site SPDSBSPracticeSite_Starter.wsp Shipments.xml
Chapter 7, "Using Business Connectivity Services"	None
Chapter 8, "Understanding Workflows"	Use solution file site SPDSBSPracticeSite_Starter.wsp
Chapter 9, "Reusable Workflows and Workflow Forms"	WideWorldImporters.png
Chapter 10, "Branding SharePoint Sites"	bg.png Solution folder contains the resulting MyStyles.css and MyPage.aspx
Chapter 11, "Working with Master Pages"	Use solution file site SPDSBSPracticeSite_Starter.wsp
Chapter 12, "Understanding Usability and Accessibility"	Index.aspx
Chapter 13, "Managing Web Content in the SharePoint Server Environment"	None
Chapter 14, "Using Controls in Web Pages"	ADRotator.xml LucernePublishing.png WideWorldImporters.png ConsolidatedMessenger.png

Minimum System Requirements

This section details the requirements for both your computer—the client computer, where SharePoint Designer should be installed—and the requirements for a computer running SharePoint 2010—the server computer, where either SharePoint Foundation or SharePoint Server is installed. If you have access to an Internet service provider (ISP) that hosts SharePoint for you or your company, or if your company has installed SharePoint on your corporate intranet, the details about the server requirements will be of little interest to you. Just ask your company for a SharePoint site that you can use while you are completing the exercises in this book, preferably a top-level site in your own site collection. If you currently have no access to a SharePoint site, the server computer requirements section that follows will help you create or get access to a SharePoint environment.

Tip You can install SharePoint Designer 2010 and SharePoint 2010 on the same computer. However, this not usual in a production environment.

Client Computer

To use this book, your client computer should meet the following requirements:

- **Processor**   500 MHz processor or higher.

- **Memory**   256 megabytes (MB) of RAM or higher.

- **Hard disk**   For the eBooks and downloads, 3 GB of available hard disk space is recommended, with 2 GB on the hard disk where the operating system is installed.

- **Operating system**   Windows 7, Windows Server 2003 R2, Windows Server 2008 R2, Windows Server 2008 with Service Pack 2, Windows Vista with Service Pack 1 or later, Windows XP with Service Pack 3.

  .NET Framework 3.5 SP1 must be installed on the client machine, which is incorporated in Windows 7 and Windows Server 2008 R2 but not in other operating systems.

- **Drive**   CD or DVD drive.

- **Display**   Monitor with 1024×768 or higher screen resolution and 16-bit or higher color depth. Use of graphics hardware acceleration requires DirectX 9.0c–compatible graphics card with 64 MB or higher of video memory.

- **Software**   Windows Internet Explorer 7 or later, or one of the supported browsers and Microsoft Silverlight. See the article "Plan browser support (SharePoint Server 2010)" at *technet.microsoft.com/en-us/library/cc263526(office.14).aspx*.

Tip Actual requirements and product functionality might vary based on your system configuration and operating system.

Note SharePoint Designer 2010 connects only to SharePoint 2010. To connect to sites based on Office SharePoint Server 2007 or earlier versions, you must use SharePoint Designer 2007. If you install SharePoint Designer 2007 and SharePoint Designer 2010 side by side, you must download the 32-bit version of SharePoint Designer 2010. Also note that 64-bit Office applications will not run if SharePoint Designer 2007 is installed; 64-bit Office 2010 applications should be used only if you are not connecting to SharePoint 2007 servers.

Client Software

In addition to the hardware, software, and connections required to run SharePoint Designer, you need the following software to successfully complete the exercises in this book:

- SharePoint Designer 2010, which is available at no cost from the Microsoft Web site *office.microsoft.com/en-us/sharepointdesigner/*
- Microsoft Visio Premium 2010
- Microsoft InfoPath Designer 2010
- Microsoft Outlook 2010
- Microsoft Access 2010
- 20 MB of available hard disk space for the practice files

Server Computer

To use this book, you must have access to a server running Microsoft SharePoint Foundation 2010 or Microsoft SharePoint Server 2010. Directions for how to install either of these products, especially for a production environment, is outside the scope of this book. However, if you do not have access to a SharePoint site and your company cannot provide you with one, you have two options:

- Download the 2010 Information Worker Hyper-V virtual machine that includes Office 2010, SharePoint Designer 2010, and SharePoint Server 2010 from Microsoft's download site (*www.microsoft.com/downloads*). Use the search keyword *2010 IW*.
- Create a temporary SharePoint environment by installing a copy of SharePoint on your computer.

Important To create a permanent installation of either a SharePoint Server or a SharePoint Foundation environment, refer to one of the following sources of information: *Microsoft SharePoint Server 2010 Administrator's Companion*, by Bill English, Brian Alderman, and Mark Ferraz (Microsoft Press, 2011) or *Microsoft SharePoint 2010 Administrator's Pocket Consultant*, by Ben Curry (Microsoft Press, 2010). For online assistance, visit the SharePoint 2010 products site on Microsoft TechNet, which can be found at *technet.microsoft.com/en-us/library/ ee428287(office.14).aspx*.

An installation of SharePoint Foundation allows you to complete the majority of exercises in this book. Appendix C, on page 503, provides a brief set of instructions for installing SharePoint Foundation 2010 on a single server with a built-in database. This configuration can be used as a temporary SharePoint environment. The server computer should meet the following requirements:

- **Operating system**   One of the following 64-bit operating systems: Windows Server 2008 R2, Windows Server 2008 R2 Enterprise, Windows Server 2008 R2 Standard, or Windows Server 2008 with Service Pack 2.

- **Processor**   64-bit; four-cores.

- **Memory**   8 GB for development or evaluation use.

- **Software**   80 GB for installation

See Also A full list of hardware and software requirements for SharePoint Foundation 2010 can be found at *technet.microsoft.com/en-us/library/cc288751(office.14).aspx*.

Tip A temporary installation of SharePoint Server 2010 on a single server with a built-in database will allow you to complete all but a very few of the exercises in this book, but you need to obtain access to a trial version of SharePoint Server or purchase a copy. More information can be found at *sharepoint.microsoft.com/Pages/Default.aspx*. The installation of SharePoint Server 2010 on a single server with a built-in database is similar to the installation of SharePoint Foundation 2010 on a single server with a built-in database. You can use the installation instructions in Appendix C as a guideline.

Using the Practice Files for the Exercises

While you work through the exercises in this book, you should have access to a SharePoint site, preferably a top-level site in your own site collection. You should be a site owner of this site. In the exercises, you create child sites below this site, and in Chapters 5, 6, 8, and 11, you use a starter solutions .wsp file to create the child site. Please refer to the instructions later in this section for how to create a practice site from the starter solutions .wsp file.

The solution file provided on the Web site contains lists, libraries, files, and pages that you use for the exercises. In chapters that require you to create a site based on the solutions file, a SET UP paragraph lists that requirement. The text also explains any preparations you need to take before you start working through the chapter, as shown here:

> **Practice Files** Before you can use the practice files in this chapter, you need to copy the book's practice files to your computer. The practice files you'll use to complete the exercises in this chapter are in the Chapter08 practice file folder. A complete list of practice files is provided in "Using the Practice Files" at the beginning of this book.

SET UP Using SharePoint Designer, open the site you created from the SPDSBSPracticeSite_Starter.wsp practice file.

Other practice files might need to be uploaded to the Site Assets library. You can use the browser or SharePoint Designer to upload the files to the Site Assets library. To use SharePoint Designer, use the following steps:

1. In the **Navigation** pane, click **Site Assets**, and then on the ribbon, click **Import Files** in the **New** group. The Import dialog box opens.

2. Click **Add File** to display the **File Open** dialog box.

3. Browse to the folder that contains the practice file. Click **Open**, and then click **OK** to close the File Open and Import dialog boxes.

Uploading the Solution WSP File

To create a practice site for a chapter based on the solution .wsp file, you first need to upload the solution .wsp file to the Solutions gallery by following these steps:

 SET UP Verify that you have sufficient rights to upload a solutions file to the Solutions gallery for the top-level site of the site collection you are using. Open the top-level SharePoint site in the browser.

1. Click **Site Actions**, and click **Site Settings** to display the site settings page.

2. Under **Galleries**, click **Solutions** to display the **Solutions** page.

   Note If you see a Go To Top Level Site Settings link under Site Collection Administration, you are not on the top-level site administration page. A site template can only be uploaded to the Solutions gallery on a top-level site. Click Go To Top Level Site Settings, and then repeat the previous step.

Upload Solution

3. On the ribbon, click the **Solutions** tab, and then click **Upload Solution** to display the **Solutions Gallery: Upload Solution** dialog box.

4. Click the **Browse** button to display the **Choose File to Upload** dialog box.

5. Navigate to the folder that contains the solution .wsp file, click **SPD2010SBS_ PracticeWeb_StarterSite.wsp**, and then click the **Open** button.

6. Click **OK**.

   The Solutions Gallery—Activate Solution dialog box is displayed.

7. On the **View** tab, click **Activate** to redisplay the Solutions page.

Creating a Site from the Solution WSP File

After you have uploaded the solution .wsp file to the Solutions gallery, you can create a child site based on the solutions file.

 SET UP In your browser, display the home page of the SharePoint site where you want to create the child site.

1. Click **Site Actions**, and then click **New Site**.

   In SharePoint Foundation, the New SharePoint Site page is displayed. In SharePoint Server, a Create page is displayed.

2. Complete the following step depending the version of SharePoint that is installed:

   a. On SharePoint Foundation, on the **Custom** tab of the **Select a template** list, select **SPD2010SBS_PracticeSite_Starter**.

   b. On SharePoint Server, in the left pane, under **Filter By**, click **Custom**, and then select **SPD2010SBS_PracticeSite_Starter**.

   Troubleshooting If you are using SharePoint Server and cannot see the Custom filter or the name of the template you uploaded, contact your site collection administrator. If you are the administrator for the site collection where you are trying to create this team site, follow the procedure in Appendix C on page 503 to display the template and then complete this exercise.

3. In the **Title** box, type a logical name for the new site—for example, **SPDSBS Practice Site**.

4. In the **URL name** box, type the same name you typed in the **Title** box.

5. Click **Create**.

   The home page of the new practice site is displayed.

 CLEAN UP Close the browser.

Removing the Solution Files

To remove the solution .wsp file from the Solutions gallery, follow these steps:

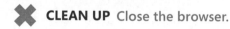 **SET UP** Verify that you have sufficient rights to delete a solution from the Solutions gallery. Open the top-level SharePoint site where you previously uploaded the solution file.

1. Click **Site Actions**, and click **Site Settings** to display the site settings page.

2. Under **Galleries**, click **Solutions**.

Note If you see a Go To Top Level Site Settings link under Site Collection Administration, you are not on the top-level site administration page. A site template can only be stored in the Solutions gallery on a top level site. Click Go To Top Level Site Settings and then repeat the previous step.

3. Point to the site template you want to remove, click the arrow that appears, and then click **Deactivate**.

   The Solutions Gallery—Deactivate Solution dialog box appears.

4. On the **View** tab, click **Deactivate**.

Deactivate

5. Point to the site template you want to remove, click the arrow that appears, and then click **Delete**. You are prompted to confirm your request. Click **OK** to complete the deletion and display the Solutions gallery.

6. Repeat steps 3 through 5 to remove each site template that you no longer want to be available for creating practice sites.

✖ **CLEAN UP** Close the browser.

Deleting a Practice Site

If you created a practice site that you no longer want, you can delete it. Follow these steps to delete a practice site:

 SET UP Verify that you have sufficient rights to delete a site. In the browser, open the SharePoint site you want to delete.

1. On the **Site Actions** menu, click **Site Settings** to display the site settings page.

2. In the **Site Actions** section, click **Delete this site** to display the **Delete This Site** confirmation page.

3. Click the **Delete** button to delete the site.

4. On the **Delete This Site** warning page, click **Delete**.

✖ **CLEAN UP** Close the browser.

Important Microsoft product support services do not provide support for this book or its practice files.

Getting Help

Every effort has been made to ensure the accuracy of this book. If you run into problems, please contact the sources listed in the following sections.

Getting Help with This Book

If your question or issue concerns the content of this book, please first consult the book's errata page, which can be accessed at:

www.oreilly.com/catalog/errata.csp?isbn=9780735627338

This page provides information about known errors and corrections to the book. If you do not find your answer on the errata page, send your question or comment to O'Reilly Media Customer Service at:

mspbooksupport@oreilly.com

Getting Help with Microsoft SharePoint Designer

If your question is about SharePoint Designer and not about the content of this Microsoft Press book, please search the Microsoft Help and Support Center or the Microsoft Knowledge Base at:

support.microsoft.com

In the United States, Microsoft software product support issues not covered by the Microsoft Knowledge Base are addressed by Microsoft Product Support Services. The Microsoft software support options available from Microsoft Product Support Services are listed at:

www.microsoft.com/services/microsoftservices/srv_support.mspx

Outside the United States, for support information specific to your location, please refer to the Worldwide Support menu on the Microsoft Help And Support Web site for the site specific to your country:

support.microsoft.com/common/international.aspx

Features and Conventions of This Book

This book has been designed to lead you step by step through all the tasks you are most likely to want to perform in Microsoft SharePoint Designer 2010. Each chapter of this book includes self-contained topics that teach you about specific program features. Most topics conclude with a step-by-step exercise in which you practice using the program. The following features of this book will help you locate specific information:

- **Detailed table of contents** Scan this list of the topics and sidebars within each chapter.

- **Chapter thumb tabs** Easily locate the beginning of each chapter by looking at the colored blocks on the odd-numbered pages.

- **Topic-specific running heads** Within a chapter, quickly locate the topic you want by looking at the running head on odd-numbered pages.

- **Glossary** Look up the meaning of a word or the definition of a concept.

- **Detailed index** Look up specific tasks and features and general concepts in the index, which has been carefully crafted with the reader in mind.

You can save time when you use this book by understanding how the *Step by Step* series shows special instructions, keys to press, buttons to click, and other information. These conventions are listed in the following table.

Convention	Meaning
SET UP	This paragraph precedes a step-by-step exercise and indicates the practice files that you will use when working through the exercise. It also indicates any requirements you should attend to or actions you should take before beginning the exercise.
CLEAN UP	This paragraph follows a step-by-step exercise and provides instructions for saving and closing open files or programs before you move on to another topic. It also suggests ways to reverse any changes you made to your computer while working through the exercise.
1 2	Blue numbered steps guide you through hands-on exercises in each topic.
1 2	Black numbered steps guide you through procedures in sidebars and in expository text.

See Also	This paragraph directs you to more information about a given topic in this book or elsewhere.
Troubleshooting	This paragraph alerts you to a common problem and provides guidance for fixing it.
Tip	This paragraph provides a helpful hint or shortcut that makes working through a task easier or information about other available options.
Important	This paragraph points out information that you need to know to complete a procedure.
Keyboard shortcut	This paragraph provides information about an available keyboard shortcut for the preceding task.
Ctrl+Tab	A plus sign (+) between two key names means that you must hold down the first key while you press the second key. For example, "Press **Ctrl+Tab**" means "hold down the **Ctrl** key while you press the **Tab** key.
Black bold	In exercises that begin with SET UP information, the names of program elements, such as buttons, commands, and dialog boxes, as well as files, folders, or text that you interact with in the steps are shown in black bold characters.
Blue bold	In exercises that begin with SET UP information, text that you should type is shown in bold blue type.

Part 1

Getting Started with Microsoft SharePoint Designer 2010

Chapter at a Glance

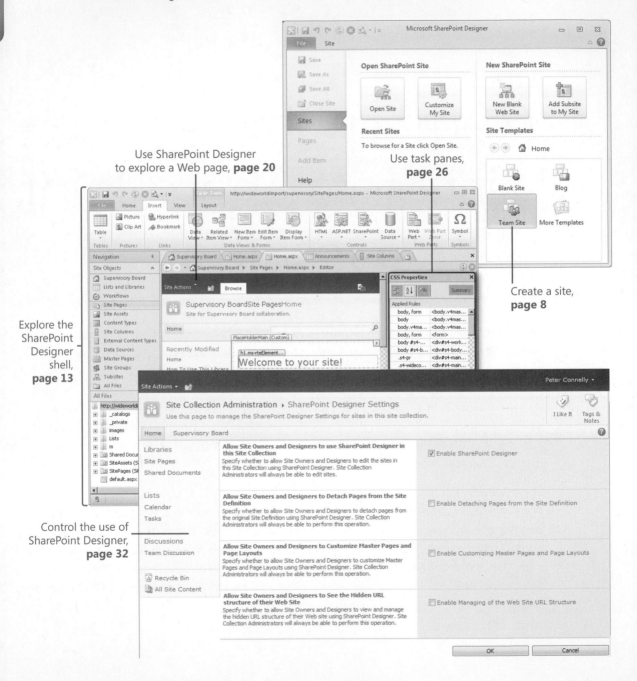

Use SharePoint Designer to explore a Web page, **page 20**

Use task panes, **page 26**

Create a site, **page 8**

Explore the SharePoint Designer shell, **page 13**

Control the use of SharePoint Designer, **page 32**

1 Exploring SharePoint Designer 2010

In this chapter, you will learn how to

✔ Understand SharePoint Designer.

✔ Use SharePoint Designer to carry out common tasks.

✔ Understand what's new in SharePoint Designer 2010.

✔ Create a site with SharePoint Designer.

✔ Explore the SharePoint Designer shell.

✔ Use SharePoint Designer to explore a Web page.

✔ Use task panes.

✔ Control the use of SharePoint Designer.

You may be reading this book because you have Microsoft SharePoint—Microsoft SharePoint Foundation 2010, Microsoft SharePoint Server 2010, or both—in your organization and want to do more with your SharePoint sites than you can achieve with only the browser. You do not know how to program SharePoint, but you want to create more complex solutions than you can achieve by using the browser and have been told that Microsoft SharePoint Designer 2010 is a tool that you can use to do this. What you've heard is true; SharePoint Designer is a powerful tool that allows you to create rich and robust applications on top of your SharePoint sites.

SharePoint Designer is now "the preferred" tool for designing powerful, no-code solutions and applications in SharePoint 2010. It is a complex tool and is designed to help you present and manipulate content to meet your business needs. It's not designed for adding static content, such as text or images to your Web pages, or for uploading documents or creating list items. You use the browser to complete those tasks. SharePoint Designer is not a tool for general use by all users who visit or have access to a SharePoint site.

To make the best use of this book, you should already be familiar with creating and modifying SharePoint sites in a browser. It is likely that you are a site or site collection owner who has little or no experience using SharePoint Designer. A few of you might be familiar with programming SharePoint solutions in Microsoft Visual Studio 2010; however, coding experience is not necessary to use this book, which focuses on producing no-code solutions. Regardless of your current skill level, the book assumes that every reader wants to learn about the powerful capabilities of SharePoint Designer 2010. Whether you are an information worker, an IT professional, or a developer, this book is for you.

Most of this book covers the mechanisms of using SharePoint Designer, but you'll also find advice and guidelines for creating successful solutions for other users. As you read this book and start to learn how to use SharePoint Designer, you'll find that you can't do without it.

Soon after you start SharePoint Designer 2010, you'll notice that the user interface (UI), known as the shell, looks quite different from SharePoint Designer 2007. SharePoint Designer 2010 uses the Microsoft Office Fluent user interface, which was designed to make it easier for users to use and find features within a product. It incorporates the ribbon and the companion feature—Backstage view—which can be accessed from the File tab.

Tip If you are unfamiliar with Microsoft SharePoint 2010, read *Microsoft SharePoint Foundation 2010 Step by Step* by Olga Londer and Penelope Coventry (Microsoft Press, 2011) before you read this book.

In this chapter you will learn what SharePoint Designer is and what common tasks you can accomplish by using it. You will create, close, and open a team site and explore the new shell in SharePoint Designer 2010. You will also see how each site has a home page.

Important You should not complete the book's exercises on a production site. You should have a practice site or, ideally, your own site collection. For more information about setting up your environment and the practice files, see "Using the Practice Files" on page xxiii.

Practice Files No practice files are required to complete the exercises in this chapter.

Understanding SharePoint Designer 2010

SharePoint Designer 2010 is a free, powerful Web-editing tool with special capabilities for building solutions with SharePoint Foundation 2010 and SharePoint Server 2010 sites. Once you connect to a SharePoint site, you can use SharePoint Designer to administer the site, create workflows, and customize pages.

Note Unlike with previous versions of SharePoint Designer, which could be used to create and customize any standards-compliant site, you cannot use SharePoint Designer 2010 to customize sites not based on SharePoint, nor can you use it to customize sites based on previous versions of SharePoint, such as Windows SharePoint Services 3.0 or Microsoft Office SharePoint Server 2007.

SharePoint Designer renders pages, like many other Web editing tools, in a document window so that you can visually amend the content in a "what you see is what you get" (WYSIWYG) environment. Also, like other Office 2010 applications and the browser when you open a SharePoint site, SharePoint Designer uses the Office Fluent user interface, including the ribbon, which displays all the tools you need—and only the tools you need—to complete specific tasks. You can use the tools provided to customize and develop business solutions based on Microsoft SharePoint Products and Technologies without the need to write code.

Tip SharePoint Foundation, SharePoint Server, and SharePoint Designer are known collectively as Microsoft SharePoint Products and Technologies.

SharePoint sites work in a different way than non-SharePoint sites you may be familiar with. Instead of using a folder on a Web server, such as c:\inetpub\wwwroot, to store site content, a SharePoint site stores the majority of the content in a set of Microsoft SQL Server databases. SharePoint Designer does not have direct access to the content that is stored in the SQL Server databases. Any modifications you make to a site using SharePoint Designer are saved in the SQL Server content databases via SharePoint Foundation or SharePoint Server. Therefore, before you can use SharePoint Designer, you need access to an environment in which SharePoint is already installed.

With SharePoint Designer, you never open files directly on the local drive, a shared network drive, or a CD. You connect to a SharePoint site with SharePoint Designer using a URL that begins with http: or https:, just as you would connect to a SharePoint site using the browser.

Using SharePoint Designer to Carry Out Common Tasks

Many of the most successful SharePoint sites are built by the users who use them—the users of the site become the designers and the developers. Many of them are created just with the use of the browser; others are enhanced with the use of SharePoint Designer. SharePoint is wonderful for producing solutions with no code. These solutions are successful because the users know what they want to achieve; they are using a site as they develop it; and they can sort out problems, including problems that can be found only by using the solution. There is no need to provide feedback to others or raise incidents with your organization's help desk.

Initially this is probably how you started building solutions, and I hope this book helps you build more successful SharePoint sites. However, once others in your organization learn of your success, you might be asked to build solutions for other users. Never forget, however, that the reason for the success of your SharePoint site is that you knew the business requirements and experienced firsthand the issues of your solution. You were also probably very passionate about your own SharePoint solution.

Part of the SharePoint technologies ethos is to allow users to easily complete tasks that are traditionally completed by highly skilled technical users—changes to sites were the domain of the IT department, the Web master, or a Web hosting company. This caused what became known as the Web master bottleneck; content on sites became dated, and the number of visitors decreased. Microsoft has provided a set of tools that you can use to quickly and easily complete common tasks on a SharePoint site. SharePoint Designer is one such tool. However, you must be sure that the way you use these tools does not reinvent the Web master bottleneck, where the bottleneck now becomes you! By transferring the knowledge necessary to maintain a site to another user who does not need to know how to use SharePoint Designer, you can remove yourself from the maintenance cycle, leaving you with more time to develop exciting solutions with SharePoint Designer.

To organize a SharePoint site to meet the business needs of you and your coworkers, you can customize lists, libraries, and the pages of a SharePoint site by using a browser. With SharePoint Designer, you can carry out similar tasks, but you can also extend those customizations. With SharePoint Designer 2010, you can now complete more tasks natively, without the need to jump back and forth between SharePoint Designer and the browser, but you can't do everything with SharePoint Designer. It complements your Web browser but does not replace it. Use SharePoint Designer to produce solutions that are easily maintainable and supportable. Typically, you can achieve 75 percent of the necessary customizations of a SharePoint site by using a browser; 15 percent require the use of SharePoint Designer, and 10 percent require a developer who is skilled in Visual Studio 2010.

Whether you are an administrator, a developer, or an information worker, some of the most compelling uses of SharePoint Designer are as follows:

- Using the Data View and Data Form Web Parts to create data-driven solutions based on *eXtensible Markup Language (XML)* and *eXtensible Stylesheet Language Transformations (XSLT)* technologies, including creating custom views of data from external systems exposed by Business Connectivity Services (BCS). If you need to use either of these Web Parts on multiple sites, you can export and import the Web Parts or make them part of the Web Part gallery. This lets you produce maintainable solutions, where you store the XSLT in a central document library and point these Web Parts to it. You can then centrally manage changes to the Web Parts you create without visiting every site that uses them.

- Connecting to other data source connections, such as *XML Web services*, databases, and lists and libraries on other SharePoint sites, including the use of *external content types (ECT)* and external lists.

- Using Web Part connections to pass data from a Web Part on one page to one or more Web Parts on another page. With Web Part connections, you can manage the data displayed on a page in a dynamic and interesting way. Using a Web browser, you can connect only Web Parts that are placed on the same page.

- Creating workflows for lists or libraries, a content type, or a site by using the built-in workflow editor—complemented by business workflow diagrams produced with Microsoft Visio 2010 and without having to write server-side code. These workflows can be exported and given to a developer with Visual Studio skills.

- Creating solutions to meet the needs of specific business processes or sets of tasks in your organization, and then reusing them as a basis for future SharePoint sites.

- Prototyping a solution to justify business expenditure. Before submitting a proposal or requesting additional resources, you can quickly create solutions with SharePoint Designer to gather requirements and verify the business process the solution must meet. You may need to export your solution and involve a developer or an administrator so that the final solution is easily deployed and managed. When you start to develop a solution using SharePoint Designer, your intention might be to create a solution that will be used immediately. However, as you work with the business, the solution might become more complex or the business might not be able to answer all of your questions, so it turns out that the solution cannot be used immediately. Essentially, you'll find that you are using SharePoint Designer as a prototyping tool. Another example of when you will discover that you are using SharePoint Designer as a prototyping tool is when you have customized a site and then you receive requests to repeat the customization again and again on other SharePoint sites. In this situation, you need to devise a solution that does not distract you from your other tasks.

- Performing one-off site customizations.

At this early stage of the book, do not to worry if this list means little to you. By the end of the book, you will understand what each item means and should review this list of common tasks that you can accomplish using SharePoint Designer.

Understanding What's New in SharePoint Designer 2010

SharePoint Designer has historically been a very powerful and useful tool. SharePoint Designer's modifications can have long-lasting implications, and the previous version of SharePoint Designer did not make this obvious to an untrained user, nor did it provide an easy method of controlling the level of modifications users could make with SharePoint Designer. Therefore, some organizations restricted the installation of SharePoint Designer to all but a few trained business users.

Microsoft has addressed this limitation by implementing a safe-by-default approach. Site definition pages can be customized (unghosted) only when a page is in advanced edit mode. Also, you can limit what users can or cannot do with SharePoint Designer at the Web-application or site-collection level by using the browser.

See Also Chapter 2, "Working with SharePoint Sites," for more information on how site collection administrators can control the use of SharePoint Designer, and Appendix C on page 503 for a list of steps that SharePoint farm administrators can use to restrict the use of SharePoint Designer at the Web-application level.

Other new features in SharePoint Designer 2010 are:

- **User interface (UI)** The SharePoint Designer user interface (UI) is redesigned and uses the Office Fluent UI, which was designed to make it easier for users to use and find features within a product. It incorporates the ribbon and Backstage view, which can be accessed from the File tab.

- **Easier management of SharePoint components** The new Navigation pane, which replaces the Folder List task pane in SharePoint Designer 2007, focuses on SharePoint artifacts and not where the artifacts are stored. You can now manipulate major SharePoint components—such as content types, site columns, and external lists—and modify site and list permissions natively within SharePoint Designer. Using SharePoint Designer to manipulate SharePoint components is now much faster and more efficient than using a Web browser to complete similar tasks.

- **New tools to help users create better composites (solutions)** Two areas of tool improvement are:

  - **Workflows** The challenge in implementing a new workflow is that the person who creates the workflow is usually not the one who defines the requirements. SharePoint 2010 addresses this challenge by allowing people to create workflows in Visio 2010 and export them into SharePoint Designer 2010, where business logic and additional rules are added. Workflows developed in SharePoint Designer can be exported from one SharePoint site and imported into another, as well as into Visual Studio 2010. This enables development and testing of the SharePoint Designer custom workflow to take place in a trusted environment before deployment to the production system. In the previous version of SharePoint, this was available only with workflows created using Visual Studio. More information on workflows can be found in Chapter 8, "Understanding Workflows," and Chapter 9, "Using Reusable Workflows and Workflow Forms."

  - *Business Connectivity Services (BCS)* Originally called the *Business Data Catalog*, BCS is now available in the base product, Microsoft SharePoint Foundation 2010. SharePoint Designer is the major tool for information workers and business analysts to define how to access external systems and create dashboards and composite applications based on data from the external systems. The BCS is detailed in Chapter 7, "Using Business Connectivity Services."

- **Performance and stability improvements** Until the release of Service Pack 2, SharePoint Designer 2007 had major performance and stability issues. Some users also complained about the code SharePoint Designer 2007 generated. Microsoft has invested heavily in this area.

A number of SharePoint Designer 2007 features are removed from SharePoint Designer 2010. Many of these features are not relevant to SharePoint sites, and since SharePoint Designer 2010 can be used only with SharePoint 2010 sites, they served no purpose. The features removed include:

- *Contributor settings* Microsoft received feedback that this feature was too complicated and rarely used. Restrictions are now controlled using permissions, the safe-by-default editing mode, and the configuration at the Web-application and site-collection level as described earlier in this section.

- **Database-related features** This includes the Database Interface Wizard that creates new database-driven Web sites, the database results Web component (also known as a WebBot), and the Database tab of the Site Settings dialog box, which on a SharePoint site displayed the message "Database properties cannot be used with this Web site."

- **Layout tables** CSS layout features have replaced the layout tables feature. If any of your upgraded SharePoint sites contains a layout table, SharePoint Designer 2010 displays the layout table functions correctly; however, you will not be able to install any new layout tables.

- **Publish, backup, and restore of Web sites; import and export of Web packages (.fwp), and *FTP* client** Many of these features were useful on non-SharePoint sites and have been removed. Expression Web is the tool to use for these features. Also, SharePoint Designer is not a server administrator's tool. The Central Administration Web site should be used to complete comparable tasks for SharePoint sites.

  Tip To package and deploy SharePoint solutions, save a site as a template or use a solutions file. You can find more information on solutions at *http://social.msdn.microsoft.com/Search/en-us?query=sharepoint+2010+solutions*. There is a 20 minute learning snack on developing solutions with Microsoft SharePoint Server 2010 at *www.microsoft.com/learning/en/us/training/format-learning-snacks.aspx#SP10*.

- **The Reports, Navigation, and Hyperlinks options available on the Sites menu and at the bottom of the Web Site tab** The error checking features in SharePoint Designer 2010 let you check for broken links, unused pages, cascading style sheets usage, and master page usage.

  See Also More information on changes to SharePoint Designer 2010 can be found at *http://technet.microsoft.com/en-us/library/cc179083(office.14).aspx*.

Creating Sites with SharePoint Designer

Usually, the first task when you build a solution is to create a site. When you create a site with SharePoint, you can choose from a number of *site templates* that incorporate pages, Web Parts, and other features that allow you to organize information, manage documents, and create workflows to support your business environment.

SharePoint Foundation 2010 has 10 built-in site templates. SharePoint Server includes these 10 site templates plus a number of other site templates. These templates form a good basis on which to create almost any SharePoint site. You should familiarize yourself with the features that sites created from these templates offer so that you know which to use as a blueprint.

When you create a SharePoint site from one of the built-in site templates, you refer to pages and files stored on each Web server. The pages and files are stored in a subfolder, named *TEMPLATE*, in the root directory, which in a default installation is *C:\Program Files\Common Files\Microsoft Shared\web server extensions\14*. When you create a SharePoint site, no files or pages are created. Instead, entries are created in tables in the SQL Server content databases that point to files in the TEMPLATE folder. The files in the TEMPLATE folder on the Web server are known as *site definitions*. Site definition files are cached in memory on the server at process startup. As a result, when you request a page that points to one of the site definitions files, it is retrieved from the server's memory. Therefore, a relatively small set of files can support a large number of SharePoint sites with many pages, resulting in improved performance.

To open a SharePoint site with your browser, you type the address of your site, known as a *URL*—for example, *http://wideworldimporters/Human_Resources or http://intranet. wideworldimporters.com/sites/teams/11*. The first portion of the URL, such as *http://wide-worldimporters* or *http://intranet.wideworldimporters.com*, is known as the *Web application*. A Web application can consist of one or more *site collections*; each site collection always has one *top-level site* and, optionally, one or more *subsites*, also called *child sites*. This hierarchy resembles the hierarchy of folders in file systems in that it is a treelike structure. Using the example mentioned earlier, *http://wideworldimporters* is the top-level site of a site collection and Human_Resources is a subsite of the *http://wideworldimporters* site collection.

In this exercise, you create a subsite by using the Team Site template.

SET UP You need the URL of a SharePoint site where you can create the new team site as a subsite. It is recommended that you do not complete the book's exercises on a production site. You should ideally have your own practice site collection. If in doubt, check with your SharePoint administrator.

Start

1. On the taskbar, click the **Start** button, point to **All Programs**, click **SharePoint**, and then click **Microsoft SharePoint Designer 2010**.

The SharePoint Designer window opens, displaying Backstage view.

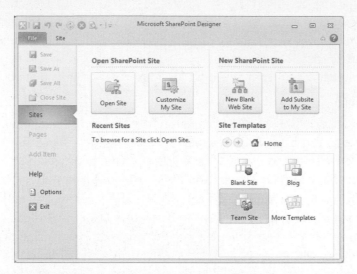

2.   Under **Site Templates**, click **Team Site**.

The Team Site dialog box opens.

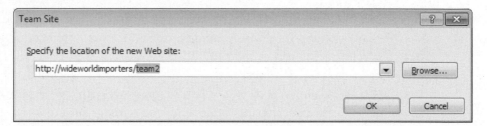

3.   In the **Specify the location of the new Web site** text box, type the name of your team site: *http://<yourwebapplicationname/path>/Human_Resources*.

The *yourwebapplicationname/path* portion of the URL is the location of the site collection that you are using for the exercises in this book. (The *path* portion might be empty.) Human_Resources is the name of the team site.

Important For the exercises in this book, I use a fictitious SharePoint site, wideworldimporters. Its URL is *http://wideworldimporters*. However, in your environment, you will use a different URL, and therefore you need to use your site location, *http://<yourwebapplication/path>* in place of *http://wideworldimporters*.

4.   Click **OK**.

A number of dialog boxes open. If prompted, type your user name and password.

When the last dialog box closes, the new team site is displayed in On Stage view in SharePoint Designer.

 CLEAN UP Close SharePoint Designer.

Best Practices for Naming URLs

Every SharePoint component is referenced by a URL, whether it is for a site, a list, or a library. When you create a new SharePoint component, do not use the following characters: \ / : * ? " < > | # { } % & <TAB> " ! ~ +. Both the browser and SharePoint Designer display a warning dialog box if you use an illegal character. When you use the browser, the message points to the illegal character you tried to use.

Note When Microsoft Silverlight is not installed, the error message appears in a dialog box. Microsoft Silverlight is a Web application framework that provides functionalities similar to those in Adobe Flash, integrating multimedia, graphics, animations, and interactivity.

The error message displayed by SharePoint Designer does not point specifically to the illegal character used.

See Also For more information about using these characters in URLs, see the Microsoft Knowledge Base article at *support.microsoft.com/default.aspx?scid=kb;en-us;905231*.

Keep a URL's name short and meaningful, and include terms that are memorable to users and terms that they might enter as search query keywords. The name can tell users about your Web site—its purpose and the type of content it contains—and helps search engines rank your site for targeted keywords. Check the spelling of words you include in the URL name and be consistent in your naming conventions; for example, don't call a picture library *pictures* in one site and *images* in another. For some SharePoint components, such as the URL for a site, you cannot change the URL later.

If your aim is to make the URL readable and the URL consists of several words, use an underscore ("_") in place of a space or remove the space and capitalize the first character in each word. For example, replace the three words *Wide World Importers*, with either *Wide_World_Importers* or *WideWorldImporters*. The underscore is the better of these options because all popular search engines and spiders understand it as a word separator.

See Also More information on SharePoint 2010 Search Engine Optimization (SEO) tips can be found at *http://blogs.msdn.com/b/opal/archive/2010/04/23/sharepoint-2010-search-engine-optimization-seo-tips.aspx*.

Although the space character is a legal URL character, there are several issues with having one or more spaces in the URL, such as the following:

- Readability. A space in the URL name is URL-encoded as *%20*, so the resulting name is difficult for people to read. A site with a URL of *s p f* would result in an encoded version of *s%20p%20f*, six extra characters.

- URL length limitation. A URL must contain no more than 260 characters. SharePoint refers to every site, list, library, list item, or document as a URL. SharePoint prefixes the document name by the document library's URL, which is prefixed by the site's URL, then by its parent's site's URL, and so on. In addition, when a user edits documents or list items, SharePoint appends the URL of the document library or list, so that when the user clicks Save or Close, the browser redirects them to the list or library in which the item was saved.

If the URL for the list or library contains two spaces, it contains six extra char-acters. Then, as the URL is appended for editing, that adds another six extra characters, making 12 extra characters. Therefore, if you consistently use long names, you'll eventually have problems, which is exaggerated if you use spaces.

● Links in e-mails. If you incorporate a URL in an e-mail message, some e-mail programs truncate the URL at the first space when sending the clickable link to the recipient, resulting in a broken link. When users click the link, they are taken to an invalid location in the browser and won't understand why they can't find the document.

Note You might see the use of dashes or hyphens ("-") to separate words in a URL name; however, hyphens are used as break points to wrap text on separate lines. URLs that contain hyphens can cause problems similar to spaces with e-mail and text editors.

Exploring the SharePoint Designer Shell

When you open SharePoint Designer (as in the previous exercise), you are presented with Microsoft Office Backstage view, which gives you access to those tasks you need to per-form on the whole site or in configuring SharePoint Designer. The title bar contains the program name or the site name, if one is open.

When you open SharePoint Designer but have not yet opened a SharePoint Web site, Backstage view is divided into five areas:

● The pane at the left includes essential management commands and product options.

● **Open SharePoint Site** Allows you to open a SharePoint 2010 site and, if you have SharePoint Server 2010 installed, customize your My Site.

● **Recent Sites** Displays the SharePoint sites that you recently opened with SharePoint Designer.

● **New SharePoint Site** Allows you to quickly create a blank SharePoint site or a sub-site beneath your My Site.

● **Site Templates** Allows you to create a site based on one of the SharePoint site templates. By default, this area shows the Blank Site, Blog, and Team Site templates. You can use the More Templates option to connect to a SharePoint site that pro-vides more site templates.

Once a site is open, On Stage view is displayed, and as in many Microsoft Office applications, it contains a number of elements, as shown here:

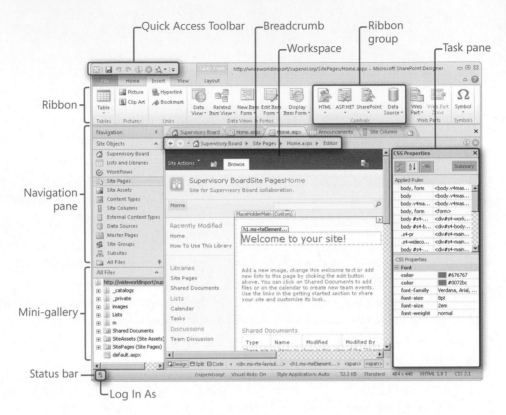

- **Quick Access Toolbar** This area can be customized to include favorite or frequently used commands. Commands that cannot be used with the information displayed in the workspace are not available.

- **Ribbon** The ribbon was introduced in Office 2007 and has been improved in Office 2010 to include some new tools and provide more flexibility. It consists of a number of task-oriented tabs; each tab contains a number of command buttons. The number of tabs shown depends on the information displayed in the workspace.

- **Ribbon group** A collection of related commands, each command has one or more images and alternative text that appears as a ScreenTip when you hover the mouse over it. The image displayed for the command depends on the size of the SharePoint Designer window. As you resize the window, the ribbon resizes, and the groups and commands expand or collapse dynamically.

- **Navigation pane** This lists SharePoint artifacts, such as a lists and libraries, workflows, and master pages. Unlike in SharePoint Designer 2007, you no longer need to know where each artifact is stored. By using the Navigation pane, you can quick-ly go to the artifact you need to work with.

● *Breadcrumb* As with any other breadcrumb on the Web, the breadcrumb in the shell provides a tool that makes it easy to navigate back and forward and keep track of where you are. The SharePoint Designer breadcrumb also allows you to navigate through related components of an artifact.

● **Workspace** In the workspace, you manipulate SharePoint artifacts, including Web pages. When a site is open, a tab appears above the workspace with the name of the site. The workspace and tab name change as you navigate between artifacts, and new tabs open as you manipulate artifacts. A Refresh button is located at the top left of the workspace, and the workspace can contain its own status bar when you are editing Web pages. The workspace has three page formats, depending on the artifact displayed:

   ○ **Settings page**   Used to configure the settings or display information for an artifact such as the open site, lists, libraries, pages, and workflows.

   ○ **Gallery page**   Used to display a list of artifacts and helps to obtain a broad view of the contents of the site. For example, if you click Site Columns in the Navigation pane, you see a list of site columns.

   ○ **Editors**   Allows you to edit artifacts such as Web pages, content types, and workflows.

● **Mini-gallery** A list of artifacts; it can be seen below the Navigation pane, similar to the gallery page.

● **Task panes** These are helper windows that you can open and use to perform cer-tain tasks with files, such as adding ASP.NET controls and managing *cascading style sheets*. Unlike in SharePoint Designer 2007, task panes do not automatically appear in SharePoint Designer 2010 when you open a Web page.

● **Status bar** The status bar contains information such as the visual aid setting, style application settings, download statistics, rendering mode, page size, cascading style sheet version, and code errors.

● **Log In As** This control allows you to sign in as a different user for testing purposes.

Tip You can switch between Backstage and On Stage view by clicking the File tab.

In this exercise, you explore the SharePoint Designer shell, open a SharePoint site, and review the backstage and startup settings of SharePoint Designer.

 SET UP Use the team site you created in the previous exercise.

Start

1. On the taskbar, click the **Start** button, point to **All Programs**, click **SharePoint**, and then click **Microsoft SharePoint Designer 2010**.

   The SharePoint Designer window opens, displaying Backstage view.

2. In the left pane, click **Options**.

   The SharePoint Designer Options dialog box opens.

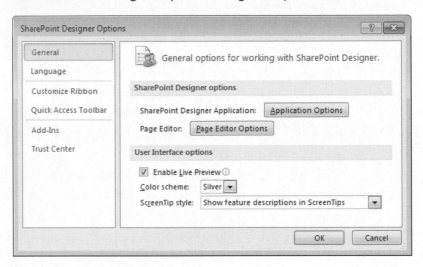

3. Click **Application Options**.

   The Application Options dialog box opens displaying the General tab, where the Startup options are listed. You use the Configure Editors tab to associate file types with programs (the default editors) on your computer. These programs are used to open a file when you double-click it or when you right-click a file and click Open.

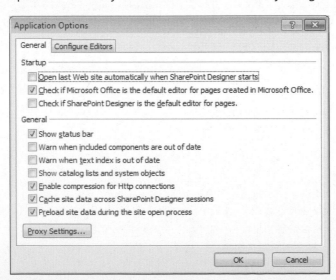

4. On the **General** tab, select the **Open last Web site automatically when SharePoint Designer starts** check box, and then click **OK** twice to close the **Application Options** and then the **SharePoint Designer Options** dialog boxes.

5. In the left pane, click **Help**.

    Options for getting help and details about SharePoint Designer, including version information and whether you are using the 32-bit or 64-bit version of SharePoint Designer, are displayed.

6. In the left pane, click **Sites,** and then under **Open SharePoint Site**, click **Open Site**.

    The Open Site dialog box is displayed.

    Tip You can use your browser to open a Web site in SharePoint Designer by clicking Site Actions and then clicking Edit In SharePoint Designer. If you click this option and do not have SharePoint Designer installed, you are asked whether you want to download and install SharePoint Designer. If you choose to install SharePoint Designer 2010 yourself and have SharePoint Designer 2007 already installed (so that you can customize earlier versions of SharePoint), you must download the 32-bit version of SharePoint Designer 2010. Please also note that 64-bit Office applications will not run if SharePoint Designer 2007 is installed.

7. In the **Site name** box, type the URL of your team site, and then click **Open**. If prompted, type your user name and password, and click **OK**.

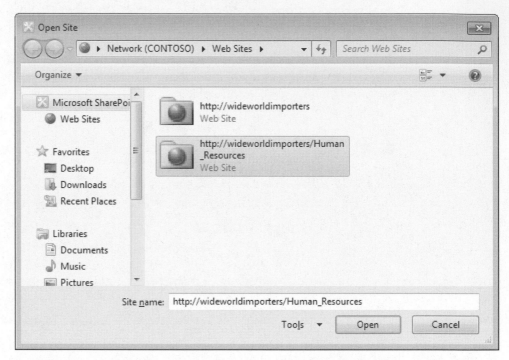

Important SharePoint Designer uses Internet Explorer's security settings to decide whether to prompt for credentials. If you are prompted for credentials when you display the site in the browser, you are prompted for credentials when you open the same site using SharePoint Designer.

The On Stage view of SharePoint Designer is displayed. The workspace contains the settings page for your team site, and the workspace tab displays the name of your site. The workspace also displays the key information for your site, such as the title and description, the Web address, the SharePoint version, server version, percentage of storage used (if a quota is set for this site), and users and groups that have permissions to your site. You'll also see a list of subsites and see whether you have the ability to customize your home page and master page and to change the theme. The ribbon's Site tab contains commands to create new SharePoint artifacts and to manage the site.

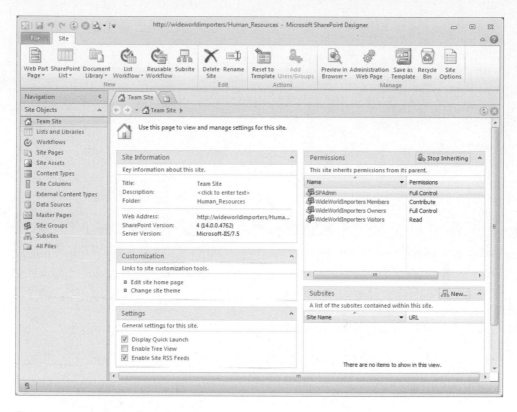

8. Click the down arrow at the right end of the Quick Access Toolbar, and then click **More Commands**.

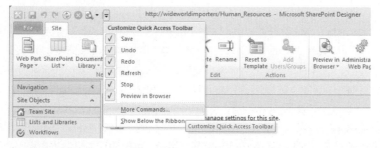

The SharePoint Designer Options dialog box opens.

9. Under **Choose command from,** select **All Commands,** and then scroll down, click **Paste Text,** and click **Add**.

Paste Text appears in the Customize Quick Access Toolbar column.

10. Click the up arrow to the right of the **Customize Access Toolbar** column so that the **Paste Text** command is below **Redo,** and then click **OK** to close the **SharePoint Designer Options** dialog box.

A dimmed Paste Text icon appears on the Quick Access Toolbar. This icon becomes activate when you have a Web page open and you place the insertion point in the Web page.

 CLEAN UP Leave SharePoint Designer open if you are continuing to the next exercise.

Using SharePoint Designer to Explore a Web Page

When you open a site you are presented with the site settings page in the workspace area. You can use this page to view and manage the settings for a site, and you can use the link in the Customization area to open the site's home page. The home page, also known as the site's default page, is the page that renders in your browser if you type the URL of a site and do not specify a specific page.

SharePoint Designer provides you with the following three views of a page:

- *Design view* displays the page as it would appear in a browser and provides a WYSIWYG editing environment. To identify page elements such as borders, margins, and padding, you can use SharePoint Designer 2010 visual aids.

- *Code view* displays the HTML tags, client-side script (such as JavaScript), and controls that SharePoint uses to display content, such as the name of the site and the Search box. The code elements are color-coded to make it easier for you to distinguish the text that users see in their browser from the code surrounding the text. Each line of code is numbered so that error messages can reference them and you can quickly identify problems.

- *Split view* divides the workspace horizontally and displays Code view at the top and Design view at the bottom.

Tip You can change the default colors for the code elements by using the Page Editor Options dialog box. You can also change the default text attributes for content you add using Design view. You will use the Page Editor Options dialog box in the next exercise.

You can use any of these three views to edit a page. When you display a page in the workspace, it is called the *editor page*, and *Editor* appears in the workspace breadcrumb.

A SharePoint site can contain a number of different types of Web pages. The types of Web pages you might be familiar with when using a browser are Web Part pages, Wiki pages, and, if you use SharePoint Server, publishing pages. These pages on a newly created SharePoint site are built from site definition files and point to files in the TEMPLATE folder, as described earlier in this chapter.

See Also For more information on editing Web Part pages and Wiki pages in the browser, see Chapter 6, "Working with Web Pages," in *Microsoft SharePoint Foundation 2010 Step by Step*. Publishing pages are covered later in this book in Chapter 13, "Managing Web Content in the SharePoint Server Environment."

The home page of a newly created team site is a Wiki page, which allows users to intermingle content with Web Parts in a rich-text editing region within the page. This region of the page, known as *PlaceHolderMain*, is saved separately from the site definition file. Therefore, when you edit the page in the browser or in SharePoint Designer in safe mode—which is the default editing mode—you are only modifying the content within PlaceHolderMain and not the content of the site definition files. Depending on your permissions, as explained in the last section of this chapter, you might be able to edit the Web page in advanced edit mode. This allows you to amend the content outside the PlaceHolderMain region. Then, when you save the Web page, a copy of the site definition file together with your amendments are stored in the SQL Server content database. These amended Web pages, known as *customized* or *unghosted* pages, no longer point to the site definition files in the TEMPLATE folder on the SharePoint servers and no longer provide the same performance benefit as site definition files. Site definition files that have not been customized are known as *uncustomized* or *ghosted* pages.

In Code view, when you are editing a page in safe mode, the code that is stored outside PlaceHolderMain and which you cannot modify is highlighted in yellow.

In this exercise, you use the Page Editor Options dialog box to configure Design and Code views and then explore a Web page.

 SET UP Using SharePoint Designer, open the team site you used in the previous exercise if it is not already open. The site's settings page should be displayed.

1. Click the **File** tab, and then click **Options** in the left pane.

   The SharePoint Designer Options dialog box opens.

2. On the **General** tab, click **Page Editor Options**.

   The Page Editor Options dialog box opens with the General tab active. This tab contains a number of settings that affect Code view. You can also change these options from the Code View toolbar. The default settings make it easy for you to work with code and find errors.

3. Click the **Default Fonts** tab.

    The default setting is to use the Unicode (UTF-8) language, which is the World Wide Web Consortium (W3C) recommendation. Depending on the size of your monitor, you might want to change the font size used in Code view.

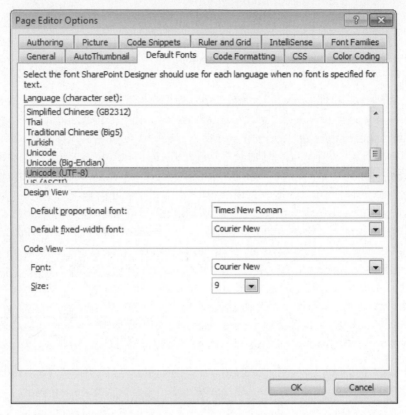

Tip Do not change the Design view font. Internet Explorer and Firefox use Times New Roman as their default font, and you want the view of a page in Design view to reflect the rendering of the page within the browser.

4. Click **OK** twice to close the **Page Editor Options** and then the **SharePoint Designer Options** dialog boxes.

    The site settings page is displayed in the workspace.

5. In the **Customization** area, click **Edit site home page**.

    The home page of the team site opens as a second tab in the workspace. The Home.aspx file is stored within the Site Pages document library. SharePoint Designer indicates this by highlighting the artifact Site Pages in orange in the Navigation pane and displaying the Site Pages mini-gallery below the Navigation pane.

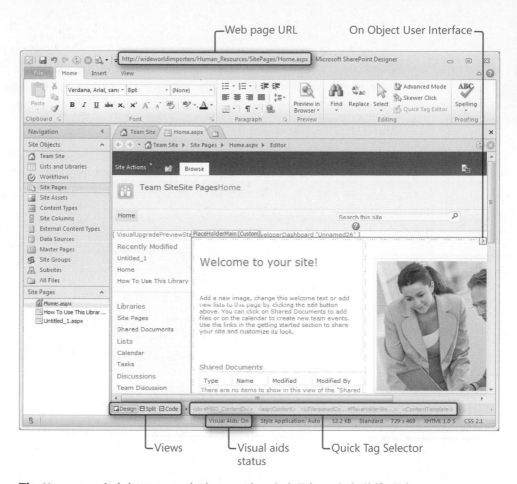

Web page URL   On Object User Interface

Views   Visual aids status   Quick Tag Selector

Tip You can switch between tabs by pressing Ctrl+Tab or Ctrl+Shift+Tab.

The title bar of the SharePoint Designer window contains the URL of the page. A purple border labeled PlaceHolderMain (Custom) is displayed with a small arrow floating to the top right of the border, known as the On Object User Interface (OOUI). The Quick Tag Selector is displayed in the workspace status area to the right of the view tabs. The SharePoint Designer window status bar identifies whether visual aids are turned on or off.

Troubleshooting If the purple border labeled PlaceHolderMain (Custom) does not appear, place the insertion point to the left of the text *Welcome to your Site!*

6. On the **View** tab on the ribbon, click **Visual Aids** in the **Workspace** group, and then click **Show**.

The status of visual aids is reversed; in other words, if they were turned on, the SharePoint Designer window status bar now indicates Visual Aids: Off.

No-Entry

7. Move the pointer over the page to where the pointer changes to the no-entry icon.

A no-entry icon identifies content that is not within the EmbeddedFormField SharePoint control. The PlaceHolderMain (Custom) region contains the EmbeddedFormField control. You cannot click or enter text at the location where the no-entry icon appears.

8. Within the **PlaceHolderMain** region, click **Shared Documents**.

The Web Part is highlighted in blue and labeled WebPartPages:XsltListViewWebPart, and the WebPartPages:XsltListViewWebPart tag becomes the last tag on the Quick Tag Selector. On the ribbon, four List View Tools tabs are displayed: Options, Design, Web Part, and Table.

9. Press **Esc** four times.

The third time you press Esc, the table cell *td,* which contains the left part of the PlaceHolderMain region, is highlighted. The final time you press Esc, the *table#layoutsTable* tag contained in the PlaceHolderMain region is highlighted. The Esc key takes you to the parent HTML tag container. On the Quick Tag Selector, a number of unavailable tags are displayed. These tags are defined outside the PlaceHolderMain region. On the ribbon, the List View Tools tabs disappear, and the Table Tools, Layout tab is displayed.

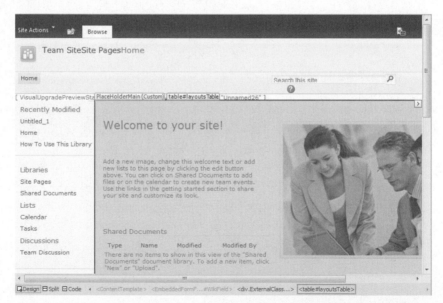

Tip SharePoint sites contain a number of controls, so it can be difficult to position your cursor exactly where you want it. Use the Esc key together with the Up Arrow, Down Arrow, Left Arrow, and Right Arrow keys to navigate around the page.

10. At the bottom of the Home.aspx document window, click **Split**.

The workspace splits horizontally and displays Code view in the upper pane and Design view in the lower pane. The table is highlighted in both views. In Code view, the code above the table tag is highlighted in yellow, indicating that you cannot amend that code.

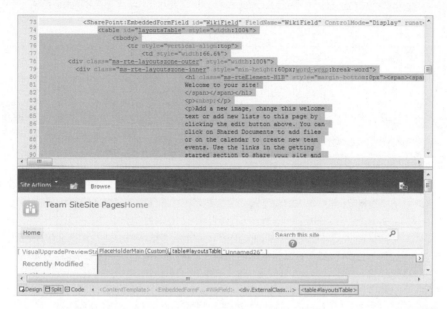

Tip You can switch between views by pressing **Ctrl+Page Up** or **Ctrl+Page Down**.

11. On the **Home** tab, click **Advanced Mode** in the **Editing** group.

Troubleshooting If the Advance Mode command is not active, you have not been given permissions by your site collection owner or SharePoint administrator to edit pages in advanced mode and will not be able to complete this step. See the last section in the chapter for more information on controlling the use of SharePoint Designer.

The word *Editor* on the workspace breadcrumb is replaced by *Advanced Editor*. The Home.aspx page refreshes, and in Code view no lines of code are highlighted in yellow.

Tip The Advanced Mode command in the Editing group is not available and cannot be used to toggle the page back to safe edit mode. To return the page to safe edit mode, you need to close and reopen the page.

12. On the **View** tab, click **Design** in the **Page Views** group. Right-click the **Home.aspx** tab, and then click **Close**.

The home page of the team site closes, leaving the Team Site tab displayed in the workspace.

 CLEAN UP Leave SharePoint Designer open if you are continuing to the next exercise.

Using Task Panes

Task panes are helper windows that you can use to perform certain tasks with Web pages. You can open, close, and move task panes to the sides of the SharePoint Designer window or make them float so that they appear in the middle of the window. You can open task panes by using the ribbon's View tab. SharePoint Designer provides 17 task panes, listed in the following table.

Task pane	Description
Tag Properties	Use to manipulate tag properties, such as HTML tags, ASP.NET controls, and SharePoint Server controls.
CSS Properties	Use when working with cascading style sheets, particularly when manipulating cascading style sheet class, ID, or tag definitions. Use as an alternative to launching the Modify Style dialog box.
Apply Styles	Use to create new cascading style sheet styles and apply existing ones to elements within pages.
Manage Styles	Use to manage cascading style sheet styles that are added to elements within pages.
Behaviors	Lists behaviors that you can add to pages. Behaviors allow you to add dynamic effects and are mostly driven by JavaScript.
Layers	Use to insert and configure layers. A *layer* is the name given to an absolute-positioned HTML division (DIV) tag. You use the DIV tag to group elements so that you can format them with styles or create animations or flyout menus.
Toolbox	Lists HTML tags, form controls, ASP.NET controls, and SharePoint controls that you can place on pages by dragging and dropping.
Data Source Details	Use to display or modify contents of the data sources by using either the *Data View Web Part* (DVWP) or *Data Form Web Part* (DFWP).
Conditional Formatting	Use to format the data in a DVWP or DFWP depending on criteria that you specify.
Find 1	Use to search and replace text, code, and HTML within a page. You can find and replace text on one page, a number of pages, or the whole site. You can also find words in the code and regular expressions.
Find 2	Displays a second search task pane. Use when you want to leave the search results in the Find 1 task pane but need to complete another search.
Accessibility	Use to check pages and sites against Web Content Accessibility Guidelines (WCAG) Priority 1 and 2 and Section 508.

Compatibility	Use to validate pages and sites for well-formed HTML/XTML or cascading style sheet versions. The Compatibility Checker currently supports CSS 2.1, 2.0, 1.0 and CSS IE6.
Hyperlinks	Use to check and fix broken links.
CSS Reports	Use to check pages for cascading style sheet errors and highlight those cascading style sheet styles that are not used.
Clip Art	Use to search for clip art.
Clipboard	Allows you to view up to 24 thumbnails of any item that can be cut or copied by an Office program (text, graphics, photographs, and more).

In this exercise, you view and manage task panes.

SET UP Using SharePoint Designer, open the team site you used earlier in this chapter. The settings page for the site should be displayed.

1. In the **Navigation** pane, click **Site Pages**.

    The Site Pages gallery page is displayed in the workspace.

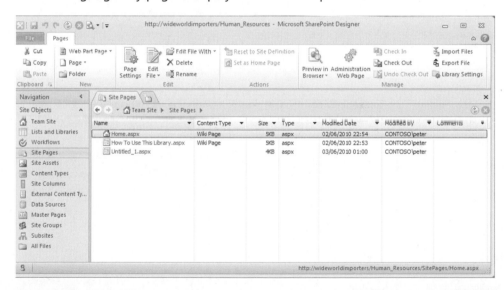

Edit File

2. Click **Home.aspx** if it is not already selected. Then, on the **Pages** tab, click **Edit File** in the **Edit** group.

    The home page of the team site opens in the workspace.

3. On the **View** tab, click **Task Panes** in the **Workspace** group, and then click **Find 1**.

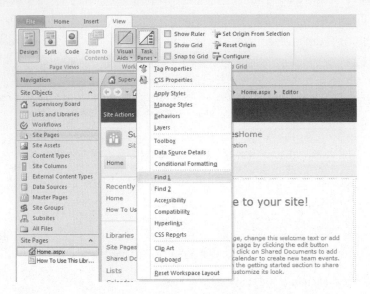

The Find 1 task pane opens, docking below the workspace.

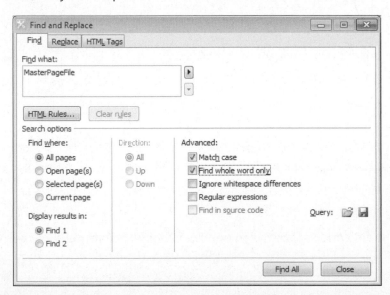

4. In the **Find 1** task pane, click the **Find and Replace** button.

The Find And Replace dialog box opens.

5. In the **Find what** box, type **MasterPageFile**, and click **All pages** under **Find where**.

6. Select the **Match case** and **Find whole word only** check boxes under **Advanced**. Clear any other options that are selected under **Advanced**.

7. Click **Find All**.

The Find And Replace dialog box closes. The status bars of both the SharePoint Designer window and the Find 1 task pane indicate the progress of the search. When the search is complete, the Find 1 task pane status bar informs you that no occurrences of *MasterPageFile* were found.

Note Because the page was displayed in Design view, SharePoint Designer searched the text that would be displayed to users when they use a browser in the search for the term MasterPageFile. It was not searching the source code for the word.

8. In the **Find 1** task pane, click the **Find and Replace** button.

The Find And Replace dialog box opens.

9. Under **Advanced**, select the **Find in source code** check box under **Advanced**.

Note When you have a page in Code view, it is possible to search all pages in your site, by first selecting **Find in source code** under **Advanced** and then **Find where**, clicking **All pages**.

10. Click **Close** to close the **Find and Replace** dialog box.

11. In the workspace status bar, click **Code**.

The home page is displayed in Code view in the workspace.

12. In the **Find 1** task pane, click the **Find and Replace** button to open the **Find and Replace** dialog box.

13. In the **Find what** box, type **MasterPageFile** (if necessary), select the **Find in source code** check box under **Advanced,** and click **All pages** under **Find where**.

The Find In Source Code check box is not available but is still selected.

14. Click **Find All**.

The Find And Replace dialog box closes, and as before, the status bars indicate the progress of the search process; the Find 1 task pane displays the results. In a newly created SharePoint site, each page refers to a master page. The number of pages returned in the results depends on the site template the site is created from and whether the site is created in a SharePoint Foundation or SharePoint Server installation.

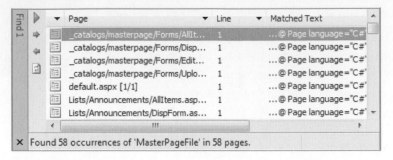

	Page	Line	Matched Text	
	_catalogs/masterpage/Forms/AllIt...	1	...@ Page language="C#"	
	_catalogs/masterpage/Forms/Disp...	1	...@ Page language="C#"	
	_catalogs/masterpage/Forms/Edit...	1	...@ Page language="C#"	
	_catalogs/masterpage/Forms/Uplo...	1	...@ Page language="C#"	
	default.aspx [1/1]	1	...@ Page language="C#"	
	Lists/Announcements/AllItems.asp...	1	...@ Page language="C#"	
	Lists/Announcements/DispForm.as...	1	...@ Page language="C#"	

✕ Found 58 occurrences of 'MasterPageFile' in 58 pages.

Next Result

15. In the **Find 1** task pane, click the **Next Result** button.

The first page in the results list opens in a new tab in the workspace in Code view, with the first instance of the text you are looking for highlighted.

Tip To continue searching the page for the next occurrence of the word, click the Next Result button; to find the previous occurrence of the search keyword, click the Previous Result button. When no more occurrences of the search keyword can be found on the current page, the next page in the results list opens in a new tab if the page is not already open. To open a specific page, double-click the page in the results list. To save your common find-and-replace searches, in the Find And Replace dialog box, click the Save Query button. To use a saved query, click the Open Query button.

16. On the **View** tab, click **Task Panes**.

Notice that the task panes displayed in the drop-down menu are grouped and separated with a horizontal line. Task panes in the same group open in the same area of the SharePoint Designer window. Task panes that open in the same area appear as tabs.

17. Use the **Task Panes** list to open the **Clipboard, Manage Styles,** and **Apply Styles** task panes.

The Clipboard task pane docks to the right edge of the SharePoint Designer window, and the Apply Styles task pane opens to the left of the Clipboard task pane, with the Manage Styles task pane represented by a tab to the right of the Apply Styles tab. The Workspace and Find 1 task panes are reduced in size.

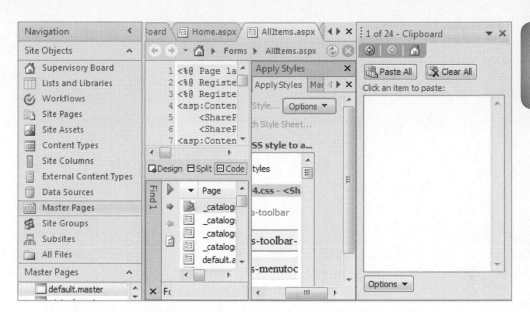

18. In the lower-left corner of the **Find 1** task pane, click the **Close** button.

Close

The Find 1 task pane closes.

Tip Close task panes when you no longer need them because they reduce the space available for the document window area.

19. In the **Apply Styles** task pane area, click the **Manage Styles** tab.

The Manage Styles task pane becomes active.

20. Move the mouse pointer over the **Manage Styles** task pane title bar so that the pointer changes to a four-way arrow. Hold down the mouse button, and drag the **Manage Styles** task pane below the workspace.

Note The Clip Art and Clipboard task panes cannot be moved or merged with the other task panes and always open in a separate window docked at the right side of the SharePoint Designer window.

21. On the ribbon's **View** tab, click **Task Panes,** and then click **Reset Workspace Layout**.

All task panes close.

22. On the **View** tab, click **Design**.

The active page is displayed in Design view.

✖ **CLEAN UP** Close SharePoint Designer.

Controlling the Use of SharePoint Designer

SharePoint is a rich and complex tool, designed to be used by information workers, business analysts, project managers, administrators, and developers—in fact, by anyone who needs to design, develop, or prototype SharePoint 2010 solutions. However, it is not a tool for everyone, and IT administrators and site collection owners will want to limit its usage at either the Web-application or site-collection level.

When a Web application is created, by default each site collection within that Web application can be modified using SharePoint Designer only by users who are members of the Site Owners and Designers site groups. However, such users are not allowed to do the following:

- Detach pages from site definitions; that is, they cannot edit Web pages in advanced mode, and therefore cannot customize (unghost) Web pages.

- Customize master pages and page layouts. The Master Page option will not be available on the Navigation pane in SharePoint Designer.

- See the hidden URL structure of their Web site. Within SharePoint Designer, users will not see the All Files option on the Navigation pane, the All Files gallery page in the workspace, or All Files in the mini-gallery. If this option is enabled but the Customize Master Pages And Page Layouts option is not allowed, then site owners and designers can see the master pages and page layouts, but they are not allowed to amend them.

  Note In SharePoint Foundation, the Designers site group is not created by default, but it can be created by using the browser or SharePoint Designer. When you create the Designers site group, map it to the design permission level.

Site collection administrators are not limited by these settings at the site-collection level. However, at the Web-application level, all users, including site collection administrators, can be prevented from using SharePoint Designer or be limited in their use of SharePoint Designer across all site collections within the Web application.

In this exercise, you configure SharePoint Designer settings at the site-collection level. You need to be a site collection owner to complete this exercise.

 SET UP You need the URL of the top-level site of a site collection.

1.   Open the root site of your site collection in the browser.

2.   Click **Site Actions,** and then click **Site Settings**.

     The site settings page is displayed.

3. Under **Site Collection Administration**, click **SharePoint Designer Settings**.

    Troubleshooting Under Site Collection Administration, if you see only Go To The Top Level Site Settings, you have opened a subsite in the browser. Click the link to go to the root site's site settings page. If you do not see the Site Collection Administration section on the site settings page, you are not a site collection owner and cannot complete the rest of this exercise.

    The SharePoint Designer Settings page is displayed.

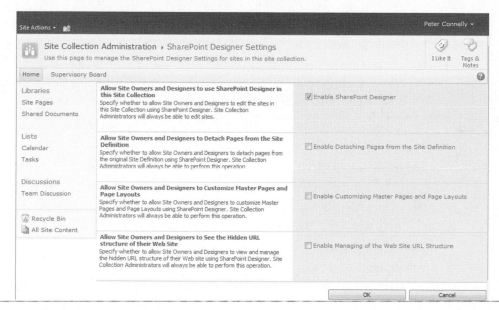

4. Select the check boxes that meet your business needs, and then click **OK**.

 **CLEAN UP** Close the browser.

See Also Appendix C on page 503 for a list of steps that SharePoint farm administrators can use to restrict the use of SharePoint Designer at the Web-application level.

Key Points

- SharePoint Designer is "the preferred" tool to design powerful no-code solutions and applications in SharePoint 2010.

- Use SharePoint Designer to produce solutions that are easily maintainable and supportable.

- SharePoint Designer is not a tool for general use by all those who visit or have access to a SharePoint site. The browser should be used to complete tasks such as adding static content (text, images, or hyperlinks) to Web pages, uploading documents, or creating and modifying list items.

- SharePoint Designer 2010 can be used only with SharePoint Foundation 2010 or SharePoint Server 2010 sites. These are server-based products and need to be installed prior to using SharePoint Designer 2010.

- SharePoint Designer 2010 cannot be used to customize non-SharePoint Web sites, nor can you use it to customize sites based on previous versions of SharePoint, such as Windows SharePoint Services 3.0 or Microsoft Office SharePoint Server 2007. Use Expression Web for non-SharePoint sites and SharePoint Designer 2007 with sites created in previous versions of SharePoint.

- SharePoint Designer can remember the last site you worked on and open it when you start the program. This is not the default configuration, but you can select this setting on the General tab of the Application Options dialog box. The Application Options dialog box can be opened by clicking Options in Backstage view.

- SharePoint Designer uses the security settings of your browser to decide whether to prompt for credentials.

- The SharePoint Designer shell consists of Backstage view and On Stage view. On Stage view consists of a number of elements, including the Quick Access Toolbar, ribbon, breadcrumb, Navigation pane, mini-gallery, workspace, task panes, and status bar.

- Web pages initially created in a SharePoint site point to files on a file system, known as *uncustomized* pages; however, when pages are customized by using SharePoint Designer, they are stored in the SQL Server databases, where they are known as *customized* pages.

- In SharePoint Designer 2010, uncustomized (site definition) pages can only be customized (unghosted) when a page is in advanced edit mode.

- A SharePoint Web application consists of one or more site collections that contain one or more Web sites.

- When a Web application is created, by default each site collection within that Web application can be modified using SharePoint Designer only by users who are members of the Site Owners and Designers site groups. However, these users cannot customize site definition pages, nor can they see the hidden URL structure of a SharePoint site.

Chapter at a Glance

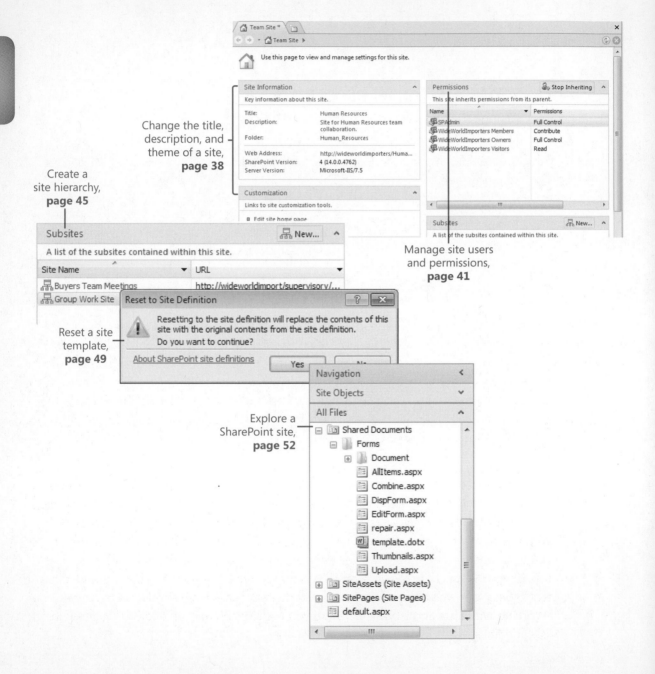

Change the title, description, and theme of a site, **page 38**

Create a site hierarchy, **page 45**

Manage site users and permissions, **page 41**

Reset a site template, **page 49**

Explore a SharePoint site, **page 52**

2 Working with SharePoint Sites

In this chapter, you will learn how to

✔ Change the title, description, and theme of a site.

✔ Manage site users and permissions.

✔ Create a site hierarchy.

✔ Delete a SharePoint site.

✔ Reset a site template.

✔ Explore a SharePoint site.

✔ Navigate a site's components.

✔ Save and use a site template.

You might be using SharePoint for your Internet, intranet, or extranet Web sites, which are built from a series of SharePoint sites. It is within these sites that you create, store, and manage your content and collaborate with other users in your enterprise. Each site can have its own security settings, functionality, content, and navigation. As you saw in Chapter 1, "Exploring SharePoint Designer 2010," these sites can be children of other sites and can have subsites underneath them. This hierarchal relationship can assist you with navigation as well as security inheritance.

In this chapter, you will see how to use Microsoft SharePoint Designer 2010 to modify a site's title, description, and theme. You will also learn how to manage who has access to a site and what they can do on the site, as well as how to manage your site hierarchy. You will learn how to make a copy of your customizations by creating a site template and how to reset your site's pages when users have customized them with SharePoint Designer so that they reflect the site template . You will explore the hidden URL structure of your Web site and review other site components, such as site columns and content types. Your work with site columns and content types leads nicely to Chapter 3, "Working with Lists and Libraries," where you use site columns and content types with lists and libraries.

> **Practice Files** No practice files are required to complete the exercises in this chapter. For more information about practice files, see "Using the Practice Files" on page xxiii.

Changing the Title, Description, and Theme of a Site

Each site has a title and description. These are important properties of a site because they appear on each page within a site and communicate to users the purpose and function of the site. They are also fundamental to making information easy to find.

SharePoint uses the text in the title and description fields to rank content items that are returned in a search result set. Users of SharePoint Server sites can create a more focused result set by using the advanced search page on the Enterprise Search site, where title and description are some of the *metadata* properties that can be selected in the property restrict list. On SharePoint Foundation sites, where there is no enterprise search, a user can, for example, type *description:oak* in the Search box to find all SharePoint components whose description property contains the word *oak*. As a site or content owner, it is important that you enter meaningful and consistent names for your site and other SharePoint components.

See Also More information on how to execute basic search queries on a SharePoint site can be found in Chapter 16, "Finding Information on the SharePoint Site," in *Microsoft SharePoint Foundation 2010 Step by Step* by Olga Londer and Penelope Coventry (Microsoft Press, 2011).

Site owners of collaboration and team sites will want to apply their own unique look and feel. Themes provide lightweight branding of a SharePoint site. Site owners can apply one of 20 out-of-the-box themes to a site. Themes reuse the theme definition and format defined in the Office Open XML standard that was introduced with Microsoft Office PowerPoint 2007 to create new themes for slide decks. No developer resource is needed; once the .thmx file is created using an Office 2010 application, it can be loaded into the Theme gallery at the top-level site of a site collection.

See Also To find how to create a theme using Office PowerPoint 2010, see, Chapter 3, "Creating and Managing Sites," in *Microsoft SharePoint Foundation 2010 Step by Step*. More information on how to plan for themes can be found at *http://technet.microsoft.com/en-us/library/ee424399.aspx*.

Using a browser on a SharePoint Server publishing site or on a site where the Publishing feature is enabled, you can create your own new themes and push them down to subsites or inherit a theme from the parent site. However, you can apply a theme to only one site by using the browser on SharePoint Foundation sites, on SharePoint Server sites that do not have the Publishing feature enabled, or when you use SharePoint Designer.

Note Themes change the colors and fonts used on a site. If you want to change other design elements, such as font size or spacing, you need to use cascading style sheets. If you want to completely change the page structure and design of your site, you need to modify or create your own master pages.

In this exercise, you modify a site's title and description and apply a theme to the site.

SET UP Using SharePoint Designer, open the team site you created and modified in Chapter 1. The settings page should be displayed in the workspace. If you did not yet create a team site, follow the steps in Chapter 1 before you start this exercise.

Rename

1. On the **Site** tab, click **Rename** in the **Edit** group.

   In the Site Information area, a box appears to the right of Title, with the site name highlighted.

2. Type **Human Resources,** and then press **Enter**.

   An asterisk appears on the Team Site tab, indicating that the properties of the site have changed but you have not saved your changes.

3. To the right of **Description**, click **<click to enter text>,** and then type **Site for Human Resources team collaboration**.

   Tip You can modify the URL of your site by clicking the text to the right of Folder, unless the site is the top-level site of a site collection. If that is the case the URL of the site cannot be modified and the Folder option is not displayed in the Site Information area.

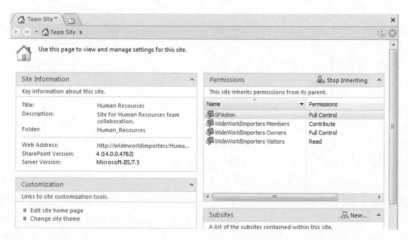

Save

4. On the Quick Access Tool bar, click **Save**.

The site settings page is refreshed, and the tab label changes to *Human Resources* with no asterisk. In the Navigation pane, the site object is labeled *Human Resources*, as is the ScreenTip that appears when you hover the mouse over the site name.

5. In the **Customization** area of the site settings page, click **Change site theme**. If prompted, type your user name and password, and then click **OK**.

A browser window opens and displays the Site Theme page.

6. In the **Select a Theme** section, click **Azure,** and then click **Apply**.

The Processing page is momentarily displayed before the site settings page is displayed, with the Azure theme applied.

Troubleshooting Cascading style sheets used on SharePoint sites can be created so that they do not support themes. This often occurs on company portal sites or an Internet site where a company wants to maintain its brand on all sites within a site collection. If the theme you choose in this exercise is not applied, check with your SharePoint administrator.

7. Under **Look and Feel**, click **Site theme**.

The Site Theme page is displayed.

8. In the **Select a Theme** section, click **Default (no theme),** and then click **Apply**.

The site settings page is displayed, with no theme applied.

 CLEAN UP Close the browser, but leave SharePoint Designer open if you are continuing to the next exercise.

Publishing Features

Publishing functionality is enabled on SharePoint Server sites when the SharePoint Server Publishing feature is activated. A *feature* is a concept introduced in Windows SharePoint Services 3.0 that allows you to activate or deactivate functionality at the level of a site, site collection, Web application, or *SharePoint farm*. The SharePoint Server Publishing feature depends on the activation of the SharePoint Server Publishing Infrastructure feature at the site-collection level. Microsoft developed both these features, which are installed when SharePoint Server 2010 is installed on each Web front end. Site owners can activate features to extend the functionality of their sites. Therefore, you can turn a SharePoint site based on the Team Site template into a publishing site by activating the SharePoint Server Publishing feature.

Managing Site Users and Permissions

SharePoint Designer provides you with more than just the ability to customize a SharePoint Foundation or SharePoint Server site. It also helps you manage and protect your sites without the need to open the browser. When you create a site in the browser, you can choose whether the site has its own security setting. However, when you create a site with SharePoint Designer, your site automatically has the same security settings as the parent site. If you are customizing a new site to meet a specific business need, or if you want to templatize your site so that you can create many other sites based on your customizations, you do not want other users to use your site until your customizations are complete and tested. In this case, you need to alter the default security settings of your site.

SharePoint permission rights, such as Manage Lists, Create Subsites, Apply Themes and Borders, and Delete Items, are grouped into permissions levels. On a specific SharePoint object, such as a site, a list, or a list item, you map a permissions level to a user or to a SharePoint group.

SharePoint Foundation has five permission levels: Full Control, Design, Contribute, Read, Limited Access, and View Only. SharePoint Server has an additional three permission levels: Manage Hierarchy, Approve, and Restricted Read. In SharePoint Designer you cannot create a permission level or change the level of a permission rights group. However, you can create and manage SharePoint groups, and you can map users and SharePoint groups to permission levels for sites, lists, and libraries. To map permission levels to list items or individual files, you need to use the browser.

See Also For more information on permissions and permission levels, see Chapter 3 and the appendix in *Microsoft SharePoint Foundation 2010 Step by Step*.

In this exercise, you change the security settings for a subsite from inheriting permissions from its parent site to using unique permissions. You also prevent the Viewers site group from accessing the site and then grant a user, such as Todd, access to the site so that he can add and modify content. You then test whether that user can use SharePoint Designer to open the site.

Important To complete this exercise, you need access to the credentials of another user account and a team site that is inheriting its permissions from its parent site.

 SET UP Using SharePoint Designer, open the team site you used in the previous exercise if it is not already open. The settings page for the site should be displayed.

Stop Inheriting

1. In the **Permissions** area of the workspace, click **Stop Inheriting**.

   A Microsoft SharePoint Designer dialog box opens.

2. Click **OK** to confirm the change.

   The dialog box closes. In the Permissions area, the Stop Inheriting button is replaced by New. A list of the SharePoint groups and users is copied from the parent site and mapped to the same permission levels as on the parent site.

   Note The Permissions column in the Permissions area references permission levels.

3. Click the icon to the left of **Viewers** to activate the **Site Permissions** tab on the ribbon, and then click **Delete** in the **Edit** group.

4. Click **OK** to confirm the change.

   The Viewers SharePoint group is not listed under Permissions.

5. In the Permission area, take note of the site group that is mapped to the **Contribute** permission level, and then click **New**.

   The Add Permissions dialog box opens.

6. In the **Choose users or groups to add** text box, type the user name or e-mail address of the user to whom you'd like to grant permissions, such as **todd**.

   Tip You can use the Check Names or the People Picker icon to ensure you enter a valid user name.

7. Under **Add users to a SharePoint group**, click the group you noted earlier that was mapped to the Contribute permission, such as **Wide World Importers Members**.

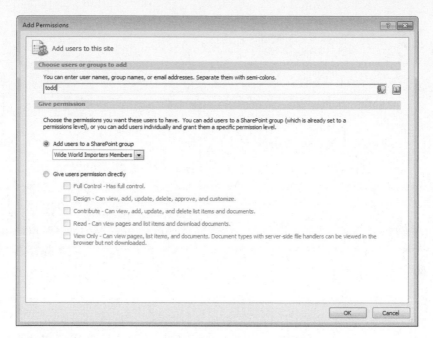

Important Editing a site group affects the membership of all sites, lists, folders, and items that are using that site group.

8. Click **OK** to close the **Add Permissions** dialog box.

A Microsoft SharePoint Designer dialog box opens.

9. Click **Yes** to view the membership of the group.

A new workspace tab opens and displays the settings page of the site group you added the user to. In the Members area is a list of all users who are a member of this site group, including the user you added in this exercise.

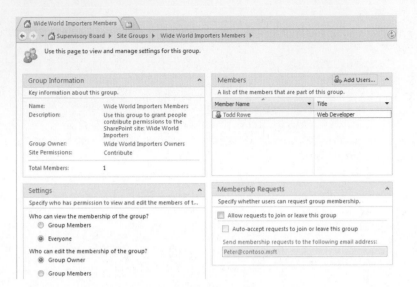

10. Click the **Log In As** button in the status bar in the SharePoint Designer window.

Log In As

11. Click **OK** in the **Log in as another user** dialog box that opens.

12. In the **Windows Security** dialog box that opens, type the user name and password of the user you granted permissions to earlier in this exercise, and then click **OK**.

A Microsoft SharePoint Designer dialog box opens stating that you do not have permission to open this Web site in SharePoint Designer.

Important SharePoint permissions are used when you access SharePoint resources in SharePoint Designer. If your user name is mapped to the Contribute permission level at the site level, you cannot open the site in SharePoint Designer. Your user name must be mapped to the Design or Full Control permission levels to use SharePoint Designer. See the section "Controlling the Use of SharePoint Designer," in Chapter 1.

13. Click **OK**.

Backstage view is displayed.

 **CLEAN UP** Close SharePoint Designer.

Creating a Site Hierarchy

A site collection consists of one or more sites. Each site is created by using as a template a site definition or a customized site definition, both of which are commonly known as *site templates*. A site collection can be created by using the browser or programmatically. You cannot use SharePoint Designer to create a site collection. You can use SharePoint Designer only to create child sites within a site collection.

See Also For a list of steps that a SharePoint administrator can use to create a site collection, see Appendix C on page 503 and refer to *Microsoft SharePoint Server 2010 Administrator's Companion*, by Bill English, Brian Alderman, and Mark Ferraz (Microsoft Press, 2011).

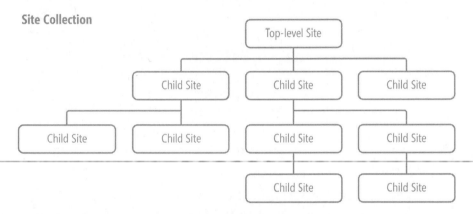

Tip The Site Content and Structure page provides a visual representation of a site collection's hierarchy. The Site Content and Structure page is available only on SharePoint sites created on SharePoint Server when the SharePoint Server Publishing Infrastructure site collection feature and the SharePoint Server Publishing site feature are activated.

Typically, in a site collection that will host a number of collaboration SharePoint sites such as blogs, document workspaces, and meeting workspaces, the top-level site of the site collection is based on the Team Site template. This top-level site could be the focal site for an entire team or department. The team or department members might have only read access to this top-level site, with a limited number of them who contribute content to the site, and one or two who act as site collection owners. As child sites are created, the number of team members who have access to the site decreases, and the proportion of members who can create and update content increases.

The first task in developing a SharePoint-based solution when you use SharePoint Designer is to create a subsite. The only information you need is the URL, also known as the *internal name*.

Tip Use the best practices specified in the sidebar "Best Practices for Naming URLs" in Chapter 1 when you specify the URL name.

In Chapter 1 you created a subsite by using Backstage view. In this exercise, you will create two SharePoint sites, one by using the ribbon and the other by using the New button on the site's settings page.

 SET UP Using SharePoint Designer, open the team site you used in the previous exercise. The settings page for the site should be displayed.

1. On the **Site** tab on the ribbon, click **Subsite**.

   The New dialog box opens. In the Specify The Location Of The New Web Site text box, Subsite is highlighted. SharePoint Designer communicates with the SharePoint site collection and retrieves a list of SharePoint site templates that you can use as a basis for your new child site. These are displayed in the central pane of the New dialog box, also known as the *site type list*. Which templates are listed depends on whether you are using SharePoint Foundation or SharePoint Server, or whether your organization has created any site templates. If you connect to another SharePoint site, you might see different SharePoint templates.

2. Type **team_meeting** over Subsite. In the central pane, click **Basic Meeting Workspace**.

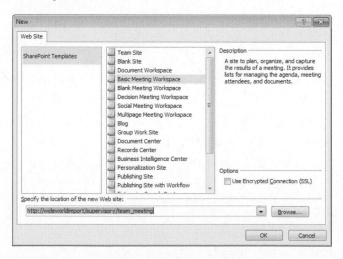

3. Click **OK**.

    Warning After you use a site template to create a site, you cannot change the site template the site is based on. If the functionality you require is not exposed through a SharePoint feature and you choose the wrong site template, you must delete the site and create it again.

    The new site opens in a new SharePoint Designer window.

4. In the **Site Information** area of the workspace, click **Basic Meeting Workspace** to the right of **Title,** and type **Buyers Team Meetings**.

    Tip When you create a site, the site's title is taken from the name of the site template. To avoid confusion about which site you are modifying, always change the title of the site as the first task after you create the site.

5. Click **<click to enter text>** to the right of **Description,** and type **Site for monthly team meeting details**.

    An asterisk appears on the site's workspace tab, indicating that some site information has changed but that you have not saved your changes.

Save

6. On the Quick Access Toolbar, click **Save**.

    The asterisk on the workspace tab disappears.

7. Click the **File** tab.

    Backstage view is displayed.

8. In the left pane, click **Close Site,** and then click **Exit.**

    The SharePoint Designer window displaying the Buyers Team Meeting site closes.

    Tip Each site you open in SharePoint Designer is displayed in its own SharePoint Designer window. With multiple SharePoint Designer windows open, it is very easy to modify a site you weren't planning to change. Try to have only one SharePoint Designer window open at a time.

9. Switch to the SharePoint Designer window displaying the team site setting page in the workspace. Notice that the Buyers Team Meeting site is listed in the **Subsites** area.

10. In the **Subsites** area, click **New**.

    The New dialog box opens. In the Specify The Location Of The New Web Site text box, Subsite is highlighted.

11. Type GroupWork over **subsite**. In the central pane, click **Group Work Site,** and then click **OK**.

    The new site opens in a new SharePoint Designer window.

12. Close the newly opened SharePoint Designer window, and switch to the SharePoint Designer window showing the team site setting page in the workspace. Notice that the **Subsites** area lists the two newly created subsites.

 CLEAN UP Leave SharePoint Designer open if you are continuing to the next exercise.

Deleting a SharePoint Site

If you no longer need or want a site, you can delete it. Be warned, however. When you delete a site, it is not sent to the *Recycle Bin*. As you saw earlier in this chapter, when you create a site using SharePoint Designer, the title of the site reflects the name of site template used to create the site. You could end up with many sites named Team Site, for example, and only by looking at each site's URL can you see which site is which. Always verify that you are deleting the correct site.

In this exercise, you delete the two SharePoint sites you created in the previous exercise. To complete this exercise, you must have completed the previous exercise or have other sites you want to delete.

SET UP Using SharePoint Designer, open the team site you used in the previous exercise if it is not already open. The settings page for the site should be displayed.

1. In the **Subsites** area of the workspace, click the icon to the left of **Group Work Site** to activate the **Site Subsites** tab on the ribbon.

2. On the ribbon, click **Delete Site** in the **Edit** group.

3. Click **OK** to confirm the deletion.

Delete Site

4. If a new SharePoint Designer window opens, close it and return to the SharePoint Designer window where the team site is open.

5. In the **Navigation** pane, click **Subsites**.

   The Subsites gallery page is displayed in the workspace.

6. Right-click **Buyers Team Meeting,** and click **Delete Site**.

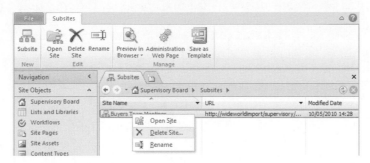

7. Click **OK** to confirm the deletion.

The Buyers Team Meeting site is no longer listed on the Subsites gallery page.

 **CLEAN UP** Leave SharePoint Designer open if you are continuing to the next exercise. Close any open Web pages.

Resetting a Site Template

As I described in Chapter 1, when you create a site based on one of the default site templates, you do not create and save any pages in the SQL Server content databases. The content databases contain only pointers to the site definition files on the Web server. These site definition pages are known as *uncustomized pages*. When you use SharePoint Designer to edit an uncustomized page in advanced edit mode, a copy of the site definition file is stored in the SQL Server content database, where your customizations can be retained.

Any customized page can be reset to the uncustomized site definition file. You can reset all customized files within a site to point to the files in the site templates defined on the Web server, or you can reset just one customized file. Resetting a customized page to the site template restores the page to its original condition. Any customizations you made with SharePoint Designer in advanced edit mode are discarded, except for customizations made to content in the PlaceHolderMain region of a wiki page or to Web Parts that are placed inside a Web Part zone in a Web Part page (as long as the Web Part zone was defined in the original site definition page).

For example, on the Home.aspx page of a team site, if you insert an image and a Content Editor Web Part (CEWP) in the PlaceHolderMain region and then reset the page, any changes you made outside the PlaceHolderMain region are discarded, but the image and the Content Editor Web Part remain, along with any customizations you made to that Web Part.

In this exercise, you reset a site definition.

SET UP Using SharePoint Designer, open the team site you used in the previous exercise if it is not already open. The settings page for the site should be displayed.

1. On the **Site** tab, click **Reset to Template** in the **Actions** group.

   The Reset To Site Definition dialog box is displayed.

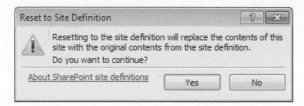

2. Click **Yes**.

   The Reset To Site Definition dialog box closes. A browser window opens. If prompted, type your user name and password, and then click OK. The Reset Page To Site Definition Version page is displayed.

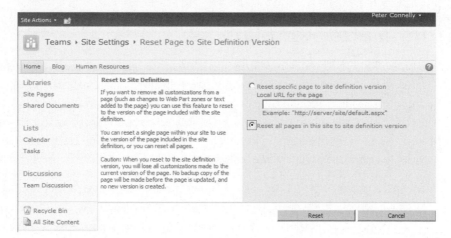

3. Select **Reset all pages in this site to site definition version,** and then click **Reset**.

   A Message From Webpage dialog box opens.

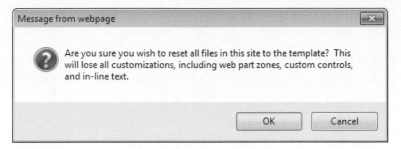

4.   Click **OK**.

 CLEAN UP Close the browser. Leave SharePoint Designer open if you are continuing to the next exercise.

Complications of Upgrading Customized SharePoint Sites

Upgrading from the previous version of SharePoint to SharePoint 2010 is not a trivial task, and the upgrade process needs to be planned and tested carefully. If you are a site owner or a solutions creator of a Windows SharePoint Services 3.0 or Microsoft Office SharePoint Server 2007 site, you might be involved in this process. The IT department will upgrade the content so that your site runs on SharePoint Foundation 2010 or SharePoint Server 2010. However, as the owner of the site, you might have to decide on when to upgrade to the new look and feel and to other customizations you or the previous owner of the site implemented.

As previously noted, SharePoint sites are different from other sites because they use site templates during the site creation process, and these site templates point to site definition files on the Web server. Customizing these site definition files was easier with SharePoint Designer 2007. During the upgrade process, when Microsoft modifies its site definitions on the Web server to include new functionality, you might not see the new functionality, depending on the pages you customized. For example, the ribbon is implemented as a control on the master page; therefore, if you customized your site's master page, the ribbon will not be available to you. Other customizations can also affect the upgrade process, so during the upgrade planning process you need to identify any customizations on your SharePoint sites and test to see the effect the upgrade process might have on them.

If you are involved in the upgrade process, you can do one of the following with your customized pages after your site is upgraded to SharePoint 2010:

● Leave the customized page as a customized page. If the customized page is a master page, pages associated with that master page will always look like a Windows SharePoint Services 3.0 or SharePoint Server 2007 page.

● Reset the customized page to the now-upgraded site definition files or pages stored on the server file system. You lose all the customizations you made to your page, and you can decide whether to reapply that customization by using SharePoint Designer 2010. This process can involve a great deal of time and effort. For example, if customizing a page takes 15 minutes and you have 100 pages, you need to allow 25 hours to customize these pages.

See Also For more information on how to handle customizations, refer to *http:// technet.microsoft.com/en-us/library/cc263203(office.14).aspx.*

Exploring a SharePoint Site

There is no one interface for SharePoint technologies; instead, you can access a SharePoint site by using a Web browser or compatible programs such as Office applications, including SharePoint Designer. You can choose the interface that suits the task you have to complete. However, depending on the program you choose, you might have a different view of the SharePoint site. If you use Microsoft Word, you see only a small portion of the Web site and its content. If you use a Web browser, you see the lists and libraries that support the collaborative nature of SharePoint, together with their content. When you use SharePoint Designer—the product that understands the most about the SharePoint infrastructure—you can see site lists and libraries that you would not see otherwise; however, you will see files but not their associated metadata, and you will not see list items.

In this exercise, you use SharePoint Designer to explore a SharePoint site.

Important To complete this exercise, you must be a site collection administrator or a site owner or designer with permissions to see the hidden URL structure of your site. See "Controlling the Use of SharePoint Designer," in Chapter 1.

 SET UP Using SharePoint Designer, open the team site you used in the previous exercise if it is not already open. The settings page for the site should be displayed.

1. In the **Navigation** pane, click **Lists and Libraries**.

The workspace displays the gallery page displaying each list or library for your site, and the workspace tab is labeled *Lists And Libraries*. The Lists And Libraries tab on the ribbon contains commands to create new lists and libraries and to edit the list.

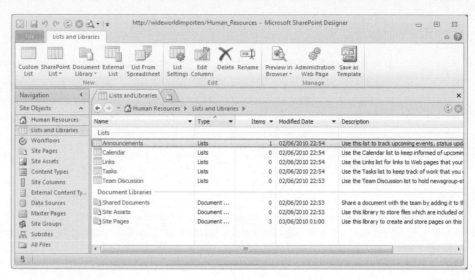

2. In the **Navigation** pane, hover over **All Files,** and click the Always Show pin that appears.

In the Navigation pane, the pin remains permanently visible to the right of All Files. The mini-gallery appears below the Navigation pane and displays the hidden URL content of the Web site, such as subsites (if they exist), folders, lists, libraries, and files. The icon that represents files depends on their extension.

Special folders are listed, such as _catalogs, _private, images, and Lists. The _catalog folder contains libraries such as those used to store Web Parts, Web site and list templates, as well as master pages.

SharePoint has a number of other folders that start with an underscore, such as _layouts and _vti, that contain images and Web pages that you can reference as links.

Warning Do not create folders for your private use with the name _layouts or _wpresources or any name that begins with _vti.

3. In the mini-gallery, click the + sign to the left of **Lists**.

The Lists folder expands, and a SharePoint-specific subfolder appears for each list created for your Web site.

4. In the mini-gallery, under the **Lists** top-level folder, click the + sign to the left of **Announcements**.

The Announcements list expands, exposing an Attachments subfolder (if attachments are enabled) and a number of Web pages that correspond to views created for the list and forms used to insert, edit, and display the properties of a list item.

5. In the workspace, in the **Lists and Libraries** gallery, under **Lists**, click **Announcements**.

The workspace tab is now labeled *Announcements*, and the workspace contains the settings page for the Announcements list. The workspace displays more information for the Announcements list than is displayed in the mini-gallery. It contains key information such as the list name and description and the number of Announcements list items. It also shows whether you can customize the list by editing the columns or modifying the permissions of the list and shows views and forms to insert, edit, and display the properties of a list item. The List Settings tab on the ribbon contains commands to create new list objects and to manage the list.

Troubleshooting The settings page for the Announcements list is displayed only if you click Announcements in the Lists And Libraries gallery page in the workspace. The settings page is not displayed if you click Announcements in the mini-gallery.

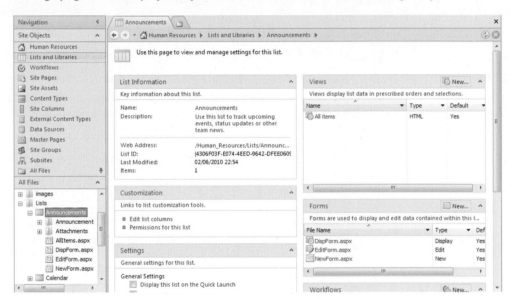

6. In the breadcrumb above the workspace, click the Back arrow.

Back Arrow

The gallery page for lists and libraries is displayed.

7. In the workspace, under **Document Libraries,** click **Shared Documents**.

The workspace tab is labeled *Shared Documents*, and the workspace now contains the settings page for Shared Documents, which is similar to the settings page for the Announcements list. As with lists, you cannot see the metadata for documents loaded into this document library. You must use the browser to see the metadata associated with the documents.

Collapse Group

8. In the **Navigation** pane, click the up arrow to the right of **Site Objects** so that the mini-gallery is displayed the full length of the **Navigation** pane. Then click the **–** sign to the left of **Announcements**.

The Announcements list collapses.

9. In the mini-gallery, click the **+** sign to the left of **Shared Documents**.

The Shared Documents top-level folder expands and exposes a subfolder named Forms and all the documents that users have uploaded to the library. (If this is a newly created team site, no documents are listed.)

10. In the mini-gallery, click the **+** sign to the left of **Forms**.

The Forms folder expands, exposing Web pages that correspond to views created for this library and forms to manipulate metadata and upload documents. A file named template.dotx is listed in the Forms folder. This file is used when you click New Document on the Document tab in the Web browser.

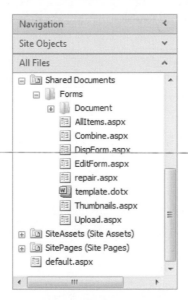

Hide pin

11. In the **Navigation** pane, click the down arrow to the right of **Site Objects**, and then click the Hide pin to the right of **All Files**.

The mini-gallery closes.

CLEAN UP Close SharePoint Designer.

Navigating a Site's Components

In the previous version of SharePoint Designer, the main object that you could customize and manage was a file. In SharePoint Designer 2010, you can manage other SharePoint objects, such as site columns, content types, external content types, and workflows. Content types and site columns are the building block of all the default lists and libraries.

Site columns introduce the concept of global column definitions. SharePoint Foundation, and therefore SharePoint Server, come with a set of default site columns that SharePoint installs when you create a site collection. These site columns are then grouped into content types that share common properties and can be used to standardize the metadata properties and use of business information across a number of lists and libraries.

Content types can include not only a group of site columns but also information policies, workflows, and the configuration of the document information panel (DIP) settings. The default content types defined at the root level of a site collection are used to create all the default lists and libraries. For example, the Document content type is used to create the Shared Documents library you find in a team site. The Document content type is based on the Item content type, which defines the Title column. In turn, the Item content type is based on the System content type, which is at the top of the content type hierarchy. Content types and site columns can be defined at the site-collection level and at the site level.

Note The SharePoint Server Managed Metadata Service (MMS) allows you to share a term store, and optionally content types, across site collections and Web applications. More information on MMS can be found at *http://technet.microsoft.com/en-us/library/ ee424402(office.14).aspx*.

External content types define data that is stored in external systems. Using SharePoint Designer to work with external content types and workflows is detailed in Chapter 7, "Using Business Connectivity Services", Chapter 8, "Understanding Workflows," and Chapter 9, "Using Reusable Workflows and Workflows Forms," later in this book.

In this exercise, you use SharePoint Designer to navigate to site components.

 SET UP Using SharePoint Designer, open the root site of a site collection.

1. In the **Navigation** pane, click **Content Types**.

    A new workspace page opens with a tab labeled Content Types and displays the gallery page for content types.

2. In the workspace, click the down arrow in the **Group** column heading, and then click **Document Content Types**.

The gallery page displays only those content types that are Document content types. The source column defines where the content types are defined. If your team site is not the root of a site collection, the source column is likely to be the Web address of the site collection.

3. In the **Name** column, under **Document Content Types**, click **Document**.

> **Troubleshooting** If you have not opened the root site of a site collection and the site you have opened has not created any content types of its own, a Microsoft SharePoint Designer dialog box opens with the name of the site where the Document content type is defined. Click OK in the dialog box, open the site in SharePoint Designer using the steps described in the first exercise of this chapter, and then repeat the steps in this exercise.

The workspace now contains the settings page for the Document content type. The Content Type Settings tab on the ribbon contains commands to edit and manage the Document content type, and the mini-gallery lists all content types.

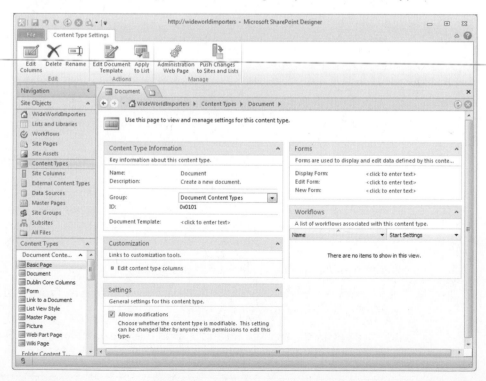

4. On the ribbon, click **Edit Columns** in the **Edit** group.

The workspace contains a gallery page displaying the columns Name and Title, which form part of the Document content type. The ribbon displays a Columns tab with commands to create, edit, and manage columns for this content type.

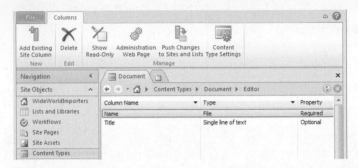

5. In the mini-gallery, scroll down, and then under **List Content Types**, click **Announcement**.

Tip To display the mini-gallery the full length of the Navigation pane, use the up arrow to collapse the Site Objects group.

The workspace now contains the settings page for the Announcement content type. This is the content type used to create all Announcements lists. Notice on the ribbon that the Edit Document Template command is not available because lists have no document template associations.

6. In the **Navigation** pane, click the arrow to the right of **Navigation**.

Collapse the
Navigation pane

The Navigation pane collapses, and the workspace expands.

7. On the breadcrumb, click the arrow to the right of **Content Types**, and then click **Basic Page**.

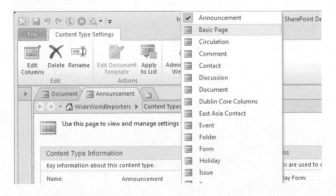

The workspace now contains the settings page for the Basic Page content type. Notice on the ribbon that the Edit Document Template command is active. The Basic Page content type is used to create a document library, and therefore it can have a document template association.

8. On the breadcrumb, click the arrow to the right of your site's name, and then click **Site Columns**.

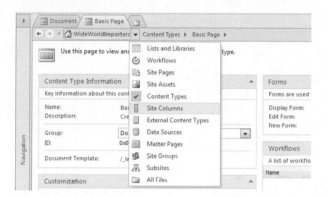

The workspace now contains the gallery page for site columns.

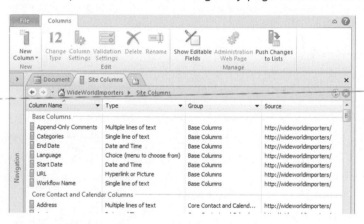

Troubleshooting If the Site Columns gallery page contains no site columns, the filter you placed earlier on the Group column (in step 2) is still active. Click the arrow in the Group column, and click All.

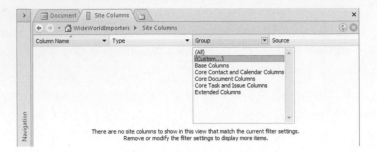

9. Click the arrow at the top of the **Navigation** pane to expand the pane.

✖ **CLEAN UP** Close SharePoint Designer.

Saving and Using a Site Template

After customizing your site by applying themes or by adding or removing lists, libraries, pages, and even subsites, you can package everything for additional reuse by making your own site template. A site template is represented by one .wsp file, which is known as a *solution file*, and is stored in the Solutions gallery at the top-level site of a site collection.

When you create a site template, you can choose to save its content, which includes list items, documents, pages, custom pages, master pages and configurations; however, a number of components are not saved, such as permissions.

You can copy solutions files from one site collection to another site collection, thereby allowing you and your users to create multiple sites based on your solution. You do not need to have server administrator privileges to install a site template solution because the Solutions gallery is a document library itself, and as such it is stored in the SQL Server content database and not in a folder on the Web server. If you are a site owner or an administrator of the top-level site, you have sufficient rights to upload a site template solution to the Solutions gallery.

Warning Solution files might contain malicious code, so use site templates only from sources you trust.

Site template solutions are based on files stored on the Web server, which means that if you copy the site template to a site collection on another server, that server must have those site definition files installed. For this reason, many people who design solutions use the team site or the blank site as their basis for creating site template solutions because these site definition files are installed with SharePoint Foundation and SharePoint Server.

Similarly, if your lists or libraries use any site collection custom content types, those content types must be re-created in the destinations site collection's Site Content Type gallery. The same is true for features that may be installed and enabled.

The .wsp file is actually a cabinet file that contains a WebTemplate\Elements file that identifies the site definition files used. Other files in the solutions file identify features that the site template might be dependent on. If you cannot create a site from a site template solutions file, and you suspect that you do not have the site definition files installed on your Web server, you can integrate this file to identify the site definition files you are missing. You might need the help of a developer to identify the cause of the problem.

Each site definition is given a number, and so is each site configuration within a site definition. You can use this information to identify the site definition a site template is based on. The template and configuration number for team and Meeting Workspace site definitions are listed in the following table.

Template	Configuration
1. STS	0 Team Site
	1 Blank Site
	2 Document Workspace
2. MPS	0 Basic Meeting Workspace
	1 Blank Meeting Workspace
	2 Decision Meeting Workspace
	3 Social Meeting Workspace
	4 Multipage Meeting Workspace

After you create a site template solution and before you allow other users to create sites from it, you should create a site based on the template and test your solution to discover whether customizations work successfully after being packaged in a site template. If necessary, also check that they work on other site collections and Web applications.

Note With SharePoint Server, you can limit the site templates that are visible. See Appendix C on page 503 for a list of steps.

In this exercise, you use SharePoint Designer to create a site template, save the site template and review its contents, and then create a site from a site template and test your solution.

SET UP Using SharePoint Designer, open the team site you used in previous exercises in this chapter, if it is not already open. The settings page for the site should be displayed.

1. On the **Site** tab, click **Save as Template** in the **Manage** group.

   The browser opens. If prompted, type your user name and password, and click **OK**. The Save As Template page is displayed.

2. In the **File name** box, type **SPDSBS_Sites**, and in the **Template name** box, type **SBS Working with Sites**.

3. In the **Include Content** section, select the **Include Content** check box, and then click **OK**.

   The Operation Completed Successfully page is displayed, stating that the Web site was successfully saved to the Solutions gallery.

4. On the **Operation Completed Successfully** page, at the end of the second para-graph, click **solutions gallery**.

   Tip If the Operation Completed Successfully page is not displayed, click Site Actions, and then click Site Settings. If you are working on a child site, under Site Collection Administration, click Go To Top Level Site Settings. On the site settings page, under Galleries, click Solutions.

5. Click **SPDSBS_Sites**. The **Save As** dialog box opens.

6. Navigate to the **Desktop,** and then click **Save**.

   The Save As dialog box closes. If the Download Complete dialog box opens, click Close.

7. On your Desktop, rename SPDSBS_Sites.wsp as **SPDSBS_Sites.cab**.

   A Rename warning dialog box opens, stating that the file might become unstable.

8. Click **Yes** to close the **Rename** warning dialog box.

9. Double-click **SPDSBS_Sites.cab** to open the cabinet file, locate **Elements.xml** in the **SPDSBS_SitesWebTemplate** path, and drag it to your desktop.

   Tip You might have to change the Explorer view to Details to see the path.

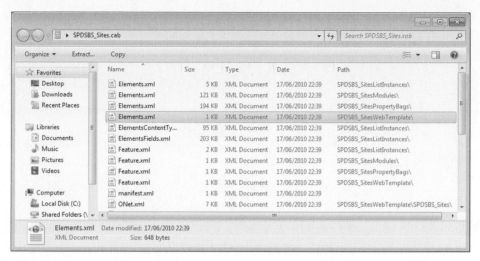

10. Right-click **Elements.xml,** and click **Edit with Microsoft SharePoint Designer**.

SharePoint Designer displays Elements.xml in the workspace.

The BaseTemplateID has a value of 1, the BaseTemplateName has a value of STS, and the BaseConfigurationID has a value of 0, which means that the SPDSBS_Sites template solution was based on the team site definition.

11. In the **Navigation** pane, click **Subsites**.

A new workspace tab opens, labeled *Subsites*.

12. On the ribbon, click **Subsite** in the **New** group.

The New dialog box opens, and in the Specify The Location Of The New Web Site text box, Subsite is highlighted. SharePoint Designer communicates with the SharePoint site collection and retrieves a list of SharePoint site templates that you can use as a basis for your new SharePoint child site. The SPDSBS_Sites site template is listed in the site type list.

Note There is no visible difference between using site template solutions and site templates stored on the Web server.

13. Type **SiteTest** over Subsite, and in the central pane, click **SPDSBS_Sites**.

14. Click **OK**.

The new site opens in a new SharePoint Designer window. Notice that the Title and Description site properties of the Human Resources site were not saved.

Preview in
Browser

15. On the **Site** tab, click **Preview in Browser** in the **Manage** group.

The browser opens and displays the home page of the new site.

✖ **CLEAN UP** Close SharePoint Designer.

Key Points

- The SharePoint site properties Title and Description communicate to users the purpose and function of a site. They are also fundamental to making information easy to find.

- Themes can be created using PowerPoint 2010. The .thmx file is then loaded in the Themes gallery at the top-level site of a site collection.

- Themes change the colors and fonts used on a site. If you want to change other design elements, such as font size or spacing, you need to use cascading style sheets.

- Cascading style sheets used on SharePoint sites can be created to not support themes.

- A number of features can be activated at the site-collection level, whereas others can be activated on a site-by-site basis.

- You can use SharePoint Designer to create and manage SharePoint groups and map users and SharePoint groups to permission levels for sites, lists, and libraries

- You cannot change the site template used to create a SharePoint site after the site is created. If the functionality you require is not exposed by a feature, you have to delete and re-create the SharePoint site using a different site template.

- You can delete child sites of a site collection by using SharePoint Designer; however, you cannot delete the top-level site of a site collection. Deleted sites are not sent to the Recycle Bin.

- You can reset customized (unghosted) pages to be uncustomized pages that point to site definition files on the Web server.

- Site components such as site columns and content types can be managed using SharePoint Designer.

- The hidden URL structure of a Web site can be viewed in the All Files mini-gallery.

- You can use site template solution files to package your solutions so that you can use them again. These files are stored in the SQL Server database and are exposed in the Solutions gallery at the top-level site of a site collection.

- Site template solution files are cabinet files with the extension .wsp. These cabinet files contain a number of files that describe how to create a site that includes your customizations.

Part 2

Working with Information

Chapter at a Glance

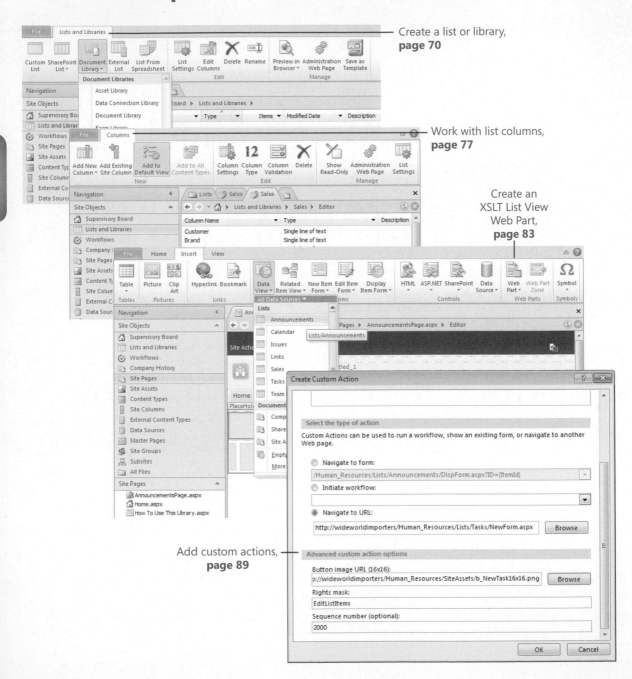

Create a list or library,
page 70

Work with list columns,
page 77

Create an
XSLT List View
Web Part,
page 83

Add custom actions,
page 89

3 Working with Lists and Libraries

In this chapter, you will learn how to

- ✔ Create lists and libraries.
- ✔ Import data into SharePoint.
- ✔ Work with list columns.
- ✔ Use calculated columns and column validation.
- ✔ Create an XSLT List View Web Part.
- ✔ Customize an XSLT List View Web Part.
- ✔ Secure a list or library.
- ✔ Add custom actions.
- ✔ Create and use site columns.
- ✔ Work with content types.
- ✔ Delete a SharePoint object.

Lists and libraries are central components in sites built on both Microsoft SharePoint Foundation 2010 and Microsoft SharePoint Server 2010. *Lists* are containers for items that have similar columns or metadata, security settings, and user interfaces for viewing and managing the items. You can use lists to manage and display information for collaboration purposes. *Libraries* are specialized lists in which each list item refers to one document. Libraries have strong document management features. Lists and libraries are core to the SharePoint infrastructure and can be used to store internal data, which enables you to build SharePoint 2010 applications in which the internal data is needed by the solution but can be configured to not be visible through the browser. This prevents users from accidentally deleting the internal data or being confused by the data's presence.

In this chapter, you will learn to identify when to use the browser and when to use Microsoft SharePoint Designer 2010 to manipulate lists and libraries. You will consolidate your understanding of lists and libraries, as well as reinforce the link between a list or a library and the XSLT List View Web Part. You will also learn how to add commands to the ribbon on list views and forms, add custom actions to list item menus, secure a list, and use site columns and content types with lists and libraries. In Chapter 4, "Creating and Modifying Web Pages," which concentrates on pages, you will learn how to create views and how to modify the pages that allow you to display, edit, and create new list items.

> **Practice Files** Before you can use the practice files provided for this chapter, you need to install them from the book's companion Web site. For more information about practice files, see "Using the Practice Files" on page xxiii.

Creating Lists and Libraries

Just as you base a new site on a site template, you base a new list or library on a list template. When you select a list template, you refer either to files on the file systems of the SharePoint Web servers or to a template file in the List Template gallery, which is stored in the Microsoft SQL Server database. Each list is created using one or more content types.

SharePoint Foundation 2010 and SharePoint Server 2010 provide a number of built-in list definitions that you can use as a basis for SharePoint lists and libraries. When you use the browser, the list definitions are grouped into four categories: Libraries, Communications, Tracking, and Custom Lists. When you use SharePoint Designer 2010, the list definitions appear in the New group on the Lists And Libraries ribbon tab and are grouped as Custom List, SharePoint List, Document Library, External List, and List From Spreadsheet.

A number of lists cannot be created by using the browser and can be seen only if you create a site from a specific site template or activate a specific feature. For example, the Circulations, Holidays, Time Card, Phone Call Memo, and Whereabouts list types are available only if you create a site based on the Group Work Site template or have activated the Group Work Lists site-level feature. Similiarly, in SharePoint Server 2010, if you create a site based on the Visio Process Repository site template, a Process Diagrams document library is created that has six content types attached. However, nothing stops you from creating a *list template* from this document library and creating your own libraries based on that list template. The group of lists created with the Group Work Site template would be more complex to reproduce because of dependencies between the different lists.

> **Tip** List templates can be created by using the list settings page in the browser or with the Save As Template command in the Manage group on the Lists And Libraries tab in SharePoint Designer.

After you create a list or library, you can perform tasks such as the following in the browser:

- View, add, modify, or delete list items, documents, or metadata.
- Modify list-level or item-level permissions.
- Add, delete, or modify columns.
- Add, delete, or modify content types.
- Create views to allow multiple perspectives on the list's or library's data.
- Create a list template from a list, including its content.

See Also More information on working with lists and libraries in the browser can be found in Chapter 4, "Working with Lists," and Chapter 5, "Working with Libraries," in *Microsoft SharePoint Foundation 2010 Step by Step* by Olga Londer and Penelope Coventry (Microsoft Press, 2011).

With SharePoint Designer, you cannot create or modify list items or the metadata associated with documents; however, unlike in the previous version, in SharePoint Designer 2010 you can create or modify list permissions, content types, columns, and site columns by using the list settings page that is displayed in the workspace when you click a list or library from the Lists or Library gallery page or the mini-gallery.

The list settings page is divided into eight areas:

- **List Information** Provides key information about a list, such as the name, description, list ID, the date that the list was last modified, and the number of items that the list contains.

- **Customization** Use to edit list columns and manage the permissions of the list.

- **Settings** Use to set the general settings of a list, such as displaying the list in the browser on the Quick Launch Toolbar or hiding the list from the browser so that it does not appear on the All Site Content page.

- **Content Types** Use to manage the association of content types with the list or library.

- **Views** Use to manage or create new list views. List views are pages that display the contents of a list. By default, most lists and libraries contain at least one view page, All Items, that displays all items in the list. Some lists contain a number of view pages, such as the tasks list, which is provided with six view pages by default: Active Tasks, All Tasks, By Assigned To, By My Groups, Due Today, and My Tasks.

- **Forms** Use to manage and create list forms. By default, most lists or libraries contain at least three forms:

  - ❍ DispForm.aspx to display the properties of a list item.
  - ❍ EditForm.aspx to edit the properties of a list item.
  - ❍ NewForm.aspx to create a new list item.

- **Workflows** Use to manage and create new list workflows.

- *Custom Actions* Use to create and manage custom actions you have added to the list item menu or on the server ribbon you see on form pages when you use the browser.

In this exercise, you create a Wiki Page library, an Issue Tracking list, and a list from an Excel worksheet. You also change the default settings of the lists and library.

  SET UP Using SharePoint Designer, open the team site you created and modified in earlier chapters. If you did not create a team site yet, follow the steps in Chapter 1 before you start this exercise.

1. In the **Navigation** pane, click **Lists and Libraries**.

   The Lists And Libraries gallery page is displayed in the workspace.

Document Library

2. On the **Lists and Libraries** tab, click **Document Library** in the **New** group, and then click **Wiki Page Library**.

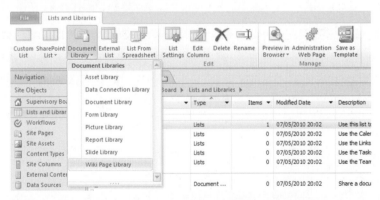

The Create List Or Document Library dialog box opens.

3. In the **Name** box, type **Wiki_Pages,** and then click **OK** to close the dialog box.

The name that you type in the Name box is used to create the URL as well as the title of the library.

See Also For information about good naming conventions, see the sidebar "Best Practices for Naming URLs" in Chapter 1, "Exploring SharePoint Designer 2010."

The Wiki_Pages library appears under Document Libraries on the gallery page.

Tip If you want to change the URL of a list or library, in the All Files mini-gallery or in the All Files gallery page, right-click the list or library, and then click Rename. All references to the old URL will be replaced with the new URL. However, if users have bookmarked or created hyperlinks to the list or library, these continue to point to the old URL. Renaming the list or library in the Lists And Library gallery page renames the title of the list or library but does not change the URL of the list or library.

4. Click **Wiki_Pages**.

The list settings page opens in the workspace and the Lists And Libraries mini-gallery appears below the Navigation pane.

5. In the **List Information** area, click **Wiki_Pages** to the right of **Name**, type **Company History**, and then press **Enter**.

An asterisk appears on the Wiki_Pages tab, indicating that the library settings have changed but you have not saved your changes.

6. Click **<click to enter text>** to the right of **Description,** and type **This wiki page library contains a set of Wiki pages that describes the history of our company,** and then press **Enter**.

Save

7. In the **Settings** area, under **Advanced Settings**, select the **Require content approval for submitted items** check box. On the Quick Access Toolbar, click **Save**.

The asterisk disappears from the tab, and the tab is now labeled Company History. In the Lists And Library mini-gallery, the wiki library is listed under Document Libraries as Company History. In the List Information area, the Web address can be seen to include Wiki_Pages.

Note This Wiki library will still be listed as Wiki_Pages in the All Files gallery and mini-gallery.

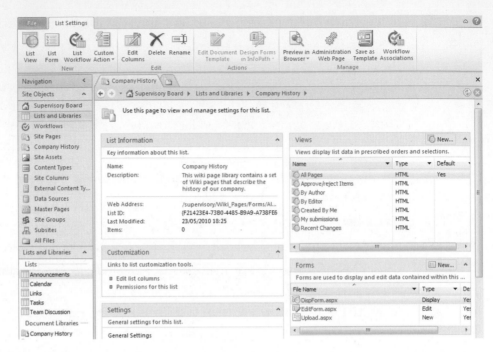

 CLEAN UP Leave SharePoint Designer open if you are continuing to the next exercise.

Creating an Issue Tracking List

SharePoint Designer provides several methods for creating lists and libraries. You can use the SharePoint List or Document Library commands in the New group on the ribbon, which appears when the following pages are displayed in the workspace:

- The site settings page
- The Lists And Libraries gallery page

Note When the All Files gallery page is displayed in the workspace and a list or library is selected, the Cut, Copy, and Paste commands in the ribbon's Clipboard group are active. However, if you attempt to create lists or libraries by using these commands, a SharePoint Designer dialog box appears stating you cannot copy lists or libraries. These commands are for creating or copying files or folders.

In this exercise, you create an Issue Tracking list.

SET UP Using SharePoint Designer, open the team site you used in the previous exercise if it is not already open.

1. In the **Navigation** pane, right-click **Lists and Libraries**, and then click **Open in New a Tab (Ctrl+Enter).**

SharePoint List

2. On the **Lists and Libraries** tab, click **SharePoint List** in the **New** group. Then, under **Tracking Lists,** click **Issue Tracking**.

    The Create List Or Document Library dialog box opens.

3. In the **Name** box, type **Issues**, and then click **OK** to close the dialog box.

    The Issues list appears under Lists on the Lists And Libraries gallery page.

4. Right-click **Issues**, and then click **List Settings**.

    The list settings page opens in the workspace, and the Lists And Libraries mini-gallery appears below the Navigation pane.

5. In the **Settings** area in the workspace, under **Advanced Settings**, clear the **Allow Attachments** check box.

    A Microsoft SharePoint Designer dialog box opens warning you that if any files are attached to list items, disabling attachments results in their deletion.

6. Click **OK**.

    An asterisk appears on the Issues tab, indicating that the list settings have changed but you have not saved your changes.

    Tip You can check the current settings of a list in the browser by clicking Administration Web Page in the Manage group on the List Settings tab on the ribbon. This opens the list settings page in the browser. You can then check the attachment settings by clicking Advanced Settings under General Settings.

7. Right-click the **Issues** tab, and then click **Save.**

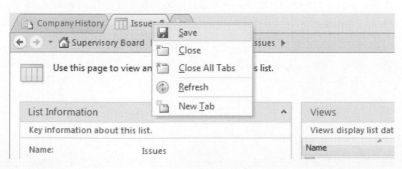

8.   On the breadcrumb, click **Lists and Libraries** to display the gallery page.

The Issues list appears under Lists.

 CLEAN UP Leave SharePoint Designer open if you are continuing to the next exercise.

Importing Data into SharePoint

In many situations you may have data in a spreadsheet and find that you need to share the data with other members of your team. SharePoint provides the ability to import data from a Microsoft Office Excel 2007 or Microsoft Excel 2010 worksheet into a SharePoint list. You can choose to import all the data in a worksheet, a range of cells, a named range, or an Excel table.

See Also Using Microsoft Office Access 2007 or Microsoft Access 2010, you can also import data to a SharePoint list. See Chapter 14, "Using SharePoint Foundation with Excel 2010 and Access 2010," in *Microsoft SharePoint Foundation 2010 Step by Step*.

In this exercise, you create a list from the data in an Excel worksheet. You also change the default settings of the lists and library.

 **SET UP** Using SharePoint Designer, open the team site you used in the previous exercise if it is not already open, and then open the Lists And Libraries gallery page.

List From
Spreadsheets

1.   On the **Lists and Libraries** tab, click **List From Spreadsheet** in the **New** group.

The browser opens and displays the New page.

2.   In the **Name** box, type **Sales**. In the **Description box,** type **This list contains Wide World Importers sales for the last year**.

3.   Click the **Browse** button.

The Choose File To Upload dialog box opens and displays your Documents folder or the last folder that you accessed.

4.   If the **Documents** folder is not displayed in the **Choose File to Upload** dialog box, click Documents in the left pane under **Libraries**.

5.   Navigate to the Chapter03 practice file folder, double-click **WideWorldImportsSaleData.xlsx**, and then click **Open**.

6.   On the **New** Web page, click **Import**.

> **Troubleshooting** If a Message From Webpage dialog box opens with the error message "An unexpected error has occurred," click OK. On the Site Actions menu, click More Options to display the Create dialog box. Under Filter By, click Blank & Custom, select Import Spreadsheet, click Create, and then repeat steps 2–6.

> Excel 2010 opens WideWorldImportSaleData.xlsx and displays the Import To Windows SharePoint Services List dialog box.

7.   From the **Range Type** list, select **Range of cells**, and then press **TAB**.

8.   In the spreadsheet, select the range of cells **A1** to **I39**, and then click **Import** in the dialog box.

> The All Items view of the Sales list is displayed.

Refresh

9.   Close the browser, and then click Refresh on the SharePoint Designer Quick Access Toolbar.

> In the workspace, in the Lists And Libraries gallery, Sales appears under Lists.

10.   In the **Navigation** pane, click **All Files**, and then in the workspace click **Lists**.

> The Lists gallery page is displayed in the workspace, and the All Files mini-gallery opens below the Navigation pane. The Issues and Sales lists appear in the List gallery page. In the All Files mini-gallery, in the root of the SharePoint site, the library Wiki_Pages (Company History) that was created in previous exercise is listed.

11.   In the **Navigation** pane, click **Lists and Libraries**, and then click **Sales**.

12.   On the **Sales** list settings page, in the **Settings** area under **Advanced Settings**, select the **Display this list on the Quick Launch**. On the Quick Access Toolbar, click **Save**.

 **CLEAN UP** Leave SharePoint Designer open if you are continuing to the next exercise.

Working with List Columns

Columns, also known as fields, determine the type of data a list or library can hold. Each column is associated with a column data type. The value stored in a column is often referred to as metadata and is used to filter and sort the data. Metadata can be indexed by SharePoint, which lets users quickly find information.

When you create a list or a library, it is provisioned with a number of site columns that are defined by one or more content types, depending on the template chosen. The site column is stored locally in the list or library as a list column. When you make changes to the column, you have your own copy of the site column, and any changes you make apply only to the column in that list or library. You enhance your list by creating your own list columns.

In this exercise, you enhance the Sales list. You change the List Price column type to Currency and the Region column type to Choice, add a calculated column named Total, and add column validation to the Quantity Purchased column.

SET UP Using SharePoint Designer, open the team site you used in the previous exercise if it is not already open, and then open the Sales list settings page.

Edit Column

1. In the **Customization** area, click **Edit list columns**.

   The workspace contains a list of columns for the Sales list. On the Columns tab on the ribbon, Add To Default View is highlighted in orange. This command is a toggle switch. When it is highlighted in orange, new columns are automatically added to the Default view.

   Tip Only those columns whose settings you can amend are listed. To see all columns for a list or library, click Show Read-Only on the Columns tab. Columns such as Created and Modified are displayed dimmed.

2. Under **Column Name**, click **List Price**. Then, on the **Columns** tab, click **Column Type** in the **Edit** group.

3. In the **List Price** row, click the down arrow that appears to the right of **Number (1, 1.0, 100)** and click **Currency**. On the Quick Access Toolbar, click **Save**.

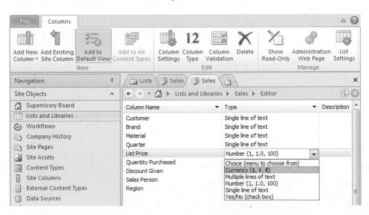

Column Settings

4. Click **List Price,** and then on the **Columns** tab, click **Column Settings** in the **Edit** group.

The Column Editor dialog box opens.

5. In the **Display format** list, select **British Pound**, if it is not already selected, and then click **OK** to close the **Column Editor** dialog box.

6. Under **Column Name**, click **Region** and then on the **Columns** tab, click **Column Type** in the **Edit** group.

7. In the **Region** row, click the down arrow that appears to the right of **Single line of text**, and click **Choice**.

8. Right-click **Region**, and click **Column Settings**. The **Column Editor** dialog box opens.

9. In the **Choices (enter each choice on a separate line)** box, type the following four lines:

East

West

Europe

Asia

10. In the **Default value** box, delete **Choice 1**, and type **West**. Then, in the **Display as** list, select **Radio buttons**.

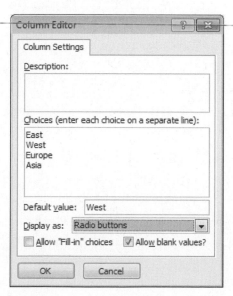

11. Click **OK** to close the **Column Editor** dialog box.

    The list of columns for the Sales list now contains the Region column.

12. Right-click the **Sales** tab, and then click **Save**.

 CLEAN UP Leave SharePoint Designer open if you are continuing to the next exercise.

Using Calculated Columns

In many scenarios, you need to display data that can be calculated from data already included in the list. This is when you use a calculated column, which uses formulas similar to those in Excel and Access. Calculated columns can contain functions, column references, operators and constants, as well as IF statements.

See Also For more information on calculated columns, see the series of blog posts titled "Taming the Elusive Calculated Column" at *www.endusersharepoint.com/2008/06/12/taming-the-elusive-calculated-column/*. For information on the maximum number of IF statements in a column, see *http://blog.pathtosharepoint.com/category/calculated-columns/*.

In this exercise, you add a calculated column to the Sales list.

 **SET UP** Using SharePoint Designer, open the team site you used in the previous exercise if it is not already open, and display the list of columns for the Sales list as described at the start of the previous exercise.

Add New Column

1. On the **Columns** tab, click **Add New Column** and then click **Calculated (calculation Based on Other Columns)**.

   The Column Editor dialog box opens.

2. In the **Insert Column** list, double-click **List Price**, and then double-click **Quantity Purchased.**

   The Formula box contains the text [List Price][Quantity Purchased].

3. In the **Formula** box, place the insertion point after the first closing square bracket (**]**) and before the second opening square bracket (**[ ),** and then type *.

   The formula should look similar to *[List Price]*[Quantity Purchased]*.

4. In the **Data type returned** list, select **Currency**, and in the **Currency format** list, select **British Pound**, if it is not already selected.

5. Click **OK**.

    The Column Editor dialog box closes, and a new column named NewColumn1, of type Calculated, appears in the workspace.

6. Click **NewColumn1** to highlight the text, type **Total**, and then press **ENTER**.

    The column NewColumn1 is renamed to Total.

7. Right-click the **Sales** tab, and then click **Save**.

 **CLEAN UP** Leave SharePoint Designer open if you are continuing to the next exercise.

Using Column Validation

By using the correct column types and setting properites such as minimum and maxium values, you can be sure your users enter data correctly. To further aid the integrity of data entered in your lists and libraries, SharePoint 2010 added new functionality for list and column validation. When a user enters data that fails the validation check, you can display a default validation error message or provide your own error messages. In the previous version of SharePoint, such validation and customized error messages were only available by customizing the data entry Web pages and using client-side scripting languages such as JavaScript or JQuery.

Similar to calculated columns, list and column validation uses formulas like those used in Excel and Access. List validation can reference data in more than one column in the list. When you configure both list and column validation, the column validation formulas are evaluated before the list validation formulas. You can also set column-level validation on a site column by using the Validation Settings command in the Edit group on the ribbon.

Note Not all column types support column validation. Supported column types are Single Line of Text, Choice (single), Number, Currency, and Date and Time.

In this exercise, you add column validation to the Quantity Purchased column and then add a new task item to test that the validation formula is correctly defined.

 SET UP Using SharePoint Designer, open the team site you used in the previous exercise, if it is not already open, and display the list of columns for the Sales list.

1. Click **Quantity Purchased**, and then on the **Columns** tab, click **Column Validation** in the **Edit** group.

    The Validation Settings dialog box opens.

2. In the **Formula** box, type **NOT(MOD([Quantity Purchased],2))**, and in the **Message** box type, **Enter an even number. Goods can only be purchased in multiples of 2.**

Validation
Settings

3. Click **OK** to close the **Validation Settings** dialog box.

4. Right-click the **Sales** tab, and then click **Save**.

5. Press **F12**, or on the **Home** tab, click **Preview in Browser** to open the Sales list in the browser.

    Tip You should make small changes and test your solution often. It is then easier to identify errors in your solution.

6. Click the **Items** tab, and then click **New Item** in the **New** group.

The Sales – New Item window appears.

7. In the **Quantity Purchased** box, type **1**, and then click **Save**.

The window remains open. Under the Quantity Purchased box, **Enter an even number. Goods can only be purchased in multiples of 2** appears.

8. Click **Cancel**, and then close the browser.

✖ **CLEAN UP** Leave SharePoint Designer open if you are continuing to the next exercise.

Creating an XSLT List View Web Part

When a list or library is created, one or more pages (known as views) are created to display the contents of the list or library. You can display a list's or library's default view by clicking the list or library's link in the Quick Launch. There are at least three other pages created, called forms. Forms allow you to view the column values of a single list item or the metadata associated with a document, add a new list item or upload a document, and edit existing list items or document metadata. You can also create your own Web pages to display the contents of lists and libraries. SharePoint Foundation provides a new Web Part to display the contents of lists and libraries, the XSLT List View (XLV) Web Part. The XLV is also available on SharePoint Server because SharePoint Server is based on SharePoint Foundation.

See Also For more information on working with views and forms, see Chapter 4.

In the previous version of SharePoint you used the List View Web Part (LVWP) to display the contents of lists and libraries. Both the XLV and the LVWP Web Parts are easy to modify using the browser. The XLV can do everything that the LVWP can do, but the LVWP is difficult to extend to produce the solutions you might need, which is why it was often converted to a Data View Web Part (DVWP). The DVWP, also known as the Data Form Web Part (DFWP), is highly customizable in SharePoint Designer, in both Design and Code views, but it is difficult to customize in the browser. In fact, you can think of the XLV as the DVWP for lists. However, you can manipulate the XLV easily in both your browser and in SharePoint Designer.

The LVWP uses Collaboration Application Markup Language (CAML) to dynamically find and display SharePoint data. This is a proprietary markup language specific to SharePoint technologies, and very few tools are available to help you write CAML. In SharePoint Designer you need to use the source code window to write CAML, and there is no

IntelliSense to help you. The XLV and the DFWP use Extensible Stylesheet Language for Transformation (XSLT), which is an open standard commonly used on Web sites. Much more documentation of XSLT exists than for CAML.

In this exercise, you create an Announcements XLV.

SET UP Using SharePoint Designer, open the team site you used in the previous exercise if it is not already open.

1. In the **Navigation** pane, click **Site Pages**.

The Site Pages gallery page is displayed in the workspace.

2. On the **Pages** tab, click **Web Part Page** in the **New** group, and then click the Web Part page that displays the ScreenTip **Header, Left Column, Body**.

Web Part Page

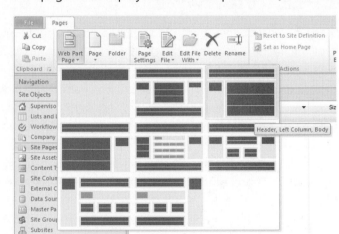

A new file, named Untitled_1.aspx, appears on the Site Pages gallery page, with the name of the file highlighted.

3. Type **AnnouncementPage.aspx**, and press **ENTER** to rename the file.

4. On the **Pages** tab, click **Edit File** in the **Edit** group.

Edit File

The Announcement page opens in edit mode, with the workspace tab labeled AnnouncementsPage.aspx. The page has three rectangles surrounded by a light-blue border. These are *Web Part zones*.

Tip Web Part zones are containers for Web Parts. The use of Web Parts and Web Part zones is discussed in Chapter 4.

5. Click in the first light-blue bordered rectangle.

The light-blue border changes to a blue border and the label Header appears above the rectangle. A purple bordered rectangle labeled PlaceHolderMain (Custom) surrounds the three Web Part zones.

Data View

6.   On the **Insert** tab, click **Data View**, and then click **Announcements**.

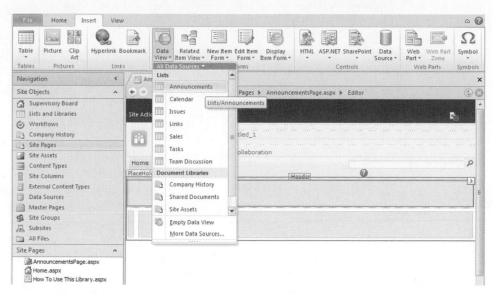

Tip The ScreenTip that is displayed when you hover the mouse pointer over Announcements in the Data View lists indicates the physical location of the list in the site. All lists are stored in the lists folder in the root of the Web site. This is discussed in Chapter 2, "Working with SharePoint Sites."

The Announcements XLV is created on the page, and the <webpartpages:XsltListView WebPart> tag is highlighted in orange on the Quick Tag Selector in the workspace status bar. In a newly created team site, one list item is displayed: "Get Started with Microsoft SharePoint Foundation!" The ribbon contains the List View Tools set of tabs: Options, Design, Web Part, and Table.

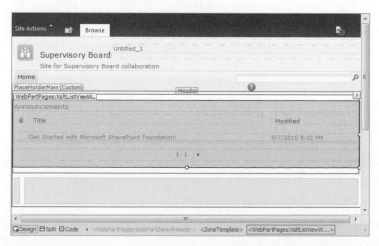

7.   On the Quick Access Toolbar, click **Save**.

> **Note** The page contains the text Untitled_1, which is the title of the page. When you renamed the page, you renamed the file name. The renaming process does not rename the title of the page.

 CLEAN UP Close any open tabs. Leave SharePoint Designer open if you are continuing to the next exercise.

Customizing an XSLT List View Web Part

All Web Parts, including the XLV, share a common set of properties that control their appearance, layout, and advanced characteristics, such as whether the Web Part can move to a different Web Part zone. XLVs have other configurable settings, such as which columns are displayed, the sort order of the list items, whether the list items are filtered, and whether items with the same value are grouped in their own section.

In this exercise, you modify the Announcements XLV to display announcements whose expiration dates are not set or have not expired. You also modify the Announcement XLV to show no more than five announcements.

SETUP Using SharePoint Designer, open the team site you used in the previous exercise, if it is not already open, and open AnnouncementsPage.aspx in edit mode with the XLV Web Part selected as described in the previous exercise.

Filter

1. On **Options** tab, click **Filter** in the **Filter, Sort & Group** group.

   The Filter Criteria dialog box opens.

2. Click the **Field Name** arrow, and in the list, click **Expires**.

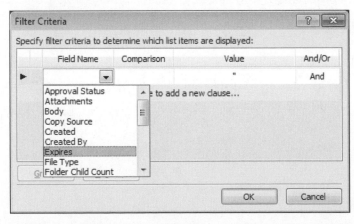

3. Under **Comparison**, click **Equals**, click the arrow that appears, and from the drop-down menu, select **Is Null**.

4.   Under **And/Or**, click **And**, click the arrow that appears, and then select **Or** from the drop-down menu.

5.   Click **Click here to add a new clause**, click the arrow that appears under **Field Name**, and then click **Expires**.

6.   Under **Comparison**, click **Equals**, click the arrow that appears, and then click **Greater than or Equal**.

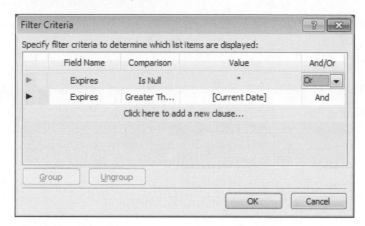

Tip To delete a filter criterion, click the arrow to its left to select the entire criteria line, and then press Delete.

7.   Click **OK** to close the **Filter Criteria** dialog box.

The Page refreshes, and the message "Updating Data View. Click Stop to Cancel" might briefly be displayed.

Paging

8.   On the **Options** tab, click **Paging** in the Paging group, and then click **Limit to 5 Items**.

The Page refreshes, and the message "Updating Data View. Click Stop to Cancel" might briefly be displayed.

Options

9.   On the **Design** tab, click **Options**, and then click **Summary Toolbar**.

The page refreshes, and the Add New Announcement link is added to the bottom of the Web Part.

Chrome Type

10. On the **Web Part** tab, click **Chrome Type**, and then click **Title Only**.

11. On the Quick Access Toolbar, click **Save**.

12. Press **F12,** or on the **Home** tab, click **Preview in Browser** to display the page in the browser.

CLEAN UP Close the browser. Leave SharePoint Designer open if you are continuing to the next exercise.

Securing a List or a Library

In Chapter 2 you learned how to manage site users and permissions and how to apply unique permissions to a site. Lists and libraries automatically inherit the permission settings from their site. If you want to change the security settings of a list or library (given that lists and libraries are just SharePoint objects, as are sites), you can use the same techniques you used in Chapter 2. You can stop inheriting the security settings from the site, and then you can remove users or SharePoint groups from the list's permission settings and add new users or SharePoint groups, mapping them to a permission level.

In this exercise, you change the security settings for a list. You also remap the permission levels of the Members site group so that users in that group can only read the contents of the list.

SET UP Using SharePoint Designer, open the team site you used in the previous exercise if it is not already open.

1. In the **Navigation** pane, click **Lists and Libraries**, and then click **Announcements**.

2. In the **Customization** area, click **Permissions for this list**.

A browser window opens and displays the permission settings for the Announcements list.

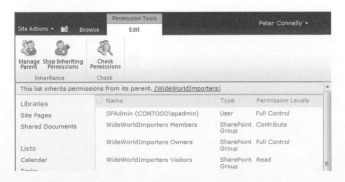

3. On the **Permissions Tools**, **Edit** tab, click **Stop Inheriting Permissions** in the **Inheritance** group.

    A dialog box opens warning you that you are about to create unique permissions for this list.

4. Click **OK** to close the dialog box.

    The page refreshes, additional groups are displayed on the server ribbon, and the status bar states that this list has unique permissions.

5. Select the check box to the left of the SharePoint group you want to amend, such as **WideWorldImporters Members**, and then click **Edit User Permissions** in the **Modify** group on the **Edit** tab.

    The Edit Permissions dialog opens.

6. Clear the check box to the left of **Contribute**, and select the check box to the left of **Read**. Click **OK**.

    The page refreshes, and the SharePoint group you amended displays Read in the Permission Level column.

 CLEAN UP Close the browser. Leave SharePoint Designer open if you are continuing to the next exercise.

Adding Custom Actions

The term *custom actions* is used twice in SharePoint Designer. First , it refers to the ability to extend SharePoint Designer workflows by adding custom actions and custom conditions created by a developer and installed on the Web server. Second, and new to SharePoint Designer 2010, it refers to the ability to add new actions to the list item menu (LIM) and the server ribbon that you see in the browser on the list views and forms. This allows you to add content to the list item menu or server ribbon without involving a developer or the IT department.

Custom actions should be added to facilitate the tasks needed to complete a business process. For example, if you commonly need to create a task item every time you create an announcement item, then place a custom action on the server ribbon of list views. Custom actions appear as buttons and can be accompanied by an image.

When you define a custom action for the list item menu or the server ribbon, you can specify a number, known as a sequence number, that defines the order in which the action appears on the list item menu or the server ribbon.

For example, in the browser, when you display an Announcements list and then select the arrow to the right of an announcement item, the list item menu contains the actions View Item, Edit Item, Alert Me, Manage Permissions, and Delete Item. On a site created using SharePoint Server, additional actions are displayed, such as Compliance Details. These default actions are also associated with a sequence number. The sequence numbers for the default actions are not visible in SharePoint Designer, but with some testing you can discover them by trying different numbers as the sequence number when you add your own actions. For example, if you want users to quickly create a new Task item by using the Tasks list's NewForm.aspx page, choose a sequence number of 50 to place the New Task Item action at the top of the item menu. A sequence number of 2,000 places the New Task Item action below the Delete Item action. To create the New Task Item action between the Edit Item and Alert Me actions, choose a sequence number between 300 and 1,000.

When you define your custom action, you can also specify a Rights Mask that defines which users can see the custom action. The Rights Mask can contain any of the SPBasePermission member names that are listed at *http://msdn.microsoft.com/en-us/library/microsoft.sharepoint.spbasepermissions.aspx*. When you want the custom action to appear for any user of the list, leave the Rights Mask empty or type **EmptyMask**.

Using SharePoint Designer, you cannot remove a custom action, add other forms of actions (such as check boxes, combo boxes, drop-down lists, text boxes, and flyout anchors), or add tabs or groups. Developers can create such actions and extend the server ribbon on pages other than the view and form pages, as well as the list item menu, by creating a feature in Visual Studio 2010 with the SharePoint Ribbon project template, which can be found at *http://code.msdn.microsoft.com/vsixforsp*. This Web site also contains a hands-on lab and a walkthrough video.

In this exercise, you upload new image files to the Site Assets library and then use those images when you add a custom action to a list item menu.

 SET UP Using SharePoint Designer, open the team site you used in the previous exercise, if it is not already open.

Import Files

1. In the **Navigation** pane, click **Site Assets**, and then click **Import Files** in the **New** group on the ribbon.

   The Import dialog box opens.

2. Click **Add File** to display the **File Open** dialog box.

3. Navigate to the Chapter03 practice file folder and use the **CRTL** or **SHIFT** key to select the images you want to import, such as b_NewTask16x16.png, b_NewAnn16x16.gif, and b_NewAnn32x32.png.

4. Click **Open**, and then click **OK** to close the **File Open** and **Import** dialog boxes.

The image files are imported.

5. In the N**avigation** pane, click **Lists and Libraries**, and then in the workspace click **Announcements** to display the list settings page in the workspace.

New

6. In the **Custom Actions** area, click **New**.

Tip The Custom Actions area is at the bottom right on the list settings page. You might need to scroll down to see it. Alternatively, collapse the Views, Forms, and Workflows areas by clicking their titles or by clicking the up arrow to the right of the area titles.

The Create Custom Action dialog box opens.

7. In the **Name** box, type **New Task Item,** and in the **Description** box, type **Custom action to create a new task item**.

8. Under **Select the type of action**, select **Navigate to URL**, and then click **Browse**.

The Insert Hyperlink dialog box opens.

9. Navigate to the Tasks list's New form by double-clicking **Lists** and then **Tasks**. Click **NewForm.aspx**.

Note You can navigate to another Web site or Internet site from this dialog box.

10. Click **OK** to close the **Insert Hyperlink** dialog box.

11. In the **Create Custom Action** dialog box, scroll down. Under **Advanced Custom actions options**, to the right of the **Button image URL (16x16)** box, click **Browse**.

The Insert Hyperlink dialog box opens.

Up One Folder

12. Navigate to **SiteAssets** by using the **Up One Folder** button to the right of the **Look In** box. Click the image you want to use, such as **b_NewTask16x16**, and then click **OK** to close the **Insert Hyperlink** dialog box.

Tip If you plan to create a site template, do not use absolute URL addresses. Instead, use the ~site token to point to the location of the file, such as ~site/SiteAssets/b_NewTask16x16.png. Then, when you create a site from your site template, the custom action will search for the image file in the new site's Site Assets library.

13. In the **Rights mask** box, type **EditListItems**.

This custom action will appear only on the item menu if the user has permission to edit list items on the Announcements list.

14. In the **Sequence number (optional)** box, type **2000**.

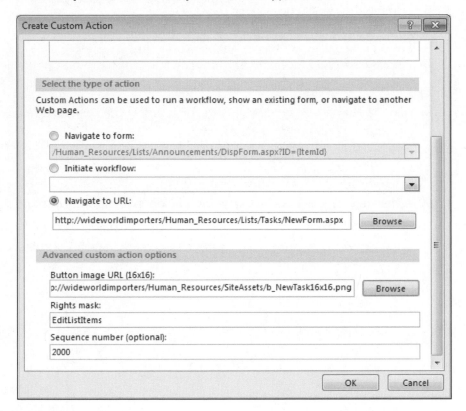

15. Click **OK**.

The Create Custom Action dialog box closes. In the Custom Actions area, the custom action New Task Item appears as a list item menu (LIM) action with a sequence number of 2,000.

 CLEAN UP Leave SharePoint Designer open if you are continuing to the next exercise.

Creating Server Ribbon Custom Actions

In the previous section, you used the New button in the Custom Actions workspace area to create a list menu item custom action. To create server ribbon custom actions on views and forms you must use the Custom Action command on the ribbon in the New group. When you create a server ribbon custom action for a view, that custom action appears on the ribbon for all view pages you create.

When you add server ribbon custom actions to list views and forms, you can optionally provide two images: 16×16 and 32×32 pixels. The smaller image is used when the browser size is reduced and the amount of space for the custom action is limited.

In this exercise, you create a server ribbon custom action for a list form.

 SET UP Using SharePoint Designer, open the team site you used in the previous exercise, if it is not already open.

Custom Action

1. On the **Custom Actions** tab, click **Custom Action** in the **New** group, and then click **Display Form Ribbon**.

2. In the **Name** box type **Add Announcement**. In the **Navigate to form** list, select the NewForm.aspx page for the list.

3. In the **Button Image URL (16x16)** box, click **Browse**, and then select the image you want to use, such as **b_NewAnn16x16**. Click **OK**. In the **Button Image URL (32x32)** box, click **Browse** and select the image you want to use, such as **b_NewAnn32x32**. Click **OK**.

4. Click **OK**.

   The Create Custom Action dialog box closes. In the Custom Actions area, the Add Announcement, Display Form Ribbon action, with a sequence number of 0, appears.

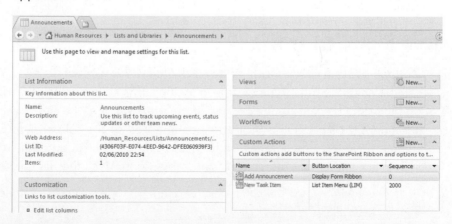

5. On the ribbon's **List Settings** tab, click **Preview in Browser**.

   Troubleshooting If the Preview in Browser command is inactive, click one of the workspace area titles or Announcements in the workspace breadcrumb.

   A browser window opens displaying the All Items view of the Announcements list.

6. Hover the mouse pointer over an announcements item, and then click the arrow that appears.

   The item menu appears with the New Task action as the last action in the list.

7. Click **View Item**.

   The View dialog box opens. On the ribbon, the Add Announcements action is the first action in the Manage group.

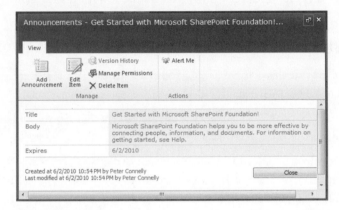

   Note To modify or delete your custom actions, select the icon to the left of the custom action to display the List, Custom Action ribbon tab, and then use the appropriate command in the Edit group.

 CLEAN UP Close the browser. Leave SharePoint Designer open if you are continuing to the next exercise.

Creating Site Columns

Although you can create a column to track data within a list or library, you might find that you need the same type of data in multiple lists. This is when you should use a site column. A site column can be defined at the site level or at the site-collection level. Child sites inherit the site columns from their parent sites, so site columns can be used across multiple sites, lists, and libraries. They enable you to define and update a column in a single place and have it affect all lists and libraries in which the site columns are used.

Tip If you need the same site column within a different site collection, you need to create it again in that site collection.

In this exercise you create a site column so that list and library owners can use it to categorize their content by country or region.

SET UP Using SharePoint Designer, open the team site you used in the previous exercise if it is not already open, and open the Sales list settings page.

1. In the N**avigation** pane, click **Site Columns**.

The Site Columns gallery page is displayed.

Troubleshooting If no site columns are displayed, click each of the column headings and then click All to remove any filter that is applied to the gallery page.

2. On the **Columns** tab, click **New Column**, and then click **Choice**.

The Create A Site Column dialog box opens.

New Column

3. In the **Name** box, type **WideWorldImporters Country/Region**.

Tip Site column names must be unique within the site collection.

4. Select **New group**, and in the **New group** box, type **SPD SBS**.

5. Click **OK**.

The Create A Site Column dialog box closes, and the Column Editor dialog box opens.

6. In the **Choices (enter each choice on a separate line)** box, type the following three lines:

East

West

Europe

7. In the **Default value** box, delete **Choice 1** and type **East**. In the **Display as** list, select **Radio buttons**.

8. Click **OK** to close the **Column Editor** dialog box.

9. Click the arrow in the **Type** column heading and select **All**. Then click the arrow in the **Group** column heading and select **SPD SBS**.

   The WideWorldImporters Country/Region site column is displayed.

Push Changes
To List

10. On the **Columns** tab, if the **Push Changes to List** command in the **Manage** group is not highlighted in orange, click **Push Changes to Lists**.

    Note By highlighting the Push Changes to Lists command, any changes to this site column will be copied to lists that use this site column. When this command is not highlighted, then only when you add this site column to a list does the list obtain the latest copy of the site column.

11. Click **Save**.

 CLEAN UP Close Sales. Leave SharePoint Designer open if you are continuing to the next exercise.

Using Site Columns

Once you create a site column, you need to add it to a list or library. You can subsequently change the site column's settings and push them to the lists or libraries that are using the site column. You can make changes to a site column at the list level. Such changes affect only the list in which the changes are made; that is, the changes made at the list level are not pushed up from the list to where the site column was created. Changes to a site column that are pushed to a list override any changes made to the site column at the list level.

In this exercise you enhance the Company History Wiki Pages library by adding a site column so that users can categorize their wiki pages by country or region.

 SET UP Using SharePoint Designer, open the team site you used in the previous exercise if it is not already open, and open the Sales list settings page.

1. In the **Navigation** pane, click **Lists and Libraries**, and then under **Document Libraries**, click **Company History**.

   The Company History list settings page is displayed in the workspace.

Edit Columns

Add Existing Site
Column

2. On the **List Settings** tab, click **Edit Columns**. Then, on the **Columns** tab, click **Add Existing Site Column**.

The Site Column Picker opens with Enter search keywords highlighted.

3. Type **wi,** and then in the **Select one of the Site Columns below** area, click **WideWorldImporters Country/Region**.

4. Click **OK** to close the **Site Columns Picker** dialog box.

5. With **WideWorldImporters Country/Region** column name selected, on the **Columns** tab, click **Column Settings**.

6. In the **Column Editor** dialog box, clear the **Allow blank values?** check box, and then click **OK**.

The Column Editor dialog box closes, and Yes appears in the Required column on the WideWorldImporters Country/Region row.

7. On the Quick Access Toolbar, click **Save**.

8. In the **Navigation** pane, click **Site Columns** to display the Site Columns gallery page. The site column WideWorldImporter Country/Region is selected.

9. On the **Columns** tab, check that the **Push Changes to Lists** command is highlighted in orange, and then click **Column Settings**.

10. In the **Choices (enter each choice on a separate line)** box, place the insertion point at the right of **West**, press **ENTER**, and then type the following two lines:

    Asia

    Africa

    The Column Editor dialog box contains five choices, and the **Allow blank values?** check box is selected.

11. Click **OK** to close the **Column Editor** dialog box, and then click **Save** on the Quick Access Toolbar.

Refresh

12. At the top of the workspace, click the **Company History** tab to display the columns editor page, and then click **Refresh** at the far right of the breadcrumb bar.

    The page refreshes as SharePoint Designer contacts the Web server. The Required column for WideWorldImporters Country/Region does not contain Yes.

    Note If you opened the Column Editor dialog box for the WideWorldImporters Country/Region list column, it would contain the five choices from the site column. Your customizations for the WideWorldImporters Country/Region list column have been overridden by the changes you made to the site column.

 CLEAN UP Close Company History. Leave SharePoint Designer open if you are continuing to the next exercise.

Creating Content Types

A content type can group site columns, define workflows and information management policies, and associate document templates with content of its type. After a content type is assoicated with a list or library, it defines the attributes of a list item, a document, or a folder. By default, both SharePoint Foundation and SharePoint Server contain a number of content types and site columns that are defined at the site-collection level. These site columns are the ones used to create the columns in your lists and libraries. By defining content types and site columns at the site-collection level, you make them available to all sites within the site collection, and they can be used to apply consistent metadata and data management policies across all sites. You can also define content types at a site level. These site columns and content types then become available to child sites of the site in which they are defined.

Content types and site columns cannot easily be copied from one site collection to another, or from one site to another. Therefore, in SharePoint Foundation, without the skills of a developer, it is difficult to apply consistent data management across a number of site collections. In SharePoint Server, you have the same restrictions. However, by using the Managed Metadata Service (MMS), term stores and content types can be created and shared across Web applications and site collections. It is important to plan your use of list columns, site columns, content types, and if you have SharePoint Server, MMS; otherwise, you might find that you are creating the same columns, site columns, and content types for each of your solutions.

See Also More information on site columns and content types can be found in Chapter 7, "Working with Lists Settings," and Chapter 8, "Working with Library Settings," in Microsoft *SharePoint Foundation 2010 Step by Step*. Information on document management planning can be found at *http://technet.microsoft.com/en-us/library/cc263266.aspx*.

In this exercise you create a content type.

 SET UP Using SharePoint Designer, open the team site you used in the previous exercise if it is not already open.

Content Types

1. In the **Navigation** pane, click **Content Types**, and then on the **Content Types** tab, click **Content Type** in the **New** group.

   The Create A Content Type dialog box opens.

2. In the **Name** box, type **Expenses**, and in the **Description** box type **Use this content type when uploading new expense claims or creating new expense claims.**

3. In the **Select parent content type from** list, select **Document Content Types**. In the **Select parent content type** list, select **Document**.

4. Select **New group**, and in the **New group** box, type **SPD SBS**.

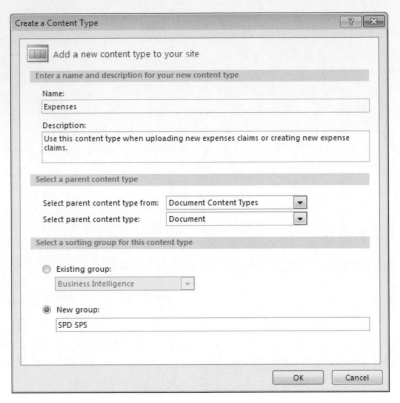

5. Click **OK** to close the **Create a Content Type** dialog box.

The Content Types gallery page refreshes.

✖ **CLEAN UP** Leave SharePoint Designer open if you are continuing to the next exercise.

Adding a Site Column to a Content Type

The settings of a content type are similar to the settings you can add to a list or library. Using SharePoint Designer, you can add, amend, or delete document templates, site columns, forms, and workflows for content types. In the browser, you can also configure information management policies and document information panel (DIP) settings. From SharePoint Designer, you can display the browser content administration page by clicking the Administration Web Page command in the Manage group on the ribbon.

By adding multiple site columns to a content type, you can associate multiple types of metadata with a particular type of content.

In this exercise you add a site column to a content type.

SET UP Using SharePoint Designer, open the team site you used in the previous exercise, if it is not already open, and open the Content Types gallery page as described in the previous exercise.

1. Click the down arrow in the **Group** column heading, and select **SPD SBS**.

    The Content Types gallery page refreshes and displays only those content types categorized in the SPD SBS group. The Expenses content type should be listed on this page.

2. Click **Expenses**.

    The Expenses settings page is displayed.

Add Existing Site Column

3. In the **Customization** area, click **Edit content type columns**. Then, on the **Columns** tab, click **Add Existing Site Column** in the **New** group.

    The Site Columns Picker dialog box is displayed, with Enter search keywords highlighted.

4. Type **wi**, and then under **Select one of the Site Columns below**, click **WideWorldImporters Country/Region**.

5. Click **OK**.

    The Site Columns Picker dialog box closes, and the WideWorldImporters Country/Region site column is listed in the Expenses gallery page.

Content Type Settings

6. On the **Columns** tab, click **Content Type Settings** in the **Manage** group.

    A dialog box opens asking whether you want to save changes to the content type Expenses.

7. Click **Yes** to save your changes.

    The Expenses content type settings page is displayed.

CLEAN UP Leave SharePoint Designer open if you are continuing to the next exercise.

Adding a Document Template to a Content Type

A document content type can have a file associated with it. This file is known as a document template. Once the content type is associated with a document library, users working in the browser can click the New command on the Documents tab. When a user clicks New, the program associated with the document template file extension opens and a copy of the document template is displayed, ready to be modified and then saved to the document library.

In this manner, a document library can contain multiple types of documents, such as invoices and purchase orders, each with their own document templates, metadata, information management policies, and workflows.

In this exercise you add a document template to a content type.

SET UP Using SharePoint Designer, open the team site you used in the previous exercise if it is not already open.

1. In the **Navigation** pane, click **All Files**.

    A new tab opens, on which folders, libraries, and pages are displayed, including a folder named _cts.

    Refresh

    Troubleshooting If you do not see the folder name _cts in the All Files mini-gallery, but other folders, such as _catalogs, are visible, then click Refresh on the SharePoint Designer Quick Access Toolbar. If the folder name _cts is still not visible, close SharePoint Designer and reopen it. If the All Files option is not available, talk to your site collection owner or Web application administrator and ask to be allowed to see the hidden URL content of the Web site. (See the section "Controlling the Use of SharePoint Designer," in Chapter 1.) If you are not allowed to see the hidden URL content, use the browser to upload the document template by navigating to the Site Content Types gallery from the site settings page. Click the Expenses content type, and then click Advanced Settings in the Settings section. In the Document Template section, click Upload A New Document Template. Then complete the exercise in the section "Associating Content Types with Lists and Libraries."

2. Click **_cts** to display the contents of the folder.

    The folder should contain a folder for each content type created for this site.

3. Click **Expenses**, and then on the **All Files** tab, click **Import Files** in the **Manage** group.

    The Import dialog box opens.

4. Click **Add File**.

    The Add File To Import List dialog box opens.

5. Browse to the folder that contains the document template you want to use, such as the Chapter03 practice file folder, and then select the file you want to import, such as **WideWorldImportersExpenses.docx**.

6. Click **Open**, and then click **OK** to close the **Add File to Import** and then the **Import** dialog boxes.

7. In the **Navigation** pane, click **Content Types**, and then click **Expenses**.

    The Expenses content type settings page is displayed.

8. In the **Content Type Information** area, to the right of **Document Template**, click **<click to enter text>**, and type **WideWorldImportersExpenses.docx**.

> **Tip** Once a document template is associated with a file name, you can use the Edit Document Template command on the Content Type Settings tab to modify the document template.

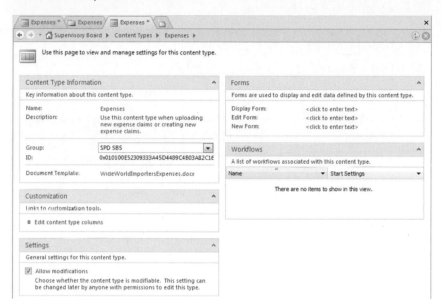

9. On the Quick Access Toolbar, click **Save**.

> **Troubleshooting** If a Microsoft SharePoint Designer warning message is displayed, stating that the content type changes to the server could not be saved and that the urlOfFile Parameter name: Specified value is not supported for the urlOfFile parameter, then you have misspelled the document template name or the file name is not stored in the _cts\Expenses folder.

 CLEAN UP Leave SharePoint Designer open if you are continuing to the next exercise.

Associating Content Types with Lists and Libraries

Once you have created a content type, you need to add the content type to a list or library. By adding multiple content types to a list or library, you can store different types of content in that list or library.

In this exercise you associate a content type with a document library.

 SET UP Using SharePoint Designer, open the team site you used in the previous exercise, if it is not already open.

1. In the **Navigation** pane, click **Lists and Libraries**, and then under **Document Libraries**, click **Shared Documents**.

    A new workspace tab opens displaying the Shared Document list settings page.

2. In the **Settings** area, under **Advanced Settings**, select the **Allow management of content types** check box.

    Tip Content types cannot be added to a list or library if the Allow Management Of Content Types check box is cleared.

Add

3. In the **Content Types** area, click **Add**.

    The Content Types Picker dialog box opens with Enter search keywords highlighted.

4. Type **ex**, and then under **Select one of the Content Types below**, click **Expenses**. Click **OK**.

    The Content Types Picker dialog box closes, and in the Content Types area Expenses is listed, with Yes in the Show On New Menu column.

5. On the Quick Access Toolbar, click **Save**.

6. Click the **List Settings** tab, and then click **Preview in Browser**.

    The browser opens and displays the Shared Documents All Items page.

7. Click the **Documents** tab, and then click the **New Document** arrow. You should see two types of documents that you can use as a basis for a new document: Document and Expenses.

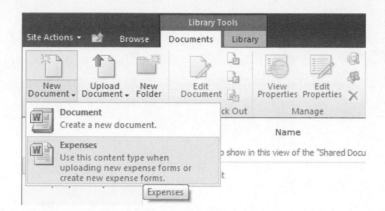

 CLEAN UP Close the Expenses and Shared Document tabs. Leave SharePoint Designer open if you are continuing to the next exercise.

See Also More information on content types can be found at *http://msdn.microsoft.com/en-us/library/ms479905.aspx.*

Deleting SharePoint Objects

You can delete many SharePoint objects by using SharePoint Designer. For example, you can delete lists, libraries, files, site columns, content types, and list columns. You cannot, however, delete list items. Any lists, libraries, pages, files, or list items that are deleted by using the browser or SharePoint Designer are stored in the Recycle Bin, from which you can restore them. When you delete SharePoint objects such as list columns, custom actions, site columns, and content types, they are not stored in the Recycle Bin, and the process of restoring them is more complex and will involve your IT department.

In this exercise, you delete a list, a file, and a list column. You then use the Recycle Bin to restore one of these SharePoint objects.

 SET UP Using SharePoint Designer, open the team site you used in the previous exercise, if it is not already open.

1. In the **Navigation** pane, click **Lists and Libraries**.

    The Lists And Libraries gallery page is displayed in the workspace.

2. Click the icon to the left of **Issues**, and then on the **Lists and Libraries** tab, click **Delete** in the **Edit** group.

    The Confirm Delete dialog box is displayed.

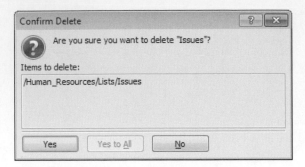

3. Click **Yes** to confirm the deletion.

   The Lists And Libraries gallery page is displayed again, and the Issues list does not appear.

4. Click the icon to the left of **Tasks**, and then on the ribbon, click **Edit Columns** in the **Edit** group.

   The Columns Editor page is displayed in the workspace.

5. Click **Task Group**, and then on the **Columns** tab, click **Delete** in the **Edit** group.

   The Columns Editor page redisplays. An asterisk appears on the tab labeled Tasks, and the Task Group column does not appear.

6. Right-click the **Tasks** tab, and click **Save**.

7. In the **Navigation** pane, click **Site Assets**. Right-click the file you want to delete, such as **b_NewTask16x16.png**, and then click **Delete**.

   Tip You can delete multiple files by selecting them with the Ctrl or Shift key and then clicking Delete on the ribbon or the item menu.

8. Click **Yes** to confirm the deletion.

Recycle Bin

9. In the **Navigation** pane, click your site's name, such as **Human Resources**, and then on the **Site** tab, click **Recycle Bin** in the **Manage** group.

   A browser window opens, and the Recycle Bin page is displayed. The list and the file you deleted should be listed on the page, but the list column you deleted does not appear in the list.

 CLEAN UP Close the browser and SharePoint Designer.

Key Points

- SharePoint Foundation and SharePoint Server provide a number of built-in list definitions that you can use as a basis for creating lists or libraries with SharePoint Designer.

- In SharePoint Designer, you can create or modify list columns, site columns, and content types and create list templates. You cannot create or modify list items or metadata associated with documents.

- Columns, also known as fields, determine the type of data that a list or library can hold. Each column is associated with a column data type.

- Using the browser or SharePoint Designer, you can create a Web Part Page based on one of the eight built-in Web Part Page templates.

- Use XSLT List View (XLV) Web Parts to display the contents of lists and libraries.

- XLV Web Parts share a common set of Web Part properties that control appearance, layout, and advanced characteristics. They also have other configurable settings, such as which columns to display and the sort order of the list items.

- Custom actions are commands that can be added to the list item menu (LIM) and the server ribbon that you see in the browser on the list views and forms. This allows you to add content to the menu item or server ribbon without involving a developer or the IT department.

- Site columns can be associated with a list or a content type.

- It is important to plan your list columns, site columns, content types, and, if you have SharePoint Server, MMS; otherwise, you might find that you create the same columns, site columns, and content types for each of your solutions.

- Any lists, libraries, pages, files, or list items that are deleted using the browser or SharePoint Designer are stored in the Recycle Bin, from which you can restore them. When you delete SharePoint objects such as list columns, site columns, and content types, they are not stored in the Recycle Bin, and the restoration process is more complex and will involve your IT department.

Chapter at a Glance

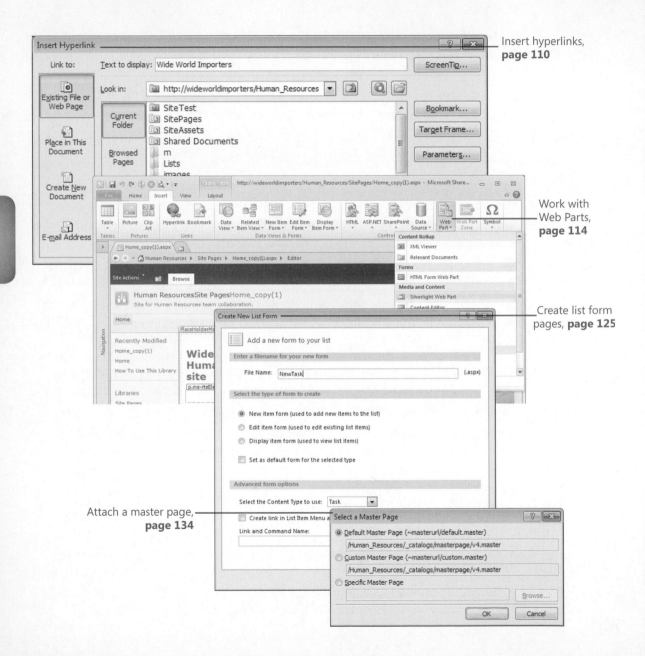

Insert hyperlinks, **page 110**

Work with Web Parts, **page 114**

Create list form pages, **page 125**

Attach a master page, **page 134**

4 Creating and Modifying Web Pages

In this chapter, you will learn how to

- ✔ Insert text, ScreenTips, hyperlinks, and images.
- ✔ Work with Web Parts.
- ✔ Change the home page for a Web site.
- ✔ Modify and create list view and list form pages.
- ✔ Create an ASP.NET page and insert a Web Part zone.
- ✔ Attach a master page.
- ✔ Manage Web pages.

With Microsoft SharePoint Designer 2010, you can create a number of different file formats, some of which you might not consider to be Web pages—for example, text and cascading style sheet files and others you might not have heard about before reading this book. Chapter 1, "Exploring SharePoint Designer 2010," explored one file type—the Wiki page. You might also be familiar with Web Part pages and, if you use Microsoft SharePoint Server, publishing pages. Publishing pages are detailed in Chapter 13, "Managing Web Content in the SharePoint Server Environment."

This chapter focuses on Wiki pages and Web Part pages, building on the information in Chapter 1. You'll learn to use the SharePoint Designer ribbon to add static content such as text, ScreenTips, hyperlinks, and images. You'll learn that Wiki pages and Web Part pages are instances of Microsoft ASP.NET 2.0 content pages and that any SharePoint content page can contain one or more Web Parts. You'll also learn how to change the appearance of a Web page by adding Web Part zones, the containers for Web Parts. And you'll learn to manage Wiki pages and Web Part pages by applying permissions, manipulating the versions of these pages, and deleting pages.

Tip You can create Web Part pages by using SharePoint Designer. Creating Wiki pages with SharePoint Designer, although not impossible, is complex. Copying an existing Wiki page or using the browser to create a Wiki page are the most efficient methods.

Practice Files Before you can use the practice files provided for this chapter, you need to install them from the book's companion Web site. For more information about practice files, see "Using the Practice Files" on page xxiii.

Inserting Text, ScreenTips, Hyperlinks, and Images

The browser is the main Web content editing tool for SharePoint. You can complete similar activities using SharePoint Designer in Design view. The standard Windows application shortcuts for the Copy, Cut, Paste, and Undo commands work in SharePoint Designer as they do in any other Windows-based program. However, when you paste contents from other programs, such as Microsoft Word, use the *Paste Text* command, which you can find by clicking the arrow on the Paste command in the Clipboard group on the ribbon, and then add your own formatting. Formatting from other programs can be verbose and might not generate the most efficient Web code.

You can add components, such as text, images, hyperlinks, ScreenTips, and alternate text. ScreenTips are useful because they provide information when users point to hyperlinks. Alternate text allows you to define text that is displayed if an image does not load or if users are unable to see images. Append a period to the end of the words you enter so that users who listen to screen readers are able to understand your pages more easily, especially when two alternative text tags are next to each other.

SharePoint Designer provides a number of tools to manage the graphics that you include on pages:

- **Image conversion** When you insert an image that is not a GIF or JPEG, SharePoint Designer by default converts the file to GIF or JPEG format, depending on the number of colors in the original image. After you insert an image, you can reformat it in SharePoint Designer by using commands on the Picture Tools, Format tab and in the Picture Properties dialog box.

- **Auto thumbnail** You can tell SharePoint Designer to create a small version of an image—a *thumbnail*—and link it to the full-size image that it represents by right-clicking an image and then clicking Auto Thumbnail. Alternatively, select the image and press Ctrl+T.

Tip You can configure the settings for both these image manipulation options by using the Picture and AutoThumbnail tabs on the Page Editor Options dialog box.

For prototyping purposes or for images on team sites, the image manipulation capabilities in SharePoint Designer should be adequate, but if you are producing a public-facing site, you might want to obtain a third-party image-editing tool. Ideally, you should resize image files in an image-editing program before inserting the images into pages, because when you resize an image by using HTML tag attributes, the original image file is downloaded to the user's computer, even though the browser renders the image file at a smaller size. This can cause a page to take more time than necessary to load the page.

Tip If you do not have a third-party tool, you can use Microsoft PowerPoint or Microsoft Picture Manager to resize your picture and reduce the size of the files.

In this exercise, you create a new page based on the home page of a team site. You then add text and quickly format it by using the commands on the Home tab. After adding a hyperlink to the text and associating a ScreenTip with the hyperlink, you will configure the hyperlink so that a new browser window opens when a user clicks the hyperlink.

 SET UP Using SharePoint Designer, open the team site you created and modified in earlier chapters. If you did not create a team site, follow the steps for creating the site in Chapter 1. The site settings page should be displayed in the workspace.

1. In the **Navigation** pane, click **Site Pages**.

    The Site Pages gallery page is displayed in the workspace.

2. Click the icon to the left of **Home.aspx**. On the **Pages** tab, click **Copy** and then click **Paste** in the **Clipboard** group.

    The file Home_copy(1).aspx appears in the Site Pages gallery page.

Edit File

3. On the **Pages** tab, click **Edit File** to open the page in edit mode, and then click the arrow to the right of **Navigation** on the **Navigation** pane.

    The Navigation pane collapses, providing you with more area in the workspace to modify the page.

4. Right-click anywhere within the **PlaceHolderMain** region, and then click **Zoom to Contents**.

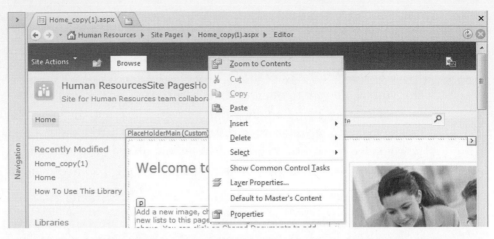

Only the code that is contained within the EmbeddedFormField control is displayed.

5. Select the text **Welcome to your site!**, and type **Wide World Importers Human Resources team site**.

An asterisk appears on the Home_copy(1).aspx tab, indicating that the page has changed but that you have not saved your changes. This type of page is commonly referred to as a *dirty page*.

Bold

Center

Hyperlink

6. Select the text **Wide World Importers Human Resources team site**. On the **Home** tab, click the **Bold** button in the **Font** group, and then click the **Center** button in the **Paragraph** group.

7. Select the text **Wide World Importers**, and then on the **Home** tab, click **Hyperlink** in the **Paragraph** group.

Tip There is also a Hyperlink command on the Insert tab in the Links group.

8. In the **Insert Hyperlink** dialog box, click **ScreenTip**.

The Set Hyperlink ScreenTip dialog box opens.

9. Under **ScreenTip text**, type text that describes the Web site, such as **Wide World Importers' intranet site**, and then click **OK** to close the **Set Hyperlink ScreenTip** dialog box.

10. In the **Address** box in the **Insert Hyperlink** dialog box, type the URL of a Web site, such as **http://wideworldimporters**, and then click **Target Frame**.

The Target Frame dialog box opens.

11. In the **Common targets** list box, select **New Window**, and then click **OK**.

The Target Frame dialog box closes. The Target Frame area at the bottom of the Insert Hyperlink dialog box *displays _blank*.

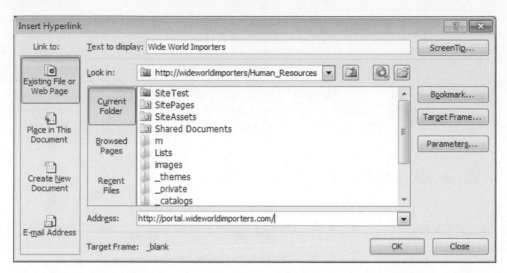

Tip Your company might have a policy about when a new browser window should be opened. Generally, you should open a new browser window only in scenarios in which you display a printable version of a Web page or large images. You can find expert usability references on this topic at *www.sitepoint.com/article/beware-opening-links-new-window/* and by using the search keywords *opening, new, browser, window, usability*.

12. Click **OK** to close the **Insert Hyperlink** dialog box.

The Insert Hyperlink dialog box closes. The text *Wide World Importers* is highlighted, and on the Quick Tag Selector, the orange <a> tag appears.

Tip If the orange <a> tag does not appear on the Quick Tag Selector, click elsewhere on the page, and then click the text *Wide World Importers*.

Save

13. On the Quick Access Toolbar, click **Save**.

A Microsoft SharePoint Designer dialog box opens, warning you that SharePoint may have removed unsafe content.

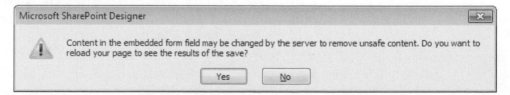

14. Click **Yes** to reload the page within the editor page.

The page refreshes, and no asterisk appears on the Home_copy(1).aspx tab.

 CLEAN UP Leave SharePoint Designer open if you are continuing to the next exercise.

> **Important** Design view in SharePoint Designer is not a true representation of what you see in a browser. Some aspects of a page might not be displayed the same or some code might not function unless you view the page in the browser. As you make changes to a Web page, you should constantly review the page in a browser and test the functionality of your changes. Every browser is different, so you should also test your page in the set of browsers with resolutions commonly used by visitors to your sites. If you have multiple browsers installed on your computer, you can use the arrow on the Preview command to preview a page in a specific browser at a particular resolution.

Working with Web Parts

In Chapter 3, "Working with Lists and Libraries," you created a Web Part page, inserted an XSLT List View (XLV) Web Part into a Web Part zone, and then customized its properties. You can add the same Web Part to a Web Part page or to a Wiki page by using the browser.

The XLV Web Part is used to display the contents of lists and libraries. Each time the data in the list or library changes, the changes are reflected in the XLV Web Part. You have likely used or seen XLV Web Parts on many pages. For example, when you create a team site, an XLV Web Part on the home page displays files stored in the Shared Documents library. When you display the contents of a task list, the All Tasks view page contains an XLV Web Part. However, you can use many types of Web Parts other than the XLV Web Part.

A Microsoft SharePoint Foundation 2010 installation has 13 built-in Web Parts: Relevant Documents, XML Viewer, HTML Form Web Part, Content Editor Web Part (CEWP), Image Viewer, Page Viewer, Picture Library Slideshow Web Part, Silverlight Web Part, Site Users, User Tasks, SQL Server Reporting Services Report Viewer, What's New, and Whereabouts. Microsoft SharePoint Server 2010 includes more than 50 additional built-in Web Parts, including Business Data List, Content Query Web Part (CQWP), Current User Filter, Excel Web Access, Visio Web Access, Indicator Details, Search Box, Top Federated Results, Web Analytics Web Part, and SQL Server Analysis Services Filter. Of course, your company may have developed its own Web Parts or purchased third-party Web Parts. A detailed description of all the Web Parts you can find in SharePoint Foundation and SharePoint Server are outside the scope of this book.

> **See Also** For more information about Web Parts, see Chapter 20, "Web Parts and Their Functionality in SharePoint Server 2010," in *Microsoft SharePoint Server 2010 Administrator's Companion* by Bill English, Brian Alderman, and Mark Ferraz (Microsoft Press, 2011).

A common mistake made by companies new to SharePoint is to spend thousands of dollars and hours of time developing custom Web Parts when one of the built-in Web Parts would meet their business needs. This is especially true given that SharePoint Designer allows you to create a Data View Web Part (DVWP), also known as a *Data Form Web Part* (DFWP), which is similar to the XLV Web Part and can be used to display and modify data from data sources such as a Microsoft SQL Server database.

See Also For more information about the Data View Web Part, see Chapter 5, "Working with Data Views." The information in Chapter 5 is also relevant to formatting the XLV Web Part.

Web Parts are also classified by where they are located:

- **Dynamic Web Parts** By using SharePoint Designer or the browser, you can place these Web Parts in the EmbeddedFormField SharePoint control on Wiki pages or in Web Part zones on Web Part pages. Dynamic Web Parts are stored separately from the page, and only when a user requests the page is the SQL Server content database queried to determine the number of dynamic Web Parts, which Web Parts are being used, where to place them on a page, and, if the page contains Web Part zones, in which Web Part zone the Web Parts should be placed.

- **Static Web Parts** These Web Parts are placed outside the EmbeddedFormField SharePoint control or outside Web Part zones. Static Web Parts can be created by using SharePoint Designer in advanced edit mode, but they cannot be created by using the browser. Static Web Parts are stored as part of the page.

In this exercise, you add, modify, and delete a Web Part.

SET UP Using SharePoint Designer, open the team site you used in the previous exercise if it is not already open. Open the home page of the team site in edit mode and zoom to view the contents by using the command on the View tab or by right-clicking the page and selecting the command from the menu. Upload the SilverlightSPDSBS.xap file to your team site's Site Assets library. See "Using the Practice Files" on page xxiii.

Web Part

1. Place the insertion point on a new line under the text, **Wide World Importers Human Resources team site,** that you added to the page in the previous exercise, and then click **Web Part** on the **Insert** tab.

2. On the **Web Part** menu, click **Silverlight Web Part**.

   The WebPartPages:SilverlightWebPart control is added to the page. On the Quick Tag Selector, the orange WebPartPagesSilverlightWebPart tag appears.

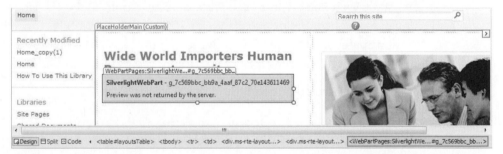

3. Double-click the Silverlight Web Part to open the **Silverlight Web Part** dialog box. Click **Configure** to open a second **Silverlight Web Part** dialog box, and in the **URL** box type **~site\siteassets\silverlightSPDSBS.xap**. Click **OK** to close the dialog box.

4. Under **Appearance** in the **Title** box, type **SPD Silverlight**. Under **Height**, select **Yes**, and type **40**.

5. Click **OK** to close the **Silverlight Web Part** dialog box.

6. Click the Silverlight Web Part, and then on the **Web Part Tools**, **Format** tab, clear the **Edit in Personal View** check box in the **Allow** group.

    Troubleshooting If the Edit In Personal View check box is not displayed, click Allow, and then clear the Edit In Personal View check box.

    Note The check boxes in the Allow list are the same check boxes as in the Advanced section of a Web Part Properties dialog box.

Options

7. In the workspace, click **Shared Documents**. On the **List View Tools**, **Design** tab, click **Options** in the **Toolbar** group, and then click **Full Toolbar**.

The Shared Documents Web Part reloads and the full toolbar is displayed.

8. Right-click **Shared Documents**, and then click **Web Part Properties**.

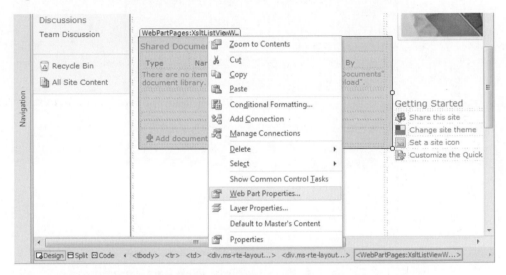

The Shared Documents dialog box opens.

9. Expand the **Layout** section, and select the **Close the Web Part** check box. Then click **OK** to close the **Shared Documents** dialog box.

10. Press **F12**, click **Yes** to save your changes, and then click **Yes** to reload your page.

Tip On some laptop computers you might need to press the Fn key with the F12 key to preview the page in the browser.

A browser window opens and displays the Silverlight Web Part with a Web Part title of *SPD Silverlight*. The Shared Documents XLV Web Part is not displayed on the page.

> **Tip** Closed Web Parts can increase the time it takes for a browser to load the page. Keep the number of closed Web Parts to a minimum and only close a Web Part when you want to temporarily hide a Web Part and its customizations. In the browser, you can find closed Web Parts by first placing a page in edit mode. Then, on the Editing Tools, Insert tab on the server ribbon, click Web Part, and under Categories, click Closed Web Parts. The Closed Web Parts category appears only if the page contains closed Web Parts. Alternatively, append *?contents=1* to the URL of the page, such as *http://wideworldimporters/SitePages/ Home.aspx?contents=1*, to display the page's maintenance page.

11. In SharePoint Designer, click the Silverlight Web Part, and then click the label **WebPartPages:SilverlightWebPart** (above the Web Part) to ensure that the **WebPartPages:SilverlightWebPart** tag is highlighted in orange on the Quick Tag Selector. Press **Delete**.

The Silverlight Web Part is removed from the page.

Properties

12. Click the Shared Documents XLV Web Part, and then, on the **List View Tools**, **Web Part** tab, click **Properties** to display the **Shared Documents** dialog box. In the **Layouts** section, clear the **Close the Web Part** check box.

Preview in Browser

13. On the Quick Access Toolbar, click **Save**. Click **Yes** to reload the page, and then click **Preview in Browser** on the **Home** tab.

A browser window opens, the Silverlight Web Part is not displayed, and the Shared Documents Web Part is displayed.

 CLEAN UP Close any open browser windows. Leave SharePoint Designer open if you are continuing to the next exercise.

Changing the Home Page for a Web Site

Each site has a home page. This is the page—such as *http://wideworldimporters*—that is displayed in your browser when you type the URL of a site and do not specify a particular page. On a newly created team site or enterprise Wiki site, the home page is configured as *Home.aspx*. On other SharePoint sites, such as a publishing site, a Visio Process Repository site, a Group Work Site, or a document workspace, the home page is *Default.aspx*. On a publishing site, the home page is also known as the Welcome page because it's the page that welcomes a visitor to the site.

Once a SharePoint site is created, you can change the home page by using SharePoint Designer or, on a site on which the Publishing feature is enabled, from the site settings page. When you need to completely redesign your home page, you should create your new home page by using a different page than the page that is the current home page. Once you complete your redesign, you can then make your new page the home page of your site.

Assuming that you save your new page in the Site Pages library, there are several ways to complete this task:

- On the Site Pages gallery page, select your new page and then, on the Pages tab, click Set As Home Page in the Actions group.

- On the Site Pages gallery page or mini-gallery, right-click your new page and then click Set As Home Page.

- In the All Files gallery page or mini-gallery, navigate to where your new page is stored, right-click your new page, and then click Set As Home Page.

  Note You need to have the rights to view the hidden URL structure of the Web site to use this method of completing the task.

- On your new page's settings page, on the Pages tab, click Set As Home Page in the Actions group.

Important When you change your site's home page, you should consider changing the name of the page so that it matches the name of the file for your previous home page. When users bookmark a site, the name of the page is part of the bookmark. If you change the home page but don't update the file name, your users will have bookmarks that are broken links, which can cause a large number of calls to your company's IT help desk, especially for the home page of your Internet site or your company's main portal intranet site.

In this exercise, you change the home page for a site and then test that the change is implemented successfully. You will then reset the site's home page.

 SET UP Using SharePoint Designer, open the team site you used in the previous exercise if it is not already open.

1. In the **Navigation** pane, click **Site Pages** to display the gallery page, and then click the icon to the left of the page that you want to set as the home page, such as **Home_copy(1).aspx**.

Set as Home
Page

2. On the **Pages** tab, click **Set as Home Page** in the **Actions** group.

   The icon to the left of Home_copy(1).aspx displays a little house.

3. Right-click **Home_copy(1).aspx**, and then click **Preview in Browser**.

   A browser window opens and displays Home_copy(1).aspx.

4. Under the site icon, click **Home**.

   The Home_copy(1).aspx page is displayed again.

5. In the ribbon, click the **Page** tab, and then click **View All Pages** in the **Page Library** group.

   The All Pages view of the Site Pages library is displayed.

6. Under the **Name** column, click **Home** to display the Home.aspx page.

7. On the ribbon, click the **Page** tab, and then click **Make Homepage** in the **Page Actions** group. A dialog box opens. Click **OK** to restore Home.aspx as the home page for the site.

 CLEAN UP Close the browser window. Leave SharePoint Designer open if you are continuing to the next exercise. Close all open workspace tabs.

Modifying a List View Page

When you create a list or library, a number of views are created. These views are Web Part pages based on files from the site's defintion—that is, they point to files in the TEMPLATE folder on the Web servers. These Web Part pages use an XLV Web Part to display all or a subset of the contents of a list or library depending on criteria defined by the metadata. These views allow you to display information in different formats without having to enter the information more than once, thereby enabling you and other users to find information easily. Each view page contains one Web Part zone named *Main* that contains one XLV Web Part.

Note Web Part pages are pages that contain at least one Web Part zone. They are not Wiki pages; therefore, to add static text or images to these pages, you need to add the CEWP or image Web Part.

The pages that define views are not stored in the Site Pages library. In lists they are stored immediately below the list container. In libraries, by using the All Files gallery page or mini-gallery, you can see them in the Forms folder for the library. By using SharePoint Designer or the browser, you can modify the XLV Web Part of view pages, and you can add other Web Parts to the Main Web Part zone. SharePoint Designer provides additional customization options, such as inserting and customizing static text and images outside the Web Part zone, but you need to display the view page in advanced edit mode. You can add additional Web Part zones and, in advanced edit mode, add Web Parts outside Web Part zones.

See Also For more information on list and library views and how to work with them in the browser, see Chapter 9, "Working with List and Library Views," in *Microsoft SharePoint Foundation 2010 Step By Step*, by Olga Londer and Penelope Coventry (Microsoft Press, 2011).

In this exercise, you modify the All Items view of a tasks list.

SET UP Using SharePoint Designer, open the team site you used in the previous exercise if it is not already open.

1. In the **Navigation** pane, click **Lists and Libraries**, and then click **Tasks**.

   The tasks list settings page is displayed in the workspace. In the Views area, six view pages are listed: Active Tasks, AllTasks, By Assigned To, By My Groups, Due Today, and My Tasks.

2. In the **Views** area, click **All Tasks** to open the page in edit mode. The workspace tab is labeled **AllItems.aspx**.

3. In the middle of the page, click **Type**.

   A blue border with the label *Main* appears, within which is the label *<webpartpages :XsltListViewWebPart>*. This label indicates that an XLV Web Part is contained within the Web Part zone Main. A purple-bordered rectangle surrounds the Web Part zones, labeled *PlaceHolderMain (Custom)*. The ribbon contains the List View Tools tabs.

4. On the **Options** tab, click **Add/Remove Columns** in the **Fields** group.

   Add/Remove
   Columns

   The Displayed Fields dialog box opens.

5. Under **Available fields**, hold down the **CTRL** key, and select two fields, such as the **Start Date** and **Task Group** fields. Click **Add**.

   The two fields, Start Date and Task Group, appear under Displayed Fields.

6. Click **Start Date**, and then click **Move Up** three times so that **Start Date** is above **Due Date**.

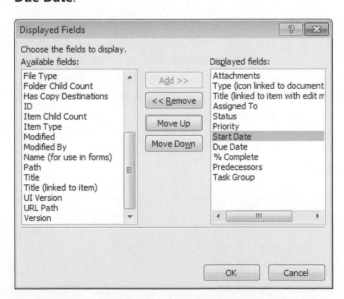

7. Click **OK** to close the **Displayed Fields** dialog box.

The workspace is displayed with the Start Date and Task Group columns visible in the Tasks XLV Web Part.

Save

Close

8. Click **Save**, and then close the **AllItems.aspx** tab by clicking the **Close** icon at the top right of the workspace. The site settings page is displayed in the workspace, and the Close icon is now dimmed.

 CLEAN UP Leave SharePoint Designer open if you are continuing to the next exercise.

Creating List View Pages

The built-in list views that are associated with a list or library might not meet all your needs. In the browser, you can use the sort and filter option on a column of a list view, but this is only a temporary solution because the next time you use the list or library, your sort or filter selections are not applied. By using both the browser and SharePoint Designer, however, you can create new list views and retain your selections. In addition, when you create list views, other formatting options become available, such as the order and visibility of columns, grouping list items in an expanded or collapsed display, or limiting the number of list items displayed.

In this exercise, you create a view for a library to display documents grouped by the person who last modified them and sorted on the modification date and file size. You then make this view the default view.

➡ **SET UP** Using SharePoint Designer, open the team site you used in the previous exercise if it is not already.

1. In the **Navigation** pane, click **Lists and Libraries**, and then under **Document Libraries**, click **Shared Documents**.

The Shared Documents list settings page is displayed in the workspace.

2. On the **List Settings** tab, click **List View** in the **New** group.

List View

The Create New List View dialog box opens.

Tip You can also create a view by using the New button in the Views area.

3. In the **Name** box, type **ByModified**.

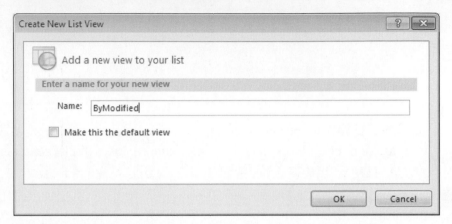

The name that you type for the view page forms part of the URL.

See Also For information about naming conventions, refer to the sidebar "Best Practices for Naming URLs" in Chapter 1.

4. Click **OK** to close the **New List View** dialog box.

The ByModified view appears in the Views area.

5. Right-click **ByModified**, click **Rename**, and then type **By Modified**. Press **ENTER**.

By Modified is the name of the view you will see in the browser.

6. Click **By Modified** to open the page in edit mode.

The workspace tab is labeled *ByModified.aspx*. A blue border with the label *Main* appears, within which is the label *<webpartpages:XsltListViewWebPart>*. This indicates that an XLV Web Part is contained within the Web Part zone Main. A purple-bordered rectangle surrounds the Web Part zones, labeled *PlaceHolderMain (Custom)*. The ribbon contains the List View Tools tabs.

Sort & Group

7. On the **Options** tab, click **Sort & Group** in the **Filter, Sort & Group** group.

The Sort And Group dialog box opens.

8. Under **Available fields**, click **Modified By**, and then click **Add**.

9. Repeat step 8 to add **Modified** and **File Size**.

10. Under **Sort order**, click **Modified By**. Then, in the **Group Properties** section, select the **Show group header** check box and click **Expand group by default** if this option is not already selected.

11. Click **Modified**. In the **Sort Properties** section, click **Descending**.

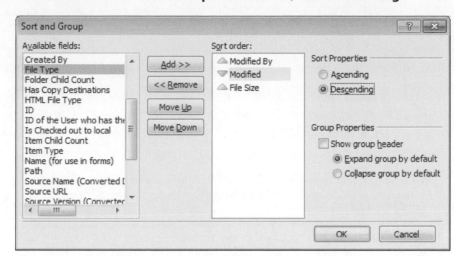

Save

12. Click **OK** to close the **Sort and Group** dialog box. On the Quick Access Toolbar, click **Save**, and then in the breadcrumb, click **Shared Documents** to open the list settings page.

Set as Default

13. In the **Views** area, click the icon to the left of **By Modified** to display the **Views** tab on the ribbon, and then click **Set as Default** in the **Actions** group.

   In the Views area, in the Default column, Yes is removed from the All Documents row and appears in the By Modified row.

Close

14. Close the **ByModified.aspx** tab by clicking the **Close** icon at the top right of the workspace.

   The site settings page is displayed in the workspace.

 CLEAN UP Leave SharePoint Designer open if you are continuing to the next exercise.

Creating and Modifying a List Form Page

When lists and libraries are created, they provide a number of built-in view pages. They also provide pages you can use to create new list items, edit and display existing list items, upload documents, create a new document, and edit and display metadata associated with documents. These pages are known as *form pages*. Like view pages, form pages consist of one Web Part zone named Main and one Web Part. These pages are displayed as dialog boxes transposed over view pages. However, if you enter the URL of a form page in the browser, you can modify it by using the browser.

View pages use an XLV Web Part, whereas most of the default form pages use a Web Part named the List Form Web Part (LFWP). In SharePoint Designer or the browser, the LFWP customization options are very limited. Unlike the XLV Web Part on view pages, the LFWP does not provide tabs similar to the List View tabs on the ribbon, so you cannot control the order in which fields are displayed or whether a field should appear.

To create a tailored data entry form that provides more customization options, you must use SharePoint Designer and create a new list form page. The list form page contains a Data Form Web Part (DFWP), which you can use to create solutions for viewing and managing data that resides internally or externally to SharePoint sites.

See Also For information about the DFWP, see Chapter 5. For information about how to use controls to provide additional data integrity checks for the data entry form, see Chapter 14 "Using Controls in Web Pages."

When you create a list form, the form does not prevent users from entering list or library data by using Datasheet view or keep users from altering metadata properties by using Microsoft Office applications. To make any additional business logic you incorporate into the list form available for other data entry methods, you need to customize those data entry methods; otherwise, you need to educate your users concerning the differences.

Important When you create your own list form using the DFWP, should you add any new columns to the list, your list form is not automatically updated with the controls to enter data into those columns. You must manually modify your list form to include the necessary text and Data View controls. For more information on controls, see Chapter 14.

In this exercise, you explore the LFWP and create a new list form page.

 SET UP Using SharePoint Designer, open the team site you used in the previous exercise if it is not already open.

1. In the **Navigation** pane, click **Lists and Libraries**, and then under **Lists**, click **Tasks**.

   The tasks list settings page is displayed in the workspace. The Forms area contains three forms: DispForm.aspx, EditForm.aspx, and NewForm.aspx. The Type column indicates the type of form (Display, Edit, or New) and whether the forms are the default forms for their type.

   Note The default New form is displayed when you click links in the browser (such as Add New Item) or on the ribbon (New Event in the New group). The default Edit form is displayed when you click Edit Item on the Item menu or on the ribbon, and the default Display form is used when View Item is clicked on the Item menu or on the ribbon.

2. In the **Forms** area, click **NewForm.aspx** to open the page in edit mode, and then click **[Preview of List Form Web Part].**

A blue border with the label *Main* appears, within which is the label *<webpartpages:ListFormWebPart>*. This indicates that an LFWP is contained within the Web Part zone Main. A purple-bordered surrounds the Web Part zones, labeled *PlaceHolderMain (Custom)*. The ribbon contains the Web Part Format tab.

List Form

3. On the breadcrumb, click **Tasks** to display the settings page in the workspace. Then, on the **List Settings** tab, click **List Form**.

The Create New List Form dialog box opens, in which you can change the purpose of the form from inserting a new list item to viewing or modifying list item metadata. You can also change the list or library that this page is associated with and create a link on the List Item menu and ribbon. The Task content type is automatically selected in the Select The Content Type To Use list.

4. In the **File Name** box, type **NewTask**.

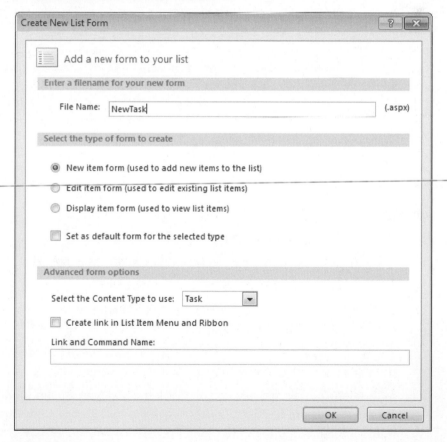

5. Click **OK.**

Troubleshooting If a Microsoft SharePoint Designer dialog box opens stating that the list changes to the server could not be saved because the file exists, choose a different name for the list form file name and repeat steps 4 and 5.

The Create New List Form dialog box closes. On the list settings page, in the Forms area, NewTask.aspx is listed as a New form that is not set as the default.

6. In the **Forms** area, click **NewTask.aspx** to open the page in edit mode.

    A blue border with the label *Main* appears, and a purple-bordered rectangle surrounds the Main Web Part zones, labeled *PlaceHolderMain (Custom)*.

7. In the **Priority** row, click the **Priority** label above the drop-down list. In the Quick Tag Selector, click the **td.ms-formbody** tag.

    The table cell that contains the Priority list is selected.

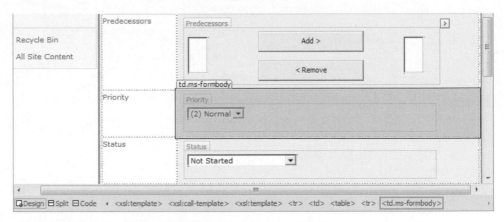

Split Cells

8. On the **Table** tab, click **Split Cells** in the **Merge** group.

    The Split Cells dialog box opens.

9. In the **Number of columns** text box, type **3**, and then click **OK**.

    Two new cells appear to the right of the Priority list.

Visual Aids

10. On the **View** tab, click the down arrow on the **Visual Aids** command, and then click **ASP.NET Non-visual Controls** if it is not already selected.

    Below each data entry control the text *[Field Description]* is displayed. If this text is not visible, you might need to turn visual aids off and then on.

11. In the status row, in the first column, click the text **Status**, and then right-click **H3.ms-standardhe**, which appears above the text **Status**. Click **Cut**, and then right-click the cell to the right of the **Priority** list and click **Paste**.

    The text *Status* is displayed in the third cell on the priority row.

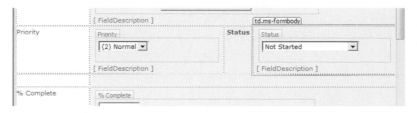

12. Click the **Status** label above the drop-down list. In the Quick Tag Selector, click the **td.ms-formbody** tag. On the **Home** tab, click **Cut**, and then right-click the cell to the right of the text **Status** and click **Paste**.

The Priority row should now contain the Priority and the Status lists, plus two text labels and two field descriptions. The row that formerly contained the Status text label and the list is now empty.

13. Right-click the empty row, point to **Delete**, and then click **Delete Rows**.

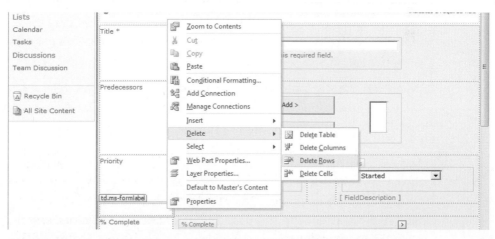

14. On the Quick Access Toolbar, click **Save**, and close the **NewTask.aspx** tab to display the site settings page.

CLEAN UP Leave SharePoint Designer open if you are continuing to the next exercise.

Creating an ASP.NET Page

The page you see in your browser when you request a page from a SharePoint site is the combination of two Microsoft ASP.NET pages: a *master page* and a *content page*.

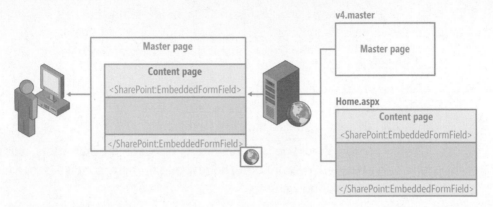

A master page is a special ASP.NET 2.0 page that you can use to share code between pages. It provides a site with a consistent appearance and navigation for each page within a site. You cannot view a master page in your browser, but you can view and customize a master page by using SharePoint Designer.

When you open a content page in Design view, the merged view of the two pages is displayed. In this view, even in advanced edit mode, you can only edit the code that the content page contains. The no-entry icon is displayed if you point to code that the master page contains. In Code view for a content page, you see only the code that the content page contains. An example of a content page is the home page of a team site, which is named Home.aspx.

When you use a browser to request a page from a SharePoint Server publishing site, it can be a combination of three ASP.NET pages: a master page, a page layout, and a content page. (In this scenario, the content page is referred to as a *publishing page*.) On the other hand, when you request a page from, say, a team site or a document workspace, two ASP.NET pages are combined: a master page and a content page. (In this scenario, the content page is referred to as a *nonpublishing page*.) You cannot modify a publishing content page by using SharePoint Designer; you must use the browser. However, you can modify the master page and page layout by using SharePoint Designer.

See Also Master pages are described in Chapter 11, "Working with Master Pages," and customizing publishing pages in Chapter 13, "Managing Web Content in the SharePoint Server Environment."

If you want to create a Web page in SharePoint Designer, you could copy an existing page, as you did earlier in this chapter. Otherwise, you need to create an ASP.NET page, associate a master page, and then insert Web Part zones (thereby creating a Web Part page) or insert the controls that make the page a Wiki page.

All built-in Web Part pages and Wiki pages use tables, but if you are concerned about accessibility, you may want to use HTML <div> tags to lay out the pages you create from scratch. Because you can insert more than one Web Part per Web Part zone, it is common practice to insert one Web Part zone to a table cell or <div> tag.

See Also For more information about page accessibility, see Chapter 12, "Understanding Usability and Accessibility."

In this exercise, you create an ASP.NET page.

 SET UP Using SharePoint Designer, open the team site you used in the previous exercise if it is not already open.

1. In the **Navigation** pane, click **Site Pages**. On the **Pages** tab, click **Page** and then click **ASPX**.

   A file, Untitled-1.aspx, is created and displayed in the Site Pages gallery page. Untitled_1.aspx is selected.

2. Type **OfficeFurniture.aspx**, and then press **Enter** to rename the page.

3. On the **Pages** tab, click **Edit File**.

Edit File

   A dialog box opens, warning that the page does not contain any regions that are editable in safe mode.

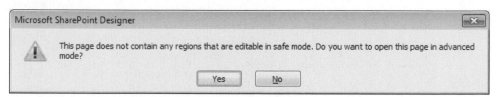

4. Click **Yes** to open OfficeFurniture.aspx page in advanced mode.

   A blue-bordered rectangle with the label *form#form1* is displayed in Design view.

5. On the workspace status bar, click **Split**.

Split

   In Code view of the page, the HTML <head> and <body> tags are surrounded by <html> tags. The <body> tags contain <form> tags.

   Tip To see the rectangle, turn on visual aids (on the View menu, point to Visual Aids, and click Show).

 CLEAN UP Leave SharePoint Designer open if you are continuing to the next exercise.

Inserting a Web Part Zone

With Wiki pages or Web Part pages, users can manipulate the content of a page by using a browser. On Wiki pages, only the content within the EmbeddedFormField SharePoint control can be modified with a browser, and on Web Part pages, only content within Web Part zones. As you develop solutions, you need to develop pages that allow you to provide content owners the ability to add their own content by using the browser. Therefore, developing your own Wiki pages and Web Part pages is important for your solution.

In Chapter 3, you saw how easy it is to use SharePoint Designer to create your own Web Part pages. You are provided with eight different layouts, but these layouts might not meet your needs—you might need to insert, delete, or modify Web Part zones on your Web Part pages or create your own Web Part page from an ASP.NET page. Developers and Web designers can use Microsoft Visual Studio 2010 to define Web Part zones in pages stored in the root directory on a Web server, or you can use SharePoint Designer to insert a Web Part zone into a new or existing page, which is stored in the SQL Server content databases when you save it.

You can insert only Web Parts into Web Part zones; you cannot insert text or images. Web Part zones have properties that affect the presentation of the Web Parts they contain, and they control the actions users are allowed to perform with the browser. These properties are detailed in the following table.

Web Part zone property	Description
Zone title	Used when storing Web Part information in the SQL Server content database. You should give each zone a meaningful and consistent title; for example, don't name the Web Part zone in a left cell *First* on one page and *Left* on another. This is particularly important if you create Web Part zones on page layouts in publishing sites.
Frame style	The default frame style for all Web Parts in the zone. This setting can be overridden by the Web Part Frame Style property.
Layout of Web Parts contained in the zone	Allows you to choose between Top-To-Bottom (Vertical Layout) or Side-By-Side (Horizontal Layout).
Browser settings for Web Parts contained in the zone	Allows you to restrict the modification of the page by browser users. By clearing the three check boxes, you effectively remove the ability to customize any Web Parts placed in the zone by using the browser.

In this exercise, you insert two Web Part zones.

SET UP Using SharePoint Designer, open the team site you used in the previous exercise if it is not already open. Open the page where you want to create a Web Part zone, such as OfficeFurniture.aspx, which you created in the previous exercise.

1. Position the insertion point where you want to add a Web Part zone, such as inside the **form#form1** rectangle.

Web Part Zone

2. On the **Insert** tab, click **Web Part Zone** in the **Web Parts** group.

   The Web Part Zone Tools, Format tab is displayed. A Web Part Zone labeled *Zone 1* appears, and the tag label *webpartpages:wikicontentweb* appears to the top right of the zone and in orange on the Quick Tag Selector. If the ASP.NET Non-Visual Controls visual aid is on, you also see the SPWebPartManager SharePoint control above the Web Part zone.

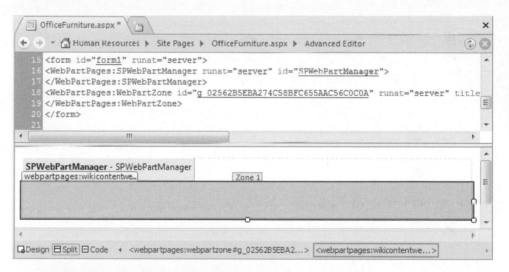

3. On the **Web Part Zone Tools**, **Format** tab, in the **Zone Title** box in the **Web Part Zone** group, delete **Zone 1** and type **Main**.

Zone Layout

4. Click **Zone Layout** in the **Layout** group, click **Side-by-Side (Horizontal Layout)**, and then click **Properties** in the **Web Part Zone** group.

   The Web Part Zone Properties dialog box opens.

5. Below **Browser settings for Web Parts contained in the zone**, clear the three check boxes.

Save

6. Click **OK** to close the **Web Part Zone Properties** dialog box, and then on the Quick Access Toolbar, click **Save**.

Note Now that OfficeFurniture contains a Web Part zone, you do not have to open the page in SharePoint Designer in advanced mode.

 CLEAN UP Leave SharePoint Designer open if you are continuing to the next exercise.

Attaching a Master Page

In the previous exercises, you created an ASP.NET page and added a Web Part zone to it, but it did not contain any SharePoint site navigation nor did it inherit any look and feel from the SharePoint site. You can envision the page you created as just the content page. It is not associated with a master page, which is the page that defines the common user interface and code. To attach a master page or to change a master page that a content page is associated with, you must open the page in advanced mode.

Each site has one master page configured as the site's master page, referred to by using the token *~masterurl/default.master*, and then all pages associated with the site's master page inherit the same look and feel. When a site is created, all pages created for the site point to the site's master page by using this token. With SharePoint Designer, you can change the master page attached to a page. If a page is not attached to a master page, you can attach the page to the site's master page or attach the page to a specific master page, such as v4.master.

See Also Changing the default master page is described in Chapter 11, "Working with Master Pages."

In this exercise, you attach a page to the site's master page.

SET UP Using SharePoint Designer, open the team site you used in the previous exercise if it is not already open. Open in advanced mode the page, such as OfficeFurniture.aspx, that you want to attach to a master page.

Attach

1. On the **Style** tab, click **Attach** in the **Master Page** group, and then click **More Options**.

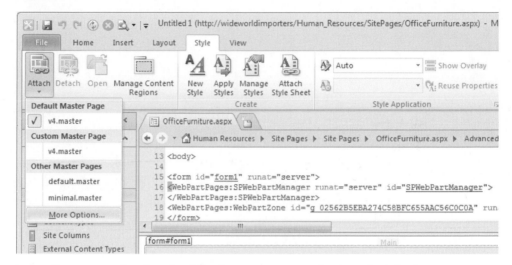

Note If your page is using the default master page, a check to the left of v4.master indicates that v4.master is configured as the site's master page.

The Select A Master Page dialog box opens.

2. In the **Select a Master Page** dialog box, select **Default Master Page (~masterurl/default.master)** if the option is not already selected.

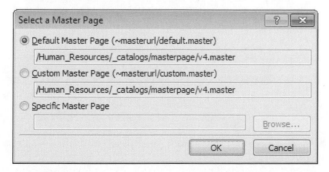

3. Click **OK**.

The Match Content Regions dialog box opens.

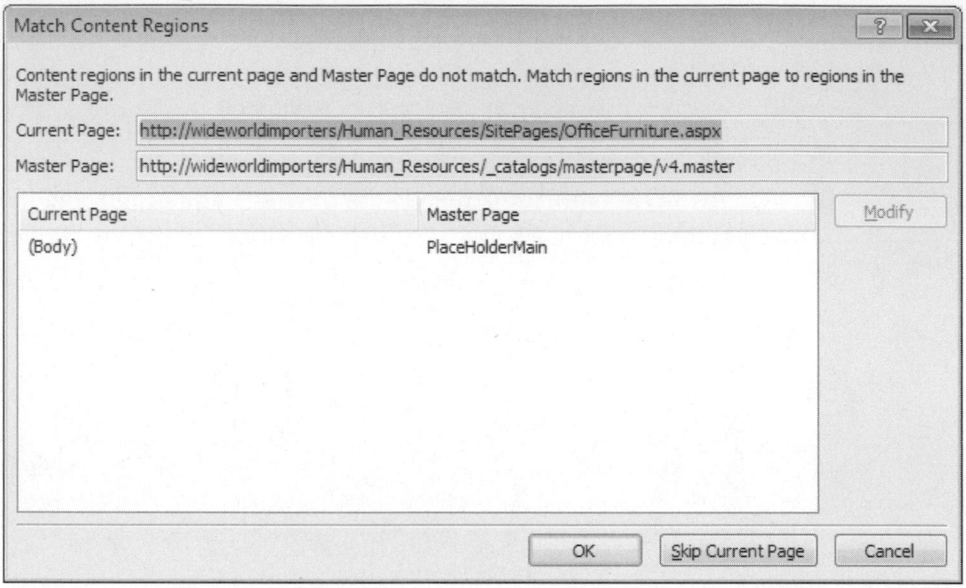

4. Click **OK** to accept the default setting of associating all the code within the HTML <body> tags of the current page, OfficeFurniture.aspx, to the content region, PlaceHolderMain on the master page.

   SharePoint Designer redisplays OfficeFurniture.aspx, which now has a SharePoint look and feel. The HTML <html>, <head>, <body>, and <form> tags are removed from the content page because they are defined in the master page.

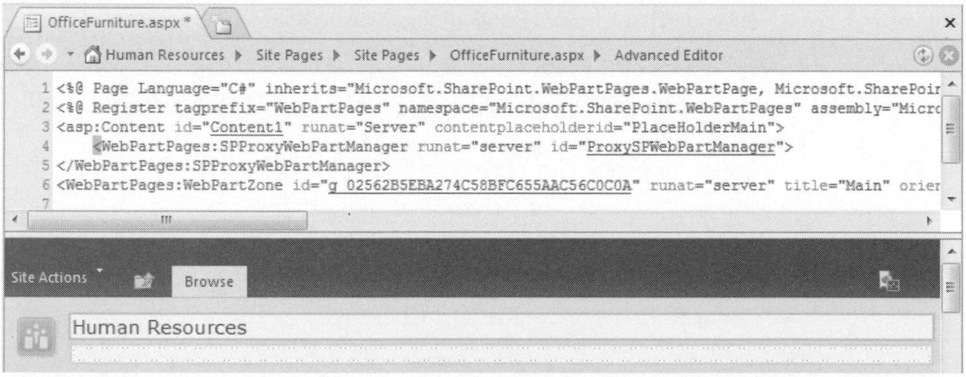

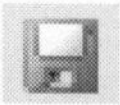
Save

5. On the Quick Access Toolbar, click **Save**, and then press **F12** to review the page in the browser.

CLEAN UP Leave SharePoint Designer open if you are continuing to the next exercise.

Managing Web Pages

As a team site owner with the default SharePoint Designer access configuration, you can manage files on a per-file basis only in the Site Pages and Site Assets libraries. These are the two main libraries you use when you develop SharePoint solutions. The Site Pages library contains your content pages, and the Site Assets library contains other files, such as images, cascading style sheets, XML files, and JavaScript files. As a site collection owner, by using the All Files option in the Navigation pane, you can access all files in all libraries.

On publishing sites, publishing pages are stored in the Pages library and not in the Site Pages library. By default, a publishing site does not contain a Site Pages or Site Assets library. However, if you open a publishing site with SharePoint Designer, both these libraries are created.

When you click a file on the Site Pages or Site Assets gallery page, the files settings page is displayed, which is divided into four areas:

- **File Information** Provides key information about the file, such as file name, created by, last modified by, file version, check in/check out status, and whether the file is based on a file from the site definiton or has been customized.

- **Customization** Use to edit the file or manage the file properties in the browser.

- **Permissions** Use to manage the permission settings for the file. By default, the file inherits its permissions from the list it is stored in, and the list commonly inherits its permissions from the site. As with the site settings page, you can use the Permissions area on the file settings page to stop inheriting permissions, thereby creating unique permissions for the file. Then you can add or remove users or SharePoint groups and configure the access rights of those users and groups to the file by using permission levels.

- **Version History** Use to restore and delete versions of a file. The version numbers are hyperlinks that open the File Version Summary dialog box. Both the Site Pages and the Pages libraries are configured with versioning enabled. The Site Pages document library uses major versions.

  Note The Pages library is configured to use major and minor (draft) versions with content approval because publishing sites are usually used as Internet sites or company portal intranet sites that need a business-approval mechanism.

  See Also Managing publishing pages is detailed in Chapter 13.

When a file's setting page is displayed, the Page tab is visible on the ribbon. This tab allows you to edit, delete, and rename the file; reset the file to the site definition; set the file as the site's home page; check in, check out, and undo the check out of the file; and preview the file in the browser. You are also given a choice of programs in which to edit the file. Any deleted files are stored in the Recycle Bin, from which you can restore them.

Important Although you have not done so in this book (because of page count constraints), you should always check out a file before you edit it and then check it in after you complete your modifications, especially when more than one person has the rights to modify the file.

In this exercise, you restore a previous version of a file, check in and check out a file, and delete a file.

SET UP Using SharePoint Designer, open the team site you used in the previous exercise if it is not already open. The exercise uses the file Home_copy(1).aspx, which was created and amended in previous exercises in this chapter. You can use another file if you want to.

1. In the **Navigation** pane, click **Site Pages** to display the gallery page, and then click **Home_copy(1).aspx**.

    The Home_copy(1).aspx settings page is displayed. The File Information area shows the current version of the file, and the Permissions area states that the file inherits permissions from its parent. The Version History area displays a number of versions of the file, although the current version of the file is not listed in the Version History area.

2. On the **Version History** area, right-click the **Modified By** column heading, point to **Arrange by**, and click **Modified Date**.

    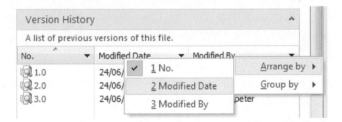

    The Version History area is redisplayed and lists the file versions in modified date order, newest to oldest.

3. Right-click the icon to the left of **1.0**, and click **Restore Previous Version**.

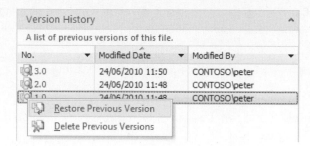

A dialog box opens warning you that the file must be checked out before a previous version of the file can be restored.

Check Out

4. Click **OK** to close the dialog box, and then on the **Page** tab, click **Check Out** in the **Manage** group.

    In the File Information area, the file version is increased, and in the Version History area the original version of the file is displayed at the top of the list.

Check In

5. Repeat step 3, and then on the **Page** tab, click **Check In** in the **Manage** group.

    The Check In dialog box opens.

6. In the **Enter comments for this version** box, type **Restoring the original version of the Home_copy(1).aspx page**, and then click **OK**.

    The Check In dialog box closes.

7. On the **Page** tab, click **Preview in Browser**.

Preview in
Browser

    A browser window opens. The modifications you made earlier in this chapter are no longer displayed, and the Welcome To Your Site! text is displayed.

8. Close the browser window. In SharePoint Designer, on the **Page** tab, click **Delete Page** in the **Edit** group.

The Confirm Delete dialog box opens.

> **Important** The Confirm Delete dialog box is different if you are deleting a page that is designated as the site's home page. When a page that is set as the home page is deleted, no page will be assigned as the home page, and the "HTTP 404, The Web Page Cannot Be Found" message is displayed in the browser when users navigate to the site. Before deleting the current home page, set another page as the home page.

9. Click **Yes** to confirm the deletion.

    If you have multiple tabs open, the workspace displays a message that SharePoint Designer cannot display the item; otherwise the Site Pages gallery is displayed.

    > **Tip** When you are closing a tab that points to a file that no longer exists, if a dialog box opens stating that the server cannot complete your request and the tab will not close, click the name of your site on the breadcrumb to display the site's setting page.

Set as Home Page

10. On the breadcrumb, click **Site Pages** if the **Site Pages** gallery is not displayed. Click the icon to the left of **Home.aspx**, and on the **Pages** tab, click **Set as Home Page** in the **Actions** group.

❌ **CLEAN UP** If you are not continuing with the next chapter, close SharePoint Designer.

Key Points

● On Wiki pages, only the content within the EmbeddedFormField SharePoint control can be modified using a browser, and on Web Part pages, only content within Web Part zones. In SharePoint Designer in advanced mode, you can modify content outside these areas.

● In the Page Editor Options dialog box, you can configure picture conversion formats, auto thumbnail creation, and settings for Design and Code views.

● Web Parts can be inserted outside Web Part zones and the EmbeddedFormField SharePoint control on content pages and on master pages by using SharePoint Designer. These are known as static Web Parts. Web Parts inserted into Web Part zones or the EmbeddedFormField SharePoint control are known as dynamic Web Parts. Details of dynamic Web Parts are stored in the SQL Server database separate from content pages and master pages.

● View pages and form pages both consist of one Web Part zone (named Main) and one Web Part. In the case of a view page, the Web Part is an XLV. In the case of a form page, it is an LFWP.

● You can create a custom data entry form by using a DFWP.

● A nonpublishing page is the combination of two ASP.NET pages: a master page and a content page.

- A SharePoint Server publishing page is a combination of three ASP.NET pages: the master page, a page layout, and a content page. You cannot modify a publishing content page by using SharePoint Designer; you must use the browser. However, you can modify the master page and page layout by using SharePoint Designer.

- Design view for a content page shows the merged view of the master page and the content page, whereas Code view shows only the code of the content page.

- In SharePoint Designer, you can create an ASP.NET page and then attach a master page to give it the look and feel of the SharePoint site.

- Any pages or files you delete in SharePoint Designer are sent to the Recycle Bin, from which you can restore them.

- SharePoint Designer saves all pages to the SQL Server content databases. You can reset pages to site definition pages if they originally pointed to them.

Chapter at a Glance

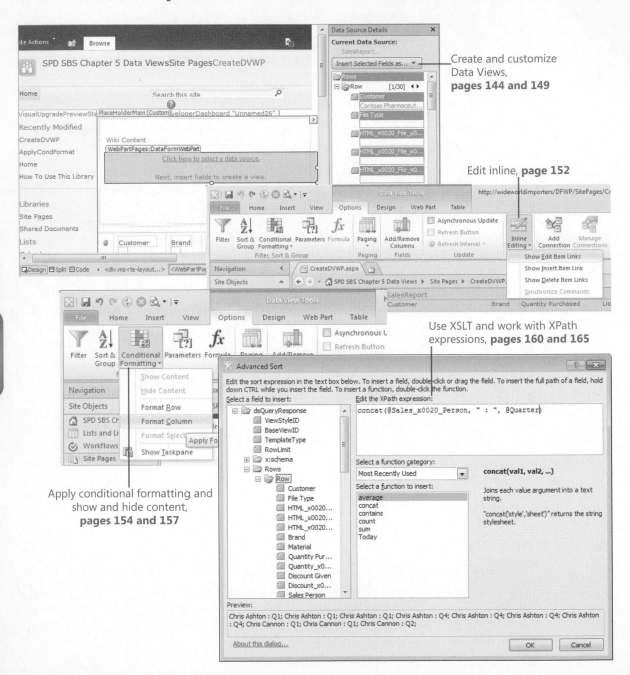

Create and customize Data Views, **pages 144 and 149**

Edit inline, **page 152**

Use XSLT and work with XPath expressions, **pages 160 and 165**

Apply conditional formatting and show and hide content, **pages 154 and 157**

5 Working with Data Views

In this chapter, you will learn how to

- ✔ Create and customize Data Views.
- ✔ Edit inline.
- ✔ Apply conditonal formating, and show and hide content.
- ✔ Use XSLT.
- ✔ Use formula columns and work with XPath expressions.
- ✔ Deploy Web Parts.

In the previous chapter, you created a custom list form, which added a SharePoint control named the Data Form Web Part (DFWP) to a Web page. You saw how easy it is to manipulate this Web Part in Microsoft SharePoint Designer 2010. The DFWP is also known as the *Data View Web Part* (DVWP), or as a *Data View*, because the DFWP can be configured to allow you to view data. The DFWP SharePoint control not only allows you to view data; it can also provide you with a form for entering data into a variety of data sources, such as Microsoft SQL Server databases, XML files, and Web services, as well as SharePoint lists and libraries. The data from these data sources is exposed as XML data, to which the DFWP applies an Extensible Stylesheet Language Transformations (XSLT) style sheet to present the data as HTML. In SharePoint Designer, the terms *Data View Web Part*, *Data Views*, and *Data Form Web Part* are all used for the same SharePoint control.

Tip XSLT is a language for formatting the presentation of XML data. Like XML, XSLT is both human-readable and machine-readable and is an open standard.

Using Data Views, you can display, edit, and modify list item data in a more flexible manner than when you use the List View Web Part (LVWP). You can use Data Views in many business scenarios for which traditionally a developer created a custom Web Part. Even if you find that the DFWP control does not meet all your business requirements, it is still a superb prototyping tool to obtain business signoff.

The XSLT List View (XLV) Web Part you created in Chapter 3, "Working with Lists and Libraries" is similar to a Data View. Therefore, many of the techniques described in this chapter can be used for either the XLV Web Part or a Data View.

In this chapter, using lists and libraries as a data source, you will create and modify Data Views. You will format the data according to specific criteria defined by the metadata and also work with the XSLT. You will also learn how to deploy the Web Parts.

Tip The XSLT List View (XLV) Web Part is very similar to the DVWP. The details in this chapter can be used to customize that Web Part, too.

> **Practice Files** Before you can use the practice files provided for this chapter, you need to install them from the book's companion Web site. For more information about practice files, see "Using the Practice Files" on page xxiii.

Creating a Data View

The Data View is a very flexible Web Part that you can create only by using SharePoint Designer. Like other Web Parts, a Data View follows these rules:

- It can be placed inside and outside EmbeddedFormField controls or Web Part zones.
- It has standard properties shared by all Web Parts, such as Title, Height, Width, and Frame State.
- Depending on the settings of the Web Part zone properties, a Data View can be relocated to other Web Part zones by using the browser.
- Web Part properties can be accessed through the browser's Web Part tool pane.
- When inside a Web Part zone, a Data View supports personal and shared views.

Additionally, you can edit the XSLT and the parameters passed to the XSLT without needing to open the page in SharePoint Designer.

The Data View and the XLV Web Part are very similar in their functionality. The XLV Web Part is used to display and modify content stored in SharePoint lists and libraries and can be created by using the browser or SharePoint Designer. The XLV Web Part is based on list views and can easily be modified in the browser or configured to use an XSLT. Data Views can be used to display and modify content in data sources, including lists and libraries.

Like the XLV Web Part, a Data View uses XSLT to present data and can be modified or deleted by using the browser. However a Data View can only be created by using SharePoint Designer, and unlike SharePoint Designer, the browser provides little help in writing XSLT.

In this exercise, you create an XLV Web Part and a Data View that display the contents of a list.

SET UP Using SharePoint Designer, open the site you created from the SPDSBSPracticeSite_Starter.wsp practice file for this book. The practice file is located in the Chapter05 practice file folder. Turn off the ASP.NET Non-Visual Controls option if it is still on by using the Visual Aids command on the View tab.

Edit File

1. In the **Navigation** pane, click **Site Pages**. Click the icon to the left of **CreateDVWP.aspx**, and then on the **Pages** tab, click **Edit File** in the **Edit group**.

Tip You can open a page in edit mode by double-clicking the icon to the left of the file name in the Site Pages gallery.

The CreateDVWP page opens in edit mode.

2. Click **Wiki Content**.

A purple border labeled *PlaceHolderMain (Custom)* surrounds a number of rectangles. The top rectangle contains the text *Wiki Content*, and the other rectangles have faint dotted borders.

Note The CreateDVWP page is a Wiki page. The top rectangle is the area that is contained in the EmbeddedFormField control and can be modified when you click Edit Page in the browser. The bottom rectangle is a Web Part zone. Although Web Parts placed in this zone can be modified by using the browser, Web Parts cannot be added or deleted from this zone with the browser. To clearly see these two rectangles in SharePoint Designer, add some text to the page when you create a Wiki page in the browser.

3. Click inside the rectangle below the rectangle that contains the text *Wiki Content*.

The Web Part zone labeled *Bottom* appears.

Data View

4. On the **Insert** tab, click **Data View** in the **Data Views & Forms** group, and then click **SalesReport**.

Troubleshooting If the Data View command on the Insert tab is not active, you have not clicked inside the faint dotted rectangle.

The SalesReport XLV is created on the page, and the <WebPartPages:XsltListView WebPart> tag is highlighted in orange on the Quick Tag Selector on the workspace status bar. Within the XsltListViewWebPart control, an HTML table appears with a number of columns, such as Customer, Brand, and Material, together with the list data in the body of the table as HTML rows and cells.

Note The XLV Web Part uses the default list view as a basis for displaying columns and content. You can then use the commands on the Design tab to modify the initial presentation of the data.

5. On the **List View Tools**, **Web Part** tab, in the **Web Part Title** box, delete **SalesReport** and type **Sales Report XLV Web Part**.

    Tip Whenever you add a Web Part to a page, always give the Web Part a unique title that describes the purpose of the Web Part. This acts as an aide-memoire when you or other team members modify the page and helps when you identify Web Part connections.

Data View

6. In the top rectangle, click below the text **Wiki Content** so that an empty <p> tag appears. On the **Insert** tab, click **Data View** in the **Data Views & Forms** group, and then click **Empty Data View**.

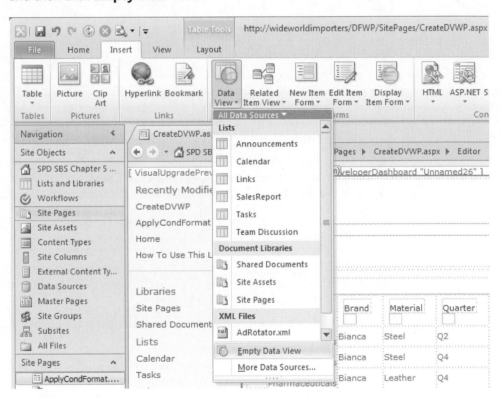

    A Data Form Web Part control is added to the page, and the <WebPartPages:DataFormWebPart> tag is highlighted in orange on the Quick Tag Selector.

7. Click **Click here to select a data source**.

    The Data Source Picker dialog box opens.

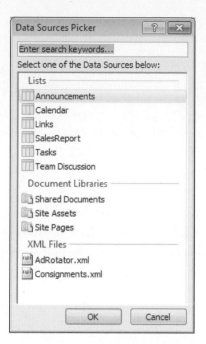

8.   Under **Lists**, click **SalesReport**, and then click **OK**.

The Data Source Details task pane opens, and to the right of Row, [1/30] denotes that the list contains 30 list items. The 1 indicates that the value of the first item is displayed below Row.

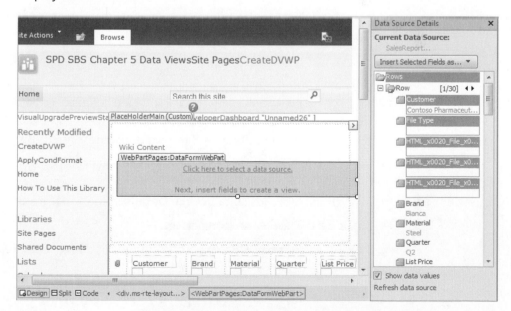

> **Tip** Unlike when you add an XLV Web Part, when you create a Data View, no criteria are used to display the list items. If you want your team members to easily amend the columns and the list item criteria in the browser, use the XLV Web Part when working with lists and libraries.

Next

9. In the **Data Source Details** task pane, to the right of **Row**, click the **Next** arrow to view the second list item's value.

   The text in the square brackets to the right of Row indicates you are now viewing the second of 30 list items.

   > **Tip** You can use the Next and Previous arrows to review the contents of the list without displaying the list in a browser.

10. In the **Data Source Details** task pane, click **Customer**. While holding down the **CTRL** key, click the fields in the following order, **Brand**, **ListPrice**, **Quantity Purchased,** and **Total Purchased**. Then click **Insert Selected Fields as**, and click **Multiple Item View**.

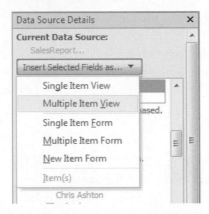

An HTML table appears in the DataFormWebPart control with the Customer, Brand, Quantity Purchased, ListPrice, and Total Purchased columns in the order you selected them, displaying sets of 10 items. The ListPrice column number is underline in red, indicating a possible spelling error. If the red underline is not displayed, click ListPrice.

> **Tip** If you find that you added more columns than you need, click Add/Remove Columns on the Options tab to remove them.

11. On the **Options** tab, click **Data Source Details** in the **Data** group.

   The Data Source Details task pane closes.

Save

12. Right-click the **CreateDVWP.aspx** tab, and then click **Save**. Click **Yes** to reload the page to see the results of the save operation.

✖ CLEAN UP Leave SharePoint Designer open if you are continuing to the next exercise.

Customizing Data Views

Data Views provide virtually limitless possibilities for formatting data. Like the XLV Web Part, Data Views do not contain data; they point to data stored elsewhere. When you request a page, SharePoint queries the SQL Server content database for the properties of the Data View to find the location of the data. Then the Data Retrieval Service obtains the data as XML, and SharePoint dynamically transforms the data to HTML as defined in the XSLT in the Data View. SharePoint Designer displays the returned XML data in the Data Source Details task pane and in Design view. You can use Design view as a visual XSLT editor, so you can manipulate the XML data in the Data View Web Part by using the same editing techniques that you used for editing static HTML in Chapter 4, "Customizing a Web Page." As you format the data in one of the HTML cells, the effect cascades to other cells within the same column.

Note The Data Retrieval Service can be configured on a Web-application-by-Web-application basis using the SharePoint 2010 Central Administration Web site. To see this site, on the Application Management page, under Databases, click Configure The Data Retrieval Service.

You can modify the DFWP in many of the same ways that you can modify the XLV Web Part, such as specifying which fields to display; filtering, sorting, and grouping data items; displaying data items in sets; or limiting the number of items that are displayed. You cannot, however, use Datasheet view for DFWPs.

Using the Data View Preview command on the Display tab, you can modify the No Matching Items template. This allows you to change the text displayed when no items are displayed in your Data View or XLV Web Part.

In this exercise, you sort and group the data displayed in a Data View, amend the text, and modify the functions used when grouping the data.

 SET UP Using SharePoint Designer, open the site you used in the previous exercise if it is not already open, and then open CreateDVWP.aspx in edit mode with the SalesReport DFWP selected.

1. In the field heading row, right-click **ListPrice**, and then click **List Price**.

2. On the **Data View Tools**, **Options** tab, click **Sort & Group** in the **Filter, Sort & Group** group.

   The Sort And Group dialog box opens.

Sort & Group

3. In the **Available fields** list, scroll down, click **Sales Person**, and click **Add**. Under **Group Properties**, click **Show group header**, and then click **Show group footer**.

4. Click **Advanced Grouping**. In the **Advanced Grouping** dialog box, select **Show column totals per group**.

5. Click **OK** to close the **Advanced Grouping** dialog box.

Tip The Show Column Totals Per Group option in the Advanced Grouping dialog box does not allow you to select which group or columns to total. It creates a formula for each column that it detects is numeric. Once the formula is created, delete those group totals or column totals that are not required or do not make business sense.

6. In the **Available fields** list, click **Quarter**, and click **Add**. Under **Group Properties**, click **Show group footer** and **Show group header.**

7. In the **Available fields** list, click **Customer**, and then click **Add**.

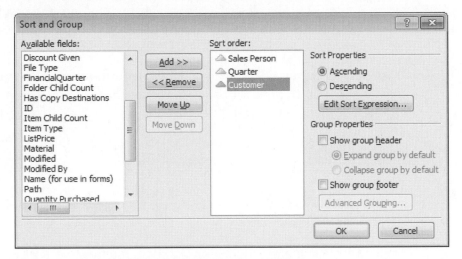

8. Click **OK**. The **Sort and Group** dialog box closes.

The CreateDVWP.aspx page refreshes, and the DVWP displays the data from the SalesReports list grouped by sales person and then by quarter. The data is ordered by customer. Totals for the Quantity Purchased, List Price, and Total Purchased columns are displayed per quarter and per salesperson.

SalesReport

Customer	Brand	List Price	Quantity Purchased	Total Purchased
⊟ **Sales Person: Chris Ashton**				
⊟ **Quarter: Q1**				
Adventure Works	Bianca	$100.00	131	$8,515.00
Adventure Works	Bianca	$100.00	300	$19,500.00
Fabrikam, Inc.	Tudor	$225.00	40	$6,120.00
Count : 5				
⊟ **Quarter: Q4**				
Blue Yonder Airlines	Milan	$35.00	138	$3,284.40
City Power & Light	Bianca	$100.00	145	$9,425.00
Contoso Pharmaceuticals	Bianca	$100.00	238	$17,850.00
Northwind Traders	Bianca	$100.00	245	$15,925.00
Count : 4				
		sum : NaN	sum : 1237	sum : NaN
Count : 7				
⊟ **Sales Person: Chris Cannon**				

Note The group footer count for sales person is correct, but the quarter count is inaccurate. The count for that group is using only the field Quarter, but to get an accurate count, the Sales Person and Quarter fields should be used to create the group. The NaN (Not a Number) entry for the List Price and Total Purchased fields occurs because the values in those fields contain nonnumeric characters—the dollar sign ($) and commas. You will correct these issues later in this chapter.

9. Double-click the first occurrence of **Count**, and type **No. of sales in Quarter**.

   The text change cascades to all group-by-quarter counts.

10. Double-click **Count** before the next **Sales Person** listed, and type **Sales per Year**.

    The text change cascades to all group-by-sales-person counts.

11. Double-click **sum** to the left of **1237**, and type **max**. Then click **1237**, click the smart icon that appears, and select **Max**.

No. of sales in Quarter : 4			td.ms-vh	
		sum : NaN	max : 1237	sum : NaN
Sales per Year : 7			⅍ ▾	
⊟ **Sales Person: Chris Cannon**			⊙ Sum	
⊟ **Quarter: Q1**			○ Count	
Northwind Traders	Milan	$35.00	○ Average	$5,346.25
Northwind Traders	Boston	$225.00	○ Max	$6,873.75
No. of sales in Quarter : 5			○ Min	
⊟ **Quarter: Q2**			Filter...	
Northwind Traders	Milan	$225.00	421	$71,043.75

The value in the Quantity Purchased column contains the maximum quantity purchased in one sale.

12. On the **Design** tab, under **Data View Preview**, click **Default Preview** in the **Preview** group, and select **'No Matching Items' Template**.

     The page refreshes. No content is displayed.

13. Select **There are no items to show in this view of the "SalesReport" list**, and type **The sales reports for this period are not available**.

14. On the **Design** tab, under **Data View Preview**, click **No Matching** in the **Preview** group, and select **Default Preview**.

✖ **CLEAN UP** Save CreateDVWP.aspx, and then click Yes to reload the page to see the results of saving it. Leave SharePoint Designer open if you are continuing to the next exercise.

Inline Editing

In Chapter 4, you created a custom list form for tailored data entry. The Data View provides other methods of data entry. By using the Insert Selected Field As list in the Data Source Details task pane, you can create a Data View as a single-item form, a multiple-item form, or a new item form.

Tip You might want to choose a multiple-item form if users like to quickly edit the data in many list items at the same time. However, some users find this form confusing.

You can also configure an existing Data View in order to edit, delete, and insert data in a list item. Unlike the single-item and multiple-item forms, which can be used only in data entry mode, a configured Data View can be used to display, edit, insert, or delete list items, where links are added to every row so that in the browser you can edit items directly in place. This is known as *inline editing*. By using the browser or SharePoint Designer, you can also configure the XLV Web Part for inline editing. Whichever method you choose for data entry, you can still filter, sort, and group the data; apply conditional formatting; or create formula columns.

When you enable inline editing for a Data View, you can customize the Edit template—the form displayed when you click Edit—and the Insert template, which is displayed when you click Insert by using the Data View Preview list on the Design tab.

Note The single-item and multiple-item modes are defined in the code on the SPDataSource SharePoint control, where the DataSourceMode attribute has a value of either ListItem or List. The Data View provides other modes, but SharePoint Designer does not expose them through its user interface. You have to modify the code directly. See *blogs.msdn.com/sharepointdesigner/archive/2007/04/24/spdatasource-and-rollups-with-the-data-view.aspx* for more information.

In this exercise, you add editing links to an existing Data View and XLV Web Part.

→ **SET UP** Using SharePoint Designer, open the team site you used in the previous exercise if it is not already open, and then open CreateDVWP.aspx in edit mode with the SalesReport DFWP selected.

Inline Editing

1. On the **Data View Tools**, **Options** tab, click **Inline Editing**, and then click **Show Edit Item Links**.

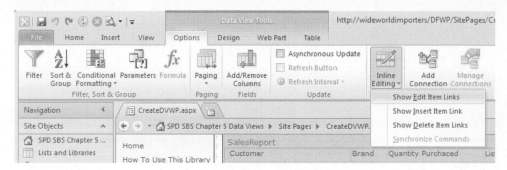

An extra column containing Edit is added to the Data View.

2. Repeat step 1 twice to select **Show Insert Item Link** and **Show Delete Item Links**.

    The first column in the DFWP contains Edit and Delete, and at the bottom of the Web Part is Insert.

3. Scroll down the page, and click **Sales Report XLV Web Part**.

4. On the **List View Tools**, **Options** tab, click **Inline Editing**.

    An extra column is added to the XLV Web Part.

5. Press **F12**, and click **Yes** to save your changes and preview the current version of the page. Then click **Yes** to reload the page.

    A browser window opens. On the Sales Report Web Part, the Edit and Delete links appear to the left of each list item, and the Insert link at the bottom of the Data View.

6. Under **Sales Person: Chris Ashton**, click **edit** to the left of **Fabrikam, Inc**.

    The Edit and the Delete links for this list item are replaced by the Save and Cancel links. List items whose values you can edit are shown as SharePoint form controls.

7. In the **Brand** list, select **Elizabethan**, and in the **Quantity** box, type **36**.

8. Click **Save**.

    The Sales report page is refreshed, and the Save and Cancel links for the list item are replaced by the Edit and Delete links. The list item displays the new values.

9. Scroll down the page to the **Sales Report XLV Web Part**. Rest the pointer over the first occurrence of **Contoso Pharmaceuticals**.

    A check box and an Edit icon appear to the left of Contoso Pharmaceuticals.

10. Click the **Edit** icon.

    The Edit icon is replaced with Save and Cancel icons. List items whose values you can edit are shown as SharePoint form controls.

11. Click the **Cancel** icon.

 CLEAN UP Close the browser. Leave SharePoint Designer open if you are continuing to the next exercise.

Applying Conditional Formatting

The Data View and XLV Web Parts offer a feature known as *conditional formatting* that you can use to alter the appearance of a set of cells or rows according to criteria that you specify. Within a Data View, you can apply conditional formatting to an HTML tag, a data value, or a range of text. The criteria you specify do not have to be based on the field being formatted.

In this exercise, you highlight list item data that is less than or equal to a specific value.

SET UP Using SharePoint Designer, open the team site you used in the previous exercise if it is not already open, and then open Stock.aspx in edit mode with the Furniture Price List DFWP selected.

Conditional
Formatting

1. In the **In Stock** column, click the **99** data cell. On the **Options** tab, click **Conditional Formatting** in the **Filter, Sort & Group** group, and then click **Format Column**.

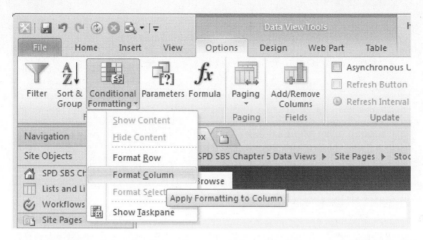

The Condition Criteria dialog box and the Conditional Formatting task pane open.

2. In the **Condition Criteria** dialog box, click the arrow below **Field Name**, and then click **In Stock**.

3. Under **Comparison**, click **Equals**, click the arrow that appears, and then click **Less Than Or Equal**.

4. Under **Value**, click **0,** and then type **10**.

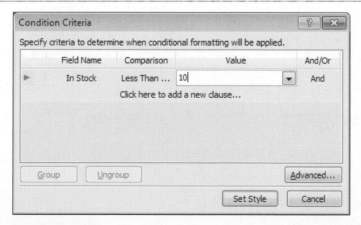

5. Click **Set Style**.

The Condition Criteria dialog box closes, and the Modify Style dialog box opens.

6. Click the **color** arrow, and select **Red**.

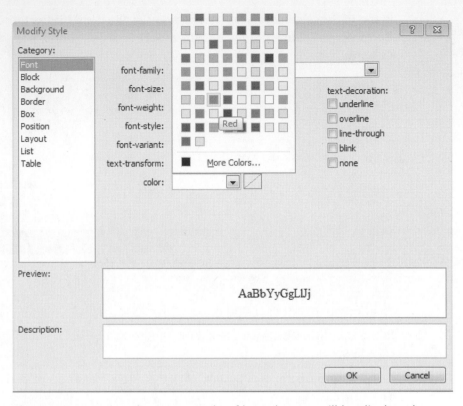

The Preview section shows a sample of how the text will be displayed.

7. Click **OK** to close the **Modify Style** dialog box.

    In the In Stock column, values less than or equal to 10 appear in a red font. In the Conditional Formatting task pane, an Apply Style When condition appears, displaying the criteria and a preview of the formatting.

8. Point to **Apply style when**, click the arrow that appears, and then click **Modify style**.

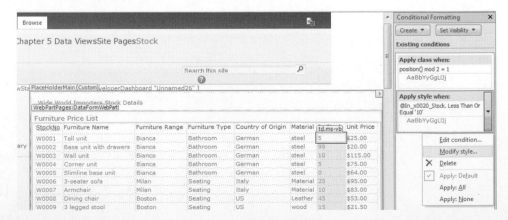

9. Under **Category** in the **Modify Style** dialog box, click **Background**, click the **background-color** arrow, and then click **Yellow**.

10. Click **OK** to close the **Modify Style** dialog box.

   In the In Stock column, values 10 or less appear in a red font with a yellow background.

11. Click **Save**, and press **F12** to review the Stock page in the browser. You might need to scroll down to see the Web Part.

 CLEAN UP Close the browser. Leave SharePoint Designer open if you are continuing to the next exercise.

Showing and Hiding Content

You can also use conditional formatting to show or hide content based on criteria. However, it is more efficient to add a filter to hide an entire row than to use conditional formatting because with filters, the data retrieval engine returns only the data you need, thereby reducing the amount of data retrieved from the SQL Server database and the processing required by the Web servers to render the page.

In this exercise, you show a sales icon when an item of stock has a sales price and the number of items in stock is greater than 10.

→ **SET UP** Using SharePoint Designer, open the site you used in the previous exercise if it is not already open, and then open Stock.aspx in edit mode.

Picture

1. Under **Furniture Name**, place the insertion point to the right of **Tall unit**. Then, on the **Insert** tab, click **Picture** in the **Pictures** group.

   The Picture dialog box opens.

2. In the **File name** box, if you are not already viewing your site, type the URL of your site, and then press **Enter**.

   The SharePoint objects for your site are displayed in the main portion of the dialog box.

3. Double-click **SiteAssets**, and then click **Sale.png**.

4. Click **Open**.

   The Picture dialog box closes, and the Accessibility Properties dialog box opens.

5. In the **Alternate text** box, type **Sale Item**, and then click **OK** to close the **Accessibility Properties** dialog box.

   A red sale image appears in all cells in the Furniture Name column.

6. Click a red sale image. In the **Conditional Formatting** task pane, click **Create**, and then click **Show content**.

   Tip If the Conditional Formatting task pane is not already open, use the Task Panes command on the View tab and then repeat step 6. You can also click Conditional Formatting on the Options tab and then click Show Content.

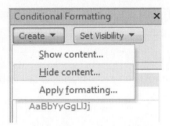

   The Condition Criteria dialog box opens.

7. Click the arrow below **Field Name**, and then click **Sale**. Leave **Equals** under **Comparison** and **Yes** under **Value**.

8. Click **Click here to add a new clause**. Click the arrow below **Field Name**, and then click **In Stock**.

9. Under **Comparison**, click **Equals**, click the arrow that appears, and then click **Greater Than**.

10. Under **Value**, click **0**, and then type **10**.

11. Click **OK**.

    The Condition Criteria dialog box closes.

    The red sale icon is displayed only for items that are a sale item and the number of items in stock is greater than 10. In the Conditional Formatting task pane, a Show Content When condition appears, displaying the criteria.

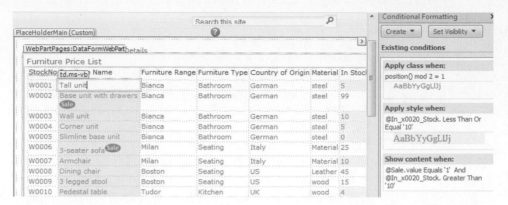

Tip The Hide Content condition is exactly the opposite of the Show Content condition. For example, in this exercise you could have used the Hide Content condition with the criteria Sale Equals '0' Or In Stock Less Than Or Equal To 10. When you need to configure multiple Hide Content or Show Content conditions in a Data View or an XLV Web Part, use only one of these conditions to describe the criteria. Using a combination can lead to confusion.

 CLEAN UP Save Stock.aspx. Leave SharePoint Designer open if you are continuing to the next exercise.

An XML Primer

XML is a language for defining and representing data of all kinds, where data is stored as text rather than in binary format. XML is an open standard that many vendors support. In contrast to HTML, XML tags describe only the data itself, not how the data should be displayed. You can choose the tag names to use as long as the XML data is well formed; that is, as long as it obeys the following set of rules:

- One root element contains all other elements.
- Each element must have matching opening and closing tags.
- Elements must use consistent capitalization; that is, they are case sensitive.
- Elements must be nested correctly; that is, no elements overlap.
- Element attribute values must be enclosed in quotation marks with no re-peating attributes in an element.

The root element in the following XML data is *Invoices*. *InvoiceNo* is known as an attribute, and *Company* and *Net* are child elements of Invoice. The content of the *Company* element is Adventure Works, whereas the element *Net* has no content.

```
<?xml version="1.0" encoding="UTF-8" ?>
<Invoices xmlns="http://consolidatedmessenger.com/finance">
    <Invoice InvoiceNo="143">
        <Company>Adventure Works</Company>
        <Net></Net>
        <![CDATA[
            function tax(){ window.open('TBD'); }
        ]]>
    <Invoice>
</Invoices>
```

When an XML document contains data that does not follow the XML rules (for example, if you want to include HTML or code in the XML document), you should include the data in an XML CDATA section to indicate that it should not be parsed as XML.

Using XSLT

Data Views use XSLT to describe how to transform the XML data that SharePoint retrieves from a data source to HTML. SharePoint first converts the XML data into an XML tree, which represents the hierarchical structure of the XML elements and attributes, known as *nodes*. The Date Source Details task pane shows this hierarchical structure in a way similar to a folder structure on a file system, with the list or library represented as a *Rows* XML element, the list item represented as a *Row* XML child element, and each field represented as an XML attribute. (In XSLT, XML attributes are prefixed with the @ symbol.) The XSLT is then used to navigate the hierarchical structure, and the *XML Path Language (XPath)* is used to select one or more nodes.

The XSLT instructions themselves are also represented as XML data. The *xsl:template* element contains a *match* attribute that defines the XPath expression used to select the set of nodes to be transformed. After a node is selected, components specify how to manipulate the XML data. These components can include HTML formatting tags and other XSLT elements. For example, in the following XSLT, the *xsl:template* element finds the *Invoice* XML element, and the HTML formats the *xsl:value-of element*. Using the XML data given as an example in the sidebar "An XML Primer," this XSLT would render Adventure Works as a new paragraph in bold font.

```
<xsl:template match="Invoice">
    <p><strong><xsl:value-of select="Company" /></strong>
</xsl:template>
```

See Also For an excellent introduction to *XSL*, visit *www.w3schools.com/xsl/* and the series of blogs by Marc D. Anderson, "Unlocking the Mysteries of Data View Web Part XSL Tags," found at *www.endusersharepoint.com/tag/xsl/*. SharePoint also has some additional functions that are documented at *msdn.microsoft.com/en-us/library/dd583143(office.11).aspx*.

In Design view, SharePoint Designer automatically generates this XSLT for you. It also provides an XSLT editor, called the XPath Expression Builder, to help you develop sophisticated solutions. This editor provides IntelliSense for XPath, making it possible for you to create XPath expressions.

In this exercise, you add a sort expression by using the XSLT editor.

SET UP Using SharePoint Designer, open the site you used in the previous exercise if it is not already open, and then open CreateDVWP.aspx in edit mode with the SalesReport DFWP selected. Close the Conditional Formatting task pane if it is open.

Sort & Group

1. On the **Data View Tools**, **Options** tab, click **Sort & Group** in the **Filter, Sort & Group** group.

    The Sort And Group dialog box opens.

2. Under **Sort order**, click **Quarter**, and then click **Remove**.

3. Under **Available fields**, scroll down, click **Add Sort Expressions**, and then click **Add**.

    The Advance Sort dialog box opens.

4. Under **Select a function to insert**, double-click **concat**.

    Troubleshooting If the function concat is not displayed in the Select A Function To Insert list, select Text/String under Select A Function Category.

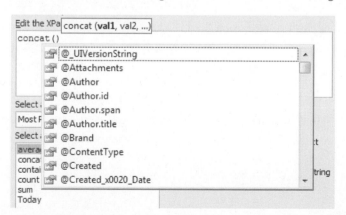

5. In the list that appears, type **@s**, and then press **Tab** to select **@ Sales_x0020_Person**.

6. With the insertion point after **@Sales_x0020_Person,** type **,** **" : "** , **@quar**, and then press **Tab** to select **@Quarter**.

The XPath expression should read *concat(@Sales_x0020_Person, " : ",@Quarter)*, and the Preview box displays the result of the expression.

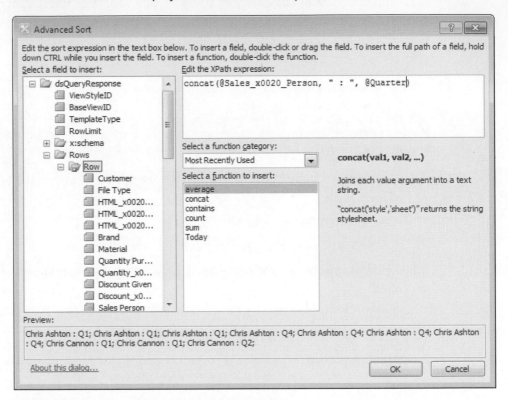

7. Click **OK** to close the **Advance Sort** dialog box.

8. In the **Sort and Group** dialog box, under **Group Properties**, click **Show group header**, and then click **Show group footer**.

9. Click **OK** to close the **Sort and Group** dialog box.

The No. Of Sales In Quarter count accurately represents the number of sales per quarter.

SalesReport				
Customer	Brand	List Price	Quantity Purchased	Total Purchased
⊟ **Sales Person: Chris Ashton**				
⊟ **Chris Ashton : Q1**				
edit delete Adventure Works	Bianca	$100.00	131	$8,515.00
edit delete Adventure Works	Bianca	$100.00	300	$19,500.00
edit delete Fabrikam, Inc.	Tudor	$225.00	40	$6,120.00
No. of sales in Quarter : 3				
⊟ **Chris Ashton : Q4**				

WebPartPages:DataFormWebPart

Save

10. On the Quick Access Toolbar, click **Save**, and then click **Yes** to reload the page to see the results.

 CLEAN UP Leave SharePoint Designer open if you are continuing to the next exercise.

Using Formula Columns

Using the browser or SharePoint Designer, you can create a calculated column. This allows you to create a column on the basis of content contained in other columns in your list or library. This aids in the task of maintaining data integrity. For example, when you use a calculated column that multiples the number of items purchased by the cost per item, the users of your solutions do not have to complete that calculation manually and type their answer into the column. However, not all the content you reference in your solution is stored in lists or libraries. For other data sources, you might not have the permissions or authority to add new columns to generate the content you want to display. This is where a *formula column* is useful.

When using Data Views or XLV Web Parts, you can create additional columns—formula columns—that present data from the data source you are working with as well as other data sources. The XPath Expression Builder is used to create formula columns.

See Also Calculated columns and formula columns can not only calculate numeric values; they can also format content and generate links to files, as long as those files follow a predictable naming convention. More examples can be found at *www.endusersharepoint.com/tag/calculated-column/*.

In this exercise, you create a formula column labeled Sale Price. The sale price is 25 percent of the unit price for those product lines in the sale. If a product line has 10 or fewer items in stock, that product line cannot be in the sale. The sale price should be formatted in dollars, with two decimal places.

SET UP Using SharePoint Designer, open the site you used in the previous exercise if it is not already open, and then open Stock.aspx in edit mode with the Furniture Price List DFWP selected.

Add/Remove
Columns

1. On the **Data View Tools**, **Options** tab, click **Add/Remove Columns** in the **Fields** group.

   The Edit dialog box opens.

2. In the **Available fields** list, scroll down, click **Add Formula Column**, and then click **Add**.

   The XPath Expression Builder dialog box opens.

3. In the **Select a field to insert** list, double-click **Unit_x0020_Price.**. Be sure you choose the field that ends in a dot.

   @Unit_x0020_Price. is displayed in the Edit the XPath Expression box.

4. In the **Exit the XPath expression** box, place the insertion point to the right of **Price.**, and then type * (1 - ((@Sale = 'Yes') and (@In_x0020_Stock. >= 10))* 0.25).

   Tip The practice file SPDSBSC05.xsl.txt contains this expression if you want to copy and paste the expression into the XPath Expression Builder dialog box.

   The Preview box displays the result of the expression.

5. Click **OK** twice. The Insert Formula and Edit Columns dialog boxes close.

   A new column is added to the DFWP. The column label is the expression you created in step 4. Only those product lines in the sale have a sales price less than the unit price.

6. In the column heading, click **@Unit**. Then click the **th.ms-vh** label that appears, and type **Sale Price**.

7. In the Sale Price column, click **15**, and then on the **Options** tab, click **Formula**.

   The Insert Formula dialog box opens and displays the expression you created in step 4. If the expression is not shown, close the Insert Formula dialog box and repeat step 7.

8. In the **Select a function** category, select **Math / Number**. In the **Select a function to insert** box, click **format-number**.

A brief description of the format-number function is displayed.

9. In the **Edit the XPath expression** box, modify the expression so that it reads
**format-number(@Unit_x0020_Price. * (1 - ((@Sale = 'Yes) and (@In_x0020_
Stock. >= 10)) * 0.25), '$#,##0.00').**

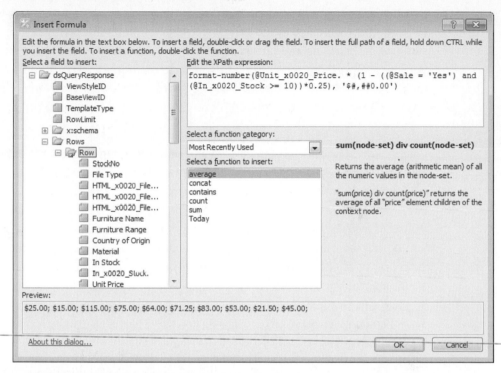

10. Click **OK**. The Insert Formula dialog box closes, and the numbers in the Sale Price
column are prefixed with a dollar sign ($) and display two decimal places.

CLEAN UP Save Stock.aspx. Leave SharePoint Designer open if you are continuing to
the next exercise.

Working with XPath Expressions

In the previous two exercises, you used the XPath Expression Builder to create formulas
to process the XML data that is returned from SharePoint when you use the Data View or
XLV Web Parts. However, you cannot create all the formulas or expressions you need by
using the XPath Expression Builder. In some cases, to get a higher degree of flexibility and
control, you need to edit the XSLT in Code view, where IntelliSense is available to help with
this task. However, you need a deep understanding of XSLT to be able to edit it directly. An

example of a situation in which you need to edit the XSLT in Code view is to work with calculated columns.

By default, SharePoint provides two columns for each numeric column. One column provides the numeric values for a list item, and the second column provides the presentation format of that numeric value. When the numeric column represents a currency, for example, the values in the presentation column contain commas, dots, and currency symbols. To calculate the sum of those currency values, you use the numeric column. If you use the presentation column to complete mathematical computations, the XPath expression results in an error, and the acronym *NaN* is displayed. The numeric column has the same name as the related presentation column but with a dot appended to the name.

Calculated columns do not have a related numeric column. Therefore, choosing the correct column to use in your XPath expressions is not a simple task. The solution that you use in the following exercise computes the function of the nodes first, capturing the results in an XSL variable as a result-tree fragment, which is subsequently transformed using the *msxsl:node-set* function that can then be used as input to the *sum* function. If you do not want to create your own XLST code, when you configure the calculated column do not select the data type returned for the formula as Currency. Instead, create an additional column to store the currency symbol, such as $, EUR, and £.

See Also Other XSLT sum solutions can be found in "Recipe 3.6. Computing Sums and Products" in the *XSLT Cookbook* by Sal Mangano (O'Reilly), which is available at *flylib.com/books.php?ln=en&n=2&p=765&c=45&p1=1&c1=1&c2=208&view=1*.

In this exercise, you use the Insert Formula dialog box and amend the XSLT code in Code view to correct two group totals that have a value of NaN.

 SET UP Using SharePoint Designer, open the site you used in the previous exercise if it is not already open, and then open CreateDVWP.aspx in edit mode with the SalesReport DFWP selected.

Formula

1. In the **List Price** column, click **NaN**, and then on the **Options** tab, click **Formula**.

   Tip You may have to click NaN again to highlight it.

   The Insert Formula dialog box opens, and in the Edit The XPath Expression box, the formula *sum($nodeset/@ListPrice)* is displayed. If the formula is not displayed, close the Insert Formula dialog box and repeat step 1.

2. Place the insertion point between **Price** and **)**, and then type a period (**.**). Click **OK**.

   The Insert Formula dialog box closes, and NaN is replaced by 760.

Tip You could use the format-number function that you used in the previous exercise to format the List Price field as currency.

Split

3. In the **Total Purchased** column, click **NaN**, and then on the View tab, click **Split**.

Tip You may have to click NaN again to highlight it.

The document window divides horizontally and displays Code view in the upper pane and Design view in the lower pane. In Code view, *<xsl:value-of select="sum($nodeset/@Total_x0020_Purchased" />* is highlighted.

4. On the Quick Tag Selector, click the **<xsl:if>**.

In Code view, the code between the opening and closing *<xsl:if test="$showfootercolumn ddwrt:cf-ignore="1">* tags is highlighted.

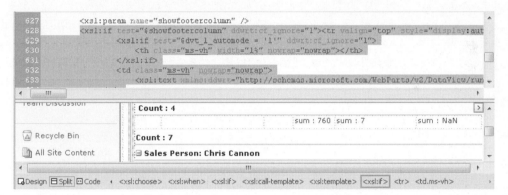

5. In Code view, place the insertion point to the left of **<xsl:if** and press **Enter** twice.

6. On the first blank line, type **<xsl:var**, and then press **Tab** to select **xsl:variable**. Press **Space**, type **n**, and then press **Tab** to select **name**.

7. Place the insertion point between the two quotation marks that appear, type **SumTotalPurchaseNodeset**, and then to the right of the second quotation mark, type >. Press **Enter** twice.

The code should look similar to the following:

```
<xsl:variable name="SumTotalPurchasedNodeset">

</xsl:template>
```

8. Using the techniques described in the previous steps, create a code segment that reads as follows:

```
<xsl:variable name="SumTotalPurchasedNodeset">
  <xsl:for-each select="$nodeset">
    <Value>
     <xsl:value-of
        select="substring-after(translate(@Total_x0020_
Purchased,',',''),'$')"/>
    </Value>
   </xsl:for-each>
</xsl:variable>
```

Tip If you do not want to type the code, the practice file SPDSBSC05.xsl.txt contains the code segments that you can copy and paste into Code view.

9. In Design view, in the **Total Purchased** column, click **NaN**. In Code view, delete the highlighted text **<xsl:value-of select="sum($nodeset/@Total_x0020_ Purchased" />**, and type the following code:

```
<xsl:value-of
  select="concat('$', sum(msxsl:node-set($SumTotalPurchasedNodeset)/
Value))"/>
```

10. In Design view, click **NaN**.

The page refreshes, and NaN is replaced by the value $80,619.40, which is the sum of purchases that the sales person Chris Ashton sold to his customers.

✖ CLEAN UP Save CreateDVWP.aspx. Leave SharePoint Designer open if you are continuing to the next exercise.

Deploying Web Parts

As you develop Data Views and XLV Web Parts, you might want to use the same formatted and filtered Web Parts on other sites within your site collection. By using the browser or SharePoint Designer, you can export a Web Part and reuse it. With both the browser and SharePoint Designer, you can save the Web Part file to the file system, and from there you can import it into a page. SharePoint Designer allows you to export a Web Part directly to the Web Part gallery.

When you edit Web pages on team sites, every time you save your modifications they are immediately visible to all users who view that page. By developing your solution on a production page, you can cause performance and rendering problems, especially if you make mistakes. You should create a test Web page and then create and modify your Data View and XLV Web Parts on that test page. When you have completed your modifications, export the Web Part and add it to the production Web page, deleting the test page if necessary.

When an XLV Web Part is saved to the Site Gallery or to a file, a dialog box opens that asks whether you want to show list data from the current Web site. If you select No, the exported Web Part uses relative addresses when referencing the list or library, which means that the Web Part can be used on any site that has a list or library with the same name. For example, if you export an XLV Web Part that displays data from the SalesReport list, the Web Part can be used on another site that has a list named SalesReport. You can use this method to display content stored on a subsite on the top-level site of a site collection, or you can move a Web Part from a test, prototype environment to a production environment. You cannot do the same with Data Views.

Warning Data Views reference a list by the list's GUID and not by its name. An exported Web Part that references a GUID results in a Web Part that will not render on another site. The Web Page where you add the Web Part might not render as well. You might also experience this error with other Web Parts. To remove the offending Web Part, append *?contents=1* to the URL of the Web page to display the maintenance page. If you want to export a Data View that exposes data from a specific list type and reuse it on a different site, where it points to a different list of the same list type, you need to edit the DataFormWebPart control in Code view. Replace all occurrences of ListID with List Name and all occurrences of the GUID value with the list name.

In this exercise, you export a Data View and add it to the home page of your Web site.

 SET UP Using SharePoint Designer, open the team site you used in the previous exercise if it is not already open, and then open Stock.aspx in edit mode with the Furniture Price List DFWP selected.

To Site Gallery

1. On the **Web Part** tab, click **To Site Gallery** in the **Save Web Part** group.

   The Save Web Part To Site Gallery dialog box opens.

2. In the **Name** box, type **SBSFurnitureSales**, and then click **OK**.

   The Save Web Part To Site Gallery dialog box closes.

3. In the **Site Pages** mini-gallery pane, right-click **Home.aspx**, and then click **Preview in Browser**.

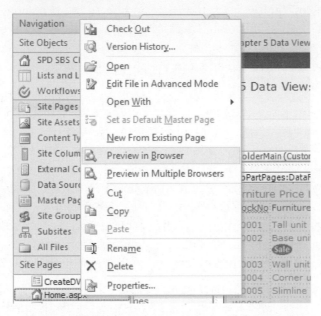

The home page of your Web site opens in the browser.

4. Click **Site Actions**, and then click **Edit Page**.

5. Place the insertion point at the bottom of the rectangle, and then on the **Editing Tools**, **Insert** tab, click **Web Part**.

The Add Web Parts area opens below the ribbon.

6. Under **Categories**, click **Miscellaneous**, and under **Web Parts** click **SBSFurnitureSales**. Then click **Add**.

The Add Web Parts area closes, and the Data View is added to the home page.

7. On the **Page** tab, click **Save & Close**.

✖ **CLEAN UP** Leave SharePoint Designer open if you are continuing to the next chapter.

Key Points

- Data Views allow you to view data and enter data in a variety of data sources.
- Data Views are also known by the names Data Form Web Parts (DFWP) and Data View Web Parts (DVWP).
- Data Views follow the same rules as other Web Parts.
- The XSLT List View (XLV) Web Part is very similar to Data Views, and many of the techniques discussed in this chapter can be used with XLV Web Parts.
- Data Views and XLV Web Parts can be configured to use inline editing. This allows users to add or edit list items without the need to open the New or Edit form pages.
- Use conditional formatting to specify criteria that alters the appearance of a set of cells in rows or columns or in selected content.
- Use conditional formatting to show or hide content on the basis of criteria you define.
- Data Views and XLV Web Parts use XSLT to transform XML data into HTML.
- You can use SharePoint Designer to import and export Web Parts. When you export Web Parts, you can save them in the Web Part gallery or on the file system.

Chapter at a Glance

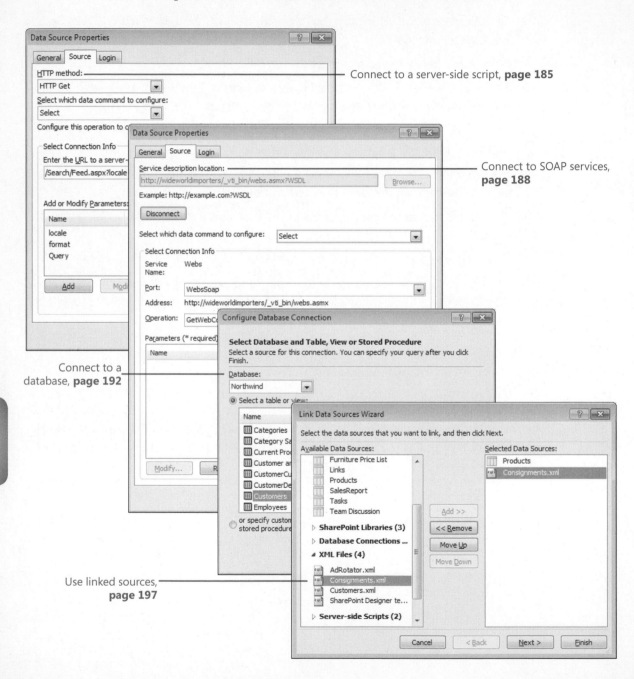

Connect to a server-side script, **page 185**

Connect to SOAP services, **page 188**

Connect to a database, **page 192**

Use linked sources, **page 197**

6 Working with Data Sources

In this chapter, you will learn how to

✔ Use data sources.

✔ Work with XML data.

✔ Connect to an RSS feed XML file.

✔ Connect to a server-side script.

✔ Connect to SOAP and REST services.

✔ Connect to a database.

✔ Use linked sources.

✔ Connect Web Parts.

When you created a Data View in Chapter 5, "Working with Data Views," the Data Sources Picker dialog box opened so that you could select a list or library on the current site. Using the Data Sources Picker dialog box, you can do more than just select lists and libraries; you can choose to access data from a variety of data sources. To create and manage the data sources shown in the Data Sources Picker dialog box, you need to use the Data Sources gallery page. Data connections control the amount of data retrieved by Microsoft SharePoint Foundation 2010 from the data sources. After data is retrieved, Data Views specify how to manipulate it by using XSLT and HTML tags.

Note In SharePoint Designer 2007, you create and manage data connections by using the Data Source Library task pane. The Data Source Library task pane has been replaced by the Data Sources gallery page. In SharePoint Designer 2007, you can also add a Data Source library from another site so that you can share its data connections rather than re-create them. This functionality is no longer available in SharePoint Designer 2010.

In this chapter, you will use the Data Sources gallery page to create data connections to a number of data sources, and you will link data sources that contain interrelated data to one another. You will also learn how to use Web Part connections.

> **Practice Files** Before you can use the practice files provided for this chapter, you need to install them from the book's companion Web site. For more information about practice files, see "Using the Practice Files" on page xxiii.

Using Data Sources

The Data Sources gallery page is an easy-to-use interface for creating, managing, and modifying data connections to data sources. These data connections describe a location and provide a query that the Microsoft SharePoint Foundation Data Retrieval Service uses to obtain data from the data sources. The Data Retrieval Service provides a layer of abstraction so that both Microsoft SharePoint Designer 2010 and Data Views do not need to differentiate between various methods of accessing data sources.

When you request a page by using SharePoint Designer 2010, it is the responsibility of the Data Retrieval Service on the Web server to return the data in an XML format that SharePoint Designer understands. SharePoint Designer interprets the XML data and displays it in the Data Source Details task pane and in Design view when the page contains any Data Views. Similarly, when you request a page by using the browser, the Data Retrieval Service provides the XML data, which SharePoint uses together with the XSLT from the Data View to provide the page that the browser renders. In the browser, when the Data View is configured to allow users to edit data, the Data Retrieval Service communicates any changes back to the data sources.

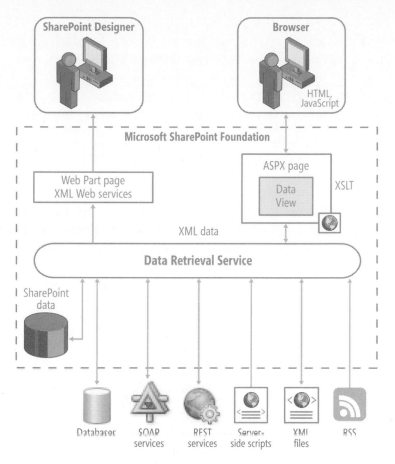

You can connect to a variety of data sources, which are grouped according to the access method they use, as described in the following table.

Data source groups	Description
SharePoint lists and libraries	Every list and library that is not hidden from the browser is listed in the Data Sources gallery page.
Database connections	When you first open the Data Sources gallery page, no connections to any databases are defined. You can create a connection to a variety of databases that reside on Microsoft SQL Server 2000 or later versions, or to any data source that uses the OLE DB protocols. You can create multiple data connections to the same database, each using a different table, view, or query.

XML files	SharePoint Designer interrogates the root of your current site and the Site Assets library for any XML files it finds. You can also import an XML file into your site or refer to an XML file in another library or on another site by using the XML File Connection command.
Server-side scripts	You can connect to server-side scripts that return XML data. For example, a *Really Simple Syndication (RSS)* feed may use a server-side script. Such RSS feeds have a URL ending in .aspx or .php. When an RSS feed has a URL ending in .xml or .ashx, use the XML file data connection method. You can connect to server-side scripts written in a variety of languages, including Microsoft ASP, Microsoft ASP.NET, PHP, and *Asynchronous JavaScript and XML (AJAX)*.
SOAP services	A SOAP service is a special site that can return XML in response to a procedural query. SharePoint itself exposes its data as a SOAP service, enabling you to create, for example, a list of announcements from the current site and its child sites, known as a rollup of announcements.
REST service	Similar to SOAP services, where data can be retrieved from a data source as XML data.
External lists	Although you cannot create external lists from the Data Sources gallery page, external lists are displayed on the page. External lists are created from *external content types (ECTs)*. Many organizations use ECTs in preference to other access methods available on the Data Sources gallery page for security reasons and because an ECT is defined once in a central location. These definitions are available for all sites and site collections. More information about external lists and ECTs can be found in Chapter 7, "Using Business Connectivity Services."
Linked sources	Many data sources contain related data. You can use this data source group to combine two or more data sources into one source.

Because of the ease with which you can connect to data sources, you should consider whether you really need all the data that your connection query returns. If you retrieve a large number of rows and columns, it might take some time for the page to render. You can use filters to limit the number of rows displayed; however, if all the data is not needed, you get better results by amending the data connection query to return a smaller portion of the data than by filtering the Data View to limit the data.

When defining a data connection, you need to consider the authentication method used to connect to the data source because this has security and infrastructure implications. For example, when you connect to a SQL Server database, you use SQL Server authentication and specify the SQL Server user name and password in the connection query defined in the data source. The user name and password are transmitted over the network in clear text, which could have security implications.

Caution When a user does not have the right to view the data, a Data View might be affected and the page itself might not render. As you create a solution by using data sources and Data Views, test your solution with users who need to access the data.

Every time you open the Data Sources gallery page, SharePoint Designer dynamically populates it with references to the site's lists and libraries and to the XML files stored in the site's root or in the Site Assets library. No other data sources are defined when you first create a site. These dynamically created definitions return all the available data. If you want to display only a subset of the data these connections provide, you must use Data View filtering methods. Alternatively, you can create copies of these dynamically created data sources and then modify them to explicitly define the data you want to retrieve.

Each data source group on the Data Sources gallery page provides a link you use to create a data connection, in which you specify the location and connection query to the data source. When you create the first data source for a site, SharePoint Designer creates a document library named the *fpdatasources library* in the _catalogs folder. This document library is visible only by using SharePoint Designer and only to those users who can see the hidden URL site structure. SharePoint Designer then creates an XML file that contains the data connection information in *Universal Data Connection (UDC)* version 1 file format, and then stores the file in the fpdatasources library. You can open these XML files in the SharePoint Designer workspace and manually modify the data connection information, but the next time you use the Data Source Properties dialog box to modify your data source, you lose any modifications you have already entered.

When you create a Data View, the data connection information is copied from the UDC file to the Data View. The Data Source Details task pane then uses the data connection information stored within the Data View to display the XML elements. Changing the UDC file or even deleting the UDC file once you have created the Data View has no effect on the Data View or the data presented by the Data View.

In this exercise, you use the Data Sources gallery page to create and modify a data connection for a SharePoint list. Then, if you have permission to see the hidden URL structure of your site, you will investigate where the information concerning data source connections is stored.

 SET UP Using SharePoint Designer, open the site you created from the SBSSPDPracticeSite_Starter.wsp practice file for this book. You might have created this site if you completed the exercises in Chapter 5. Otherwise, create a site from the practice file that is located in the Chapter06 practice file folder. For information on how to create a site from the practice file, see "Using the Practice Files" on page xxiii.

1. In the **Navigation** pane, click **Data Sources**.

   The Data Sources gallery page is displayed in the workspace.

Copy and Modify

2. In the workspace, under **Lists**, click the icon to the left of **Announcements**, and then on the **Data Sources** tab, click **Copy and Modify** in the **Actions** group.

   The Data Source Properties dialog box opens.

3. Under **Query**, click **Fields** to open the **Included Fields** dialog box.

4. In the **Included Fields** list, hold down the **Shift** or **Ctrl** key and click all but the **ID** field. Click **Remove** so that only ID appears in the list.

5. In the **Available fields** list, hold down **Ctrl**; click **Title**, **Body**, and **Modified By**; and then click **Add**.

6. Click **OK** to close the **Included Fields** dialog box.

7. In the **Data Source Properties** dialog box, click the **General** tab. In the **Name** box, type **AnnouncementsTitleBody**.

8. Click **OK** to close the **Data Source Properties** dialog box.

   The AnnouncementsTitleBody data source appears under Lists on the Data Sources gallery page.

Always Show pin

9. If you are able to see the hidden URL structure of your site, hover the mouse pointer over **All Files** in the **Navigation** pane, and click the **Always Show** pin that appears.

   In the Navigation pane, the pin remains permanently visible to the right of All Files. The All Files mini-gallery appears below the Navigation pane and displays the hidden URL structure of the Web site.

10. In the mini-gallery, click the + sign to the left of **_catalogs** and click the + sign to the left of **fpdatasources**.

    The fpdatasources library appears, containing AnnouncementsTitleBody.xml.

11. In the **All Files** mini-gallery, right-click **AnnouncementsTitleBody.xml**, click **Open With**, and then click **SharePoint Designer (Open as XML)**.

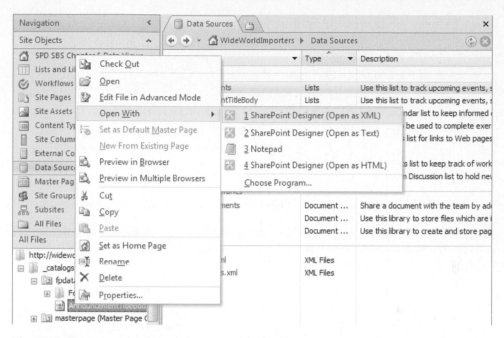

The XML file opens in the workspace with the data connection location and query information specified as XML data, all on one line.

12. Right-click within the workspace, and then click **Reformat XML**.

The XML data is redisplayed, indented and with each XML element on a new line. The *DataSourceControl* element contains the data connection information.

![CLEAN UP] **CLEAN UP** Close the AnnouncementsTitleBody.xml file and save it if you are prompted to do so. Leave SharePoint Designer open if you are continuing to the next exercise.

Working with XML Data

Using the Data Sources gallery page, you can work with XML data stored in XML files. If these files are located in the Site Assets library or in the root of your site, SharePoint Designer dynamically creates a data connection for each file, and these data connections appear on the Data Sources gallery page under XML Files. Also, if you import an XML file into one of those locations, a corresponding connection automatically appears on the Data Sources gallery page. As you delete or add XML files in the Site Assets library or the root of the site, the data connections dynamically appear and disappear from the Data Sources gallery page. When you store an XML file in any other location, you need to create an XML file data connection for that file before you can use the data in a Data View.

Note When you work with an XML file as a data source, the XML file must contain only well-formed XML; otherwise, it might cause errors. In addition, the XML file must contain and conform to a schema, or it must contain data from which a schema can be inferred.

If you do not want to retrieve all the data from the XML file, as with lists and libraries, you can copy and modify the data connection details. However, if you delete the XML file, the copy of the XML file data connection remains listed on the Data Sources gallery page. If you click Show Data in an empty Data View that uses the copy of the data connection, an error message appears in the Data Source Details task pane.

On the Data Sources gallery page you cannot delete a dynamically created data connection. You can only amend its properties or copy and modify the data connection details.

Tip Whenever you create or modify a data connection, it is good practice to check that you configured the data connection correctly by using an empty Data View and the Data Source Details task pane.

In this exercise, you add an XML file from your file system to the Site Assets library. You use the Data Source Details task pane to view the contents of the XML file and explore the dynamic creation of data connections.

SET UP Use the Shipments.xml file. This practice file is located in the Chapter06 practice file folder. Using SharePoint Designer, open the site you used in the previous exercise, and then open the Data Sources gallery page if it is not already open.

XML File Connection

1. Click the icon to the left of **Announcements**, and then on the **Data Sources** tab, click **XML File Connection** in the **New** group.

    The Data Source Properties dialog box opens.

2. On the **Source** tab, click **Browse** to open the **File Open** dialog box.

3. Navigate to the Chapter06 practice file folder, and then click **Open**.

A Microsoft SharePoint Designer message box opens, asking if you want to import the file.

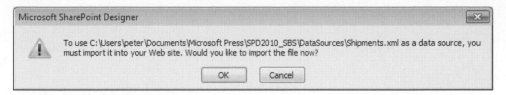

4. Click **OK** to import the file.

The Microsoft SharePoint Designer message box closes, and the Import dialog box opens.

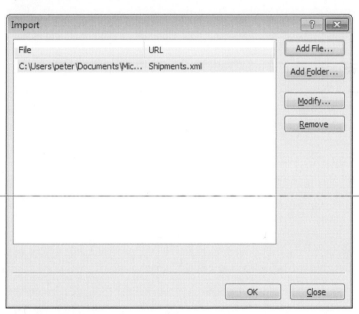

5. Click **Modify** to open the **Edit URL** dialog box.

6. In the **File location within your web** text box, type **SiteAssets/Shipments.xml**.

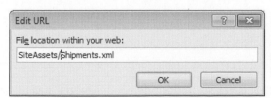

7. Click **OK** twice to close the **Edit URL** and **Import** dialog boxes.

On the Data Sources gallery page, the Shipments.xml data connection appears under XML Files.

8. In the **Navigation** pane, click **Site Pages**, and then double-click the icon to the left of **DataSourceTest.aspx** to open the page in edit mode.

9. In the **PlaceHolderMain** region, click **Click here to select a data source**. In the **Data Source Picker** dialog box, under **XML Files**, click **Shipments.xml**, and then click **OK**.

The Data Source Details task pane appears, displaying an XML root element named *Shipments*, with a child element named *Shipment* that contains a number of item child elements. The first five elements are selected.

10. If you are able to see the hidden URL structure of your site, in the **All Files** mini-gallery, expand both **_catalogs, fpdatasources** and the **SiteAssets (Site Assets)** libraries.

   The Shipments.xml file is listed in the Site Assets library. There is no corresponding UDC XML file in the fpdatasources library.

11. In the **Navigation** pane, click **Site Assets**. Right-click **Shipments.xml**, and then click **Delete**.

12. Click **Yes** to confirm the deletion, and then in the **Navigation** pane, click **Data Sources**.

   Shipments.xml disappears from both the Site Assets library and the Data Sources gallery page.

 **CLEAN UP** Leave SharePoint Designer open if you are continuing to the next exercise.

Connecting to an RSS Feed XML File

You can use the XML File Connection command on the Data Sources tab to connect to an XML file located on an external server. You do not import the XML file to your site; instead, you link the external XML file to the site by using its URL.

One popular external XML file is the one produced by an RSS feed. (Servers that publish their content as XML data that conforms to the RSS format are said to have an RSS feed.) Many Internet-facing servers produce RSS-formatted XML data as either an XML file or a server-side script that produces RSS-formatted XML data.

Note Starting with Windows SharePoint Services 3.0, lists and libraries can expose their content by using RSS.

In this exercise, you retrieve data published by an external server by linking to an XML file connection.

Important In this exercise, you access an RSS feed over the Internet. To complete this exercise, you must have Internet access.

 SET UP Using SharePoint Designer, open the site you used in the previous exercise. Open the DataSourceTest.aspx page and Data Sources gallery page if they are not already open.

XML File
Connection

1. Click in the **Data Sources** gallery page to activate the commands on the **Data Sources** tab, and then click **XML File Connection**.

    The Data Source Properties dialog box opens.

2. On the **Source** tab, in the **Location** text box, type **http://blogs.msdn.com/b/ sharepointdesigner/rss.aspx**.

    Warning For you to connect to a URL on the Internet, your SharePoint Server administrator might have to configure on the SharePoint server(s) the *web.config* for proxy server settings.

3. Click the **General** tab, and in the **Name** text box, type **SharePoint Designer team blog**.

4. Click the **Login** tab, and verify that the **Don't attempt to authenticate** option is selected.

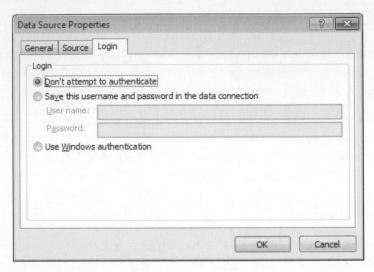

5. Click **OK**.

   The Data Source Properties dialog box closes.

   The SharePoint Designer Team Blog data connection appears in the Data Sources gallery. If you are able to see the hidden URL structure of your site, you also see in the All Files mini-gallery a corresponding UDC XML file listed in the fpdatasources library.

6. Click the **DataSourceTest.aspx** tab.

7. In the **PlaceHolderMain** region, click **Click here to select a data source**. In the **Data Source Picker** dialog box, under **XML Files**, click **SharePoint Designer team blog**, and then click **OK**.

   The Data Source Details task pane appears if it is not already open. It displays an XML root element named *rss*, with a child element named *channel* that contains a number of item child elements.

   Tip When connecting to data over the Internet, SharePoint Designer might appear to be locked. This could be caused by network problems and/or the poor performance of the server providing the XML data. To speed your design process, set the Data View to show sample data on the Design tab, and clear the Show Data Values option at the bottom of the Data Source Details task pane.

 CLEAN UP Leave SharePoint Designer open if you are continuing to the next exercise.

Connecting to an RSS Feed Server-Side Script

With the popularity of RSS feeds, many products support that XML data format, with the result that many organizations are using the RSS XML data schema as a basis for exposing data not traditionally considered RSS data. These companies use server-side scripts to produce the XML data because scripts allow more control over the data.

The XML data produced by server-side scripts can depend on parameter values. The values transmitted to the external server are either appended to the end of the URL, known as the *HTTP GET method*, or provided in the body of the request, known as the *HTTP POST method*. The HTTP GET method uses simple queries to retrieve (GET) data and is the safer method as far as the external server is concerned. The HTTP POST method is usually used to send (POST) data or instructs the external server to manipulate the data.

Whether you want to view (which in database terminology is referred to as *select*), insert, update, or delete data on the external server, you use the Data Source Properties dialog box to configure each command.

When you create data connections by using either XML files or server-side scripts, you might need to configure the authentication method to access the XML data. The Data Source Properties dialog box provides a choice of four options:

- **Don't Attempt To Authenticate** Use this option for external servers that accept anonymous access or if users must supply their user names and passwords.

- **Save This Username And Password In The Data Connection** Use this option if the XML data is password protected and you want anyone to be able to access the data without being prompted for a user name and password. The user name and password are transmitted over the network as clear text, so you might need to contact your IT department to add further infrastructure security.

- **Use Windows Authentication** Use this option when SharePoint 2010 and the XML file are located on the same server.

- **Use Single Sign-On Authentication** At the time of writing this book, this option, although available, does not work with data sources. Use ECTs if you want to use this authentication method. More information on external lists and ECTs can be found in Chapter 7.

In this exercise, you retrieve XML data by using a server-side script connection.

SET UP Using SharePoint Designer, open the site you used in the previous exercise. Open the DataSourceTest.aspx page and the Data Sources gallery page if they are not already open.

1. Open your browser. In the address box, type **http://technet.microsoft.com**.

    The Microsoft TechNet site opens.

2. In the search box, type **sharepoint designer 2010**, and then press **Enter** to display the search results.

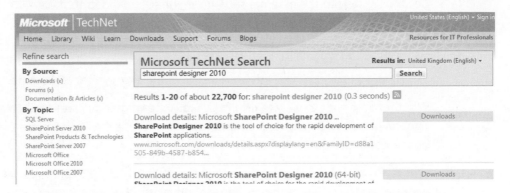

3. In the **Results** row, right-click the **RSS** icon, and then click **Copy Shortcut**.

RSS Icon

4. In SharePoint Designer, with the **Data Sources** gallery page displayed in the workspace, click **REST Service Connection** in the **New** group on the **Data Sources** tab.

    The Data Source Properties dialog box opens.

5. Right-click the **Enter the URL to a server-side script** box, and then click **Paste**.

6. Click the **Add or Modify Parameters** list box.

    The parameters from the server-side script appear in the Add Or Modify Parameters list box. The *Query* string has a value of *sharepoint+designer+2010*.

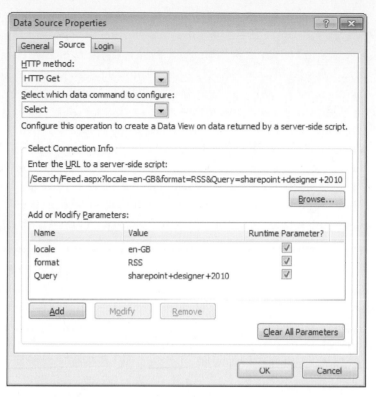

7. On the **General** tab, in the **Name** box, type **Microsoft TechNet Search**.

8. Click **OK** to close the **Data Source Properties** dialog box.

   The Microsoft TechNet Search data connection appears on the Data Sources gallery page under RSS, REST, Server Scripts.

9. Click the **DataSourceTest.aspx** tab.

10. In the **PlaceHolderMain** region, click **Click here to select a data source**. In the **Data Source Picker** dialog box, under **RSS, REST, Server Scripts**, click **Microsoft TechNet Search**, and then click **OK**.

    The Data Source Details task pane displays a number of item elements. Each item element displays information returned by the TechNet Search site as the result of searching for the terms *sharepoint designer 2010*.

✖ **CLEAN UP** Leave SharePoint Designer open if you are continuing to the next exercise.

Connecting to SOAP Services

A SOAP service, also known as an *XML Web service*, transports XML data between computer systems by using *Simple Object Access Protocol (SOAP)* over HTTP or HTTPS. SharePoint can act as a SOAP service requester or client—that is, it can request XML data from a SOAP service and present the data by using a Data View. As with server-side scripts, the requester can send XML data, instructions (known as *methods*), parameters, and values to the XML Web service provider, depending on how the SOAP service is written. The methods and parameters that a SOAP service supports are described in a *Web Service Description Language (WSDL)* file. If a SOAP service supports data manipulation, you will be able to select, insert, update, or delete data on the XML Web service provider by using the Data Source Properties dialog box to configure each command.

SharePoint also acts as a SOAP service provider, exposed as an ASP.NET Web service, to supply XML data to other computer systems. Using SharePoint Designer, you can build client-side applications that use ASP.NET Web services to request data that is not stored in your team site. The SharePoint SOAP service interface query mechanism requires the use of Collaborative Application Markup Language (CAML), which is a proprietary markup language specific to SharePoint technologies. The retrieval of some data might be quite complex and require the skills of a developer.

SharePoint 2010 introduces new methods of providing data to remote systems—the client-side object model and the SharePoint Foundation REST interface. These two providers should be used in preference to the legacy ASP.NET Web services. However, the SharePoint Foundation REST interface, which is detailed in the next section, can only retrieve information from lists and libraries; developer skills are needed to use the client-side object model. Still, you might find the SharePoint Foundation and SharePoint Server Web services useful as you build your solutions with SharePoint Designer.

See Also More information about SharePoint Foundation and data access for client applications can be found at *msdn.microsoft.com/en-us/library/ff798473.aspx*. Information about SharePoint 2010 Web services can be found at *msdn.microsoft.com/en-us/library/ee705814.aspx*.

In this exercise, you add a SOAP service connection as a data source.

 SET UP Using SharePoint Designer, open the site you used in the previous exercise. Open the DataSourceTest.aspx page and the Data Sources gallery page if they are not already open.

SOAP Service Connection

1. Click the **Data Sources** gallery page to activate the commands on the **Data Sources** tab, and then click **SOAP Service Connection**.

   The Data Source Properties dialog box opens.

2. In the **Service description location** box, type **http://<site>/_vti_bin/webs. asmx?wsdl**, where <site> is the URL of the top-level site of a site collection. For example, <site> might be wideworldimporters. Then click **Connect Now**.

> **Tip** If you cannot connect to the SOAP service connection or you get an error message that the server returned a nonspecific error or that the Web Part cannot be viewed using the browser, check the spelling of the server name and the SOAP service _vti_bin/webs. asmx?wsdl. If you forget to type **?wsdl** after the name of the SOAP service, SharePoint Designer appends it to the URL. You can connect to other SOAP services at a child-site level, in which case the service description location becomes, for example, *http://<site>/_ vti_bin/lists.asmx*, where <site> is the child site you created using the practice .wsp file for this chapter, such as *wideworldimporters/datasources*.

SharePoint Designer connects to the server hosting the SOAP service and populates the dialog box with the responses it receives from the SOAP service provider.

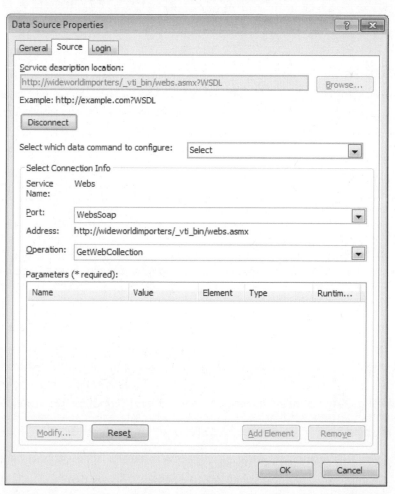

3. Click **OK** to close the **Data Source Properties** dialog box.

   The Webs On <site> data connection appears under SOAP Services on the Data Sources gallery page.

4. Click the **DataSourceTest.aspx** tab.

5. In the **PlaceHolderMain** region, click **Click here to select a data source**. In the **Data Source Picker** dialog box, under **SOAP Services**, click **Webs on <site>**, and then click **OK**.

   The Data Source Details task displays an XML root element named *soap:Envelope*, which contains a number of child elements. Each Web element contains the title and URL of a site within the site collection.

 CLEAN UP Leave SharePoint Designer open if you are continuing to the next exercise.

Connecting to REST Services

A *Representational State Transfer (REST)* service is similar to a SOAP service in that it allows the transport of XML data between computer systems. However, unlike a SOAP service, REST supports only the four basic application methods—GET, POST, PUT, and DELETE—although a verb-tunneling technique can hide operations from HTTP and submit PUT and DELETE requests as a POST request. This enables computer systems to transfer XML data over networks that block HTTP verbs other than GET and POST. The XML data is transferred through a REST service in a standardized form, known as *ATOM syndication format*, whereas SOAP services use a nonstandard schema. In theory, the REST service is more portable.

Note The term REST was introduced in 2000 by Roy Fielding, one of the principal authors of the HTTP specification, to describe the undocumented architectural design principles of the World Wide Web.

Just as SharePoint can act as a SOAP service provider and client, so it can act as a REST service provider and client. This lets you use SharePoint Designer to create solutions that consume XML data from REST services, including XML data retrieved from SharePoint REST interfaces. The number of SharePoint REST interfaces is small compared to the number of SharePoint SOAP service interfaces. The two SharePoint 2010 REST interfaces are as follows:

● **ListData.svc** Provides access to list and library data.

● **ExcelRest.aspx** Allows for easy discovery of and access to data and objects within a spreadsheet. This REST interface is available only if you have the Enterprise edition of SharePoint Server.

See Also More information about using the SharePoint 2010 REST interface can be found at *msdn.microsoft.com/en-us/library/ff798339.aspx*. Information about the Excel Services REST interface can be found on the Microsoft Excel product team blog site at *blogs.msdn.com/b/ excel/archive/tags/REST+API/.*

REST uses URL-based syntax to retrieve XML data. The syntax is predictable and therefore can be inferred by a technically savvy user. The syntax format to retrieve data using ListData.svc is *http://<site>/_vti_bin/ListData.svc/<list name>(<row>)/<column name>/<options>*, where the terms to the right of ListData.svc are optional. For example, *http://wideworldimporters/_vti_bin/ListData.svc/SalesReport(1)/Brand* returns only the value in the Brand column of the first row of the SalesReport list.

You can append query strings to the URLs to specify filter criteria or query logic. For example, the following URL returns values from the Customer, Brand, and Quantity Purchased columns from the SalesReport list for those customers whose name starts with C: *http://wideworldimporters/_vti_bin/ListData.svc/SalesReport?$filter=startswith(Custom er, 'C')&$select=Customer,Brand,QuantityPurchased*

Tip A REST query is case sensitive and spaces are removed; therefore, the spelling of lists, libraries, and column names may not be as you expect. A useful option when you are creating a REST query for the first time is to use the $metadata parameter. This parameter allows you to see the schema for the list data, which you can use to check your spellings. For example, *http://wideworldimporters/_vti_bin/ListData.svc/$metadata.*

In this exercise, you create a REST service connection.

SET UP Using SharePoint Designer, open the site you used in the previous exercise. Open the DataSourceTest.aspx page and the Data Sources gallery page if they are not already open.

REST Service
Connection

1. Click the **Data Sources** gallery page to activate the commands on the **Data Sources** tab, and then click **REST Service Connection**.

   The Data Source Properties dialog box opens.

2. In the **Enter the URL to a server-side script** box, type **http://<site>/_vti_bin/ ListData.svc**, where <site> is the URL of a SharePoint site. For example, <site> might be wideworldimporters or wideworldimporters/DataSources.

3. On the **General** tab, in the **Name** box, type **Lists and Libraries on site**.

4. On the **Login** tab, select **Save this username and password in the data connection**. Type a user name and password combination that has access to the site.

   Important The user name and password are sent over the network as clear text, which is a security risk.

5. Click **OK** to close the **Data Source Properties** dialog box.

6. Click **OK** in the warning message that states that the user name and password will be sent as clear text over the network to the computer running SQL Server.

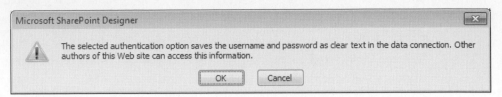

The Lists And Libraries On Site data connection appears under RSS, REST, Server Scripts on the Data Sources gallery page.

7. Click the **DataSourceTest.aspx** tab.

8. In the **PlaceHolderMain** region, click **Click here to select a data source**. In the **Data Source Picker** dialog box, under **RSS, REST, Server Scripts**, click **Lists and Libraries on site**, and then click **OK**.

The Data Source Details task pane displays an XML root element named *service*, which contain *workspace* and *collection* child elements. The *collection* child element contains the href (URL) and title of each list or library within the site, including any hidden lists or libraries. Notice that any list or library that has spaces in its name has those spaces removed when it's referred to in the REST interface.

Troubleshooting If an error message is displayed in the Data Source Details task pane that the server returned a nonspecific error, type **http://<site>/_vti_bin/ListData.svc** in the address box in your browser. If this results in an error message stating "'System.Data.Services. Providers.IDataServiceUpdateProvider' could not be loaded from an assembly," it is likely that the correct version of ADO.NET Data Services is not installed. Be sure to install ADO.NET Data Services Update for .NET 3.5 SP1, which can be found on Microsoft's download center at *www. microsoft.com/downloads*. Be sure you install the correct update for the operating system you are running on your SharePoint server.

 CLEAN UP Leave SharePoint Designer open if you are continuing to the next exercise.

Connecting to a Database

You can create a database connection by using SharePoint Designer. After the data connection is defined, you can use it to present data from that database in Data Views. A connection wizard steps you through creating the definition for how SharePoint should connect to a database. The information you provide includes the name of the server that is hosting your database and the authentication method to use to retrieve the data. Using this wizard, you can connect to Microsoft SQL Server databases or databases that use the OLE DB provider. Alternatively, you can create a custom connection string to make other database providers available, such as Microsoft .NET Framework Data Providers for ODBC and Oracle. Your SharePoint server administrator might install other providers.

See Also Information on custom connection strings can be found at *www.connectionstrings. com/sharepoint*. This site also contains information about connection strings used to connect to databases other than SQL Server databases.

When connecting to a SQL Server database you cannot use Windows authentication or the SharePoint Server single sign-on service, named Secure Store Service (SSS). You are limited to using a SQL Server authentication user name and password, which are sent over the network in plain text. The user name and password are also stored in the UDC file stored in the fpdatasources library and are saved as text within the Data View. All users who view the data using the Data View can access the database by using that user name and password.

The Business Connectivity Service (BCS) does not have these authentication restrictions, so most companies use the BCS to create external content types (ECTs) to connect to databases.

Tip Use the Data Sources gallery page to create database connections when you are prototyping your solutions, when the data is not sensitive, or when you do not need to connect to a data source from multiple SharePoint sites. If you do deploy a solution in your production environment that uses a data sources database connection, be sure the SQL Server user name has minimum privileges and has access only to the database that the database connection is related to.

In this exercise, you create a database connection to a SQL Server database.

 SET UP Your database administrator needs to provide you with a SQL Server computer name, database name, table name, and SQL Server credentials for you to complete this exercise. By default, SQL Server is configured to use only Windows authentication. To use SQL Server credentials, which is required for the database data source connection to work, your database administrator needs to change the SQL Server authentication configuration to use both SQL Server and Windows authentication. Your database administrator might want to use the Northwind sample database, which can be found at Microsoft's download site, *www.microsoft.com/ downloads*, by using the search keywords *northwind sample databases*.

 SET UP Using SharePoint Designer, open the site you used in the previous exercise. Open the DataSourceTest.aspx page and the Data Sources gallery page if they are not already open.

Database
Connection

1. Click in the **Data Sources** gallery page to activate the commands on the **Data Sources** tab, and then click **Database Connection**.

    The Data Source Properties dialog box opens.

2. On the **Source** tab, click **Configure Database Connection**.

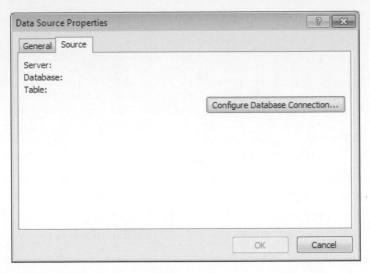

The Configure Database Connection dialog box opens.

3. In the **Server Name** box, type the name of the server on which the database is located.

4. In the **Provider Name** list, check that the provider **Microsoft .NET Framework Data Provider for SQL Server** is selected.

5. In the **Authentication** section, leave the default option selected, and enter the SQL Server user name and password combination that has access to the database.

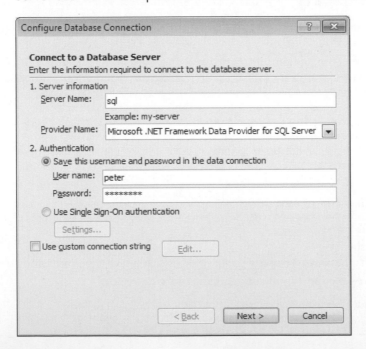

Warning On a site hosted by SharePoint Foundation 2010, the Authentication section does not have the second option, Use Single Sign-On Authentication. On SharePoint Server this option is available, but it is not usable. Single sign-on, now known as Secure Store Service, can be used only with external content type data sources.

6. Click **Next**.

7. Click **OK** in the warning message that states that the user name and password will be sent as clear text over the network to the computer running SQL Server.

Troubleshooting If the SharePoint server is unable to connect to the SQL Server database, a Server Error dialog box is displayed, stating that an authentication error occurred, the login information might be incorrectly entered, you might not have permissions to access the SQL Server database, or the requested authentication method might not be supported. Click OK to close the dialog box, and then check the information you entered in the Configure Database Connection dialog box. If the problem persists, you need to contact your database administrator.

The Select Database And Table, View Or Stored Procedure page of the Configure Database Connection dialog box is displayed.

8. In the **Database** list, select the database that contains the data you want to access; for example, **Northwind**.

The Select A Table Or View list is refreshed and displays the tables and views available in the database you selected.

9. Click the table or view that contains the data you want to retrieve; for example, **Customers**.

> **Tip** If you choose a table or view, SharePoint will create the SQL statements to connect to the database. You can provide our own SQL SELECT, UPDATE, INSERT INTO, and DELETE statements or stored procedures. Using stored procedures is more secure than using SQL statements and should be used in production environments.

10. Click **Finish**.

The Configure Database Connection dialog box closes. On the Source tab of the Data Source Properties dialog box, the server name, database name, and table name are displayed. The Query section displays a list of the fields that are returned when you use this data connection. You can use the Query section to customize the SQL statements.

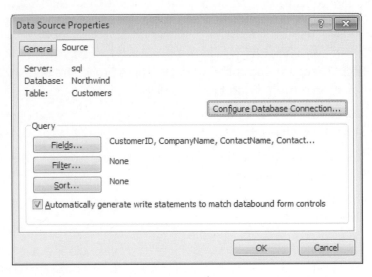

11. Click **OK**.

The Data Source Properties dialog box closes. The <table> on <database name> data connection—for example, Customers on Northwind—appears under Database Connections on the Data Sources gallery page.

12. Click the **DataSourceTest.aspx** tab.

13. In the **PlaceHolderMain** region, click **Click here to select a data source**. In the **Data Source Picker** dialog box, under **Database Connections**, click <table> on <database name> (for example, **Customers on Northwind**), and then click **OK**.

The Data Source Details task pane displays an XML root element named *ds-QueryResponse*, which contains *NewDataSet* and *Row* child elements. The *Row* child element contains the column names from the table or view you selected.

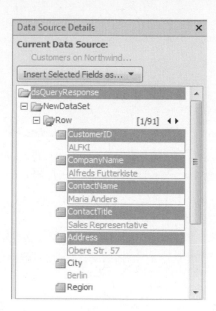

 CLEAN UP Leave SharePoint Designer open if you are continuing to the next exercise.

Using Linked Sources

Most organizations have data sources that contain interrelated data. For example, before customers purchase products, you might have to prepare estimates. After they place their orders, you have to prepare invoices. And, of course, you need to know where to send the products. The estimate, the invoice, and the customer contact information all contain related data. In the Data Sources gallery, you can combine two or more related data sources so that you can expose the data in one Data View.

SharePoint Designer provides you with two options for combining related data:

- **Merge** Use to combine data sources with the same set of fields. For example, you might store invoice data in many locations.

- **Join** Use to combine data sources that have one field in common. For example, a customer reference number might link the customer details data source and the invoice details data source.

In this exercise, you combine two data sources into one linked data source and then display the data from the linked data source in a Data View.

> **SET UP** Using SharePoint Designer, open the site you used in the previous exercise. Open the DataSourceTest.aspx page and the Data Sources gallery page if they are not already open.

Linked Data Source

1. On the **Data Sources** tab, click **Linked Data Source**.

   The Data Source Properties dialog box opens.

2. Click **Configure Linked Source** to start the **Link Data Sources Wizard**.

3. In the **Available Data Sources** list, under **SharePoint Lists**, click **Products**, and then click **Add**. Under **XML Files**, click **Consignments.xml**, and then click **Add**.

   Note Consignments.xml is a file stored in Site Assets. This means that the data connection for this XML file was dynamically created when you created the site from the practice .wsp file.

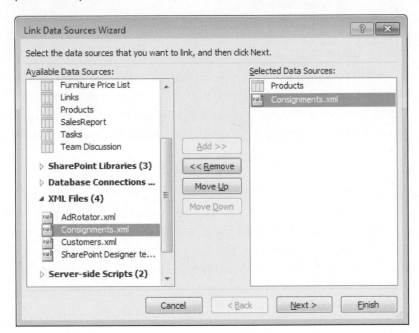

4. Click **Next** to display the next page of the **Link Data Sources Wizard**.

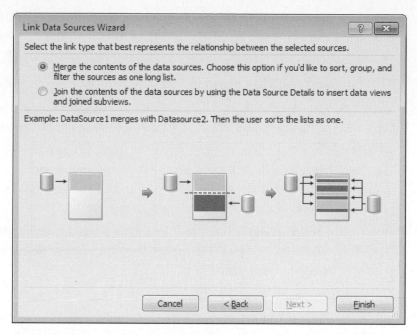

5. Click **Join the contents of the data sources by using the Data Source Details to insert data views and joined subviews**, and then click **Finish**.

    The Link Data Sources Wizard closes. The Data Source Properties dialog box displays two data sources, Products and Consignments.xml.

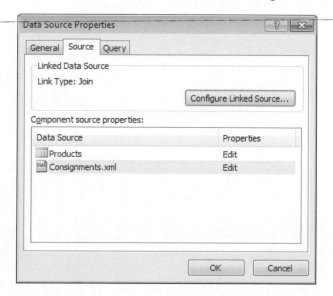

6. On the **General** tab, in the **Name** box, type **Consignments**, and then click **OK** to close the **Data Source Properties** dialog box.

   The Consignments linked data source appears in the Data Sources gallery page.

7. Click the **DataSourceTest.aspx** tab.

8. In the **PlaceHolderMain** region, click **Click here to select a data source**. In the **Data Source Picker** dialog box, under **Linked Sources**, click **Consignments**, and then click **OK**.

   The Data Source Details task pane displays an XML root element named *dsQuery-Response*, with two child elements, *Products* and *Consignments*. You may have to scroll down to see the *Consignments* child element.

9. In the **Data Source Details** task pane, under the **Products** element, click **Title**. Hold down the **Ctrl** key, click **Description**, then click **Insert Selected Fields as**, and then click **Multiple Item View**.

   The DataFormWebPart control shows data from the Products list.

Insert Right

10. In the **DataFormWebPart** control, click **Description**, and then on the **Table** tab, click **Insert Right** in the **Rows & Columns** group.

11. Click a cell in the second row of the new column. In the **Data Source Details** task pane, under the **Shipments** child element, hold down the **Ctrl** key and click **ConsignmentNumber**, **CustomerName**, and **CollectionDate**. Click **Insert Selected Fields as**, and then click **Joined Subview**.

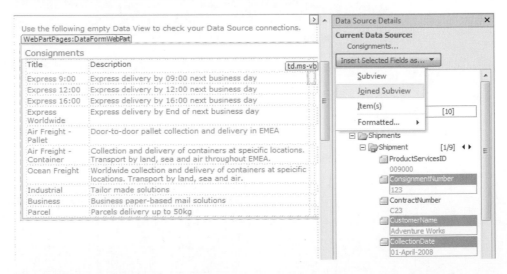

The Join Subview dialog box opens.

12. Under **Row**, click **ProductServicesID**, and under **Shipment**, click **ProductServicesID** to join the Products list items to the consignment data.

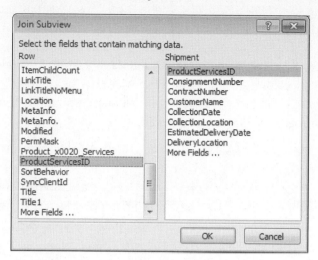

13. Click **OK** to close the **Join Subview** dialog box.

The DataFormWebPart control shows the columns from the Products list and data from the Consignments.xml file.

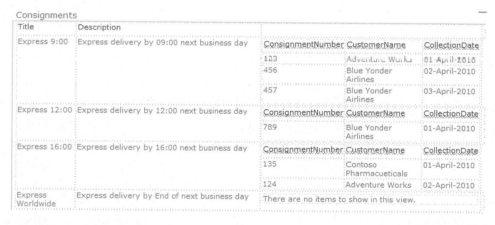

 **CLEAN UP** Close and save DataSourceTest.aspx. Close the Data Source Details task pane. Leave SharePoint Designer open if you are continuing to the next exercise.

Connecting Web Parts

Web Parts, including the XSLT List View (XLV) and Data View Web Parts, can exchange data—even when different companies produce the Web Parts, and as long as they adhere to the Web Part connection interface specification. One Web Part acts as a data provider, and the other acts as a consumer of the data. A Web Part developer can choose to implement both the consumer and provider interfaces, one of the interfaces, or neither interface. You can use a browser or SharePoint Designer to connect Web Parts, but SharePoint Designer provides you with additional options.

Typically, you connect Web Parts so that when you click an item in one Web Part, the contents in one or more other Web Parts change. The data sources that supply content to both provider and consumer Web Parts must share a common field that you use to link the Web Parts. When you use the browser or SharePoint Designer, you do not need to display this common field in both Web Parts to create the Web Part connection. By using SharePoint Designer, you can connect two Web Parts on the same page as well as Web Parts on different pages.

Note A Web Part cannot be connected to itself, either directly or through a series of Web Part connections.

In this exercise, you create a Web Part connection to a Web Part on another page.

 SET UP Using SharePoint Designer, open the site you used in the previous exercise if it is not already open.

1. In the **Navigation** pane, click **Site Pages**, and then double-click the icon to the left of **Products.aspx** to open the page in edit mode.

2. In the **PlaceHolderMain** region, click **Products** to select the **XsltListViewWebPart**, and then on the **Web Part** tab, click **Add Connection** in the **Connections** group.

   The Web Part Connections Wizard starts.

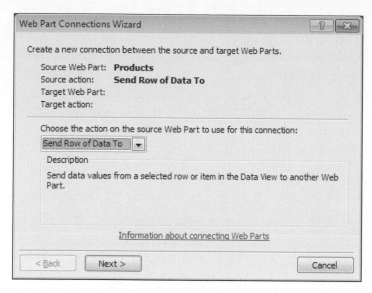

3. Click **Next** to display the second page of the **Web Part Connections Wizard**.

> **Note** The first option, Connect To A Web Part On This Page, is not available because no other Web Parts are on this page.

4. Click **Browse** to open the **Edit Hyperlink** dialog box.

5. Double-click **SitePages**, and then click **Consignments.aspx**.

The Address text box now contains SitePages/Consignments.aspx.

6. Click **OK** to close the **Edit Hyperlink** dialog box.

In the Web Part Connections Wizard, the Page box contains Consignments.aspx.

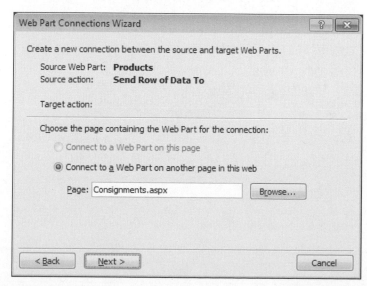

7. Click **Next** to display the third page of the **Web Part Connections Wizard**. Leave **Target Web Part**, **Consignments.xml** and **Target action**, **Get Filter Values From** selected, and then click **Next** to display the fourth page of the **Web Part Connections Wizard**.

8. Click the last cell under **Columns in Products**. Click the down arrow that appears in the cell, scroll down the list, and then click **ProductServicesID**.

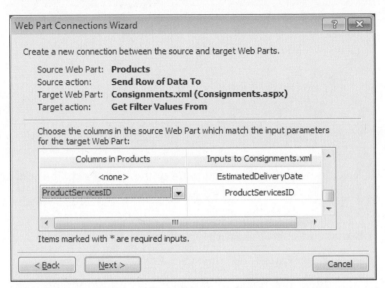

9. Click **Next** to display the fifth page of the **Web Part Connections Wizard**, and then click **Finish** to close the **Web Part Connections Wizard**.

   Both Products.aspx and Consignments.aspx open with an asterisk on their page tabs.

10. Save both pages.

   Tip If the asterisk reappears on the tab when you try to save the pages, close the Consignments.aspx tab and click Yes to save changes.

11. Display **Products.aspx** in the browser.

A two-way diagonal arrow appears to the left of each row.

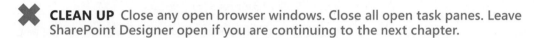
Two-way arrow

12. Under **Express**, click the two-way diagonal arrow to the left of **Express 9:00**.

The Consignments.aspx page is displayed in a Multiple Item Form Data View format, showing three consignments for the Express 9:00 delivery service.

Tip To use SharePoint Designer to remove a Web Part connection, click the Web Part, and then on the Web Part tab, click Manage Connections to display the Web Part Connections dialog box. Select the connection you want to remove, and then click Remove.

✖ CLEAN UP Close any open browser windows. Close all open task panes. Leave SharePoint Designer open if you are continuing to the next chapter.

Key Points

- With the Data Sources gallery page, you can create and manage data connections to a variety of data sources, including lists, libraries, XML files, RSS feeds, server-side scripts, SOAP services, REST services, and databases.

- Data connections describe a location and query that the SharePoint Data Retrieval Service uses to obtain data from a data sources.

- The Data Retrieval Services on the Web server return data in an XML format that SharePoint Designer and Data Views understand.

- SharePoint Designer dynamically creates a data connection for each list, library, and XML file in the Site Assets library or at the root of the site.

- You can copy and modify a data connection, specifying a different set of fields, filters, or sort order for a specific data source.

- The fields and filters defined in a data connection control the amount of data that is retrieved from the data source. Consider carefully your data connection configuration to minimize the load on the Web servers, the amount of data transmitted over the network, and the time to render a page.

- Web Parts, including XLV Web Parts and Data Views, can exchange data by using Web Part connections.

Chapter at a Glance

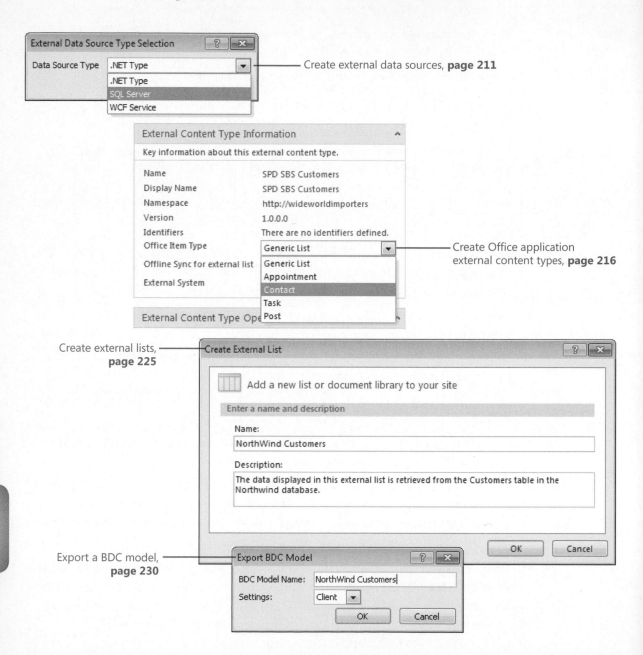

External Data Source Type Selection

Data Source Type .NET Type

.NET Type
SQL Server
WCF Service

Create external data sources, **page 211**

External Content Type Information

Key information about this external content type.

Name   SPD SBS Customers
Display Name   SPD SBS Customers
Namespace   http://wideworldimporters
Version   1.0.0.0
Identifiers   There are no identifiers defined.
Office Item Type   Generic List

Generic List
Appointment
Contact
Task
Post

Offline Sync for external list
External System

Create Office application
external content types, **page 216**

External Content Type Ope

Create external lists,
page 225

Create External List

Add a new list or document library to your site

Enter a name and description

Name:

NorthWind Customers

Description:

The data displayed in this external list is retrieved from the Customers table in the
Northwind database.

OK   Cancel

Export a BDC model,
page 230

Export BDC Model

BDC Model Name: NorthWind Customers

Settings: Client

OK   Cancel

7 Using Business Connectivity Services

In this chapter, you will learn how to

✔ Create database external data sources.

✔ Create external content types.

✔ Create Office application external content types.

✔ Create and manage external lists.

✔ Work with Office application external content types.

✔ Export and use the BDC model.

✔ Create a profile page and use associations.

✔ Manage external content types.

Microsoft Office SharePoint Server 2007 introduced functionality that allows companies to present data from back-end applications on Web pages and as column values in lists and libraries. The Microsoft *Business Connectivity Services (BCS)*, originally called the *Business Data Catalog*, was one component of this functionality and is now available in both Microsoft SharePoint Foundation 2010 and Microsoft SharePoint Server 2010. The definitions that allow BCS to connect to back-end applications can also be used to reveal external data in Microsoft Office 2010 applications, including Microsoft Outlook 2010, Microsoft Access 2010, Microsoft SharePoint Workspace 2010, Microsoft Word 2010, Microsoft InfoPath 2010, and Microsoft Excel 2010. Microsoft SharePoint Designer 2010 is one of the main tools you use to create these BCS connection definitions, and you can also use it to create views and data entry forms with the Data Form Web Part (DFWP).

In this chapter you will learn what BCS is. You learn how to define external data sources and how to create external content types from those data sources. You also learn how to create an external content type that can work with Office 2010 applications. Using these external content types, you will learn how to create an external list and how to export and use the BDC model so that you can import the model into other SharePoint environments or use it with Office applications. Readers who have the Enterprise edition of

SharePoint Server 2010 will learn how to create profile pages and use associations, which can be used with Business Data Web Parts.

> **Practice Files** Before you can use the practice files in this chapter, you need to install them from the book's companion Web site. For more information about practice file requirements, see "Using the Practice Files" on page xxiii.

What Is Business Connectivity Services?

BCS bridges the gap between various applications that a company uses and the company's need to surface key business data from those applications into SharePoint. These applications can include Siebel, CRM, and SAP, and the data from the applications needs to appear in SharePoint sites, lists, search functions, and user profiles. In the context of BCS, these applications are known as *external systems*. By using BCS, a company can accomplish the following objectives:

- Reduce or eliminate the code required to access line-of-business (LOB) systems.

- Achieve deeper integration of data in places where a user works.

- Centralize deployment of connection definitions for use by both BCS and Office applications. This capability is a major advantage of BCS over the connection methods described in Chapter 6, "Working with Data Sources," where each site owner needs to acquire connection details of the external system data.

- Reduce latency to access and manipulate data. Once an external system is defined in BCS, the connection definition is available in all site collections in Web applications within the same service application group. Then, in the browser, data from the external systems can be presented by using the XSLT List View (XLV) Web Part on Web pages and **business data columns** in lists and libraries. On SharePoint Server Enterprise edition, the Business Data Web Parts are available to present data from the external systems. In addition, users who can use SharePoint Designer on their sites can create a DFWP. Both an XLV Web Part and a DFWP can be used to create views or data entry forms that can create, read, update, and display (CRUD) data from the external systems.

- Centralize data security and auditing.
- Perform structured data searches when a company uses SharePoint Server.

Note You cannot complete the BCS central administration of external systems by using SharePoint Designer. Your server administrator can delegate these tasks to you, but you need to use the SharePoint 2010 Central Administration Web site to complete these tasks. The description of these tasks are outside the scope of this book.

See Also More information on managing BCS from a SharePoint administrator's perspective can be found in *Microsoft SharePoint 2010 Administrator's Companion*, by Bill English, Brian Alderman, and Mark Ferraz (Microsoft Press, 2011) and at *technet.microsoft.com/en-us/library/ ee661742.aspx*.

The BCS is divided into three areas:

- **Connectivity** Before you can access data from an external system, SharePoint must know how to connect to that external system and the authentication method to use. Then you can define the data you want to use from the external system. The connection information is stored in a *Business Data Connectivity (BDC)* model that is used to create *external content types (ECT)*, also known as entities.

- **Presentation** External data can be presented in Office 2010 applications and in SharePoint by using *external lists*, business data columns, business data search, user profile properties, and Web Parts. An external list is created from an ECT. The connectivity layer of BCS, the BDC layer, uses the information in the ECT to connect to the external system to display the data in the external list.

- **Tools** SharePoint Designer 2010 and Microsoft Visual Studio 2010 are ECT designers, as are some third-party tools, such as BCS Meta Man from LightningTools, which can be found at *lightningtools.com/*. The ECT is the basic building block for using external data within SharePoint. These tools allow information workers, business analysts, and developers to define the BDC model, author the ECT, and create dashboards and composite applications based on data from the external systems.

See Also You can learn more about external content types in the SharePoint SDK at *msdn. microsoft.com/en-us/library/ee556391(office.14).aspx* and on the Microsoft Business Connectivity Services Team blog at *blogs.msdn.com/b/bcs*.

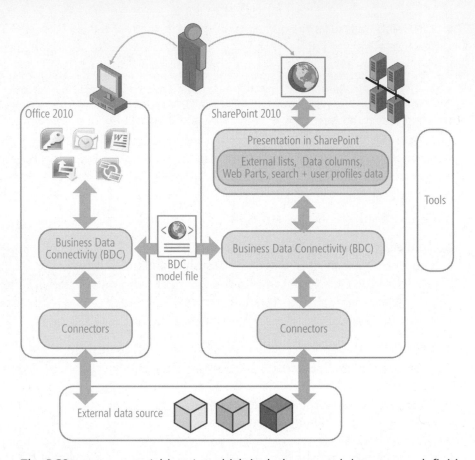

The BCS components (objects)—which include external data source definitions, ECTs, and their associated operations—are stored centrally in a BCS SQL Server database, known as the *BDC Metadata Store*. Therefore, once they are created, the BCS components are available for use by other sites. Because BCS components are not stored as part of a site, they are not included in a site template. However, you can export the definitions into an XML file known as the *BDC model file*. Then, using the SharePoint 2010 Central Administration Web site or Windows PowerShell, the BDC model can be imported into a SharePoint installation. You use the BDC model file when you want to connect directly to the external system from an Office 2010 application.

The easiest and most effective way to connect to an external system is to use SharePoint Designer. The advantage of using BCS over the methods described in Chapter 6 is that you need to define external data source connections only once as an ECT, and then you can use that ECT on many sites. You also have the capability of using single sign-on when the Secure Store Service (SSS) is configured on a SharePoint Server 2010 installation. The disadvantage is that you need to enlist the assistance of the server administrator, because ECTs are stored centrally in the BDC Metadata Store, and not everyone in your organization will have permissions to create or modify ECTs. (In comparison, site owners can create site-level data source definitions, and you do not need any special permissions assigned to you by the server administrator.)

To connect and retrieve data from an external system, the following tasks are required:

- Create an external data source connection.
- Define the operations to retrieve, modify, and delete content stored in that data source as appropriate to your business requirements.
- Create an ECT based on an external data source.
- Use the ECT to present the data from the external data source as an external list, an external data column, a Web Part, or within an Office application.

Creating Database External Data Sources

To connect to external systems, you need to know the data source type, connection properties, and the operations you want to use on the data. The following data source types can be used:

- Databases
- Cloud-based services
- Windows Communication Foundation (WCF) endpoints
- Web services
- .NET assemblies that can gather data from multiple sources
- Custom external systems that have a nonstatic interface that changes dynamically

With SharePoint Designer you can only define external systems that use the data source types SQL Server, .NET, and WCF Service. To define external systems using other data source types, you must use an alternate tool.

See Also You might have external systems that you want to connect to using SharePoint Designer but that do not provide an interface that you can use. One method to work around this situation is to expose the data from your external system as a Web service. The Microsoft Business Connectivity Services team has a two-part blog titled "Making Web Services BCS Friendly." The first part of the series can be found at *blogs.msdn.com/b/bcs/ archive/2009/11/18/making-web-services-bcs-friendly-part-1.aspx.*

The connection properties include the authentication mechanism you are going to use to connect to the external data source. External data sources are not an integral component of a SharePoint installation, so you need to configure the authentication method that will be used to retrieve, modify, and delete (if appropriate) the data from an external data source. In SharePoint Designer the following BCS authentication modes can be defined:

- **User's Identity** When a user requests a SharePoint page that displays data from an external data source, SharePoint sends the user's credentials to the external data source and allows the external data source to decide whether that user is allowed access. In most installations, to use Windows authentication credentials, your server administrator needs to configure a computer network authentication protocol named Kerberos; otherwise, a login-failed message is displayed. Your server administrator might know this authentication mode as *PassThrough*.

- **Impersonate Windows Identity** Both this and the next authentication mode require the use of SSS and are available only on SharePoint Server.

- **Impersonate Custom Identity** Credentials mapped in a database are sent to the external data source.

- **BDC Identity** SharePoint passes a special user name to the external data source for authentication purposes. This user name has a high level of privileges on a SharePoint installation. Therefore, Microsoft does not recommend the use of this authentication mode, and it is disabled by default. BDC Identity is also known as *RevertToSelf.*

See Also For more information on authenticating to your external system and the BCS built-in permissions, see the Microsoft Business Connectivity Services team blogs at *blogs.msdn.com/b/ bcs/archive/2010/03/12/authenticating-to-your-external-system.aspx*, *blogs.msdn.com/b/bcs/ archive/2009/11/24/permissions-in-business-connectivity-services.aspx*, and *blogs.msdn.com/b/ ericwhite/archive/2010/06/18/consuming-a-claims-enabled-wcf-web-service-as-an-sharepoint- 2010-external-content-type.aspx.*

You can define or modify external data sources only by using the Operations Design view of an ECT settings page. To define external system content source definitions, ECT operations, and ECTs in SharePoint Designer, your server administrator must give you the Edit permission on the Metadata Store.

In this exercise, you create an external data source for a SQL Server database.

SET UP Before you can complete this exercise, you must obtain from your server administrator the name of the computer running SQL Server, the database name, and the authentication method that you use to connect to the database. Your database administrator might want to use the Northwind sample database, which can be found at Microsoft's download site (*www.microsoft.com/downloads*) by using the search keywords northwind sample databases.

 SET UP Using SharePoint Designer, open the site you created and modified in earlier chapters. If you did not create a team site, follow the steps in Chapter 1 before you begin this exercise.

1. In the **Navigation** pane, click **External Content Types**.

   The External Content Types gallery page is displayed in the workspace. The workspace might be empty if no ECTs have been created.

External Content Types

2. On the **External Content Types** tab, click **External Content Type** in the **New** group.

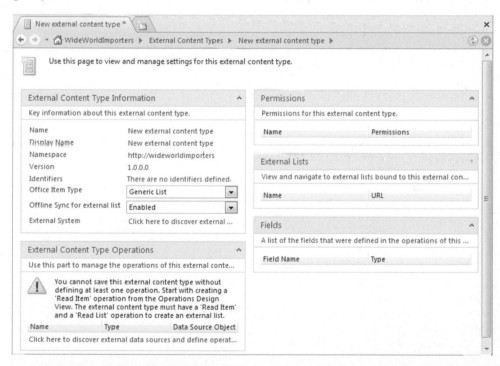

   The External Content Type settings page is displayed with an asterisk on the label. On the External Content Types tab, the Operations Design View command in the View group is active.

3. In the **External Content Type Information** area, to the right of **External System**, click **Click here to discover external data sources and define operations**.

The ECT Operation Designer view is displayed. On the External Content Types tab in the Views group, the Summary View command is active and the Operations Design View command is inactive.

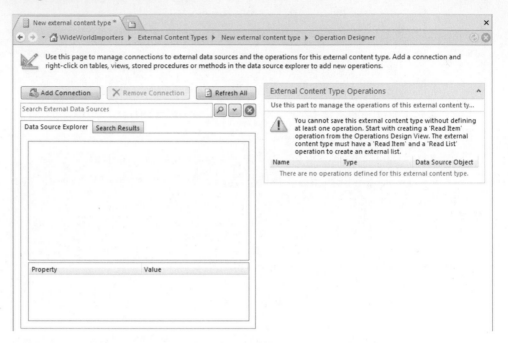

Tip You can switch between the ECT Summary and Operations Design views by using the two commands in the Views group on the External Content Types tab.

4. Click **Add Connection**.

The External Data Source Type Selection dialog box opens.

5. In the **Data Source Type** list, select **SQL Server**.

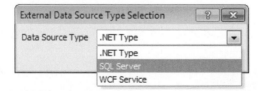

6. Click **OK.**

The SQL Server Connection dialog box opens.

7. In the **Database Server** box, type the name of the server computer. In the **Database Name** box, type the name of your SQL Server database (such as **Northwind**), and in the **Name (optional)** box, type **SPD SBS NorthWind** so that

you can identify the connection. Next, select the authentication method you are going to use to connect to the SQL Server computer.

8. Click **OK** to close the **SQL Server Connection** dialog box.

In the Operations Design view, SPD SBS NorthWind is displayed on the Data Source Explorer tab.

Note The database is now registered centrally as an external system and can be used by other users in other sites. In the SharePoint 2010 Central Administration Web site, the external system is named *northwind*. Your server administrators might also see an external system named SharePoint-<databasename>-<userid>-<guid>, where <database> is the name of the SQL Server database,<userid> is the user name of the person who created the external system, and <guid> is a randomly generated number. For example, the full name might be SharePointDesigner-northwind-Peter-22e0dc02-e54c-4084-9f04-719dbbaccf39. This entry in the BDC Metadata Store is created if a connection definition is created prior to the external creation of the ECT.

9. Expand **SPD SBS NorthWind**, **Tables**, **Orders** and **Columns**. Then click **ShipName**.

The schema of the external system is displayed, including primary keys for each table and the properties for each field. The Data Source Explorer can be used to explore SQL Server database views and routines.

Summary View

10. On the **External Content Types** tab, click **Summary View** in the **Views** group.

✖ CLEAN UP Leave SharePoint Designer open if you are continuing to the next exercise.

Creating External Content Types

When you create an ECT, you can select the external data source (if it was previously defined) or define a new content source and the create, read, update, and display (CRUD) operations you want to execute on that external data source. SharePoint Designer provides you with an Operations Wizard to create the access methods you want for your solution. The Operations Wizard consists of three pages:

- **Operation Properties** Consists of the operation name, operation display name, and operation type. When you create operations for a database external data source, there is an option to create all operations by running the operations wizard once. In this scenario, the operation properties are automatically generated, and the operation names will be Create, Read Item, Update, Delete, and Read List.

- **Parameters** On this page you can select the fields, known as *elements*, you use in your solution. The Properties section displays properties you can modify for each data source element, including the identifier name, field name, and name of the field when it is displayed in the browser. You must select at least one field to be shown in the external item picker control. By default, all fields are shown in the external item picker. If the external data source has a large number of fields, displaying them all in the external item picker might confuse users. Therefore, it is better to select a small set of elements that best describes an item.

- **Filter Parameters** Use to optimize the data that is returned from the external system. The filter types available are Comparison, Limit, Page Number, Timestamp, and Wildcard. For string data types, use the Wildcard filter type because this is translated internally to a LIKE clause in queries to get the data.

Once the operations for the data source are configured, you have created a BDC model. When you click the Save command, the BDC model is stored in the BDC Metadata Store.

In this exercise, you create operations for a data source and define the parameters the operations use.

SET UP Using SharePoint Designer, open the site you used in the previous exercise if it is not already open. Display the Summary view of the external content type you created in the previous exercise.

1. In the **External Content Type Information** area, to the right of **Name**, click **New external content type**, and type **SPD SBS Orders**.

2. To the right of **Display Name**, click **New external content type**.

The text *SPD SBS Orders* is copied to the right of Display Name.

Troubleshooting If an External Content Type Rename Confirmation dialog box is displayed, stating that an ECT with the name SPD SBS Orders already exists, click Yes to rename your content type to SPD SBS Orders (xx), where xx are your initials.

Operations
Design View

3. On the **External Content Types** tab, click **Operations Design View** in the **Views** group. On the **Data Source Explorer** tab, expand **SPD SBS NorthWind** and expand **Tables**, if it is not already expanded.

4. Right-click a table, such as **Orders**, and then click the operation you want to create, such as **Create All Operations**.

Note Database connections have the Create All Operations option available. The option is not available in other data source types.

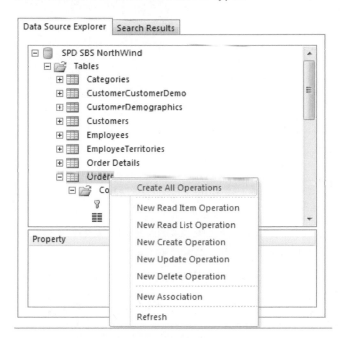

The All Operations dialog box opens. In the Errors And Warnings box is a list of errors and warnings that let you know what information still needs to be provided to complete the operation specification.

5. Click **Next**.

   The second page of the All Operations dialog box—Parameters Configuration—is displayed.

6. Under **Data Source Elements**, select **OrderDate**, and be sure you have not cleared the check box to the left of **OrderDate**.

7. Under **Properties**, in the **Display Name** box, place the insertion point between **Order** and **Date**, and then press **Space**. Then select the check box to the right of **Show In Picker**.

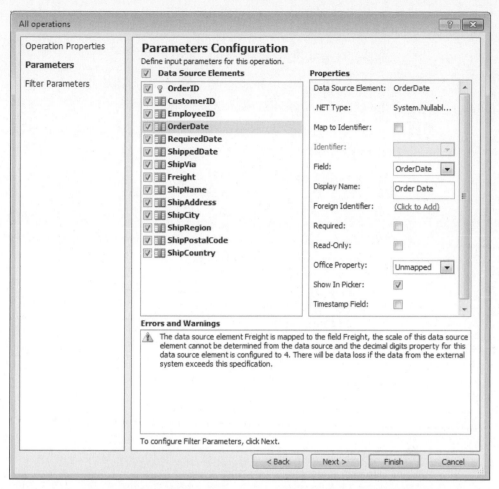

8. Repeat step 7 so that the display names of the fields **OrderID**, **CustomerID**, and **ShipName** are **Order ID**, **Customer ID** and **Ship Name**, and that all three fields will appear in the picker. Click **Next**.

    The third page of the All Operations dialog box—Filter Parameters Configuration—is displayed.

9. Click **Add Filter Parameter**.

    The OrderID element is listed under Filter Parameters, and the properties of OrderID are displayed under Properties.

10. Under **Properties**, to the right of **Filter**, click **Click to Add**.

    The Filter Configuration dialog box opens.

11. In the **New Filter** box, delete **Filter**, and then type **Top 100 Orders**. Then, under **Filter Properties**, in the **Filter Type** list, select **Limit**.

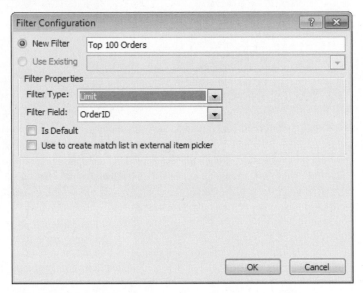

12. Click **OK**. The Filter Configuration dialog box closes.

    In the All Operations dialog box, under Properties, Top 100 Orders: Limit is displayed to the right of Filter.

13. Under **Properties**, in the **Default Value** list, highlight the text **<<None>>,** and type **100**.

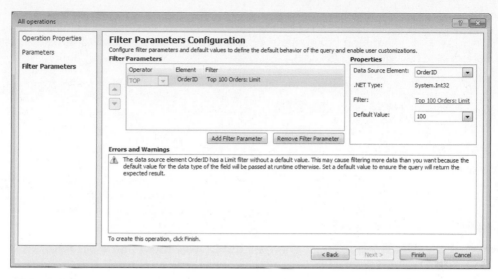

14. Click **Finish**.

    The All Operations dialog box closes. In the External Content Type Operations area
    of the Operations Design view, the five operations—Create, Read Item, Update,
    Delete, and Read List—are displayed. On the External Content Types tab, the com-
    mands in the Operation group are now active.

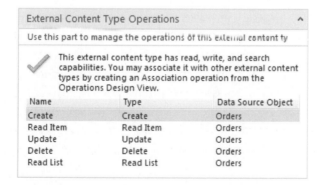

Note The operations, data source element, and parameter information are now
registered centrally as a BDC model and can be used by other users in other sites.
In the SharePoint 2010 Central Administration Web site, the BDC model is named
SharePoint-<databasename>-<userid>-<guid>, where <database> is the name
of the SQL Server database,<userid> is the user name of the person who created
the external system, and <guid> is a randomly generated number (for example,
SharePointDesigner-northwind-Peter-22e0dc02-e54c-4084-9f04-719dbbaccf39).

Save

15. On the Quick Access Toolbar, click **Save**.

A dialog box is displayed briefly, stating that SharePoint is storing the ECT to the BDC Metadata Store.

Troubleshooting If an error dialog box is displayed stating that saving the ECT failed, you are probably saving an ECT without connecting it to an external content source and have not defined at least one operation on that content source. Complete the previous two exercises, and then return to this step.

The label name changes to SPD SBS Orders, and the asterisk disappears.

 CLEAN UP Leave SharePoint Designer open if you are continuing to the next exercise.

Creating Office Application External Content Types

Microsoft made it possible to display external data in Office applications. You can also take the external data offline by using Microsoft Outlook and Microsoft SharePoint Workspace. A user can connect external lists with these two Office applications. Behind the scenes, a BDC model is packaged and deployed to the user's computer. Microsoft categorizes this type of a solution, in which a user clicks a button to deploy the BDC model, as a *BCS simple solution*. To assist in tight integration, especially with Microsoft Outlook and external lists, before you define the operations of an ECT, you must specify whether a user is allowed to take the data presented in an external list offline. You also need to configure the Office item type, of which there are four:

● Appointment

● Contact

● Task

● Post

When you define the data source operations, you map data source elements to Office properties. The mapping of elements to Office properties can be configured only when an operation is created. You cannot change the Office item type or the mappings after the operations are created. Be sure you plan the current and future use of your ECTs before you create them. Also, you can only choose to map those elements that have a compatible Office properties data type.

In this exercise, you create a new ECT and map it to the Contact Office item type.

SET UP Using SharePoint Designer, open the team site you used in the previous exercise if it is not already open.

External Content Type

1. In the **Navigation** pane, click **External Content Types**, and then on the **External Content Types** tab, click **External Content Type**.

2. In the **External Content Type Information** area, to the right of **Name**, click **New external content type**, and then type **SPD SBS Customers**.

3. To the right of **Display Name**, click **New external content type**. SPD SBS Customers is copied to Display Name.

4. In the **Office Item Type** list, select **Contact**.

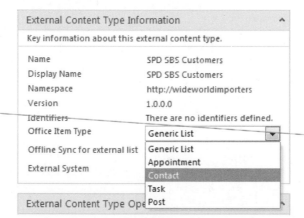

5. In the **External Content Type Information** area, to the right of **External System**, click **Click here to discover external data sources and define operations**.

   The Operations Design view of the ECT is displayed.

6. On the **Data Source Explorer** tab, right-click a table, such as **Customers**, and then click the operation you want to create, such as **Create All Operations**.

7. In the **All operations** dialog box, click **Next**.

   The Parameters Configuration page is displayed.

8. Under **Data Source Elements**, select **CompanyName** (be sure you do not clear the check box), and then under **Properties**, in the **Office Property** list, select **Company Name (CompanyName)**.

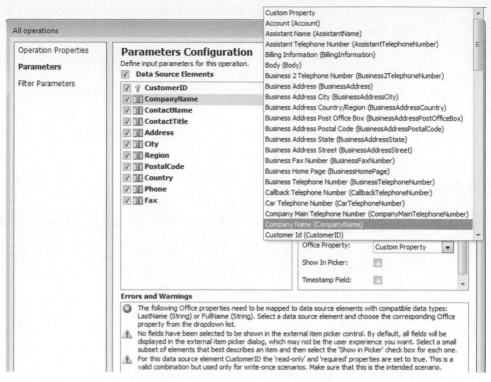

9. Repeat the previous step to map the following data resource elements to matching Office properties:

Data source element	Office property
Contact Name	Full Name (FullName)
Contact Title	Job Title (JobTitle)
Address	Business Address (BusinessAddress)
City	Business Address City (BusinessAddressCity)
Region	Business Address State (BusinessAddressState)
Postal Code	Business Address Postal Code (BusinessAddressPostalCode)
Country	Business Address Country/Region (BusinessAddressCountry)
Phone	Business Telephone Number (BusinessTelephoneNumber)
Fax	Business Fax Number (BusinessFaxNumber)

10. Click **Next**, and then click **Finish**.

The All Operations dialog box closes, and the five operations are listed in Operations Design view.

11. Right-click the **SPD SBS Customers** tab, and then click **Save**.

12. On the workspace breadcrumb, click **External Content Types**.

The External Content Types gallery page is displayed.

 **CLEAN UP** Leave SharePoint Designer open if you are continuing to the next exercise.

Creating and Managing External Lists

No matter which version of SharePoint 2010 you have installed, the preferred method of displaying data from external data sources is to use an external list. Depending on the operations you have specified in an ECT, an external list can provide CRUD capabilities. The external list can also be added to a SharePoint page as an XLV Web Part or a Data View. This lets you configure additional columns, conditional formatting, and sorting and grouping in the browser and in SharePoint Designer.

Note If you have SharePoint Server 2010 Enterprise edition, you can also use the Business Data Web Parts.

You create external lists by using the browser, SharePoint Designer, Windows PowerShell, or code. After you create these lists, you will find that they have similar functionally to other SharePoint lists. However, you cannot associate RSS feeds to external lists. There is also no Datasheet view, nor can you bind workflows to the data—because the data is not in SharePoint, you cannot trigger workflows on data changes. However, using SharePoint Designer, you can create a site, list, or reusable workflow that accesses one or more external lists.

Although you might have permissions to create a BDC model, an ECT, and external lists, you might not be able to see the data in the external list or on a page that contains an external list XLV Web Part. Using the SharePoint 2010 Central Administration Web site, a server administrator can set permissions on data source elements, and once you have created an ECT, your SharePoint installation can be configured to not allow anyone to see the data from the external data source. However, other systems or users—those using Office applications, for example—might be able to connect directly to the external system without using the BCS permissions you have configured in SharePoint. You might need to contact your server administrator before you can progress further with your solution.

External lists can be created and managed from the Lists And Libraries gallery page, the Data Sources gallery page, and from the ECT settings page.

In this exercise, you create an external list and a new list view page for that external list. You will check that you have permission to the ECT before modifying the list view.

 SET UP Ask your SharePoint server administrator to give you permissions to the two ECTs you created in the previous exercises. For a list of steps that a SharePoint administrator follows to set permissions on an ECT, see Appendix C on page 503 and refer to Chapter 18, "Aggregating External Data Sources," in *Microsoft SharePoint 2010 Administrator's Companion*.

 SET UP Using SharePoint Designer, open the site you used in the previous exercise, and then open the External Content Types gallery page if it is not already open.

External List

1. Click the icon to the left of **SPD SBS Customers**, and then on the **External Content Types** tab, click **External List** in the **New** group.

   The Create External List dialog box opens.

2. In the **Name** box, type **NorthWind Customers**, and in the **Description** box type **The data displayed in this external list is retrieved from the Customer table in the Northwind database**.

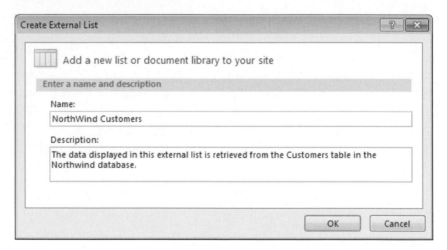

3. Click **OK**.

   The NorthWind Customers list settings page is displayed. In the Views area, one view is listed: SPD SBS Customers Read List. In the Forms area, three forms are listed, DispForm.aspx, EditForm.aspx, and NewForm.aspx. The view and the three forms use the XLV Web Part to display and update data on the external system.

4. On the **List Settings** tab, click **List View** in the **New** group.

   The Create New List View dialog box opens.

5. In the **Name** box, type **ByCountry**.

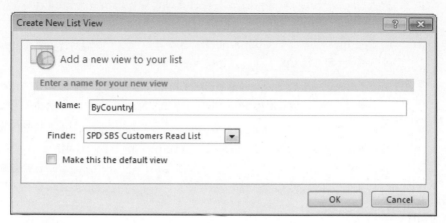

6. Click **OK**.

The Create New List View dialog box closes. In the Views area, ByCountry appears.

7. In the **Navigation** pane, click **External Content Types**, and then click **SPD SBS Customers**.

The contents of the Permissions area should contain your name or a group of which you are a member and show that you have at least Edit, Execute, and Selectable In Client permissions. The External Lists area contains the name of the external list you created in step 2.

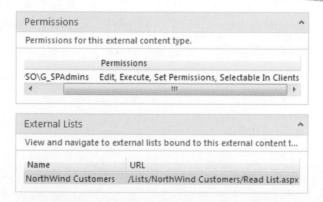

Go to List

8. In the **External Lists** area, click **NorthWind Customers**, and then on the **External Content Types** tab, click **Go to List** in the **Lists & Forms** group.

The NorthWind Customers list settings page is displayed.

9. In the **Views** area, click **ByCountry**.

TheByCountry.aspx page opens in edit mode.

Note When your site is created on a SharePoint Server installation, you have the option of replacing the existing browser forms with InfoPath forms by clicking the Design Forms In InfoPath command on the List Settings tab.

10. In **Design** view, click **CustomerID**, and then on the **List View Tools, Options** tab, click **Sort & Group**.

11. In the **Sort and Group** dialog box, under **Available fields**, click **Country**, and then click **Add**. Under **Group Properties**, click **Show group header**. Click **OK**.

The Sort And Group dialog box closes, and the XsltListViewWebPart displays the contents from the Northwind database grouped by country.

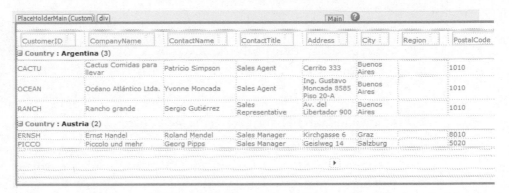

Note The XLV Web Part in SharePoint Designer will show only five items from the Northwind database, even though the Customer table has more rows. When you use the browser to request ByCountry.aspx, the rows returned are grouped in sets of 30 items.

12. Save **ByCountry.aspx**, and then on the **Navigation** pane, click **Data Sources**.

The Data Sources gallery page opens. NorthWind Customers is displayed under External Lists.

 **CLEAN UP** Leave SharePoint Designer open if you are continuing to the next exercise.

Working with Office Application External Content Types

Whenever you create an ECT, you must test whether your data source definitions are correct. For an Office application ECT—one for which you selected an Office item type, mapped elements to Office properties, and enabled offline use of the external data—this means connecting the external data to an Office 2010 application, such as Outlook or SharePoint Workspace. In Outlook, for example, depending on the Office item type chosen, the external list can be shown in the Contacts, Calendar, or Tasks pane, as well as in the SharePoint External Lists folder. If you mapped a data source element to the Office e-mail property, you should be able to use Outlook to send an e-mail message to the person whose e-mail address is stored in the external data source.

Note Connecting an external list to Outlook or SharePoint Workspace can only be done from SharePoint Server 2010 with an Enterprise Client Access License. All other servers, including SharePoint Foundation 2010, are not supported by Microsoft.

Office clients have a SQL Server Compact Edition client database installed that caches external data and allows both online (connected) access and offline (disconnected, or cached connection mode) access. If amendments are made while the client is offline, they are stored in the client data cache and committed to the external data source when the client is next online. External lists, unlike other types of lists you connect to, are not controlled by the Outlook Send/Receive settings. External lists are synchronized by default every six hours. When you right-click an external list in Outlook, you can see the synchronization status and when the data was last refreshed from the external system. You can then force synchronization.

See Also The Microsoft Business Data Connectivity Services team blog "Deploying BCS Simple Solutions," found at *blogs.msdn.com/b/bcs/archive/2010/02/25/deploying-bcs-simple-solutions.aspx*, contains details on using external lists with the Connect to Outlook and Sync to SharePoint Workspace options. The MSDN article found at *msdn.microsoft.com/en-us/library/ff677562.aspx* details the use of Excel 2010 with BCS.

In this exercise, you connect an external data source to Outlook. You need Outlook 2010 to complete this exercise.

 SET UP Using the browser, open the site you used in the previous exercise.

1. On the **Quick Launch**, under the **Lists** section, click the name of the external list, such as **NorthWind Customers**.

2. On the **List Tools**, **List** tab, click **Connect to Outlook** in the **Connect & Export** group.

Connect to
Outlook

> **Troubleshooting** If you do not see the Connect To Outlook option, return to the SPD SBS Customers ECT, and in the External Content Type Information area, be sure that the Office Sync For External List option is set to Enabled. Save your changes, and then repeat step 1.

3. If a **Microsoft Office Customization Installer** dialog box is displayed, click **Install** to verify the installation, and then click **Close**.

Outlook opens, and you might be asked to supply your user name and password. In the Outlook navigation pane, under **SharePoint External Lists,** the

<site> - <External List name> list is displayed, where <site> is the name of the site on which the external list was created. Customer details are shown in the main pane.

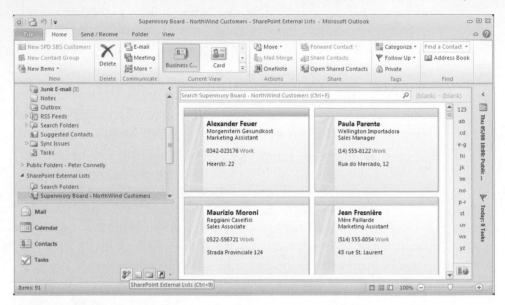

Solution

Troubleshooting If the external list does not appear in the Outlook navigation pane, press **Ctrl** + **F9** or click the Solutions icon at the bottom of the navigation pane.

4. In the Outlook navigation pane, select **Contacts**.

Under **My Contacts,** the <site> - <External List name> list is displayed

Note When you connect a list or library to Outlook, the list or library appears in its respective area of the Outlook navigation pane. Calendars appear in the Calendar pane under Other Calendars; tasks appear in the Tasks pane under Other Tasks; and Contacts lists appear in the Contacts pane under Other Contacts. Discussion lists and libraries appear in a folder in the Mail pane under SharePoint Lists.

 CLEAN UP Close Outlook and close the browser.

Exporting and Using the BDC Model

External content types are metadata objects defined in the BDC model XML file, which usually has the extension *.bdcm*. The BDC model is usually created by a business analyst, a developer, and a database administrator (DBA). Among them, they have the knowledge of the external data source as well as how the data will be used. They might not create the BDC model on the SharePoint installation where it is finally needed. They might create it in a development or prototype environment. Also, even though the BDC model can be created using SharePoint Designer, and part of that creation process stores the BDC model in the BDC Metadata Store, the BDC model may have been created for use with an Office application. Therefore, you need a mechanism for exporting a BDC model from one SharePoint system to another (default export) and to an Office application (client export).

SharePoint Designer can be used to export BDC models that it creates; however, it cannot be used to import BDC models into SharePoint. That is a job for the server administrator and the SharePoint 2010 Central Administration Web site. Again, whatever environment a BDC model is planned for, it must be tested.

Note Not all Office client applications can write to an external system, even though the external system supports the operations and the operations are correctly modeled in the BCS. For example, for Word 2010, BCS exposes read-only data in content controls that map to external data columns in a SharePoint document library. Also, you can import a BDC model into Access 2010 to create read-only tables.

In this exercise, you export a BDC model and then use it to create a linked table in Access 2010. You need Access 2010 to complete this exercise.

 SET UP Using SharePoint Designer, open the site you used in previous exercises.

1. On the **Navigation** pane, click **External Content Types**.

   The External Content Types gallery page is displayed.

Export BDC
Model

2. Click the icon to the left of **SPD SBS Customers**, and then on the **External Content Types** tab, click **Export BDC Model** in the **Manage** group.

   The Export BDC Model dialog box opens.

3. In the **BDC Model Name** box, type **NorthWind Customers**, and in the **Settings** list, select **Client.**

4. Click **OK**. The File Save dialog box opens.

5. Navigate to **Documents**. In the **File name** box, remove the space between **NorthWind** and **Customers** and change the file extension from **bdcm** to **xml** so that the file name appears as **NorthWindCustomers.xml**. Click **Save**.

6. Open Access 2010. The Backstage view of Access is displayed.

7. With **Blank database** selected under **Available Templates**, in the **File Name** box type **SPDSBS.accdb**, and then click **Create**.

8. Right-click the **Table1** tab, and then click **Close**.

More

9. On the **External Data** tab, click **More** in the **Import & Link** group, and then click **Data Services**.

The Create A Link To Data Services dialog box opens.

10. Click **Install new connection**.

The Select A Connection Definition File dialog box opens.

11. Navigate to **Documents**, select NorthWindCustomers.xml, and then click **OK**.

The Select A Connection Definition File dialog box closes, and under Create Link To Data Services, SPD SBS NorthWind is listed.

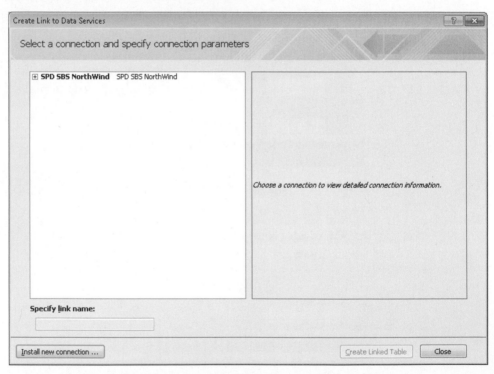

12. Expand **SPD SBS NorthWind**, and then click **SPD SBS Customers**.

The column names from the Customers table are displayed.

13. Click **Create Linked Table**.

The Create A Link To Data Services dialog box closes, and in the Access navigation pane, under Tables, the linked table SPD SBS Customers is listed.

14. Double-click **SPD SBS Customers**.

A tab labeled SPD SBS Customers opens and lists the contents from the Northwind database Customers table.

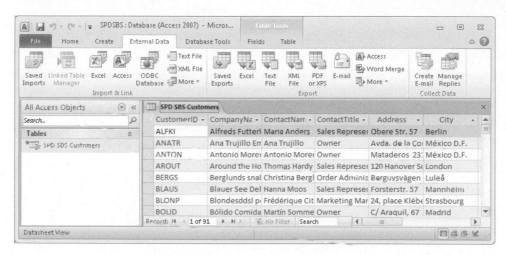

 CLEAN UP Close Access. Leave SharePoint Designer open if you are continuing to the next exercise.

Creating a Profile Page

After you create a BDC model, you need to create a profile page for each ECT, which you can use to view a single row of data from the external system. On the Enterprise edition of SharePoint Server 2010, it is very easy to create a profile page by using SharePoint Designer or the SharePoint 2010 Central Administration Web site, which also creates an external data action named View Profile. This external action is the default action for the ECT. If a user clicks an external data item, she is redirected to the profile page. The profile page consists of a Business Data Item Builder and a Business Data Item Web Part. These Web Parts are available only if you are using the Enterprise edition of SharePoint Server 2010.

Because ECTs can be used on many sites, it is common practice for all profile pages to be hosted at one location. On SharePoint Server, this location is configured by using the SharePoint 2010 Central Administration Web site. For you to create and modify a profile page in SharePoint Designer, the hosted location must be configured and you must have, at minimum, the Add And Customize permission for the hosted location. For a list of steps that a SharePoint administrator can follow to configure the hosted location, see Appendix C on page 503 and refer to Chapter 18 in *Microsoft SharePoint 2010 Administrator's Companion.*

Note For users to render the profile page in the browser, they need read-only permissions on the hosted location.

At first glance, it also seems easy to create a profile page for ECTs created on SharePoint Foundation or the Standard edition of SharePoint Server 2010. When the settings page for an ECT opens in SharePoint Designer, the Create Profile Page command is active. However, when you click the command, a "Server could not complete your request" message appears, with an empty Details dialog box. This message is not a true indication of the error. Ideally, the Create Profile Page command would be inactive for sites created on SharePoint Foundation or the Standard edition of SharePoint Server. To simulate the Create Profile Page command, you need to create a page using Data Views and then create custom actions as detailed in Chapter 3, "Working with Lists and Libraries." Alternatively, a SharePoint server administrator can create an external custom action by using the SharePoint 2010 Central Administration Web site.

Another issue is that after you create a profile page, within SharePoint Designer it is not obvious that one has been created or where it is hosted if one does exist. If you try to create a profile page and one does exist, a dialog box opens asking whether you want to overwrite the page. However, you still do not know the hosted location of the profile page. You can ask your SharePoint server administrator where the page is located or check the location by creating, for example, an *external data column* on an existing list and then looking at the URL where the profile page is located.

An external data column allows you to add data from an ECT to a standard SharePoint list. In SharePoint Server 2007, external data columns were referred to as *business data columns*. You can create many column types in SharePoint Designer, but this does not include external data columns. You can rename and delete external data columns in SharePoint Designer, but you cannot create them. To check whether your profile page was successfully created, you need to use the browser.

Note If an external data column is added to a document library, the column can be made available as a content control in Word 2010. More information can be found at *blogs.msdn. com/b/bcs/archive/2010/02/15/surfacing-business-data-in-word-2010-using-external-data-columns-and-the-external-item-content-control.aspx.*

In this exercise, you create a profile page and test that the profile page was successfully created.

SET UP Using SharePoint Designer; open the site you used in previous exercises if it is not already open.

1. On the **Navigation** pane, click **External Content Types**, and then click **SPD SBS Customers**.

2. On the **External Content Types** tab, click **Create Profile Page** in the **Profile Page** group.

   The Profile Page Creation dialog box opens temporarily while the profile page is created.

   Troubleshooting If you receive an error that the profile page cannot be created until the host site is defined, contact your SharePoint server administrator to configure the hosted location.

3. Open your site in the browser, and then on the Quick Launch, click a list, such as **Tasks**.

   The All Tasks list view page is displayed.

4. On the **List Tools**, **List** tab, click **Create Column** in the **Manage Views** group.

   The Create Column dialog box opens.

Create Column

5. In the **Column name** box, type **Customers**, and then under **The type of information in this column is,** select **External Data**.

   The Create Column dialog box is displayed again.

6. In the **Additional Column Settings** section, in the **External Content Type** box, type **SPD SBS Customers**, and then click the icon to the right of the box that displays the ScreenTip **Check if External Content Type exits**.

7. In the **Select the Field to be shown on this column** list, select **CompanyName** and leave the check box **Link this column to the Default Action of the External Content Type** selected.

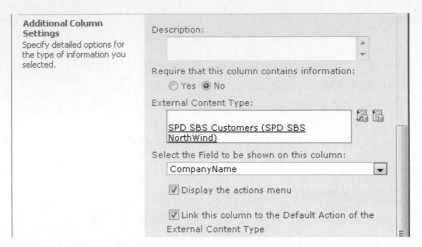

8. At the bottom of the dialog box, click **OK**.

   The All Tasks list view now contains a column labeled Customers.

9. Click **Add new item** to open the **Tasks—New Item** dialog box.

10. In the **Title** box, type **Profile Page Check.** In the **Customers** box, click the second icon to the right of the box, which has the ScreenTip **Select External Item(s).**

    The Choose SPD SBS Customers—Webpage Dialog dialog box opens.

11. Select the first item in the list, click **OK,** and then click **Save**.

    A new task item is added to the All Tasks list view.

12. Under the **Customers** column, click the arrow to the left of the customer's name, and click **View Profile**.

The profile page you created in step 2 is displayed. The URL of the page will have the format *http://<host location>/_bdc/http__<site>/SPD%20%SBS%20Customers. aspx?CustomerID=<value>*, where <site> is the URL of the site where you created the ECT, and <value> is the primary key to retrieve the customer details from the Northwind database.

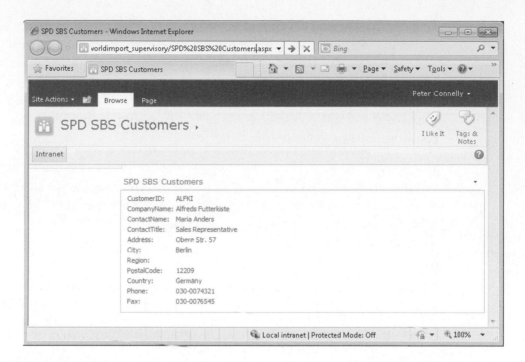

 CLEAN UP Close the browser. Leave SharePoint Designer open if you are continuing to the next exercise.

Using Associations

Associations can be created when there is a relationship between two ECTs, such as customers and orders. Each customer can have one or many orders. This is known as a *one-to-many relationship*. These ECTs could define data from the same external system or two different ones. Customer details might be stored in a CRM system, and order details in a separate external system. Defining an association in an ECT documents this relationship. You do not need to create an association in an ECT to use linked data sources when joining or merging data and displaying the data in a Data View. (See Chapter 6 for more information.) However, you must create an association if you want to use the Business Data Related List Web Part to provide a relationship—a Web Part connection—between the Business Data Related List Web Part and a Business Data List Web Part.

To create an association, at least one field must be common to both ECTs—for example, orders can be identified with a unique customer. Usually the relationship is configured so that the customer field in the orders ECT uses the same value that is the *primary key* field in the customers ECT. The customer field in the orders ECT is known as a *foreign key*. In the Northwind database, the primary key in the Customers table is *CustomerID*, and the foreign key in the Orders table is *CustomerID*. It is common practice to design tables so that the primary key and a foreign key have the same column names—this help identify relationships between tables. You can also create cascading associations. An example of a cascading association is when a customer has many orders and each order consists of many products.

You can use SharePoint Designer to create one-to-many associations when the relationship is defined using foreign keys, including self-referential associations (relating instances of the same external content type). Alternative tools can be used to create other relationships, such as one-to-many and many-to-many relationships, when foreign keys are not used or where a primary key is made from multiple columns, known as a *composite key*.

Warning In an association between two ECTs, SharePoint 2010 cannot ensure the referential integrity between the ECTs, unlike linking two tables in a relational database, where business logic can be used.

On database-based ECTs, you create the association on a table—the same table used to create the other operations. For ECTs based on a Web service or WCF, you create the association on the appropriate Web method. You can add filter parameters to a database-based ECT association but not to a WCF-based association. Reverse associations—that is, you provide an order ID and return the customer associated with that order—cannot be created on a database-based ECT.

See Also The Microsoft Business Connectivity Services team has released a blog post on associations and SharePoint Designer at *blogs.msdn.com/b/bcs/archive/2010/01/15/tooling-associations-in-sharepoint-designer-2010.aspx*. Two short videos on associations and Web Parts are available at *www.youtube.com/watch?v=YibQVIgJQG4* and *www.youtube.com/watch?v=WWvTLXW3lw0*.

In this exercise, you create an association.

 SET UP Using SharePoint Designer, open the team site you used in the previous exercise if it is not already open.

1. In the **Navigation** pane, click **External Content Types**. On the gallery page, click the ECT in which the foreign key is defined, such as **SPD SBS Orders**.

   The SPD SBS Orders settings page is displayed.

Operations
Design View

2. On the **External Content Types** tab, click **Operations Design View**.

3. In the **Data Source Explorer**, expand **SPD SBS NorthWind**, and then expand **Tables**. Right-click **Orders**, and then click **New Associations**.

   Important Always create an association on the ECT that is on the many side of the one-to-many relationship. This is the ECT in which the foreign key is defined, also known as the child ECT.

   The Association Wizard opens.

4. In the **Association Name** box, type **GetOrdersForCustomer**, and in the **Association Display Name** box, type **Get Orders for Customer**.

5. To the right of **Related External Content Type**, click **Browse**.

   The External Content Type Selection dialog box opens.

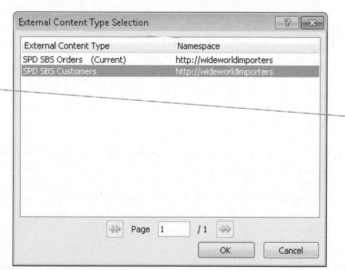

6. Click **SPD SBS Customers** in the **External Content Type** picker, and then click **OK**.

   The External Content Type Selection dialog box closes, and in the Operations Design view, under Related Identifier, CustomerID appears and is automatically mapped to the foreign key for the Orders ECT.

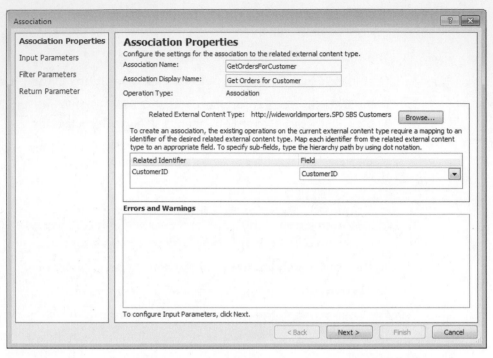

7. Click **Next** to display the **Input Parameters** page of the **Association** Wizard.

   An error message is displayed in the Errors And Warnings box, stating that a data source element that represents the identifier CustomerID of the external content type needs to be selected.

8. Under **Data Source Elements**, click **CustomerID**, and then under **Properties**, select the option **Map to Identifier**.

   The error message in the Errors And Warnings box disappears.

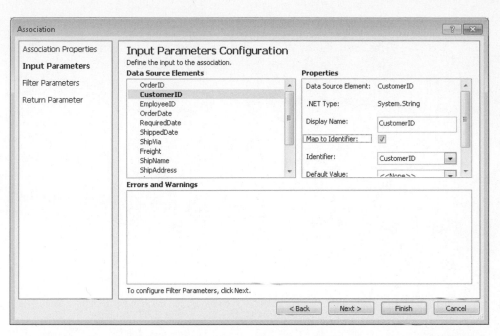

9. Click **Next** twice. The **Return Parameter Configuration** page of the **Association** Wizard is displayed.

10. Under **Data Source Elements**, select **OrderID**. Do not clear the check box. Under **Properties**, select the check box for **Map to Identifier**, if it is not already selected.

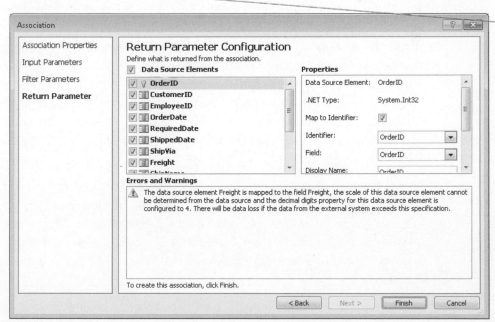

11. Click **Finish.**

The Association Wizard closes. In the External Content Type Operations area, the GetOrdersByCustomer association is listed.

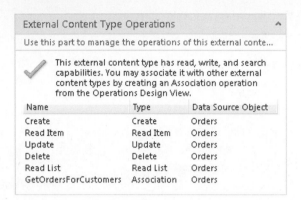

 CLEAN UP Save the SPD SBS Orders ECT. Leave SharePoint Designer open if you are continuing to the next exercise.

Managing External Content Types

In SharePoint Designer you can manage ECT data sources, remove operations and associations, and manage filters by using Summary or Operations Design view. In Summary view, you can switch the ECT to another compatible external system and edit connection properties such as those specific to the default or client connection, the database server name, the database name, and the authentication method. You can also view, but not modify, BCS permissions and field properties. In Operations Design view, by using ribbon commands you can remove connections, edit and remove operations, create external lists, and create list view pages as an ASPX page or, if you have the Enterprise edition of SharePoint Server, as InfoPath forms. You can also create profile pages in Operations Design view.

You can also manage external lists using the Lists And Libraries gallery page or the Data Sources gallery page. You can also go to the ECT in the External Lists area, click on the external list, and then click Go To List on the External Content Types tab. You can delete an external list, and the list is removed from SharePoint. The data in the external system is not deleted, however, because the external list is just presenting the data from the external systems.

In this exercise, you delete an ECT, modify connection properties, and change the filter criteria for a Read List operation.

SET UP Using SharePoint Designer, open the site you used in the previous exercise if it is not already open, and then open the ECT gallery page.

1. Click **SPD SBS Orders**.

2. On the **External Content Types** tab, click **Edit Connection Properties**.

   The Connection Properties dialog box opens.

Edit Connection
Properties

3. In the **Other Properties** section, click **Specify Number of Connections**, and then click **OK**.

   The Connection Properties dialog box closes.

Operations
Design View

4. If the **Connection Property Change Confirmation** dialog box opens, click **Yes**. Otherwise, on the **External Content Types** tab, click **Operations Design View**. In the **External Content Types Operations** area, in the **Name** column, click **Read List**, and then on the **External Content Types** tab, click **Edit Operation**.

5. If the **Data Source Discovery Confirmation** dialog box opens, click **Yes** to connect to the data source metadata store.

   The Operation Properties page of the Read List Wizard opens.

6. Click **Next** to display the **Filter Parameters Configuration** page of the **Read List** Wizard. Under **Properties**, to the right of **Filter**, click **Top 100 Orders Limit**.

   The Filter Configuration dialog box opens.

7. In the **Filter Properties** section, in the **Filter Type** list, select **Comparison**, and then in the **Operator** list, select **Greater Than**.

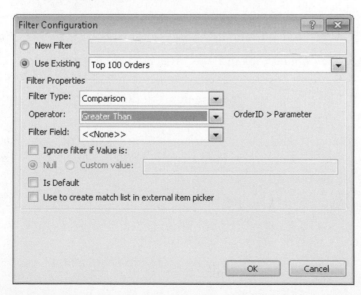

8. Click **OK**. The Filter Configuration dialog box closes.

9. In the **Default Values** box, type **11000**, and then click **Finish**. The Read List Wizard closes.

Summary View

10. On the **External Content Types** tab, click **Summary View**, and then on the Quick Access Toolbar, click **Save**.

    In the External Content Type Information area, the version number changes from 1.0.0.0 to 1.2.0.0.

11. On the workspace breadcrumb, click External Content Types. On the gallery page, right-click **SPD SBS Orders**, and then click **Delete**.

12. Click **Yes** to confirm the deletion of all versions of SPD SBS Orders from the BDC Metadata Store.

    The SPD SBS Orders ECT is removed from the External Content Types gallery page.

 CLEAN UP Leave SharePoint Designer open if you are continuing to the next exercise.

Key Points

- The Business Connectivity Service (BCS) bridges the gap between various applications that a company uses and the need to surface key business data from those applications into SharePoint.

- SharePoint Designer 2010 and Visual Studio 2010 are external content type (ECT) designers.

- The ECT is the basic building block for using external data within SharePoint.

- The BCS components (objects)—external data source definitions, ECTs, and their associated operations—are stored centrally in a BCS SQL Server database known as the BDC Metadata Store. Once created, the BCS components are available for use by other sites.

- The mapping of data source elements to Office properties can only be configured at operation creation; you cannot change the Office item type or the mappings once the operations are created

- Although you might have permissions to create the BDC model, ECTs, and external lists, you might not be able to see the data in the external list or on a page that contains an external list XLV Web Part.

- The preferred method of displaying data from external data sources is to use external lists.

- External lists can be created and managed from the Lists And Libraries gallery page, the Data Sources gallery page, and from the ECT settings page.

- Depending on the operations you have specified in an ECT, the external list can provide create, read, update, and delete (CRUD) capabilities.

- An external list can be added to a SharePoint page as an XLV Web Part or a Data View. This lets you configure additional columns, conditional formatting, and sorting and grouping in the browser and in SharePoint Designer.

- On the Enterprise edition of SharePoint Server 2010, you can create a profile page by using SharePoint Designer or the SharePoint 2010 Central Administration Web site.

- An external data column allows you to add data from an ECT to a standard SharePoint list.

- External content types are metadata objects defined in the BDC model XML file, which usually has the extension *.bdcm*.

- SharePoint Designer can be used to export a BDC model from one SharePoint system to another (default export) and to an Office application (client export).

- Create an association if you want to use the Business Data Related List Web Part to provide a relationship—a Web Part connection—between the Business Data Related List Web Part and a Business Data List Web Part.

Part 3

Using Workflow

Chapter at a Glance

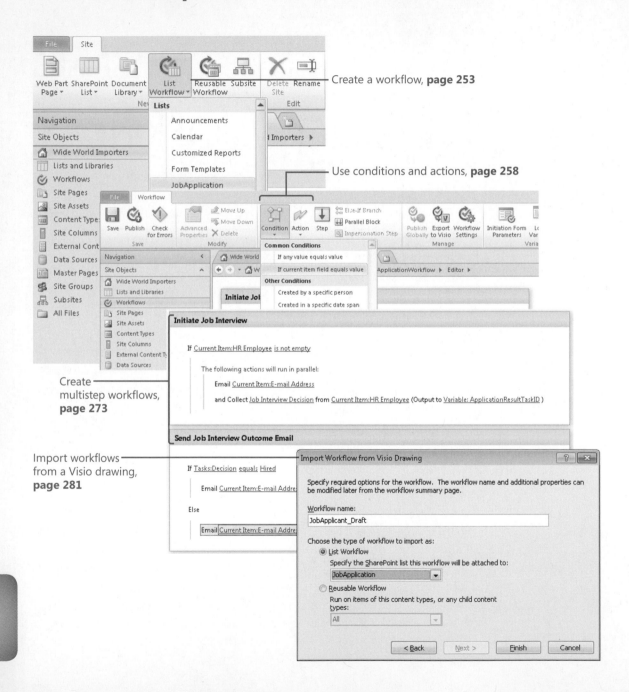

Create a workflow, **page 253**

Use conditions and actions, **page 258**

Create multistep workflows, **page 273**

Import workflows from a Visio drawing, **page 281**

8 Understanding Workflows

In this chapter, you will learn how to

- ✔ Work with workflows.
- ✔ Create workflows with SharePoint Designer.
- ✔ Use actions and conditions.
- ✔ Modify a workflow.
- ✔ Create a multistep workflow.
- ✔ Use Microsoft Visio to map a workflow.
- ✔ Import and export workflows from and to Visio.
- ✔ Remove and delete workflows.

The workflow technology included in Microsoft SharePoint Foundation 2010 and Microsoft SharePoint Server 2010 can help you automate new and existing business processes. With the workflow editor in SharePoint Designer 2010, you can create workflows in a user-friendly way that is completely visual and doesn't require advanced knowledge about software development. Workflows created by using SharePoint Designer are known as *user-defined workflows* to differentiate them from workflows that are created by a developer in Microsoft Visual Studio 2010. You can also create workflows in Microsoft Visio Premium 2010, which you can then import in SharePoint Designer 2010.

In this chapter you will learn how to work with the workflow editor and settings pages in SharePoint Designer, including the commands on the Workflow tab and the building blocks of any SharePoint Designer workflow—actions and conditions. After that, I discuss the creation of a full-blown, multistep workflow. You will learn how to deploy, modify, and delete workflows; how to create various workflow types (list workflows, site workflows, and reusable workflows); and how to export a reusable workflow as a template that can become a starting point for creating workflows in Visual Studio 2010. The chapter finishes with a discussion of SharePoint Designer and Visio 2010 integration points.

Mastering the creation of workflows in SharePoint Designer may take some time, but it is well worth the effort.

See Also This chapter assumes that you are familiar with the built-in workflows in SharePoint 2010. If you want to revise the built-in workflows by using the browser, see Chapter 11, "Working with Workflows" in *Microsoft SharePoint Foundation 2010 Step by Step* by Olga Londer and Penelope Coventry (Microsoft Press, 2011). You can also find information about using workflows in SharePoint Server 2010 at *technet.microsoft.com/en-us/sharepoint/ff819861.aspx*.

> **Practice Files** Before you can complete the exercises in this chapter; you need to copy the book's practice files to your computer. A complete list of practice files is provided in "Using the Practice Files" at the beginning of this book.

Working with Workflows

All workflow functionality provided by SharePoint Foundation 2010 or SharePoint Server 2010 is built using the version of *Windows Workflow Foundation (WF)* included in the *Microsoft .NET Framework 3.5*. You cannot install the 2010 versions of SharePoint products on a server without the .NET Framework 3.5 being installed first.

Warning To use SharePoint Designer to create workflows, you must have the .NET Framework 3.0 installed on your computer. Windows 7 includes this version. If you are using Windows Vista, you might need to install the .NET Framework 3.0 before you can work with workflows in SharePoint Designer. The .NET Framework is available from the Microsoft Download Center, *www.microsoft.com/downloads*.

Workflow Foundation offers all kinds of functionality required for building enterprise-level workflows, such as built-in support for transactions, tracking, and notifications. Workflow Foundation does not act as a stand-alone application but always works with a program, which in this instance is SharePoint Foundation. Because SharePoint Server is built on SharePoint Foundation, it too has workflow capabilities.

In the same way that you can base a new site, list, or library on a template, you can base a new workflow on a workflow template. These templates are implemented as features that can be activated or deactivated by using the browser or programmatically. A workflow feature is available only when a workflow template is activated.

You can think of a workflow as a series of tasks that produces an outcome. SharePoint Foundation and SharePoint Server provide a number of built-in workflow templates that define tasks and outcomes. SharePoint Foundation ships with a single, generic list workflow template—the three-state workflow that can be used across multiple scenarios. SharePoint Server contains in addition the following list workflow templates and site workflow templates:

- List workflow templates

  - **Approval**   Workflows created from this template provide an approval mechanism for documents. Two versions of this template are included: the Approval—SharePoint 2010 workflow template, which provides a visualization of a workflow instance's progress in an embedded Visio 2010 image, and the Approval workflow template, which is provided for compatibility with lists or libraries that were upgraded from a previous version of SharePoint or for a SharePoint 2010 installation in which the Visio service application is not activated.

  - **Collect Feedback**   Workflows created from this template route documents for review. Reviewers can provide feedback, which is compiled and sent to the document owner when the workflow instance is complete. As with the Approval workflow template, two versions of this template are included: Collect Feedback—SharePoint 2010 and Collect Feedback.

  - **Collect Signatures**   This template provides a mechanism for collecting digital signatures needed to complete a Microsoft Office document. Two versions of this template are also included: Collect Signature—SharePoint 2010 and Collect Signature.

  - **Disposition Approval**   Provides an expiration and retention mechanism that allows you to decide whether to retain or delete expired documents. This workflow can be started only by using the browser.

  - **Group Approval**   Similar to the Approval workflow. Available only in East Asian versions of SharePoint Server.

  - **Translation Management**   Provides a mechanism for document translation by creating copies of the documents to be translated and assigning tasks to translators. This workflow is available only when you create a Translation Management library.

  - **Publishing Approval**   Routes a page for approval.

- Site workflow templates   You must have the View Web Analytics Data permission to start workflows instances created from either of these two site-workflow templates.

  - **Schedule Web Analytics Alerts**   Sends e-mail messages to alert recipients about specific analytics data changes.

  - **Schedule Web Analytics Reports**   Schedules selected reports to be sent via e-mail to reviewers. You can specify reviewers, the frequency of the reports, and additional information.

See Also For more information about the built-in workflows, refer to *technet.microsoft.com/ en-us/library/cc263148(office.14).aspx.*

Tip When you create a site, you might find that a workflow is not available. For example, the three-state workflow is not immediately available in a SharePoint Server installation. A site collection administrator can activate the three-state workflow feature by using the Site Collection Administration: Features page, which is available from the site settings page at the top-level site of a site collection.

The browser, SharePoint Designer, and Visual Studio use the term *workflow* for a work-flow template, a workflow process, and an instance of a workflow, which can be confus-ing. You must infer what you are working with according to the context. For example, when you associate a workflow (template) with a SharePoint component, such as a site, list, library, or content type, you create a workflow (process). A workflow (instance) is created automatically or manually for a site, list item, or document that exists in the SharePoint component where you create the workflow (process).

When you associate one of the built-in workflow templates with a SharePoint compo-nent such as a list, library, content type, or site, you can customize the workflow in a lim-ited fashion by using the browser to define the exact process that needs to be executed to meet your business needs. When the first instance of a list or library workflow runs, a column is created, allowing you to monitor individual workflow instances as they prog-ress through the workflow process.

See Also Workflows cannot be created on an external list. You can find more information on using workflows with Business Connectivity Services at *blogs.msdn.com/b/bcs/ archive/2010/01/20/using-sharepoint-workflows-with-business-connectivity-services-bcs.aspx* and *blogs.msdn.com/b/bcs/archive/2010/01/29/using-sharepoint-workflows-with-business-connectivity-services-bcs-sandboxed-workflow-actions.aspx.*

A workflow instance starts when a workflow event is triggered. Depending on the configu-ration of the workflow process, an instance of a workflow can start in the following ways:

- Manually from the browser or an Office client application. Although you can see documents in SharePoint Designer, you cannot manually start workflow instances with SharePoint Designer. Similarly, you cannot start a workflow instance on a list item in SharePoint Designer—for the basic reason that you cannot see list items in SharePoint Designer.

- Automatically when you create or save a major version of a document. This method of starting a workflow is not available on lists. It is available only for libraries that have major and minor versioning enabled.

- Automatically when you create a new list item or document.

- Automatically whenever you change a list item or document.

Although doing so is not strictly required, most workflows use both a task and a history list while the workflow process runs. Workflows add tasks to a task list so that users can keep track of all the work required to complete the workflow process for a particular workflow instance. The history list keeps track of the workflow instances that are running or have been completed for a given list item or document.

See Also Before creating workflows in SharePoint Designer, you should carefully plan what you want to achieve and determine whether SharePoint Designer is the correct tool. More information on planning workflows can be found at *technet.microsoft.com/en-us/library/ cc288553.aspx.*

Creating Workflows with SharePoint Designer

SharePoint Designer includes a workflow editor and a Workflow Settings page that you use to create and configure workflow templates and workflows. SharePoint Designer 2010 has several improvements over the previous version:

- A number of built-in workflows templates can also be used as *globally reusable workflows*, and, therefore, can serve as the starting point for workflows created in SharePoint Designer. You can learn more about globally reusable workflows in Chapter 9, "Using Reusable Workflows and Workflow Forms."

- The creation of workflow templates that can be used as starting points for workflows.

- Supports multiple and custom outcomes from a single task. Basically, rather than having a simple approve/reject outcome, a task can have any number of outcomes.

- Workflows are now able to impersonate other users during the execution of workflow steps. This allows workflow designers to temporarily raise permissions to access functionality not available with limited or unknown user permissions.

- Workflows are now able to operate on document sets; that is, a single workflow can be started for an entire group of documents.

The workflow editor, like other SharePoint Designer components, operates within the scope of a SharePoint site, so to create a workflow you must open the SharePoint site in which you want to create the workflow. You can then create a workflow by using the workflow editor, depending on your permission level and whether the SharePoint server administrator has enabled user-defined workflows through the SharePoint 2010 Central Administration site.

See Also For a list of steps that a SharePoint administrator can use to create a site collection, see Appendix C on page 503.

You create a workflow in Backstage view or on the site settings page. Click List Workflow or Reusable Workflow on the Site tab, or click Workflows in the Navigation pane, and then use the ribbon.

The following type of workflows can be created by using SharePoint Designer:

● **List workflow** Allows you to create a workflow process that is attached to a single list or library within the site. This is the only type of workflow you can create in SharePoint Designer 2007, and it will still probably be the most popular type in SharePoint Designer 2010.

● **Reusable workflow** Allows you to create a workflow template that can be attached to a content type. Workflows of this type can be used in different lists or libraries.

● **Site workflow** Allows you to create a workflow process that operates on the site-level context itself.

● **Import Visio workflow** Allows you to import and export workflow processes between Visio Premium 2010 and SharePoint Designer 2010.

In this exercise, you create a list workflow in SharePoint Designer and associate it with a specific library.

 SET UP Using SharePoint Designer, open the site you created from the SBSSPDPracticeSite_Starter.wsp practice file.

List Workflow

1. On the **Site** tab, click **List Workflow** in the **New** group, and then click a document library, such as **JobApplication,** where you'd like to create a list workflow.

   Troubleshooting If you cannot see your list or library in the drop-down list, click the Refresh icon on the Quick Access Toolbar. If your list or library still does not appear, check that you have opened the correct site in SharePoint Designer.

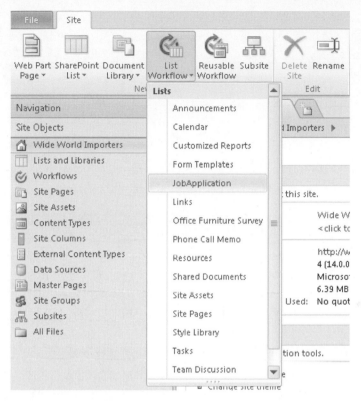

The Create List Workflow—Shared Documents dialog box opens.

2. In the **Name** box, type the name of your workflow, such as
    JobApplicationWorkflow, and in the **Description** box, type **A simplified job ap-
    plication workflow**. Click **OK**.

    Warning The name of your workflow is used to create a new column in your library. Be
    sure that a column with this name does not already exist.

    A Downloading Data dialog box briefly appears as information is downloaded from
    the SharePoint server. A new tab labeled *JobApplicationWorkflow* opens, with an
    asterisk indicating that the workflow has not been saved. This is the workflow edi-
    tor. In the Step 1 area, an orange horizontal line flashes.

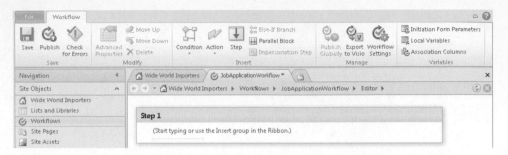

The Workflow tab contains basic functions for working with SharePoint Designer workflows, organized in the following groups:

○ **Save**   Contains commands to save the workflow you are modifying, publish a workflow to a SharePoint site, and check whether the workflow contains any errors.

○ **Modify**   Contains commands to view and modify the properties of the selected action or condition; to move up a selected action, step, or condition; to move down a selected action, step, or condition; and to delete a selected action, step, or condition.

○ **Insert**   Contains commands to add a condition, an action, or a step to a workflow. You also use commands in this group to add an Else-If branch to a workflow, to add a parallel block to a workflow, and to insert a step in the workflow that runs actions and conditions in the workflow in the context of the user who last edited the workflow, known as the *workflow associator*. Usually a workflow runs in the context of the user who starts the workflow.

Warning A change in the permissions of the last editor of the workflow might affect the impersonation steps within the workflow. You can find more information about impersonation steps at *technet.microsoft.com/en-us/library/ee428324(office.14). aspx#BKMK_UserStep*.

○ **Manage**   Contains commands to convert a workflow to a globally reusable workflow, to export a workflow to a Visio 2010 *Workflow Interchange* (.vwi) file that can be imported in Visio 2010, and to switch from the workflow editor to the Workflow Settings page.

○ **Variables**   Contains commands to create and manage initiation form parameters, local variables, and association columns. Local variables are typically used within the workflow. Association columns allow you to automatically create columns for a list when a workflow is associated with that list.

3. On the **Workflow** tab, click **Workflow Settings** in the **Manage** group.

Workflow
Settings

The Workflow Settings page is displayed. Each workflow has a collection of settings that you can view and manage via the Workflow Settings page. The page contains five areas:

- ○ **Workflow Information**   Use this area to change the name and description of the workflow. This area also displays the workflow type (list, site, or reusable) and the associated item. When you view a list workflow, the associated item is the list. When you view a reusable workflow, the associated item is the content type the workflow is attached to, and when you view a site workflow, there is no associated item.

- ○ **Customization**   This area contains links to the workflow editor and, depending on the type of workflow, links to the list settings page of the associated list, task list, or history list.

- ○ **Settings**   Use this area to create a new task list or to select a list you want to use as a task list. You also use this area to create or select a list to be used to store the history of the workflow. The Settings area for a reusable workflow can be used to select the language the workflow applies to. When the Show Workflow Visualization On Status Page option is enabled, the SharePoint status page in the browser displays a Visio diagram (generated by using Visio services).

- ○ **Start Options**   This area is used differently for each type of workflow. For a list workflow, use it to allow a workflow to be started manually, automatically when an item is created, or automatically when an item is changed. For a site workflow, the list item options are not available, which makes sense because site workflows don't operate on the list-item level. The only option available for a site workflow lets you specify whether to start the workflow manually. For a reusable workflow, this area allows you to explicitly disable one or more of the list start options.

- ○ **Forms**   This area lists forms used in the workflow.

  See Also More information on workflow forms can be found in Chapter 9.

4. If your site was created on an installation that uses the Enterprise edition of SharePoint Server 2010, in the **Settings** area, select the **Show workflow visualization on status page** check box.

5. In the **Start Options** area, clear the **Allow this workflow to be manually started** check box, and select **Start workflow automatically when an item is created**.

Tip To collect information from a user when he or she manually starts a workflow, you need to specify a set of initiation parameters by clicking the Initiation Form Parameters command, which appears on both the Workflow and the Workflow Settings tab. These initiation parameters must have default values if the workflow is to be configured to start automatically. You can design the data entry form that users see when they start the process, and you can customize this form in SharePoint Designer as you would any other page. If the site is created on an installation of the Enterprise edition of SharePoint Server and Office Forms Server is configured, you can use an InfoPath form.

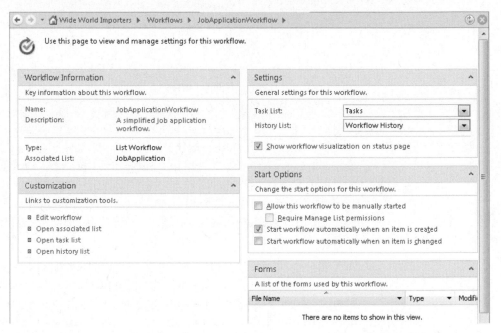

6. On the **Workflow Settings** tab, click **Save**, and then click **Edit Workflow** in the **Edit** group.

Save

The workflow editor is displayed.

CLEAN UP Leave SharePoint Designer open if you are continuing to the next exercise.

Using Actions and Conditions

When you create a workflow, you define one or more *workflow steps*. In each step, you define the set of *workflow actions* that need to be performed and a *workflow condition* that triggers the workflow actions. The combination of a condition and the associated actions is known as a *workflow rule*. In workflow terminology, both conditions and actions are *workflow activities*, where an activity is an event that needs to occur, such as sending an e-mail message or writing log information. Actions and conditions are the essential building blocks for creating workflows in SharePoint Designer.

SharePoint 2010 provides you with a set of conditions and actions that you can use to create your workflows. A condition is a kind of filter. For example, if the condition is true, the associated action or actions are executed. The conditions available to your workflow depend on the workflow type; for example, the condition that checks the size of a file is available only on list workflows, and specifically on lists and libraries that allow attachments.

An action defines a set of tasks that needs to be completed. Actions can be configured to run in serial or parallel. When you run actions in serial, an action starts only if the preceding one is complete. When you run actions in parallel, known as a parallel block, all actions start at the same time. SharePoint Designer divides built-in actions into six action categories:

- **Core Actions** Contains common activities that you use in many workflows. These activities allow you to manipulate dates and times, build a form to collect information from users, and write information to the history list. This category has three changes from SharePoint Designer 2007:

  - **Add a Comment** A new action, Add a Comment can be used to leave informative comments for reference purposes to help users who are coauthoring the workflow.

  - **Send Document to Repository** Only available on libraries and for the Document content type.

  - **Set Workflow Status** The default options are Canceled, Approved, and Rejected. You can also add your own.

- **Document Set Actions** A new action category specific to SharePoint Server 2010 sites. Document sets are groups of documents that have a specific meaning as a group and share a specific life cycle. For instance, all documents related to a certain legal matter can be grouped as a document set.

- **List Actions** Contains actions that allow you to manipulate list items, including creating, copying, and deleting list items. These actions can be applied to documents within libraries because libraries are just special lists. This category also includes specific document-related actions, such as undoing a check out. A number of new actions are included in the category concerning records, permissions, deleting draft items, and pausing the execution of a workflow while waiting for a change in a document's check-out status.

- **Relational Actions** A new category for SharePoint Server 2010 sites. It contains only one built-in action: Lookup Manager of a User. This action looks at the SharePoint user's profile and returns that user's manager from the profile. The user profile Manager property is usually populated from Active Directory after profile synchronization has occurred. The Manager field will be empty if the relevant field in Active Directory contains no value.

- **Task Actions** Contains actions that allow you to assign a task to a specific user or to a group. This category contains three new actions that start a custom approval, task, or feedback process. These three actions are similar to the globally reusable workflows, such as *Approval—SharePoint 2010* and *Collect Feedback—SharePoint 2010*. The globally reusable workflows represent a more complete solution. For example, the three new task actions do not give you the ability to reassign a task or change request. Use a new action if the globally reusable workflows do not meet your needs. Use the *Start Custom Task Process* action if you want a configuration similar to the approval task actions but not the logic.

- **Utility Actions** A new category in SharePoint 2010 that contains actions that can be used to manipulate strings and dates. The four extract substring actions replace the SharePoint Designer 2007 Build Dynamic String core action.

See Also An overview of the default workflow conditions and actions can be found in Appendix A on page 481.

If the set of built-in conditions and actions does not meet your business needs, you can add new conditions or actions that are called *custom activities*. Custom activities can be created only by using Visual Studio 2010 or a third-party tool.

In this exercise, you build the first step of a workflow that includes one condition, a parallel block, and one action.

SET UP Using SharePoint Designer, open the site you used in the previous exercise if it is not already open. Display the workflow editor page for the JobApplicationWorkflow.

1. Click **Step 1**, type **Initiate Job Interview**, and then press **Enter**.

2. On the **Workflow** tab, click **Condition** in the **Insert** group. Under **Common Conditions**, click **If current item field equals value**.

Condition

   Tip You can have multiple conditional blocks, each with its own set of branches in each step. Conditional blocks can occur one after another, or you can create conditional blocks inside one of the other branches.

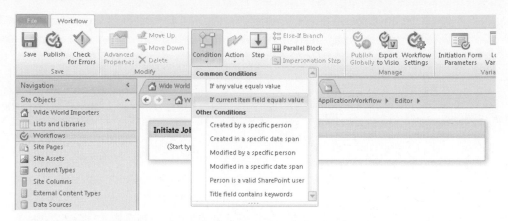

The Initiate Job Interview area contains two rectangles. The text *If Field Equals Value* appears in the top rectangle, with a flashing horizontal line immediately below the text.

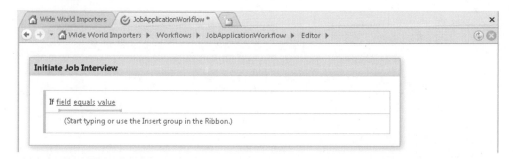

3. Click **field** to display a list of columns in the JobApplication list, and then scroll down and click **HR Employee**. Click **equals**, and then click **is not empty** in the list that appears.

> **Tip** You do not have to specify a condition for a workflow. There might be circumstances when you require an action to always occur. For example, you might want to create a new list item in the history list when a workflow starts and when it finishes.

Parallel Block

4. Click **Start typing or use the Insert group in the Ribbon**, and then on the **Workflow** tab, click **Parallel Block** in the **Insert** group.

A new rectangle is added to the step containing the text *The Following Actions Will Run In Parallel*.

Actions

5. On the **Workflow** tab, click **Action**. Under **Core Actions**, click **Send an Email**.

> **Troubleshooting** If at any time the Action command is not enabled, check that your insertion point is placed where you can insert an action. The SharePoint editor displays rectangles to help you identify steps as well as If, Else, Else-if, and parallel blocks.

The text *Then Email These Users* appears.

6. Click **these users** to open the **Define E-mail Message** dialog box. To the right of the **To** box, click the **Address Book** icon to display the **Select Users** dialog box. Click **Workflow Lookup for a User**, and then click **Add**.

The Lookup For Person Or Group dialog box opens.

7. In the **Data source** list, verify that **Current Item** is selected, and in the **Field from source** list, click **E-mail Address**.

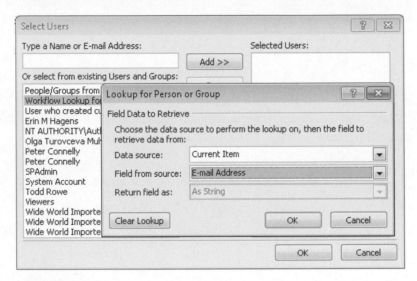

8. Click **OK** twice.

The Lookup For Person Or Group and the Select Users dialog boxes close. In the Define E-mail Message dialog box, the To box is unavailable and displays Current Item:E-mail Address.

9. To the right of the **Subject** box, type **Invitation to job interview**.

Note To create a subject line that contains values from the current item and static text, click the ellipsis button to the left of the Formula button.

10. In the box below the formatting options, type **Dear** and then at the bottom of the **Define E-mail Message** dialog box, click the **Add or Change Lookup** button.

The Lookup For String dialog box opens.

11. In the **Data source** list, verify that **Current Item** is selected, and in the **Field from source** list, scroll down and select **Job Applicant Name**. Click **OK** to close the **Lookup for String** dialog box.

12. In the **Define E-mail Message** dialog box, place the insertion point at the end of the line after the square bracket, press **Enter** twice, type **On behalf of Wide World Importers, I invite you to a job interview at** , and then click **Add or Change Lookup**.

13. In the **Data source** list, verify that **Current Item** is selected, and in the **Field from source** list, scroll down and select **Job Interview Date**. Click **OK** to close the **Lookup for String** dialog box.

14. Place the insertion point at the end of the line after the square bracket, and type **If you have any questions, please feel free to contact me.** Then press **Enter** twice, type **Kind regards** and then press **Enter**.

15. Click **Add or Change Lookup**. In the **Data source** list, verify that **Current Item** is selected, and in the **Field from source** list, scroll down and select **HR Employee**. Click **OK** to close the **Lookup for String** dialog box.

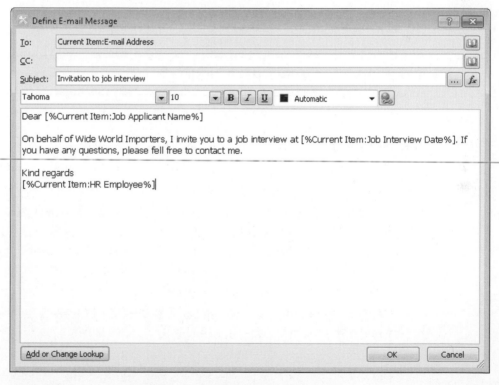

16. Click **OK** to close the **Define E-mail Message** dialog box.

In the workflow editor, the *Actions* text is replaced with *Email Current Item:E-mail Address*.

Initiate Job Interview

If <u>Current Item:HR Employee</u> <u>is not empty</u>

The following actions will run in parallel:

Email <u>Current Item:E-mail Address</u>

Note You can also configure actions and conditions by using the Advance Properties command on the Workflow tab.

 CLEAN UP Save the workflow. Leave SharePoint Designer open if you are continuing to the next exercise.

Modifying a Workflow

Any business process is likely to change; therefore, you will need to modify any associated workflows. You can modify a workflow by using the Workflow Settings page or the workflow editor page .In the workflow editor, as you move the cursor over the workflow, an orange horizontal line flashes to indicate an insertion point where you can add actions, conditions, and steps. You can also use the keyboard to move the insertion point. Pressing **Shift+End** moves the insertion point to the end of an If section. **Shift+Home** moves the insertion point to the first action in the If section, and **Ctrl+Home** or **Ctrl+End** moves the insertion point to the beginning or end of the entire workflow.

In the Modify group on the Workflow tab, you can use the Move Up and Move Down commands to rearrange the workflow logic. You can move steps or conditions, but the movement of these components is restricted. For example, you cannot move a nested step outside its current step. You should be sure you have the insertion point in the correct position in your workflow when you create steps and conditions.

Tip If you want to relocate steps and conditions and the Move Up and Move Down commands are not available—for example, when a condition is the first condition in a step—you can amend the .xoml files or explore exporting and modifying your workflow in Visio or Visual Studio.

As you modify your workflows, they can become complex and difficult to maintain. When you modify complex workflows, they are easy to break, and the amount of time you take to test them will increase. Troubleshooting problems can be challenging because SharePoint Designer has no debugging mechanism. Try to keep workflows as simple as possible, and use the Add a Comment and Log to History List actions to add comments to your workflow and help you diagnose a problem you might have.

If you modify a workflow that is already in use, you might possibly break instances of the workflow that are already running. Therefore, before modifying a workflow, you should make the workflow unavailable to users. (Do not delete it.)

See Also For information about removing a workflow from a list or library, see "Removing and Deleting Workflows" later in this chapter.

In this exercise, you modify an existing workflow.

 SET UP Using SharePoint Designer, open the site you used in the previous exercise if it is not already open. Display the site settings page.

Edit Workflow

1. In the **Navigation** pane, click **Workflows**. Under **List Workflow**, click the icon to the left of **JobApplicationWorkflow**. On the **Workflows** tab, click **Edit Workflow** in the **Edit** group.

   The workflow editor page is displayed.

2. Click **Email**, and then press **Shift+End**. Type **col**, and then press **Enter**.

   The text *and Collect Data From This User (Output To Variable:collect)* appears.

3. Click **data** to open the **Custom Task Wizard**, and then click **Next**.

4. In the **Name** box, type **Job Interview Decision**, and in the **Description** box, type **Please indicate whether the job applicant is to be hired or rejected**.

5. Click **Next,** and then click **Add**. The Add Field dialog box opens.

6. In the **Field name** box, type **Decision**. From the **Information type** list, select **Choice (menu to choose from)**.

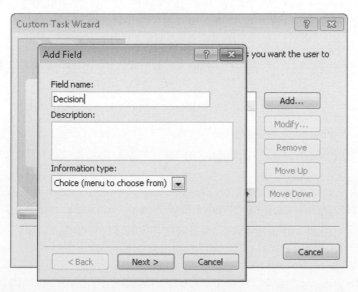

7. Click **Next**. The Column Settings dialog box opens.

8. On separate lines, type **Hired and Rejected**, and verify that **Drop-down menu** is selected in the **Display as** list.

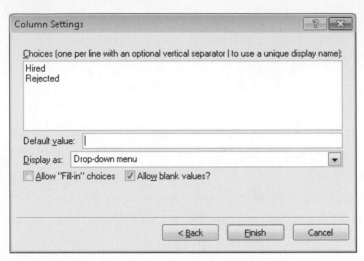

9. Click **Finish** twice to close the **Column Settings** dialog box and the **Custom Task Wizard**.

10. In the workflow editor, click **this user**. The Select Users dialog box opens.

11. Click **Workflow Lookup for a User**, and then click **Add**.

    The Lookup For Person Or Group dialog box opens.

12. In the **Data source** list, verify that **Current Item** is selected. In the **Field from source** list, select **HR Employee**, and in the **Return field as** list, select **Login Name**.

13. Click **OK** twice to close the **Lookup for Person or Group** and the **Select Users** dialog boxes.

14. In the workflow editor, click **Variable:collect**, and select **Create a new variable**.

    The Edit Variable dialog box opens.

15. In the **Name** box, type **ApplicationResultTaskID**, and then click **OK**.

    Tip When a workflow contains multiple variables, devise a naming convention that documents the stage in the workflow when the variable is used and the data it will hold. This helps you when you modify the workflow.

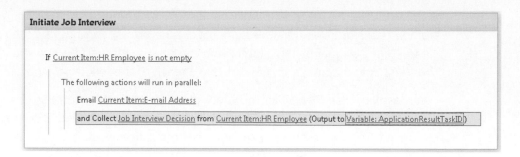

 CLEAN UP Save the workflow. Leave SharePoint Designer open if you are continuing to the next exercise.

Deploying Workflows

As you develop your workflow—and certainly before you use a workflow in production—you should publish and test your solution. The Workflow tab provides you with a command that checks the validity of your workflow. When you click the Check For Errors command, either a dialog box appears to inform you that the workflow contains no errors, or asterisks (*) appear before and after the incorrect value, which is displayed in red text. After completing the workflow validity check, you can publish the workflow. If during the publishing process, errors with the workflow are found, a Workflow Errors Found dialog box opens, and you have the option to save the workflow in a draft state or return to the workflow editor to correct the errors.

You might need to publish the workflow a number of times before the workflow meets your business needs. Each time you publish a workflow, a copy of the workflow is created. This enables workflow instances that are running with the previous version of the workflow to complete. The previous versions are renamed using a date and time stamp. You cannot see previous versions of the workflow in SharePoint Designer, but they are visible in the browser by navigating to the Workflow Settings page. After you have sign-off from the business that the workflow is correctly configured, you can use the browser to remove the previous versions.

You might also need to complete other tidy-up tasks. For example, the Collect Data from a User action creates a new content type on the tasks list that is visible in the browser on the New Item list. You might want to configure this content type so that it is not visible because it might confuse users of the task list.

For each list, site, or reusable workflow, SharePoint creates a folder in the Workflows library. The Workflows library is hidden from the browser and can be seen only in SharePoint Designer by those users who can see the hidden URL site structure. Each workflow folder contains at least one file of each of the following types:

- **.aspx or .xsn** These files represent forms used for data entry by users. You can configure these forms as you can any other form. However, redeploying the workflow could overwrite the files, and your customization would be lost.

- **.xoml** This is the main workflow markup file, which contains the *Extensible Application Markup Language (XAML)* that Windows Workflow Foundation uses. This file describes the activities included in the workflow.

- **.xoml.rules** This file contains details of the workflow rules.

- **.xoml.wfconfig.xml** This file includes the site and list or library details, as well as the workflow start configuration settings.

Caution If you delete any of these files, the workflow might fail to deploy. For example, if you delete the .xoml.wfconfig.xml file, the workflow loses its association with the list or library. You might think that this is a method of associating the workflow with a list or library different from the one you originally associated it with. However, to reassociate the workflow with a list or library, you need to revisit all the conditions and actions and reassociate them with columns and the values held within those columns. This is a large task if you have many conditions and actions, and you then have to retest the workflow thoroughly to ensure that you have not missed anything.

SharePoint 2010 contains a just-in-time compiler that uses the declarative code files in the workflow folder to create a workflow process the first time a workflow instance is started on an item. SharePoint 2010 retains the compiled workflow in memory until it is called again, which speeds performance.

The hidden Workflows library does have major versioning enabled, so theoretically, you can restore a previous version of a file. However, this library does not have any view pages, which means that you cannot use the browser to restore a file. You can, however, use SharePoint Designer to restore previous versions if you have access to the hidden URL structure of your site. Because the files as a group define a workflow, restoring just one file could break your workflow. As you can with any other list or library, you can make a copy of the workflow folder in the hidden Workflows library. Therefore, before modifying a workflow, if you have access to the hidden URL structure of your site, you can create a copy of the workflow folder. This copy does not appear in the browser or in Office client applications unless you open it using the workflow editor and then use the Publish command on the ribbon.

In this exercise, you validate, deploy, and test a workflow. You then remove the task content type created by the workflow from the new tab and explore the files that are created as part of the deployment process.

 SET UP Using SharePoint Designer, open the site you used in the previous exercise if it is not already open. Display the workflow editor page for the JobApplicationWorkflow.

Check for Errors

1. On the **Workflow** tab, click **Check for Errors** in the **Save** group.

   A message box informs you that the workflow is valid.

   Troubleshooting If errors are reported, check your workflow against the previous exercise and then repeat step 1.

Publish

2. Click **OK** to close the message box, and then on the **Workflow** tab, click **Publish** in the **Save** group.

   A Microsoft SharePoint Designer dialog box opens, displaying the progress of the publishing process.

   When the publishing process is complete, the progress window closes.

Workflow Settings

Preview in Browser

3. On the **Workflow** tab, click **Workflow settings**, and then in the **Customization** area, click **Open associated list**.

   The JobApplication list settings page is displayed.

4. On the **List Settings** tab, click **Preview in Browser**.

   The browser opens, and the All Items view of the list is displayed.

5. Click **Add new item**. In the **JobApplication—New Item** dialog box, use the following data to create a new item, and then click **Save**.

Job Applicant Name	Paula Bento
Description	Paula Bento is a very intelligent person with an extensive resume.
E-mail Address	paula@contoso.com
Job Interview Date	Choose a date in the future
HR Employee	Select a user name

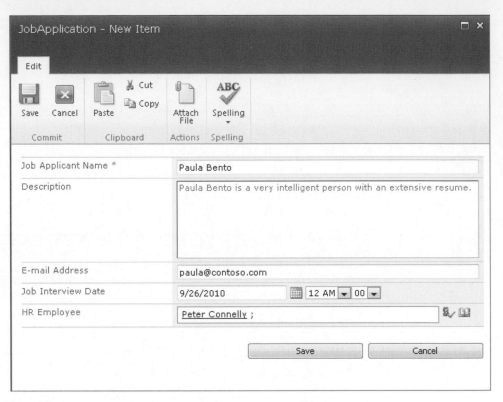

The All Items view of the JobApplication list is displayed with an extra column labeled *JobApplicationWorkflow*. Refresh your browser window if the column does not appear.

6. In the **JobApplicationWorkflow** column, click **In Progress** to display the **Workflow Status: JobApplicationWorkflow** page.

If your organization has the Enterprise edition of SharePoint Server and you choose to show workflow visualization, a Visio representation of the workflow will be displayed in the Workflow Visualization section, with icons indicating In Progress or Completed. In the Tasks section one task is displayed, and in the Workflow History section there are no workflow history events. You can use the Workflow Visualization, Tasks, and Workflow History sections to track the progress of the workflow instance.

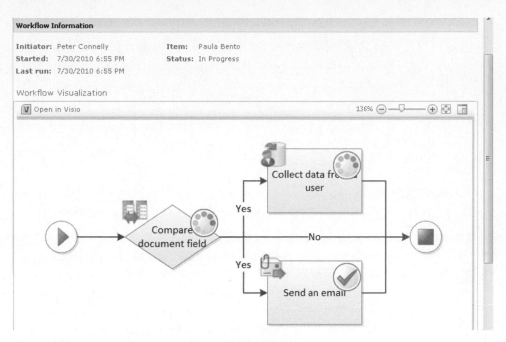

7. In the **Tasks** section, click **Job Interview Decision**.

The Workflow Task dialog box is displayed.

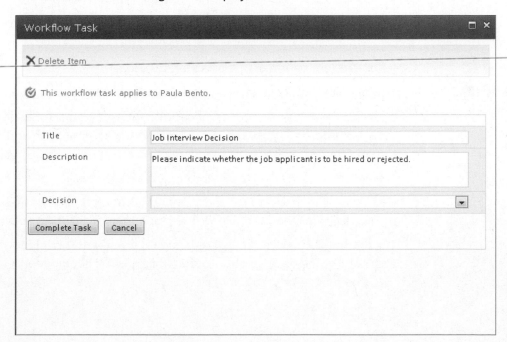

8. In the **Decision** list, select **Hired**, and then click **Complete Task**.

   The Workflow Status: JobApplicationWorkflow page is displayed. In the Visio workflow visualization, the condition and the two actions have green check marks indicating that they are complete. In the Tasks section, in the Outcome column, the task item has a status of Completed.

9. On the Quick Launch, under **Lists**, click **Tasks**.

   The All Tasks view of the tasks list is displayed. One Job Interview Decision task is listed.

10. Return to SharePoint Designer, where the **JobApplication** list settings page is displayed. In the **Workflows** area, click **JobApplicationWorkflow**.

    The Workflow Settings page is displayed. The Forms area contains one file, which is used to modify the task item that's used to collect data from a user. In the Start Options area, if the Allow This Workflow To Be Manually Started check box is selected, a second file appears, which is used to start an instance of this workflow. If you have the Enterprise edition of SharePoint Server 2010, the files will be InfoPath .xsn files; otherwise, they will be .aspx files.

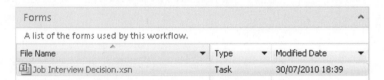

11. In the **Customization** area, click **Open task list**.

    The tasks list settings page is displayed.

Show on New
Menu

12. In the **Content Types** area, click the icon to the left of **Job Interview Decision**. On the **Lists, Content Types** tab, click **Show on New Menu** to clear the check box for the content type.

    The Yes in the Show On New Menu column disappears.

13. If you have permission to see the hidden URL structure of your site, click **All Files** in the **Navigation** pane. Click **Workflows**, and then click **JobApplicationWorkflow**.

    The JobApplicationWorkflow gallery page is displayed. The folder contains the files produced by the deployment process, which include the one form file, three .xoml files, and optionally Visio (.vdw) files.

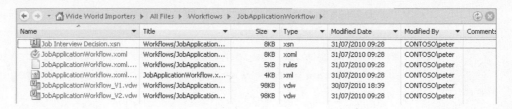

 CLEAN UP Close the browser. Leave SharePoint Designer open if you are continuing to the next exercise.

Creating a Multistep Workflow

Most business processes need more than one step; that is, the rules defined in one step must be completed before the rules in the second step can start. For example, a bank must complete several financial and security checks before creating an account for a customer.

You have seen that each step has one or more conditions, and each condition has one or more actions. A step can also consist of multiple branches, so that if condition A is true, one set of actions is executed, and if condition B is true, another set of actions is executed. However, a branch cannot extend from one step to another. To create multiple conditions, you click Else-If Branch on the Workflow tab.

In this exercise, you add a second step, which contains one condition, an Else branch, and two actions.

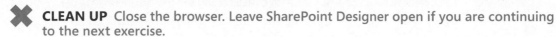 **SET UP** Using SharePoint Designer, open the site you used in the previous exercise if it is not already open. Display the workflow editor page for the StarterWorkflow.

Step

1. Place the insertion point below the **Initiate Job Interview** rectangle, and then on the **Workflow** tab, click **Step** in the **Insert** group.

   A rectangle named Step 2 appears.

2. Click **Step 2**, type **Send Job Interview Outcome Email**, press **Enter**, type **any**, and then press **Enter** again.

   The If Any Value Equals Value condition is selected, and the text and *If Value Equals Value* appears.

Define workflow lookup

3. Click the first occurrence of **value**, and then click the **Define workflow lookup** button.

   The Define Workflow Lookup dialog box opens.

4. In the **Data source** list, select **Association: Task List**, and in the **Field from source** list, select **Decision**.

Define workflow
lookup

5. In the **Find the List Item** section, in the **Field** list, select **ID**, and in the **Value** list, click the **Define workflow lookup** button. The **Lookup For Integer** dialog box opens.

6. In the **Data source** list, select **Workflow Variables and Parameters**, and in the **Field from source** list, select **Variable: ApplicationResultTaskID**.

7. Click **OK**.

The Lookup For Integer dialog box closes, and Variable: ApplicationResultTaskID appears in the Value box.

8. Click **OK**. The **Define Workflow Lookup** dialog box closes.

The text *Value* is replaced with *Tasks:Decision*.

9. Click **value**, and select **Hired**. Then, on the **Workflow** tab, click **Else-If Branch** in the **Insert** group.

Else-If Branch

10. Place the insertion point below the **If** condition, but in the same rectangle as the **If** condition, type **send an**, and then press **Enter**. Repeat this step to insert a **Send an E-mail** action below the **Else** branch.

11. Click **these users** in the **If** branch, and then use the steps in the exercise in "Using Actions and Conditions" earlier in this chapter to create a congratulations e-mail message. Click **these users** in the **Else** branch to create a decline-to-hire e-mail message.

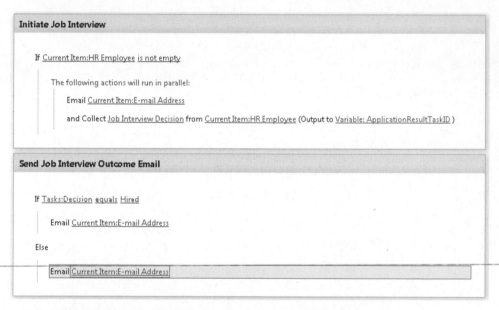

Initiate Job Interview

If Current Item:HR Employee is not empty

    The following actions will run in parallel:

        Email Current Item:E-mail Address

        and Collect Job Interview Decision from Current Item:HR Employee (Output to Variable: ApplicationResultTaskID)

Send Job Interview Outcome Email

If Tasks:Decision equals Hired

    Email Current Item:E-mail Address

Else

    Email Current Item:E-mail Address

Publish

12. On the **Workflow** tab, click **Save**, and then click **Publish**.

CLEAN UP Close the JobApplicationWorkflow tab. Leave SharePoint Designer open if you are continuing to the next exercise.

Creating a Site Workflow

In the previous version of SharePoint, all workflows were document-centric. Not all workflows are like that, however, and to cater to other scenarios, SharePoint 2010 now supports site workflows. Site workflows operate within the context of a SharePoint site and are not attached to a specific list, where workflow instances operate on list items or files. Site workflows can be started manually or programmatically, but not automatically.

There are two general conditions that initiate site-workflow actions:

- Check for some value within the SharePoint site
- Check whether a user is a valid SharePoint user

These conditions are quite generic and allow for the creation of a wide range of site workflows. For example, you could design a site workflow that creates a list of tasks the next time a valid SharePoint user logs on. These tasks could remind the user to perform actions such as filling in profile information, advising a user to create an alert on a list, or requesting a user to fill in a survey. Site workflows can be created by using Visual Studio 2010 or SharePoint Designer 2010. In SharePoint Designer, the actions you can use in a site workflow are similar to the actions you can use for a list or reusable workflow, except you cannot use actions that work on the current item, such as *Set Content Approval Status* and *Set Field in Current Item*.

In this exercise, you create a new site workflow and then use the browser to start the site workflow.

SET UP Using SharePoint Designer, open the site you used in the previous exercise if it is not already open. Display the workflow gallery page.

Site Workflow

1. On the **Workflows** tab, click **Site Workflow** in the **New** group.

   The Create Site Workflow dialog box opens.

2. In the **Name** box, type **SPD SBS Site Workflow**, and then click **OK**.

   The workflow editor opens.

3. Add conditions and actions to complete the logic of your workflow. For example, add the action **Add a Comment**, and then click **comment text** and type **Test Workflow**.

4. On the **Workflow** tab, click **Save**, and then click **Publish**.

5. Open your SharePoint site in the browser. Click **Site Action**, and then click **View All Site Content**. The All Content page is displayed.

6. To the right of the **Create** link, click **Site Workflows**.

   The Workflows page is displayed.

7. Under **Start a New Workflow**, click **SPD SBS Site Workflow**.

   The SPD SBS Site Workflow initiation page, which contains two buttons, Start and Cancel, is displayed.

8. Click **Start**.

   The Workflows page is displayed. Under My Completed Workflows, SPD SBS Site Workflow is listed as Completed.

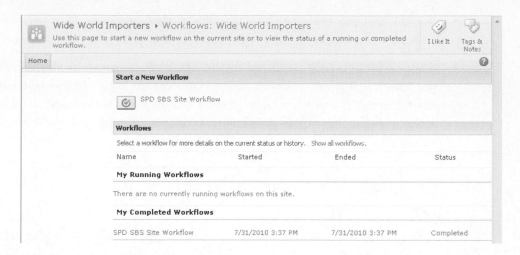

 CLEAN UP Close the browser. Leave SharePoint Designer open if you are continuing with further exercises in this chapter.

Using Visio to Map a Workflow

Another improvement in workflow technology in SharePoint 2010 is the ability to work with a workflow using Visio Premium 2010. This gives you a head start in creating a workflow by importing a Visio 2010 diagram into SharePoint Designer, where you add further details to make the workflow run in a SharePoint 2010 environment. Using Visio and SharePoint Designer together can improve communications between users who have knowledge of SharePoint 2010 and SharePoint Designer and users who are familiar with business processes.

Business users can use Visio Premium 2010 to document a business process that they want to create as a SharePoint workflow. However, they cannot use Visio shapes of any type. With Visio Premium 2010, a new template is available called Microsoft SharePoint Workflow, which allows the creation of SharePoint workflows in Visio. The conditions and actions are listed in three separate Visio stencils: SharePoint Workflow Terminators, SharePoint Workflow Conditions, and SharePoint Workflow Actions. Each workflow must have one workflow Start shape and one workflow Terminate shape and a connector connected to the two workflow shapes. The Start shape must not have incoming connections, and the Terminate shape must not have outgoing connections.

Unlike SharePoint Designer, Visio cannot connect to the SharePoint site where you want to create the workflow, and it does not retrieve dynamically a list of the available conditions and actions. Therefore, the conditions and actions in Visio might not represent the full selection of conditions and actions that are available when you use SharePoint Designer to create and modify workflows. Visio also has no shape that represents steps.

After a workflow is documented in Visio, you cannot directly deploy the Visio workflow diagram to a SharePoint site to create a working workflow. You need to export the diagram from Visio as a Visio Workflow Interchange (.vwi) file and then import the workflow file into Visual Studio 2010 or SharePoint Designer to complete the configuration of a SharePoint workflow.

The .vwi file is a ZIP file containing the .xoml files and some additional information that is used exclusively by Visio. If you change the extension of the .vwi file to .zip, you can open the file and find the following files inside:

- **[Content_Types].xml** This file contains a listing of the files found in the .vwi document.

- **workflow.vdx** This file contains a Visio-in-xml format snapshot of the workflow.

- **workflow.xoml** This file contains the workflow definition itself.

- **workflow.xoml.rules** This file contains workflow rule definitions.

See Also A 15-minute video is available on Microsoft's MSDN Channel 9 that describes how Visio and SharePoint Designer can be used to create a workflow. The video can be found at *channel9.msdn.com/learn/courses/Office2010/ClientWorkflowUnit/ VisioSharePointDesignerWorkflow/.* Also, the Microsoft Visio product team has a series of blogs on SharePoint workflow authoring in Visio Premium 2010 at *blogs.msdn.com/b/visio/.*

In this exercise, you create a workflow using Visio 2010 and export this workflow as a Visio Workflow Interchange (.vwi) file.

 SET UP Open Visio 2010. Backstage view should be displayed with New selected.

1. On the **New** tab in Backstage view, under **Template Categories**, click **Flowchart**, and then click **Microsoft SharePoint Workflow**.

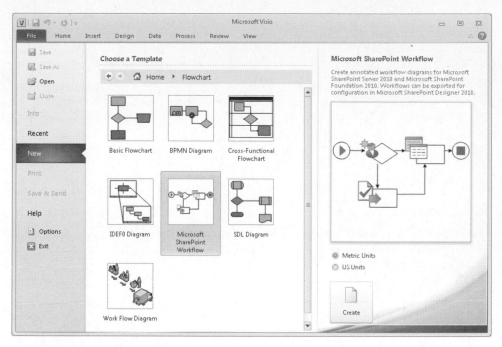

2. In the right pane, click **Create**.

   A blank template opens with three stencils in the Shapes pane: SharePoint Workflow Actions, SharePoint Workflow Conditions, and SharePoint Workflow Terminators.

3. In the **Shapes** pane, under **SharePoint Workflow Terminators**, click **Start**. Hold down the mouse button, and drag the **Start** shape to the left side of the template drawing area.

Connector

4. Repeat step 3 to add the **Terminate** shape to the right of the drawing area. Then, on the **Home** tab, click **Connector** in the **Tools** group, and drag a line from the **Start** shape to the **Terminate** shape.

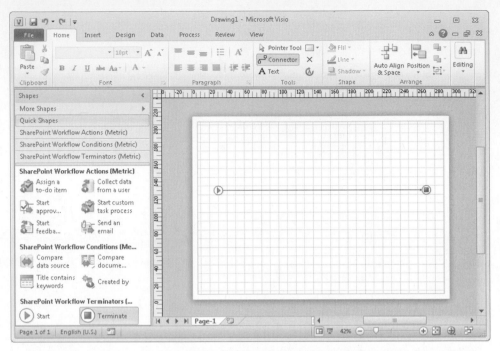

5. In the **Shapes** pane, under **SharePoint Workflow Conditions**, click **Compare data source**. Drag it to the drawing area to the right of the **Start** shape and place it on the line connecting the **Start** shape to the **Terminate** shape.

    The connecting line automatically connects the Start shape to the Compare Data Source shape, which is automatically connected to the Terminate shape.

6. In the **Shapes** pane, under **SharePoint Workflow Actions**, click **Send an Email**, and drag it to the drawing area to the right of the **Compare data source shape**.

7. Right-click the line connecting the **Compare data source** shape and the **Send E-mail** shape, and then click **Yes**.

8. Click the bottom corner of the **Compare data source** shape, and drag a line to the **Terminate** shape. Then right-click the connecting line, and click **No**.

9. On the **Home** tab, click **Pointer Tool** in the **Tools** group. Double-click **Compare data source**, and type **HR Employee Assigned?** Then double-click **Send an E-mail**, and type **Send E-mail to Job Applicant with Job Interview date and HR Employee name**.

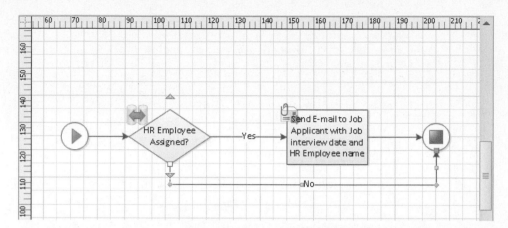

Check Diagram

10. On the **Process** tab, click **Check Diagram** in the **Diagram Validation** group.

A Microsoft Visio dialog box opens stating No Issues Were Found In The Current Document.

Note If your workflow has issues, an Issues task pane opens at the bottom of the Visio window. The component in error is highlighted. The Issues pane can be opened or closed by using the Issues Window check box in the Diagram Validation group on the Process tab.

Export

11. Click **OK**. On the **Process** tab, click **Export** in the **SharePoint Workflow** group.

The Export Workflow dialog box opens.

12. Navigate to **Documents**. In the **File name** box, type **JobApplicant_Draft**, and then click **Save**.

 CLEAN UP Close Visio and click Don't Save if prompted to save the drawing.

Importing a Workflow from Visio

After you export a .vwi file from Visio, you can import it into SharePoint Designer. You then need to configure the conditions and actions by using the workflow editor and settings pages. In real-world scenarios, this means that a business analyst sits down with the customer and comes up with a design for a workflow by using Visio 2010. The business analyst then passes the end result, a Visio Workflow Interchange file, to a workflow designer, who uses SharePoint Designer 2010 to add the missing configuration pieces.

Note When you import a workflow from Visio and the workflow already exists in SharePoint Designer, the workflow editor or settings pages must not be open. The Import Workflow From Visio Drawing dialog box opens, warning you that the workflow already exists on the site and that when you confirm the import, the existing workflow will be replaced and the operation cannot be undone.

In this exercise, you import a Visio workflow diagram into SharePoint Designer.

SET UP Using SharePoint Designer, open the site you used in the previous exercise if it is not already open.

Import From
Visio

1. In the **Navigation** pane, click **Workflows**, and then on the **Workflows** tab, click **Import from Visio** in the **Manage** group.

   The Import Workflow From Visio Drawing dialog box opens.

2. Click **Browse**, and navigate to **Documents**. Click **JobApplicant_Draft.vwi**, and then click **Open**.

3. Click **Next**, and then in the **List Workflow** list, select the list or library you want to attach the workflow to, such as **JobApplication**.

4. Click **Finish**.

   The JobApplicant_Draft workflow editor opens, displaying one step, one condition, and one action.

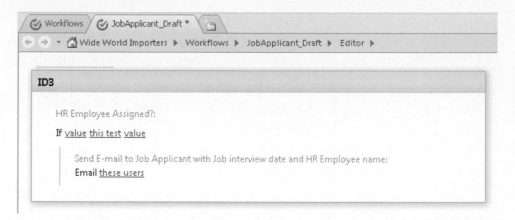

Note The Visio SharePoint workflow shapes do not contain shape data, so the text you add to conditions and actions is presented as comments in SharePoint Designer. You cannot configure conditions and actions that were added in Visio.

CLEAN UP Save and then close the JobApplicant_Draft workflow. Leave SharePoint Designer open if you are continuing to the next exercise.

Exporting a Workflow to a Visio Drawing

In the previous two sections, a Visio drawing was exported and then imported into SharePoint Designer. You can also create a workflow using SharePoint Designer 2010 and export this workflow to a .vwi file. A business analyst can modify the workflow in Visio, and then you can import it back to SharePoint Designer. However, the amendments made by the business analyst are only comments to the conditions and actions. When you import the Visio diagram into SharePoint Designer, the configurations of the conditions and actions might not match the comments. You need to check the configurations of the condition and actions to be sure they match.

Warning You cannot use a .vwi file to export a workflow from one site and import it to another site. To move workflows between sites, use Save As Template (.wsp file) to save the file as a template instead of a Visio workflow drawing. However, only reusable workflows can be saved as templates. If you are creating workflows that you need to use on other lists, libraries, or sites, use a reusable workflow.

In this exercise, you export a workflow from SharePoint Designer and import it into Visio.

SET UP Using SharePoint Designer, open the site you used in the previous exercise if it is not already open.

Export to Visio

1. In the **Navigation** pane, click **Workflows**. The Workflow gallery page is displayed.

2. Under **List Workflow**, click the icon to the left of **JobApplicationWorkflow**, and then on the **Workflows** tab, click **Export to Visio** in the **Manage** group.

   The Export Workflow To Visio Drawing dialog box opens.

3. Verify that the **File name** box contains **JobApplicantWorkflow**. Navigate to **Documents**, and then click **Save**.

4. Open Visio. In Backstage view, under **Template Categories**, click **Flowchart**, and then click **Microsoft SharePoint Workflow**. Click **Create**.

   A blank template opens with three stencils in the Shapes pane: SharePoint Workflow Actions, SharePoint Workflow Conditions, and SharePoint Workflow Terminators.

Import

5. On the **Process** tab, click **Import** in the **SharePoint Workflow** group.

   The Import Workflow dialog box opens.

6. Navigate to **Documents**, click **JobApplicantWorkflow.vwi**, and then click **Open**.

   The SharePoint workflow diagram appears in the drawing area.

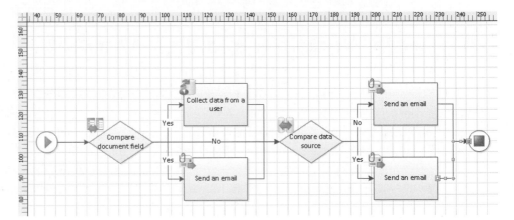

CLEAN UP Close Visio and click Don't Save if prompted to save the drawing. Leave SharePoint Designer open if you are continuing to the next exercise.

Removing and Deleting Workflows

Business processes do not last forever, and neither will your workflows. Deleting a workflow disrupts the execution of any running workflow instance, so before you delete a workflow in SharePoint Designer, you must first prevent the creation of new workflow instances and then wait for workflow instances that are still in progress to complete. SharePoint Designer does not provide a mechanism to manage workflow instances; you must use the browser.

When all the workflow instances are complete, you can remove the workflow from the site, list, or library with which it is associated. When you delete a list workflow, you also delete the column that was created to monitor workflow instances as they progress through the workflow. You do not delete any task content types that were created or any site columns that were added when you created associated columns.

See Also Associated columns are described in Chapter 9.

Removing a workflow from a list or library does not delete it. You can still access it using SharePoint Designer. When you next publish the list workflow in SharePoint Designer, it is attached to the list or library again.

See Also More information on how to perform common workflow administration tasks can be found at *technet.microsoft.com/en-us/library/cc531334.aspx*.

In this exercise, you prevent the creation of new instances of a list workflow and then delete the workflow.

SET UP Using SharePoint Designer, open the site you used in the previous exercise if it is not already open.

1.   In the **Navigation** pane, click **Workflows**, and then under **List Workflow**, click the workflow you want to delete, such as **JobApplicationWorkflow**.

     The Workflow Settings page is displayed.

2.   In the **Customization** area, click **Open associated list**.

     The list settings page is displayed.

Administration
Web Page

3.   In the **Workflow** area, click the icon to the left of **JobApplicationWorkflow**, and then on the **List**, **Workflows** tab, click **Administration Web Page**.

     The browser opens and displays the Workflow Settings page. The page contains a link for each workflow published from SharePoint Designer and the number of workflow instances currently in progress for each workflow.

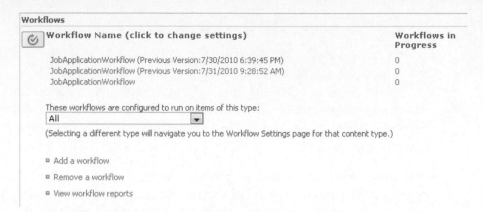

4. Click **Remove a workflow** to display the **Remove Workflows** page.

5. To the right of **JobApplicationWorkflow**, click **No New Instances**, and then click **OK**.

   Tip By clicking No New Instances, you prevent the creation of any new workflow instances.

   The Workflow Settings page is displayed.

6. In SharePoint Designer, with **JobApplicationWorkflow** still selected in the **Workflows** area, on the **List**, **Workflows** tab, click **Delete**.

   The Confirm Delete dialog box opens.

Delete

7. Click **Yes** to delete the workflow.

   Note Using Delete on the List, Workflows tab deletes the workflow from the list. This operation is the same as removing a workflow by using the browser. The workflow is still available using SharePoint Designer.

8. In the **Navigation** pane, click **Workflows**.

9. Under **List Workflow**, click the icon to the left of workflow you want to delete, such as **JobApplicationWorkflow**, and then on the **Workflows** tab, click **Delete**.

   The Confirm Delete dialog box opens, stating that this operation will also remove all workflow history data for this workflow.

Delete

10. Click **Yes** to delete the workflow.

> **Tip** Deleting a workflow from the Workflow gallery page or the Workflow Settings page deletes the folder and the .xoml and form files from the Workflows library. Therefore, just as with any other list or library, when you delete items from the Workflows library, the items are moved to the Recycle Bin, from which you can restore them. To reattach a workflow to a list (if it is a list workflow), publish the workflow.

 CLEAN UP Save the workflow. Leave SharePoint Designer open if you are continuing to the next chapter.

Key Points

- SharePoint Foundation and SharePoint Server use the Windows Workflow Foundation to provide workflows.

- SharePoint Foundation and SharePoint Server provide a set of built-in workflow templates usually associated with a tasks list and a history list. SharePoint Designer 2010 can reuse some of these workflows.

- You can use three tools to create custom SharePoint 2010 workflows: SharePoint Designer 2010, Visual Studio 2010, and Visio Premium 2010.

- You can create different types of workflows using SharePoint Designer 2010: list workflows, reusable workflows, and site workflows.

- SharePoint Designer 2010 allows you to create workflows using an extensive set of actions and conditions that are available out of the box.

- SharePoint 2010 workflows know how to impersonate other users with elevated privileges during workflow execution.

- SharePoint 2010 workflows can operate on document sets.

- Try to keep workflows as simple as possible. Use the *Add a Comment* and *Log to History List* actions to comment your workflow and to help you diagnose problems you may have.

- SharePoint Designer 2010 allows you to create, publish, copy, modify, and delete workflows.

- You can export SharePoint Designer 2010 workflows to Visio 2010, and also import Visio 2010 workflow diagrams into SharePoint Designer 2010.

- You cannot change or delete a workflow without running the risk of disrupting existing instances of a workflow. Use the browser to configure the workflow to allow the current instances of the workflow to complete and prevent the creation of new instances.

Chapter at a Glance

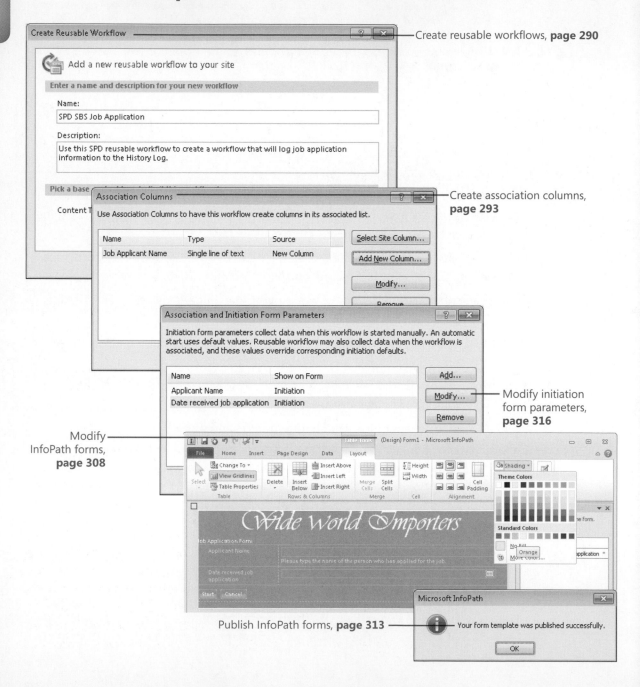

Create reusable workflows, **page 290**

Create association columns, **page 293**

Modify initiation form parameters, **page 316**

Modify InfoPath forms, **page 308**

Publish InfoPath forms, **page 313**

9 Using Reusable Workflows and Workflow Forms

In this chapter, you will learn how to

- ✔ Create and use reusable workflows.
- ✔ Create association columns.
- ✔ Use workflow templates.
- ✔ Reuse and create globally reusable workflows.
- ✔ Create initiation and association forms.
- ✔ Retrieve values from initiation forms.
- ✔ Modify and publish InfoPath forms.
- ✔ Modify initiation form parameters.
- ✔ Modify association forms.
- ✔ Add association fields to initiation forms.
- ✔ Modify task forms.

In the previous chapter, you learned about workflow-related features provided by SharePoint 2010 and SharePoint Designer 2010 and how to create workflows in SharePoint Designer 2010. That's not all there is to know about working with workflows in SharePoint Designer.

This version of SharePoint Designer has many workflow-related improvements over the previous version, in which the biggest drawback was the lack of workflow reusability. SharePoint Designer 2007 was mostly used for ad-hoc workflows that could only be created on lists and libraries. These workflows could not be easily transferred to other lists or libraries, even within the same site. With SharePoint Designer 2010, you can attach SharePoint Designer workflows to lists, libraries, content types, or sites, and you can even export them to Microsoft Visual Studio. This makes the workflow editor and settings page in SharePoint Designer an ideal starting point for custom workflows, which might or might not evolve into Visual Studio workflows.

In this chapter, you will learn how to create reusable workflows; how to reuse out-of-the-box workflows; and how to create and modify initiation, association, and task forms. You'll also learn how workflows created by SharePoint Designer can be used in various integration and deployment scenarios. When you finish reading this chapter, you'll be ready to create sophisticated workflows without writing a single line of code.

> **Practice Files** Before you can use the practice file in this chapter, you need to copy the book's practice files to your computer. The practice file you'll use to complete the exercises in this chapter is in the Chapter09 practice file folder. A complete list of practice files is provided in "Using the Practice Files" at the beginning of this book.

Creating and Using Reusable Workflows

The biggest problem with the previous version of SharePoint Designer was that you could only create workflows that were attached to a specific list or library. SharePoint Designer 2010 allows you to create reusable workflows. You can attach a reusable workflow to a specific content type, which makes the workflow available to any list or library associated with that content type.

On the Workflow Settings page, you can specify whether you want the reusable workflow to use workflow visualization, and in the Start Options area, you can specify which start options cannot be used when the reusable workflow is associated with a list or library.

In this exercise, you create a reusable workflow and then use the browser to associate it with a list.

 SET UP Using SharePoint Designer, open the team site you created and modified in earlier chapters. If you did not yet create a team site, follow the steps in Chapter 1.

Reusable Workflows

1. In the **Navigation** pane, click **Workflows**, and then on the **Workflow** tab, click **Reusable Workflow** in the **New** group.

   The Create Reusable Workflow dialog box opens.

2. In the **Name** box, type **SPD SBS Job Application**, and in the **Description** box, type **Use this SPD reusable workflow to create a workflow that will log job application information to the History Log**.

3. In the **Content Type** list, select the content type that you want to associate with this workflow, such as **Document**.

Warning After you save the reusable workflow, you cannot change the content type.

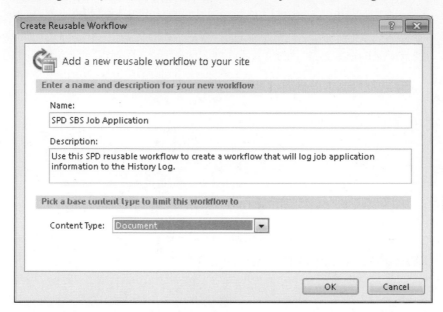

4. Click **OK**. The SPD SBS Job Application workflow editor is displayed.

Action

5. On the **Workflow** tab, click **Action**, and then under **Core Actions**, select **Log to History List**.

Display Builder

6. Click **this message**, and then click the **Display builder for this parameter** button that appears.

The String Builder dialog box opens.

7. In the **Name** box, type **Job Applicant resume:**, and then click **Add or Change Lookup**. In the **Field from source** list, scroll down, select **Name (for use in forms)**, and then click **OK** twice.

The Lookup For String and String Builder dialog boxes close.

8. On the **Workflow** tab, click **Save**, and then click **Publish**.

Workflow
Associations

9. In the **Navigation** pane, click **Lists and Libraries**, click a list or library associated with the content type you selected in step 3, such as **Shared Documents**, and then on the **List Settings** tab, click **Workflow Associations** in the **Manage** group.

A browser window opens displaying the Workflow Settings page.

10. In the **These workflows are configured to run on items of this type** list, select the content type you selected in step 3, such as **Document**, and then click **Add a workflow**. The Add A Workflow page is displayed.

11. In the **Select a workflow template** list, select **SPD SBS Job Application**, and in the **Type a unique name for this workflow** box, type **JobHistory**.

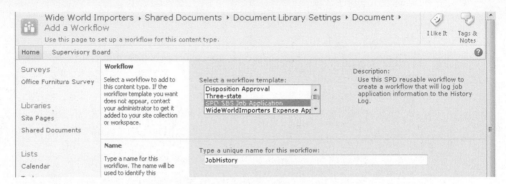

Tip When a workflow will be heavily used, it should have its own task list.

12. At the bottom of the page, click **OK**.

The Workflow Settings page is displayed and lists the JobHistory workflow.

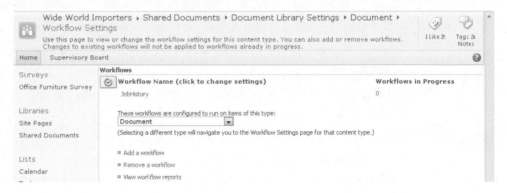

CLEAN UP Close the browser. Leave SharePoint Designer open if you are continuing to the next exercise.

Creating Association Columns

When a reusable workflow is bound to a content type, the columns specified by that content type can be used in the workflow. If you choose to bind a reusable workflow to all content types, only those columns that are shared by all content types are available. However, a workflow might require a number of other columns. To ensure that any list or library with which you associate a reusable workflow has the columns the workflow needs, you can use the Association Column command to bind those columns to the workflow. Association columns are added automatically to a list or library and guarantee that the columns are available so that the workflow can complete. Association columns can be existing site columns or new site columns. The new site columns are classified under the Custom Columns group in the Site Columns gallery.

In this exercise, you create an association column.

 SET UP Using SharePoint Designer, open the site you used in the previous exercise if it is not already open.

1. In the **Navigation** pane, click **Workflows**. Under **Reusable Workflow**, click the workflow for which you want to create an association column, such as **SPD SBS Job Application**.

2. On the **Workflow Settings** tab, click **Association Columns**.

   Association Columns

   A Microsoft SharePoint Designer dialog box opens, stating that changing the association columns for this workflow can cause new instances of existing associations to fail.

3. Click **OK** to confirm that you want to create an association column.

   The Association Columns dialog box opens.

4. Click **Add New Column**.

   The Add Column dialog box opens.

   Note You can modify new columns only by using the Association Columns dialog box. Once the workflow is published, the new column becomes an existing column and can be modified only by using the Site Column gallery in SharePoint Designer or in the browser.

5. In the **Field name** box, type **Job Applicant Name**, and in the **Description** box, type **This field should contain the name of the person who has applied for the job**.

6. Click **Next**, and then click **Finish**.

The Association Columns dialog box contains one association column, Job Applicant Name.

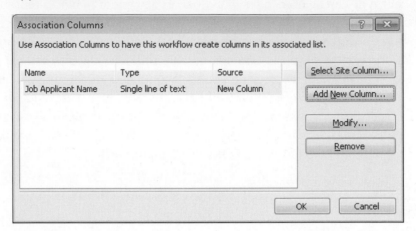

7. Click **OK**.

The Association Columns dialog box closes.

8. On the **Workflow** tab, click **Save**, and then click **Publish**.

✖ CLEAN UP Close SharePoint Designer.

Using Workflow Templates

In this section you will learn how to create the ultimate form of a reusable workflow. SharePoint Designer allows you to save a reusable workflow as a .wsp file, also known as a *SharePoint solution file*, in the Site Assets library. Using the browser, you can download the .wsp file and import it into Visual Studio 2010, where you can use the workflow as a template and a starting point for further development.

See Also A walkthrough on how to import a SharePoint Designer reusable workflow into Visual Studio can be found at *msdn.microsoft.com/en-us/library/ee231580.aspx*.

You can also give the workflow template .wsp file to a site collection owner, who can upload the file to the Solutions gallery at the top of a site collection and activate it so that it becomes visible as a site feature. Site owners can then activate that feature and use the workflow as a list workflow template within that site.

Note The list workflow template will be available only for the content types that the reusable workflow is associated with.

In this exercise, you save a workflow as a .wsp solution file.

 SET UP Using SharePoint Designer, open the site you used in the previous exercise if it is not already open.

1. In the **Navigation** pane, click **Workflows**, and then under **Reusable Workflow**, click the workflow you want to save as a template, such as **SPD SBS Job Application**.

 2. On the **Workflows** tab, click **Save as Template** in the **Manage** group.

A Microsoft SharePoint Designer dialog box opens stating that the template has been saved to the Site Assets library.

Save as Template 3. Click **OK**.

CLEAN UP Close SharePoint Designer.

Reusing Globally Reusable Workflows

Creating a workflow that already exists in SharePoint 2010 is a waste of time and could make you look foolish, especially to your manager. Before starting to create a workflow, you should take time to familiarize yourself with the workflows that are available out of the box. In addition to many useful out-of-the-box workflows, SharePoint 2010 contains a special category of workflows called *globally reusable workflows*. The word *reusable* means that you can make a copy of a globally reusable workflow in SharePoint Designer 2010 and customize the workflow in many different ways. This lets you take a workflow that is thoroughly tested by the Microsoft SharePoint product team and modify it so that it suits your specific business requirements. (In real-world scenarios, you will often find that the existing workflows approach but do not exactly match the business requirements you have.)

Reusable workflows are only reusable within the scope of the site where they are published. A *globally* reusable workflow is reusable throughout the entire site collection. If you need a workflow that is reusable across multiple site collections, Web applications, and/or SharePoint farms, you need to create a workflow template.

Microsoft SharePoint Foundation 2010 does not provide any preconfigured globally reusable workflows, but you can still create your own using SharePoint Designer. Microsoft SharePoint Server 2010 ships with the following globally reusable workflows. These globally reusable workflows are the workflow templates that you use in the browser, and they define one action:

- **Approval workflow** Uses the Start Approval process action and provides an approval mechanism for documents that allows you to assign tasks serially (one after the other) or in parallel (at the same time). Using this workflow, you can approve, reject, or reassign a document. You can also request a change to the document that is the subject of the approval process.

- **Collect Feedback workflow** Uses the Start Feedback Process action and provides a feedback mechanism for documents that allows you to collect review comments for a given document.

- **Collect Signatures workflow** Uses the Start Custom Task process and provides a mechanism for collecting digital signatures for completing a document. You can use digital signatures to provide assurance of the authenticity, integrity, and origin of the document.

Important Do not modify the out-of-the-box globally reusable workflows. Your users will assume that these workflows run as described on Microsoft's Web site, in end-user training courses, and in books about SharePoint Server. When you need to modify a globally reusable workflow, make a copy of the workflow and modify the copy.

For each globally reusable workflow, SharePoint creates a document library in the *wfpub* library, which is stored in the *_catalogs* folder in the root site of a site collection. These libraries are hidden from the browser and can be seen only in SharePoint Designer by users who can see the hidden URL site structure.

Warning When you modify and then save a reusable or globally reusable workflow, the workflow is not available to be associated with a list, library, or content type until you successfully publish the workflow.

In this exercise, you create a copy of the globally reusable Approval workflow.

Important You can complete this exercise only if you have a site created on SharePoint Server 2010.

 SET UP Using SharePoint Designer, open the root site of a site collection.

1. In the **Navigation** pane, click **Workflows**.

   The Workflow gallery is displayed.

Copy & Modify

2. Under **Globally Reusable Workflow**, click the icon to the left of the globally reusable workflow you want to copy, such as **Approval—SharePoint 2010**, and then on the **Workflows** tab, click **Copy & Modify** in the **Manage** group.

Note You can create a copy of a globally reusable workflow at the root site of a site collection or at a subsite.

A Microsoft SharePoint Designer dialog box might open, warning you that the globally reusable workflow you selected is read-only.

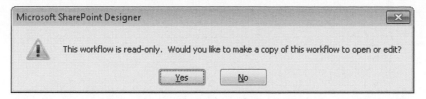

3. Click **Yes** to confirm that you want to make a copy of the workflow to open or edit.

The Create Reusable Workflow dialog box opens.

4. In the **Name** box, type the name of the workflow, such as **WideWorldImporters Expense Approval**.

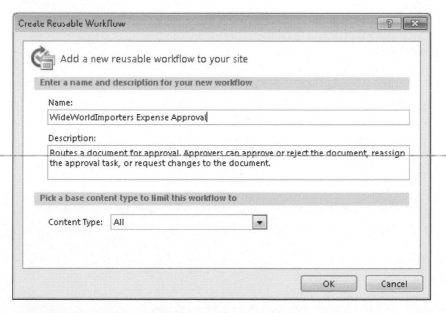

5. Click **OK**. The Create Reusable Workflow dialog box closes. The workflow editor page opens and displays one step, which defines a configured Start Approval Process action.

See Also More information on the Start Approval Process action can be found in Appendix B on page 491.

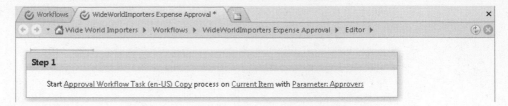

6. Press **CTRL+S** to save the workflow, and then on the workspace breadcrumb, click **Workflows**.

The Workflows gallery page is displayed, and WideWorldImporters Expense Approval is listed under Reusable Workflow.

Troubleshooting If the new globally reusable workflow is not listed in the gallery, click the Refresh button.

 CLEAN UP Leave SharePoint Designer open if you are continuing to the next exercise.

Creating Globally Reusable Workflows

In addition to reusing built-in globally reusable workflows, you can create your own. First you create a reusable workflow, which might be a new reusable workflow or a copy of a globally reusable workflow, such as the one you copied in the previous exercise. Then you convert the reusable workflow to a globally reusable workflow.

Important You can create globally reusable workflows only at the root site of a site collection and not in a subsite.

In this exercise, you create a globally reusable workflow and verify that it is available in a child site of the site collection.

SET UP Using SharePoint Designer, open the root site of a site collection if one is not already open, and then open the Workflow gallery. To complete this exercise, you also need a subsite under the root of the site collection and a document library that contains at least one document.

Workflow
Settings

1. In the Workflow gallery, click the icon to the left of the reusable workflow you want to convert to a globally reusable workflow, such as **WideWorldImporters Expense Approval**, or use the workflow you created earlier, **SPD SBS Job Application**. Then, on the **Workflows** tab, click **Workflow Settings**.

Publish Globally

2. On the **Workflow Settings** tab, click **Publish Globally** in the **Manage** group.

A Microsoft SharePoint Designer dialog box opens, indicating that publishing a workflow to the global workflows catalog will make it reusable on every site in the site collection.

3. Click **OK** to confirm the global publication of the workflow.

   A dialog box is displayed while the conversion process occurs.

4. On the workspace breadcrumb, click **Workflows**.

   The Workflows gallery is displayed. The reusable workflow you converted, such as WideWorldImporters Expense Approval, is displayed under Globally Reusable Workflow and Reusable Workflow.

5. Open the browser, and navigate to the child site where you want to test the globally reusable workflow you created in step 2.

Workflow
Settings

6. On the Quick Launch, click **Shared Documents**, and then on the **Library** tab, click **Workflow Settings** in the **Settings** group.

   The Workflow Settings page is displayed.

7. Click **Add a workflow**.

   The Add A Workflow page is displayed. In the Workflow section, under Select A Workflow Template, the WideWorldImporters Expense Approval workflow is listed.

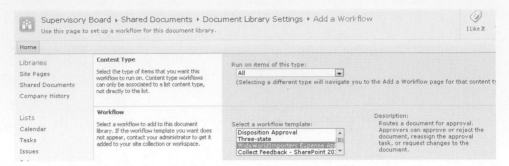

8. In the **Workflow** section, select **WideWorldImporters Expense Approval**, and in the **Name** section, type **Expense Approval**. Click **Next**.

   The Expense Approval association form is displayed.

Check Name

9. In the **Approvers** section, type the name of a user, and then click the **Check Name** icon to verify that the name you entered is a valid user name for your installation. In the **Request** box, type **Please review the expenses document**, and then in the **Duration Per Task** box, type **5**.

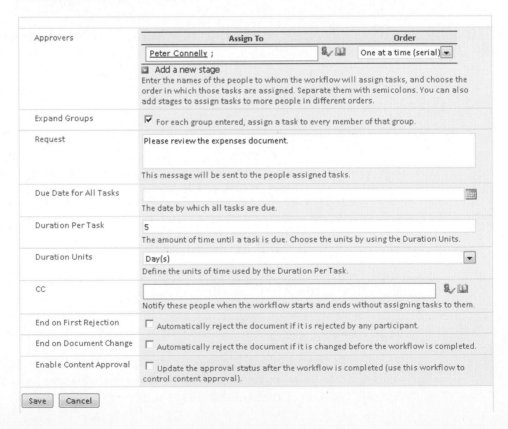

10. Click **Save**.

    The Workflow Settings page is displayed. Under Workflow Name, Expense Approval appears with no workflow instances in progress.

11. On the Quick Launch, click **Shared Documents**, point to a document, click the arrow that appears, and then click **Workflows**. In the **Start a New Workflow** section, click **Expense Approval**.

    The Expense Approval initiation form is displayed.

12. Click **Start**.

    The Shared Documents By Modified view is displayed. An extra column, labeled Expense Approval, appears in the view, with a status of In Progress for the document you chose in step 11.

 CLEAN UP Close all SharePoint Designer windows.

Creating Initiation and Association Forms

During the normal execution of a workflow created by SharePoint Designer 2010, a number of types of forms might be displayed:

- Association
- Initiation
- Task

The basic function of these types of forms is to collect data from a user. In this section, you will take a closer look at the creation of initiation and association forms.

Content owners and site administrators are the target audience for association forms. A workflow can have a single association form that is shown each time a user associates that workflow to a specific list, library, or content type. This allows you, as a workflow designer, to let users define default values or specify at workflow-association time other information that can be used when a workflow instance is started.

Note Only reusable and globally reusable workflows have an association form. List and site workflows are associated with a list or site as part of the workflow-creation process, so an association form is not needed.

Association forms and initiation forms can be—but don't have to be—identical. Association forms are targeted toward content owners or the user who manages the list, library, or content type, whereas initiation forms are targeted toward end users who manually start a workflow instance. You can use initiation forms to override default values that are specified in the association forms by content owners. You can also use initiation forms to collect information that is critical for running a workflow and known only by the end user. When a workflow instance is automatically started, the initiation form is not displayed, and the workflow process uses the values the administrator entered in the association form. If additional information needs to be collected from the end user once the workflow instance has started, this is the purpose of task forms.

The ease with which you can create and enhance initiation and association forms is one of the most remarkable improvements in SharePoint Designer 2010. The questions you ask on initiation and association forms can be of various types:

- Single line of text
- Multiple lines of text
- Number
- Date and time
- Choice
- Yes/No
- Person or group
- Hyperlink or picture
- Assignment stages

Most of these question types are similar to list column types, with the exception of the assignment stages type. A workflow passes through various stages, where each stage requires actions to be performed by one or more people. When multiple people are required to complete an action within a single stage, you need to decide whether the people should perform the actions one at a time (serially) or all at once (parallel). You use the assignment stages question type in this situation to collect the information you need. An example of an assignment stages question appears in the Approvers section of the Approval reusable workflow association or initiation form. These forms contain a repeatable section that allows you to add Approvers sections (also known as *assignment sections*) as needed. You can also remove assignment stages or add them before or after an existing stage by clicking the arrow that appears when you hover the mouse pointer over an assignment stage.

In this exercise, you create a workflow initiation form and verify its creation by using the browser.

SET UP Using SharePoint Designer, open the SharePoint site where you created the SPD SBS Job Application workflow. Display the workflow settings for the workflow.

Initiation Form
Parameters

1. On the **Workflow Settings** tab, click **Initiation Form Parameters** in the **Variables** group.

   The Association And Initiation Form Parameters dialog box opens.

2. Click **Add**. The Add Field dialog box opens.

3. In the **Field name** box, type **Applicant Name**, and in the **Description** box, type **Please type the name of the person who has applied for the job**.

4. Leave the default values in the **Information type** and **Collect from parameter during** lists; that is, **Single line of text** and **Initiation (starting the workflow)**.

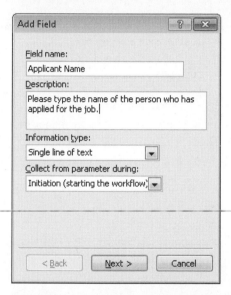

Note When using the Association And Initiation Form Parameters dialog box for a list or site workflow, the Add Field dialog box does not display the Collect From Parameter During list. For list and site workflows, only initiation forms are created, so any field you add will be an initiation form parameter.

5. Click **Next**. The Column Settings dialog box is displayed.

6. Leave the **Default value** box empty, and click **Finish**.

   Warning If you want the workflow to start automatically instead of manually, you must provide default values for all the initiation parameters. Otherwise, a warning dialog box is displayed when you publish the workflow.

7. Repeat steps 3 to 6 to add a field with a **Field name** of **Date received job application**, an information type of **Date and Time**, and a default value of **Today's date**. Clear the check box for **Allow blank values**.

The Association And Initiation Form Parameters dialog box displays two initiation form parameters.

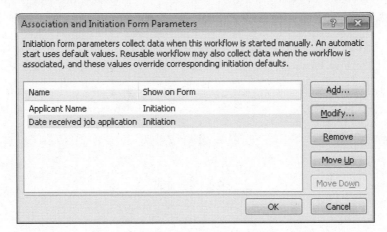

Note You can change the order of the form parameters by using the Move Up and Move Down buttons.

8. Click **OK**. The Association And Initiation Form Parameters dialog box closes.

In the Forms area, SPD SBS Job Application.xsn is displayed with an asterisk, indicating that the form has changed since you opened the Workflow Settings page in the workspace. This form uses Microsoft InfoPath 2010 technology. If you are using SharePoint Foundation, the form's name will be SPD SBS Job Application.aspx. The form always takes its name from the name of the workflow.

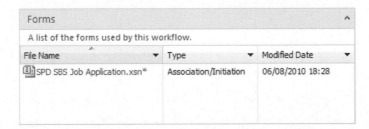

Note If this is a new workflow, the forms are not created until you publish the workflow.

9. Press **CTRL+S**, and then on the **Workflow Settings** tab, click **Publish** in the **Save** group.

Publish

10. Open the browser and navigate to the **Shared Documents** library with which you associated the SPD SBS Job Application reusable workflow.

11. In the browser, point to a document, click the arrow that appears, and then click **Workflows**. In the **Start a New Workflow** section, click **JobHistory**.

The initiation form is displayed.

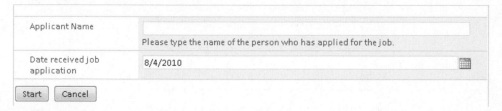

12. Click **Cancel**.

 CLEAN UP Leave the browser and SharePoint Designer open if you are continuing to the next exercise.

Retrieving Values from Initiation Forms

Creating initiation and association forms is meaningless unless you know how to retrieve values specified in those forms by end users and then use those values within your workflows.

In this exercise, you check whether a value has been typed into a field on an initiation form. You then store the value in a column and write the value of an initiation form parameter to the workflow's history list. Using the browser, you then verify the workflow.

 SET UP Using SharePoint Designer, open the site you used in the previous exercise if it is not already open. Display the workflow editor for the SPD SBS Job Application workflow you created in a previous exercise.

1. With the insertion point in **Step 1**, above the **log** action, type **if a**, and press **Enter**.

The text *If Value Equals Value* appears, and the Log action is prefixed with *Then*.

Define workflow lookup

2. Click the first **value** link, and then click the **Define workflow lookup** button that appears.

The Define Workflow Lookup dialog box opens.

3. In the **Data source** list, select **Workflow Variables and Parameters**. In the **Field from source** list, select **Parameter: Applicant Name**.

4. Click **OK** to close the Define Workflow Lookup dialog box, and then click **equals**. Select **is not empty**.

   The text *If Value Equals Value* is replaced with *If Parameter:Applicant Name Is Not Empty*.

5. Place the insertion point below **If**, type **set f**, and then press **Enter**.

   The text *Set Field To Value* appears.

Define workflow lookup

6. Click **field**, and then select **Job Applicant Name**. Click **value**, and then click the **Define workflow lookup** button that appears.

7. Repeat steps 3 and 4. Select the data source **Workflow Variables and Parameters**, and then select **Parameter:Applicant Name** in the **Field from source** list. In the **Return field as** list, select **As String**.

8. Click **Job Applicant resume:[%Current Item**. The String Builder dialog box opens.

9. In the **Name** box, with the insertion point to the right of **Name%]**, type **and the date received was:**, and then click **Add or Change Lookup**. Repeat steps 3 and 4 to add **Parameter: Date Received job application**, formatting the return field as **Long Date**. Click **OK**.

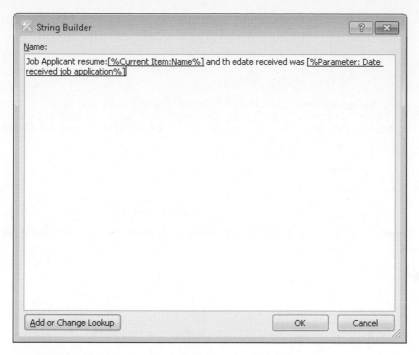

10. Click **OK** to close the **String Builder** dialog box.

Publish

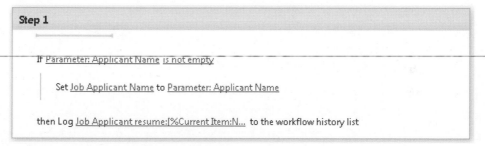

11. On the **Workflow** tab, click **Publish**.

Tip Publishing a workflow also saves any modifications you have made to the workflow.

12. In the browser, display the **Shared Documents All Document** view, point to a document, click the arrow that appears, and then click **Workflows**. In the **Start a New Workflow** section, click **JobHistory**.

The initiation form is displayed.

13. In the **Name** box, type **Peter Connelly**, and then click **Start**.

A column labeled JobHistory has been added to the view, with a status of Completed.

14. Point to the document that you used in step 12, click the arrow that appears, and then click **View Properties**.

A dialog box opens and displays the properties of the document. One of the properties is named Job Applicant Name, and it has the value Peter Connelly.

15. Click **Close**, and then in the **JobHistory** column, click **Completed**.

The Workflow Status page is displayed. In the Workflow History section, in the Description column, the text created by the workflow appears.

CLEAN UP Leave SharePoint Designer open if you are continuing to the next exercise.

Modifying an InfoPath Form

If your SharePoint site is hosted on SharePoint Server 2010, SharePoint Designer creates the workflow forms as Web-compatible InfoPath form template .xsn files (which are basically CAB files) that store the set of files required to correctly render the forms. When rendered in the browser, the form templates are loaded into a Form Services Web Part. In SharePoint Designer, you do not see the .aspx page that contains the Form Services Web Part; you see only the form templates that are created. If you look at the Address box in the browser when you display an initiation form, you will see that the .aspx page that is used is *_layouts/IniWrkflIP.aspx*. For an association form, the .aspx page is *_layouts/CstWrkflIP.aspx*.

Note You can check the contents of an .xsn file by changing the extension to .cab, as you did with the .wsp file in Chapter 2, "Working with SharePoint Sites." You will see that it mostly contains .xml, .xsl, and .xsd files, which is good from an interoperability point of view, and makes it relatively easy for other applications to interact with InfoPath forms.

The InfoPath 2010 form templates created by SharePoint Designer do not unleash the full power of InfoPath. You can take any InfoPath form created by SharePoint Designer— including list views and list forms—and use InfoPath to transform the form into something that looks quite different.

Note The InfoPath user interface uses the terms *form* and *form template* interchangeably. Don't let this confuse you. To be precise, SharePoint Designer 2010 builds form templates. Form services use a form template to display the form that is filled in by end users. Whenever SharePoint Designer 2010 refers to forms, it is really referring to form templates.

InfoPath 2010 is split into two applications: Microsoft InfoPath Designer 2010 and Microsoft InfoPath Filler 2010. To modify an InfoPath form created by SharePoint Designer, you need a copy of InfoPath Designer 2010. InfoPath Designer makes it very easy to change the look and feel of a form, and it also lets you add data validation rules, functions, and external data sources. However, when you are modifying workflow forms in InfoPath Designer, only a subset of the program's features are available. Binding existing controls to new external data sources is overruled during workflow execution because the workflow instance will not have access to the values of new controls.

See Also For a quick review of using InfoPath 2010, see Chapter 15, "Using SharePoint Foundation with InfoPath 2010," in *Microsoft SharePoint Foundation 2010 Step By Step* (Microsoft Press, 2011). To find more about developing solutions using InfoPath 2010, visit *msdn.microsoft.com/en-us/library/ff604966.aspx*.

In this exercise, you modify an InfoPath initiation form.

SET UP Using SharePoint Designer, open the site you used in the previous exercise if it is not already open. Display the workflow settings for the SPD SBS Job Application workflow you modified in the previous exercise. To complete this exercise, you need access to Microsoft InfoPath Designer 2010 and to the practice file WideWorldImporters.png in the Chapter09 practice file folder.

1. In the **Forms** area, click the initiation form you want to modify, such as **SPD SBS Job Application.xsn**.

InfoPath opens. A dialog box opens as the form is downloaded, and then the form is displayed in Design view. In the Fields task pane, the red asterisk to the right of Date Received Job Application indicates that this field cannot be blank.

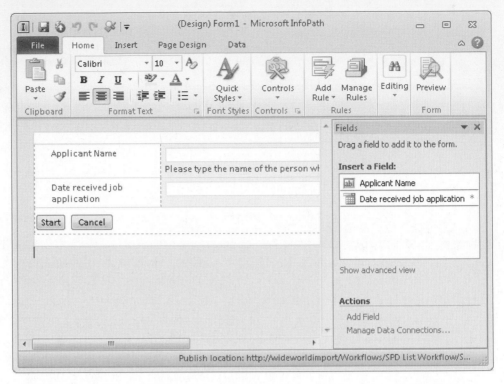

Picture

2.   Place the insertion point above the rectangle that contains the text **Applicant Name**, press **Enter**, and type **Job Application Form**. Then place the insertion point on the line above **Job**, and on the **Insert** tab, click **Picture** in the **Illustrations** group.

The Insert Picture dialog box opens.

3.   Navigate to the **Chapter09** practice file folder. Select **WideWorldImporters.png**, and click **Insert**.

An image is added above the text *Job Application Form*.

4.   Click the image, and then press **CTRL+E** to center the image on the form. Click the small square attached to the top-left corner of the form to highlight the form, and then on the **Table Tools**, **Layout** tab, click **Shading** in the **Color** group, and select **Orange**.

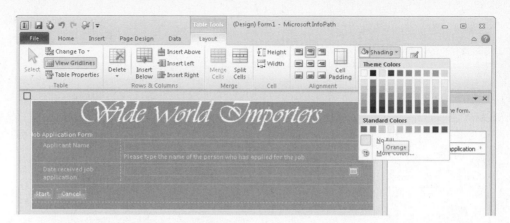

Control
Properties

5. On the **Page Design** tab, click the **Themes** down arrow, and select one of the themes, such as **Professional Classic**.

6. Click the box to the right of **Applicant Name**, and then on the **Control Tools**, **Properties** tab, click **Control Properties** in the **Properties** group.

    The Text Box Properties dialog box opens.

7. On the **Advanced** tab, in the **ScreenTip** box, type **Enter job applicant name**.

8. Click **OK**. The Text Box Properties dialog box closes.

Manage Rules

9.   Click the box to the right of **Date received job application**, and then on the **Control Tools**, **Properties** tab, click **Manage Rules** in the **Rules** group.

The Rules task pane opens.

10. Click **New**, and then select **Validation**.

11. In the **Details for** box, delete **Rule 1**, and type **JobDateRule**. Then, under **Condition**, click **None**.

The Condition dialog box opens.

12. Click **is equal to**, and select **is greater than**. Click the third box, and select **Use a formula**.

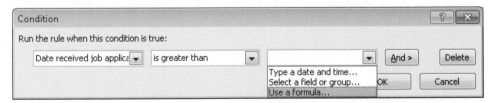

13. In the **Insert Formula** dialog box, type **now()**, and then click **OK** twice.

The Insert Formula And Condition dialog boxes close.

14. In the **Rules** task pane, in the **ScreenTip** box, type **Enter a date not in the future**.

> **Tip** You can use the Preview command on the Home tab or on the Quick Access Toolbar to view the form before you publish it.

 CLEAN UP Leave InfoPath and SharePoint Designer open if you are continuing to the next exercise.

Publishing an InfoPath Form

After you complete your form modifications in InfoPath, you need to save and publish your changes. The easiest way to publish an InfoPath form is to use the Quick Publish command, which is on the InfoPath Quick Access Toolbar and in Backstage view. The first time you use the Quick Publish command for a form, you are prompted to save the form. You can store the form in a document library, on the file system, or in a shared folder.

When SharePoint Designer creates the form template for the workflow initiation form, it effectively publishes the form template. When you open the form template from the publish location in InfoPath Designer, you do not need to specify the publish location. When you modify the initiation form in InfoPath and republish it, you have not modified the logic of the SharePoint workflow, and you do not need to republish the workflow using SharePoint Designer. When you publish the form template using InfoPath, changes to the form take effect immediately. When you start a new workflow instance, you see the modified form.

See Also Microsoft's Channel 9 Web site contains a number of SharePoint 2010 and InfoPath 2010 workflow-related videos. Navigate to *channel9.msdn.com/*, and enter the keywords *SharePoint designer 2010 workflows InfoPath*.

In this exercise, you save and publish an InfoPath initiation form. Then you verify the modification using the browser.

 SET UP Using SharePoint Designer, open the site you used in the previous exercise. Display the initiation form you modified in the previous exercise using InfoPath Designer if it is not already open.

1. Click the **File** tab to display Backstage view.

    The Info section is highlighted, and Backstage view displays the Form Information page. The Publish Your Form section shows the location where the form will be published.

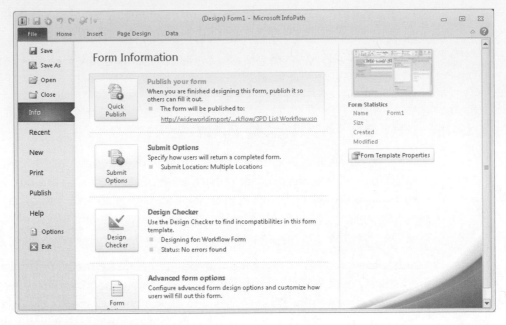

2. Click **Design Checker**.

   The On Stage view in InfoPath is displayed. The Design Checker task pane opens and indicates that there are no errors or messages.

   Tip If error messages are displayed, be sure that you complete the steps in the previous exercise.

3. Click the **File** tab. In Backstage view, with the **Info** tab selected, click **Quick Publish** under **Form Information**.

   If you did not save the form previously, a Microsoft InfoPath dialog box opens, informing you that you must save the form template before it can be published.

4. Click **OK**.

   The Microsoft InfoPath dialog box closes, and the Save As dialog box opens.

5.   Navigate to your **Documents** folder. In the **File name** box, delete **Template**, and type **SPDListInitiationFormTemplate.xsn**. Click **Save**.

A Saving dialog box is displayed while InfoPath saves the form template. Then a Microsoft InfoPath dialog box opens, indicating that the form template was published successfully.

6.   Click **OK**.

7.   In the browser, open the site you are using for this exercise, and display the **Shared Documents All Documents** view. Point to a document, click the arrow that appears, and then click **Workflows**. In the **Start a New Workflow** section, click **JobHistory**.

The initiation form is displayed.

8.   Move the mouse pointer over the **Applicant Name** box.

The text *Enter Job Applicant Name* appears.

9.   In the **Date received job application** box, type a date in the future, and then press Tab.

A red-dashed border appears around the date box, and if you move the pointer over the date box, a ScreenTip is displayed.

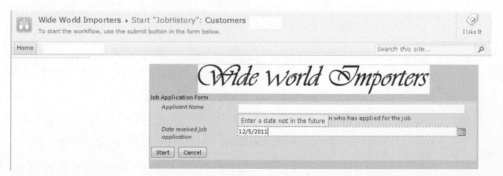

10.   Click **Start**.

A Warning dialog appears, stating that the form cannot be submitted.

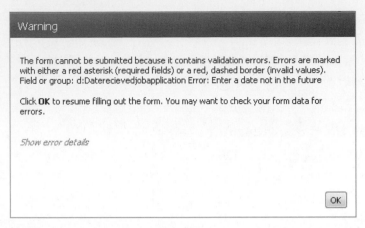

Warning

The form cannot be submitted because it contains validation errors. Errors are marked with either a red asterisk (required fields) or a red, dashed border (invalid values).
Field or group: d:Daterecievedjobapplication Error: Enter a date not in the future

Click **OK** to resume filling out the form. You may want to check your form data for errors.

Show error details

OK

11. Click **OK**, and then click **Cancel**.

 CLEAN UP Close InfoPath Designer and the browser.

Modifying Initiation Form Parameters

You can modify, delete, or add initiation form parameters by using SharePoint Designer. However, if you have customized your initiation form—whether it is an .aspx form or an InfoPath form template—your modifications are not automatically applied to the customized form. You can modify the customized form to match the modification you made to the initiation form parameters, or you can delete the customized form and let SharePoint Designer regenerate the form when you publish the workflow.

In this exercise, you modify initiation form parameters. You then modify the InfoPath initiation form to add a new initiation form parameter.

 SET UP Using SharePoint Designer, open the site you used in the previous exercise if it is not already open. Display the workflow settings for the SPD SBS Job Application workflow.

Initiation Form Parameters

1. On the **Workflow Settings** tab, click **Initiation Form Parameters**.

   The Association And Initiation Form Parameters dialog box opens.

2. Under **Name**, click **Date received job application**, and then click **Modify**.

   The Modify Field dialog box opens.

3. In the **Description** box, type **Enter the date the job application was received**. Click **Next**, and then click **Finish**. In the **Association and Initiation Form Parameters** dialog box, click **Add**.

The Add Field dialog box opens.

4. In the **Field** name box, type **Applicant Address**, and in the **Information type** list, click **Multiple lines of text**. Click **Next**, and then click **Finish**.

5. Click **OK**.

    The Association And Initiation Form Parameters dialog box closes.

Publish

6. On the **Workflow Settings** tab, click **Publish**.

    The Workflow Form Update Required dialog box opens, stating that the file SPD SBS Job Application.xsn has been customized using InfoPath and might not be compatible with this workflow because of field changes.

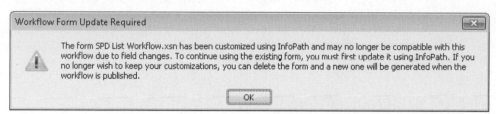

Tip If you accidentally delete your workflow template in SharePoint Designer, you can restore it by opening your saved workflow template in InfoPath Designer and then re-publishing it. You can also use the browser to navigate to the site's Recycle Bin and restore the template from there.

7. Click **OK** to close the **Workflow Form Update Required** dialog box. In the Forms area, the text (*needs update*) appears to the right of SPD SBS Job Application.xsn.

8. In the **Forms** area, click **SPD SBS Job Application.xsn**.

    InfoPath opens and displays the form in Design view. The Update Fields dialog box opens, stating that one or more fields in the workflow form have changed and that InfoPath will update the set of available fields, but that you may need to modify your form view to add or remove the updated fields.

9. Click **OK**.

    The Fields task pane refreshes, and the field Applicant Address appears.

10. Right-click below the **Date received** text box, point to **Insert**, and then click **Rows Below**.

11. With the new row selected, in the **Fields** task pane, hold down the mouse button and drag **Applicant Address** to the new row.

Tip If the new row is not selected when you add Applicant Address, both the title and the text box for the Applicant Address field might appear in the second column.

In the first cell of the new row, the text *Applicant Address* appears, and the Applicant Address control appears in the second cell.

Save

12. On the Quick Access toolbar, click **Save**. Navigate to your **Documents** folder. Accept the default file name **Template**, and then click **Save**.

Quick Publish

13. On the Quick Access Toolbar, click **Quick Publish**. When a dialog box opens stating that the template was published successfully, click **OK**.

CLEAN UP Save the form and then close InfoPath. Leave SharePoint Designer open if you are continuing with the next exercise.

Modifying an Association Form

When you use a globally reusable workflow or a reusable workflow, you create an association form as well as an initiation form. Each form is stored as a separate InfoPath view within the same InfoPath form template.

In this exercise, you modify an association form.

SET UP Using SharePoint Designer, open the site you used in the previous exercise if it is not already open. Display the workflow settings for the **SPD SBS Job Application** workflow.

1. In the **Forms** area, click the form template you want to modify, such as **SPD SBS Job Application.xsn**.

InfoPath opens. A dialog box opens as the form is downloaded, and then the form is displayed in Design view.

2. On the **Page Design** tab, in the **View** list in the **View** group, click **Start (default)**, and then click **Associate**.

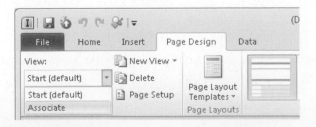

3. On the **Page Design** tab, click one of the themes, such as **Professional Classic**.

4. Press **CTRL+Shift+Q** to quickly publish the form template. Click **OK**, and then click **Save** to save the form template.

5. If you have saved an InfoPath template with the same name, a Microsoft InfoPath form opens, warning you that you are about to overwrite an existing template. Click **Overwrite**.

6. When a dialog box opens stating that the template was published successfully, click **OK**.

    Warning If errors are found with a globally reusable or a reusable workflow during the SharePoint Designer publishing process, the workflow is disassociated from any lists or libraries it is associated with. This can be catastrophic for a workflow that is associated with many lists or libraries. Knowing which lists or libraries a workflow is associated with isn't easy, until calls come in to your help desk support team, and users complain that they once could start a workflow and now they cannot. You must test your changes on a copy of the workflow prior to applying them to a live workflow. Before publishing a workflow, determine whether there are any errors by clicking the Check For Errors command. Also, if you have made any modifications to initiation or association form parameters, update the InfoPath form before publishing the workflow in SharePoint Designer.

 CLEAN UP Close InfoPath and SharePoint Designer.

Adding Association Fields to Initiation Forms

You can add, modify, and delete initiation form parameters, association form parameters, or both by using SharePoint Designer. Because the initiation form and the association form are views in the same InfoPath form template, all the initiation and association form parameters can be used in either view. When SharePoint automatically generates the two views, it adds to a view only those controls that map to the appropriate form type. However, using InfoPath Designer, you can add one or more association fields to an initiation form and then manipulate the association field. This is very useful when you want to inform end users about choices content owners or site administrators made, but you don't want to allow end users to change those choices.

If the association field placed on the initiation form is a text box control, you can use the display tab on the Text Box Properties dialog box to specify the control as read-only. However, you should change the appearance of the association field so that the user interface clearly indicates that the field is read-only. Other types of controls require more manipulation on your part to prevent end users from changing the values of the association fields.

In this exercise, you add an association field to an initiation form.

SET UP Using SharePoint Designer, open the root site of a site collection where you previously created a globally reusable workflow. Display the Workflows gallery.

Initiation Form
Parameters

1. Under **Globally Reusable Workflow**, click **WideWorldImporters Expense Approval**, and then on the **Workflow Settings** tab, click **Initiation Form Parameters**.

The Association And Initiation Form Parameters dialog box opens. All but three parameters are shown on both forms. The three parameters—End On First Rejection, End On Document Change, and Enable Content Approval—are shown only on the association form.

2. Click **Cancel**, and then in the **Forms** area, click **WideWorldImporters Expense Approval.xsn**.

InfoPath Designer opens and displays the initiation form for the WideWorldImporters Expense Approval workflow.

Insert Below

3. In the first column, click **CC**, and then on the **Table Tools**, **Layout** tab, click **Insert Below**.

4. On the **Home** tab, in the **Controls** group, scroll down and click **Calculated Value**.

5. Click **OK** to close the **Insert Calculated Value** dialog box.

A rectangle with a dashed-line border, is added to the left cell in the new row.

Control
Properties

6. Click the rectangle, and then on the **Control Tools**, **Properties** tab, click **Control Properties**.

The Calculated Value Properties dialog box opens.

7. Select **Text**, and in the box, type **If the document is rejected by any participant, then the document is automatically rejected.**

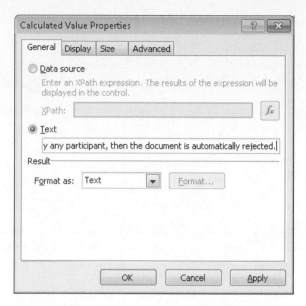

8. Click **OK**. The Calculated Value Properties dialog box closes.

Manage Rules

9. On the **Properties** tab, click **Manage Rules** to open the **Rules** task pane. Click **New**, and then click **Formatting**. Under **Condition**, click **None**.

    The Condition dialog box opens.

10. Click **myFields**, and then click **Select a field or group**.

    The Select A Field Or Group dialog box opens.

11. Click **End of First Rejection**, and then click **OK**.

12. In the **Condition** dialog box, click the third list, and click **FALSE**. Click **OK** to close the **Condition** dialog box.

13. In the **Rules** task pane, scroll down, and then select **Hide this control**.

14. Press **CTRL+Shift+Q** to quickly publish the form template. Click **OK**, and then click **Save** to save the form template.

15. Click **Overwrite**, and when a dialog box opens stating that the template was published successfully, click **OK**.

16. On the **Home** tab, click **Manage Rules** to close the **Rules** task pane.

✖ **CLEAN UP** Close InfoPath. Leave SharePoint Designer open if you are continuing to the next exercise.

Modifying Task Forms

A type of workflow form is the task form. These forms are created when you assign tasks in your workflows by using actions such as *Assign a Form to a Group*, *Collect Data from a User*, and *Start Approval Process*. Task forms are listed in the Forms area of the Workflow Settings page, where the workflow's association and initiation forms are listed. Modifying task forms is identical to modifying association forms and just as impressive.

In this exercise, you modify a workflow task form.

 SET UP Using SharePoint Designer, open the site you used in the previous exercise if it is not already open. Display the workflow settings for the WideWorldImporters Expense Approval globally reusable workflow.

1. In the **Forms** area, click **Approval Workflow Task_x0028_en-US_x0029_Copy 1.xsn**.

    Tip The number shown on your file might be greater than one.

    InfoPath Designer opens and displays the task form. This form contains a number of different views that are used to display other forms when the Request Change or the Reassign Task buttons is clicked.

2. On the **Page Design** tab, under **View** in the **Views** group, click **Main (default)**, and select **Reassign Task**.

3. On the form, click **Reassign Task To**, and then click the small square attached to the top-left corner of the form that appears.

Borders

4. On the **Table Tools**, **Layout** tab, click **Borders** in the **Color** group.

    The Borders And Shading dialog box opens.

    Note No one command can change the theme, shading, and borders for all views. To replicate any modifications across a number of views, you need to modify each view separately.

5. Under **Style**, click the gray line. Under **Presets**, click **Outline**, and then click **Inside**.

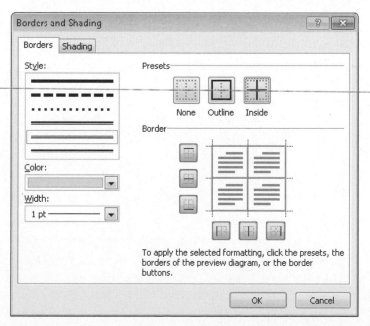

6. Click **OK**. The Borders And Shading dialog box closes.

 CLEAN UP Publish and save the form, overwriting the previous version of the file. Close InfoPath. Leave SharePoint Designer open if you are continuing to the next chapter.

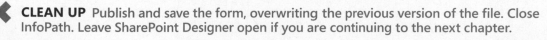

Key Points

- Reusable workflows can be saved as workflow templates and can be imported into Visual Studio 2010 for further enhancement or installed directly on other SharePoint site collections.

- Globally reusable workflows can be copied and modified.

- Do not modify the out-of-the box globally reusable workflows.

- You can create your own globally reusable workflows that can be used throughout a site collection.

- Initiation forms are used by end users, and association forms are used by content owners and site administrators.

- SharePoint Designer 2010 makes it easy to create initiation, association, and task forms.

- InfoPath Designer 2010 can be used to create compelling list views and list forms as well as workflow initiation, association, and tasks forms.

Part 4

Advanced Customizations

Chapter at a Glance

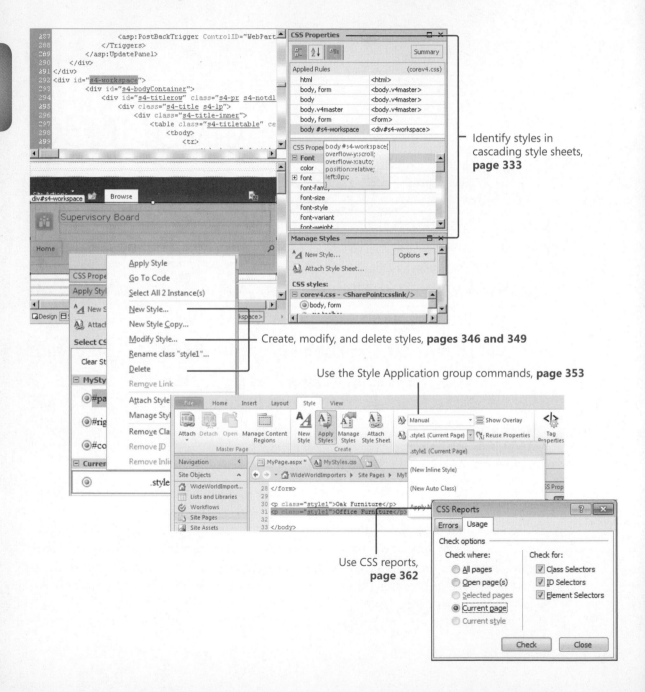

Identify styles in cascading style sheets, **page 333**

Create, modify, and delete styles, **pages 346 and 349**

Use the Style Application group commands, **page 353**

Use CSS reports, **page 362**

10 Branding SharePoint Sites

In this chapter, you will learn how to

- Set the CSS and Color Coding Page Editor options.
- Identify styles in cascading style sheets.
- Identify styles on content pages.
- Create and attach CSS files.
- Create a functioning HTML page.
- Create styles.
- Modify and delete styles.
- Use the Style Application group commands.
- Understand SharePoint's CSS inheritance.
- Use IntelliSense to add a CSS.
- Use CSS reports.

Branding a Microsoft SharePoint Foundation 2010 or Microsoft SharePoint Server 2010 site is more than just applying a theme or adding a logo. You can brand your site at many different levels, but why do you want to brand your site in the first place?

The look and feel of SharePoint 2010 has improved greatly from previous versions, but when SharePoint 2010 is initially installed, it still does not provide the look and feel of Web sites that users see on the Internet. Organizations as well as users want their SharePoint sites to look similar to those they work with on a public-facing site. They also want their Internet or extranet sites to be consistent with their company's intranet site and other marketing collateral they produce, such as letterhead, brochures, presentations, and business cards.

Most sites also include more than text. They are designed so that users can interact with them and to convey information in an engaging manner. This applies especially to Internet sites and a company's intranet or portal sites. Many companies hire an outside advertisement agency to develop their overall look and feel (brand). If you visit SharePoint sites on the Internet, you will see that almost any look is possible. The visual presentation of your site is one of the areas in which you need to invest time.

Note SharePoint Web sites on the Internet include *www.ferrari.com* and those at *www. wssdemo.com/LivePivot/.*

Like most industry-standard sites, SharePoint sites use cascading style sheets (CSS). SharePoint Designer contains one of the best cascading style sheet editors available. Microsoft Visual Studio 2010, Microsoft Visual Web Developer 2010 Express, and Microsoft Expression Web use similar cascading style sheet editing tools. Even when you use these tools, branding a site takes some time, especially if you are new to branding and have never tried to change the look and feel of a SharePoint site before. It is generally recommended to complete only minimal branding and customizations on individual sites.

In this chapter, you will explore the cascading style sheet editing options for SharePoint Designer 2010. By using the cascading style sheet task panes and the ribbon, you will learn how to identify, modify, and create styles. Next, you will create a style sheet and attach it to a page. You will also look at style inheritance on SharePoint sites and use CSS reports.

Important To complete many of the exercises in this chapter, you must have permissions to detach pages from site definitions and customize master pages. See the section "Controlling the Use of SharePoint Designer," in Chapter 1, "Exploring SharePoint Designer 2010."

> **Practice Files** Before you can use the practice file in this chapter, you need to copy the book's practice files to your computer. The practice file you'll use to complete the exercises in this chapter is in the Chapter10 practice file folder. A complete list of practice files is provided in "Using the Practice Files" at the beginning of this book.

Setting the CSS and Color Coding Page Editor Options

SharePoint Designer uses a set of configuration options to know how it should apply cascading style sheet tags to your page. You can change these default settings in the Page Editor Options dialog box. This dialog box has 12 tabs, some of which you saw in Chapter 4, "Creating and Modifying Web Pages." Here, you'll explore the tabs related to cascading style sheets.

You can choose from many options. For example, you can configure SharePoint Designer to generate styles automatically, or you can create styles yourself. You can also limit SharePoint Designer so that it modifies only those styles that it creates automatically and no others. Usually, the default settings for these options work well, so you might not need to change them. However, you should know what SharePoint Designer is doing on your behalf, because it might not be quite what you want.

In this exercise, you explore the different tabs of the Page Editor Options dialog box that relate to cascading style sheets.

 SET UP Using SharePoint Designer, open the team site you created and modified in earlier chapters. If you did not yet create a team site, follow the steps in Chapter 1.

1. Click the **File** tab, and then in the left pane, click **Options**.

   The SharePoint Designer Options dialog box opens.

2. Under **SharePoint Designer Options**, with **General** selected, click **Page Editor Options**.

   The Page Editor Options dialog box opens.

   Tip When you have a page open in edit mode in the workspace, you can open the Page Editor Options dialog box by clicking CSS 2.1 in the SharePoint Designer status bar.

3. Click the **CSS** tab.

   This tab displays the options that SharePoint Designer uses when creating and modifying styles on your pages.

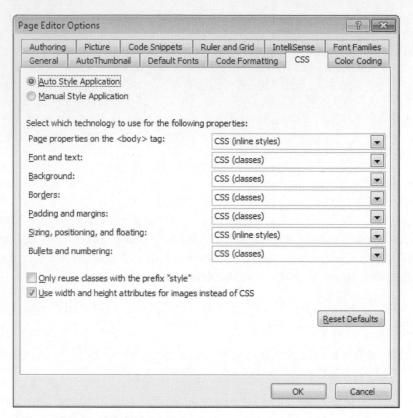

4. Click the **Color Coding** tab.

This tab displays the code coloring options that SharePoint Designer uses in the Code and Design views of the workspace. For each display item, you can select the foreground (text) and background colors. You can also make the text bold, italic, or underlined.

5. Click the **Authoring** tab.

This tab displays document properties. In the Default Document Types section, the Default Document Type is set to HTML, and the Default SharePoint Document Type is set to Web Part Page. In the Doctype And Secondary Schema section, Document Type Declaration is set to XHTML 1.0 Strict, Secondary Schema to IE 6.0, and CSS Schema to CSS 2.1.

6. Click **OK** twice.

The Page Editor Options and the SharePoint Designer Options dialog boxes close.

✖ **CLEAN UP** Leave SharePoint Designer open if you are continuing to the next exercise.

What Is CSS?

CSS separates the look and feel from the content in your Web pages. Think of CSS as a smart language that browsers use to format the font color or size of elements, and which you can use to position elements on the page. Today, all browsers support CSS and CSS functions in the same way in SharePoint Foundation 2010 and SharePoint Server 2010, as they do with other Web platforms.

Note In previous versions of SharePoint, a theme consisted of a CSS file(s) and images. In SharePoint 2010, themes are defined as in other Microsoft Office applications. More information on SharePoint themes can be found at *www.toddbaginski.com/blog/archive/2009/11/02/how-to-create-a-custom-theme-for-sharepoint-2010.aspx.aspx*.

Style sheets are made up of style rules that consist of a selector, followed by a property value. The selector can be one of three types—an HTML tag (element), a class, or an ID—and is followed by a declaration block. When a style begins with a dot (.), it is called a class. When a style begins with a hash tag or a number sign (#), it is called an ID. When the selector appears by itself, it is an HTML tag. The following table contains examples of declarations for the three selector types.

Type	Selector	Declaration block
HTML tag (element)	H1	{ font: normal 1em Verdana, Arial sans-serif;}
Class	.header	{ background-color: #336699; height: 50px;}
ID	#logo	{ position: relative; float: left; padding: 5px;}

Note IDs can be used only one time on a page, whereas classes can be used many times on a page. Also, an ID can contain a dash or a digit, but the first character after the # cannot be a dash or a digit.

A declaration block contains one or more style declarations that have a single property and value pair—for example, `background-color: #4c4c4c`. Each declaration is separated by a semicolon. You can have multiple properties within a selector. If you have more than one value within a property and that value has more than one word, the words should be surrounded by quotation marks—for example, "Times New Roman". If the words are separated with a dash, quotation marks are not needed.

Note CSS selectors, declarations, and property and value pairs are case-insensitive.

You can combine selectors in different ways. For example, you could have several CSS element declarations for the HTML H1 tag and a class declaration that applies only to the HTML H1 tag found in a <div> tag.

```
<style> .header h1 { font-weight: bold; } </style>
<div class="header">
    <h1>This is my text</h1>
</div>
```

Styles can be defined within an HTML tag using the *style* attribute; these are known as inline styles. All other styles reside in the page within a <style> block or in a separate file that can be attached to the page. Files that contain styles usually have the extension .css.

Styles can be defined multiple times on a page or in a CSS file, and many CSS files can be attached to a page. Each style can apply a different property value to an element. For example, a <div> tag could have multiple class styles assigned to it, each defining a different color.

Styles use inheritance rules, cascade order, and *CSS specificity*, which browsers use to determine which style to apply. For example, a tag takes on the style of its parent, so if the color property is specified for the <body> tag but not the <p> tag, the text within the <p> tag uses the style defined for the <body> tag. Cascade order specifies the order in which styles are applied. Cascading style sheet files are applied in a specific order and read sequentially, and then styles defined on the page are applied in sequential order. In general terms, the style used by the browser to render an element's font color is the style that last defined the color property. CSS specificity adds a few more rules to this equation, in that each selector is given a value: an ID selector has more power than an element or class selector. In a group of nested selectors, these values are used to decide which style attributes to apply.

SharePoint Designer displays style information in a number of task panes. It identifies the selector types and whether a style is defined with a tag (inline) by using color icons. Refer to the following table for examples.

Icon	Type	Description and examples
● (Yellow)	Inline	This is the simplest of styles and affects only the tag in which it is defined. Use this style type if you do not plan to use this styling elsewhere. <p style="text-align: center;">
● (Blue)	Elements	This style affects all instances of the specified element (tag) on the page. body { font-family: "Trebuchet MS", Verdana, Arial; }
● (Green)	Classes	This style is applied to those elements that reference it. .ms-quicklaunch { background-color: #d6e8ff; } The tag that references the style looks similar to: <div class="ms-quickLaunch">
● (red)	IDs	This style can be used only once per page. It is usually reserved for structural elements: #page_content { font-weight: 700; } The tag that references the style looks similar to: <div id="page_content">
◉	Style in use	SharePoint Designer places a gray circle around the style icon if the style is used on the page.

See Also Learning resources on how to use cascading style sheets can be found at *www.w3schools.com/css/* and *www.csszengarden.com*. For more information about the order in which styles are applied, search on the keywords *CSS specificity* in any search engine.

Tip The quickest way to learn more about cascading style sheets is to work in Split view as much as you can.

Identifying Styles in Cascading Style Sheets

In Chapter 4, "Creating and Modifying Web Pages," you saw that when you use a browser to request a page from a site, it combines two Microsoft ASP.NET pages: a master page and a content page. Master pages provide a consistent look and feel across your site. You can include style information in a master page, but its good practice to use a style sheet that is linked to the master page. Both SharePoint Foundation and SharePoint Server contain a large number of style rules—the majority of which are class or ID declarations—that are stored in cascading style sheet files. To brand SharePoint Foundation or SharePoint Server sites, you need to get to know these files and the declarations they contain. This is where SharePoint Designer can help you.

Tip Not all styles are exposed in SharePoint Designer, specifically those dynamically created by controls. It is only when a page is rendered in the browser that you can see the styles and the elements to which they are applied. You might find it useful to use tools that complement those that SharePoint Designer provides. One such tool is the Internet Explorer Developer toolbar, which in Internet Explorer 8 can be activated by pressing F12.

For most branding tasks, the style file corev4.css (which is the main cascading style sheet file) defines most of the styles you need to customize your site. You should not amend this file—it contains more than 7,000 lines of code—but create your own style file that contains only those styles from the SharePoint style sheets you need to modify. You can link this file to your master page by using the HTML <link> tag or the SharePoint control CssRegistration. Then the browser applies your style rules before or after the browser applies the rules defined in corev4.css. You can store a style file in the Style Library at the root of each site collection or in your site's Site Assets library. Developers can also create a .wsp solution file to deploy a style file.

Tip To identity which style rules are associated with which tags, you must display the page on which the tags are defined. Because each page you request is a combination of a master page and a content page, this could be either the master page or the content page.

In this exercise, you identify styles used on a master page.

SET UP Using SharePoint Designer, open the team site you used in the previous exercise if it is not already open. The settings page for the site should be displayed.

1. In **Navigation** pane, click **Master Pages** to display the gallery page in the workspace.

Check Out

2. Click the icon to the left of **v4.master**. On the **Master Page** tab, click **Check Out** in the **Manage** group, and then click **Edit File** in the **Edit** group.

Edit File

The v4.master page opens in the workspace. The controls on the page are displayed and surrounded by a purple line. The label for the active control, PlaceHolderMain, appears above a purple box. In the Quick Tag selector area on the workspace status bar, the PlaceHolderMain tag is highlighted in orange.

In the Master Pages mini-gallery below the Navigation pane, a green check mark appears to the left of v4.master, indicating that the file is checked out.

Tip If the control names do not appear, verify that Template Region Labels is selected on the Visual Aids menu. Using visual aids can help as you build your master page, but if you find them distracting, simply clear the options you do not want to show.

Task Panes

3. On the **View** tab, click the down arrow on the **Task Panes** command in the **Workspace** group, and then click **CSS Properties** to open the **CSS Properties** task pane. No CSS information is displayed.

4.   Repeat the previous step to open the **Manage Styles** task pane, on which the style file **corev4.css** appears. The style rules used on the master page are identified by a gray circle.

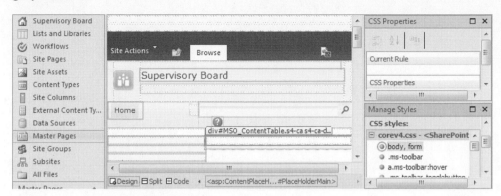

Tip By default, the Manage Styles task pane lists the style rules in the order in which they appear in their style sheet. When you have multiple style sheets, each style sheet is listed separately. If the current page does not appear in the Manage Styles task pane, then it currently contains no style rules. To make the page appear in the list, add a style block (<style>...</style>) to the <head> tags for the page. When viewing style rules by order, you can move the styles by dragging them up or down in the Manage Styles task pane. moving a style that is defined on the page to make it a style defined in a file, and vice versa.

Split

5.   On the **View** tab, click **Split** if the workspace is not already in Split view, and then click in the Code view portion of the workspace.

6.   Press **CTRL+F** to open the **Find and Replace** dialog box. Under **Find what**, type **s4-workspace**, and then click **Find Next**. Click **Close** to close the **Find and Replace** dialog box.

In Code view, the s4-workspace ID tag is highlighted in the line *<div id="s4-work-space">*, and in the Quick Tag Selector area, the <div#s4-workspace> tag is highlighted in orange.

In the CSS Properties task pane, to the right of Applied Rules, a link to corev4.css is displayed, indicating that the current master page is linked to corev4.css. Under Applied Rules, six style rules are listed in the order in which they were applied. The first rule applied is placed at the top of the list.

Tip You can click the corev4.css link in the CSS Properties task pane to open the style sheet as a new tab within the workspace.

7.   In the **CSS Properties** task pane, under **Applied Rules**, point to **body #s4-work-space** so that a ScreenTip appears with the rule's declarations.

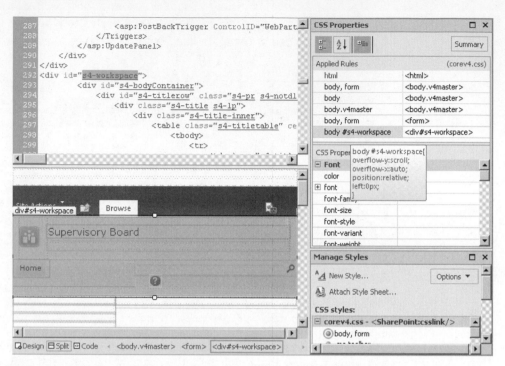

Tip You can right-click a style, and a context-sensitive list of options is displayed that allow you to go to the code, create a new style, copy a style, or modify the style. When you click a class or ID style, you will see additional options, such as those to rename the class and remove an ID.

8. In the **CSS Properties** task pane, click the **Summary** button.

    A summarized list of all properties appears.

9. In the **Manage Styles** task pane, click **Options**, and select **Show Styles Used in Current Page**.

    The Manage Styles task pane refreshes. All CSS elements (IDs) and classes are identified by a gray circle.

10. In the **Manage Styles** task pane, click **Options**, and then click **Categorized by Type**.

    The style types are listed in a treelike structure grouped by elements and classes. Elements have a blue circle to the left of the element name, and classes are identified by a green circle.

11. In the **Manage Styles** task pane, scroll down, and under **Classes**, right-click **.s4-title**, and then click **Select All 1 Instance(s)**.

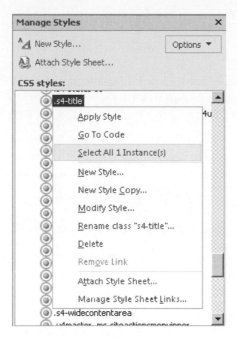

In the Quick Tag Selector area, the tag <div .s4-title s4-lp> is highlighted in orange. In the Code view portion of the workspace, the section of code between the matching <div> and </div> tags is highlighted, and in the Design view portion of the workspace, a purple rectangle appears around an area of the page that maps to that section of code.

At the bottom of the Manage Styles task pane, the Selected Style Preview box shows the effect of the style rule when it is applied to content.

Note The HTML <div> tag is used as a block-level container that holds a part or section of a Web page that can contain content and more HTML tags. Many of the HTML <table> tags used in Windows SharePoint Services are replaced in SharePoint Foundation by <div> tags. By associating a CSS element with a block-level container, you can apply a separate style than for the rest of the page. It allows you to manage and manipulate that section of the page more easily than if it were defined as a set of <table> tags, and also makes it easier for you to create pages that comply with accessibility standards.

See Also More information on accessibility can be found in Chapter 12, "Understanding Usability and Accessibility."

12. In the **Manage Styles** task pane, point to **.s4-title** so that a ScreenTip appears with the styles for the rule.

Show alphabetized

Show set properties on top

13. In the **CSS Properties** task pane, click the **Show Alphabetized List** and **Show set Properties on Top** icons. Also click the **Summary** button if it is not already selected.

In the CSS Properties task pane, the Applied Rules section shows the classes that are applied to the <div> section before the .s4-title class. In the CSS Properties section, the declarations defined in the .s4-title rule appear in blue bold text, with multiple rules listed for the Padding property. When the properties are repeated several times, this means they have been defined in a different style sheet or more than once in the same style sheet. The second Padding property in the list overrides the first property—the one with a red line through it.

Tip When you click a CSS property, the style that defines the property is surrounded by a blue rectangle in the Applied Rules section.

14. In the **CSS Properties** task pane, point to the **padding** property that has a red line through it so that a ScreenTip appears with the name of the rule overriding this property: **.s4-title**.

CLEAN UP Close v4-master; click No if you are asked to save your changes. Leave SharePoint Designer open if you are continuing to the next exercise.

Identifying Styles on Content Pages

When you display a content page in SharePoint Designer, although Design view displays a merged copy of the master page and the content page, you can only identify CSS styles for components that are stored in the content page. To identify the components that are stored in the content page, use the Code view for the page.

In this exercise, you identify styles used on a content page.

 SET UP Using SharePoint Designer, open the team site you used in the previous exercise if it is not already open. The settings page for the site should be displayed.

1. In the **Navigation** pane, click **Site Pages**, and then double-click the icon to the left of **Home.aspx** to open the page.

In the workspace, the tab is labeled *Home.aspx*, and in the Code view portion of the workspace, some of the code is highlighted in yellow. The page is open in safe mode.

The CSS Properties task pane contains no rules or properties, and the Manage Styles task pane contains element and class rules that are used on the Home.aspx page. These rules are defined in corev4.css, wiki.css, and menu-21.css, which are linked to the master page that is attached to the current page. The Manage Styles task pane contains no reference to the current page, which means that no style rules are defined in the current page.

Advanced Mode

2. On the **Home** tab, click **Advanced Mode** in the **Editing** group to access all the code defined in the Home.aspx content page and to access those page elements in Design view.

The page refreshes, and the code in the Code view portion of the workspace is no longer highlighted.

3. In the Design view portion of the workspace, click the name of the site.

A purple rectangle surrounds the site name with the label *PlaceHolderSiteName (Master)*. The Quick Tag Selector area in the workspace status bar contains no tag information, and no rules are listed in the CSS Properties task pane.

OOUI

4. To the right of your site's name, click the OOUI arrow to open the **Comment Content Tasks** list.

The Common Content Task list displays a link named Create Custom Content.

Note The presence of (Master) in the label name and the link Create Custom Content in the Common Content Tasks list indicate that the area surrounded by the purple rectangle maps to a control whose content is defined on the master page. Therefore, no CSS style information is displayed in the CSS Properties task pane.

5. Click in the Code view portion of the workspace, and then press **CTRL+F** to display the **Find and Replace** dialog box.

6. Under **Find what**, type **PlaceHolderMain**, and then click **Find Next**. Click **Close** to close the **Find and Replace** dialog box.

   In Code view, PlaceHolderMain is highlighted, and in Design view, a purple rectangle surrounds the related area with the label *PlaceHolderMain (Custom)*. In the Quick Tag Selector area, the <asp:Content> tag is highlighted in orange.

7. In Design view, click inside the **PlaceHolderMain** section.

   The CSS Properties tasks pane displays information in the Applied Rules and CSS Properties sections.

   Note The presence of (Custom) in the PlaceHolderMain label indicates that the area surrounded by the purple rectangle maps to a control defined on the master page, but on this page, the rectangle contains its own unique content, together with any CSS style information, and not content from the master page. If you were to display the Common Content Task list, the link would be named Default To Master's Content.

   See Also More information on master pages can be found in Chapter 11, "Working with Master Pages."

 CLEAN UP Close all open task panes. Leaving v4.master checked out, close v4.master and Home.aspx, and click No if you are asked to save your changes. Leave SharePoint Designer open if you are continuing to the next exercise.

Creating and Attaching CSS Files

Different types of styles can be created: styles inline within HTML tags, styles internal to the page, and styles external to the page. Use inline styles very sparingly. They are defined within the element you want to style—for example, *<div style="position: absolute; top 10px;">*. Using inline styles is in direct contradiction to the purpose of using a style sheet.

Inline styles override styles defined in style sheets and mean that you cannot restyle that part of your page without editing the page. The disadvantages of using inline styles are that they require more maintenance, are less flexible, and increase the size of the page.

Use internal style sheets if you have a small style change for a page layout or a particular page. The styles are placed within the <style> tags inside the <head> tags at the top of a page. The disadvantages of using an internal style sheet are that they require more maintenance, are less flexible, and increase the size of the page.

The preferred method of adding styles is to use an external style sheet. A CSS file is linked to a page. The link is placed in the <head> section of the page, usually after the CSS Link SharePoint control. An external style sheet is easier to maintain, more flexible, and does not increase the size of your page.

Tip An alternative to using an internal style sheet is to add a <div> tag around the HTML or section to which you want to apply a specific look and feel. Assign the <div> tag with a unique ID, and when you create styles in your style sheet, place that ID in front of the style. The only time the style is applied is when the browser sees a <div> tag with that ID. Using this method, you can still have special styling for a particular page, retain ease of maintenance for the page, and keep the file size for your page manageable.

By placing styles in a file, you can centrally manage those styles and apply the same styles to a number of pages. Both SharePoint Foundation and SharePoint Server make heavy use of styles that reside in files. You can create a new style sheet in the following ways:

- By using the Assets tab when you display the Site Assets library view in the workspace

- By using the Style tab

- In the New Style dialog box, which you can open from the Apply Styles and Manage Styles task panes and when you select Apply Style from the Target Rule list in the Style Application group

When you create styles in a cascading style sheet file, you need to attach the file to a page to apply those styles to the page. Again SharePoint Designer provides you with many ways to complete this task. For example, you can use the Attach Style command on the Style tab, or you can use links in the Apply Styles and Manage Styles task panes. When you attach a file, <link> tags are placed in the <head> tags.

In this exercise, you attach a cascading style sheet file to a page.

SET UP Using SharePoint Designer, open the team site you used in the previous exercise if it is not already open. The settings page for the site should be displayed.

1. In the **Navigation** pane, click **Site Assets** to display the gallery page for the Site Assets library.

Asset

2. On the **Assets** tab, in the **New** group, click the down arrow for the **Asset** command, and then click **CSS**.

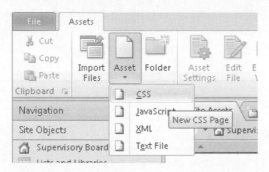

A file named Untitled_1.css appears. The name of the file is selected.

3. Type **MyStyles.css**, and then press **Enter** to rename the file.

4. In the **Navigation** pane, click **Site Pages**. On the **Pages** tab, click the **Page** command down arrow, and then click **ASPX**.

Page

A file named Untitled_1.aspx appears, with the name of the file selected.

5. Type **MyPage.aspx**, and then press **Enter** to rename the file.

6. With **MyPage.aspx** selected, click **Edit File** on the **Pages** tab. Click **Yes** to confirm that you want to open the page in advanced edit mode.

Edit File

The page opens in the workspace, and the <form#form1> tag is highlighted in the Quick Tag Selector area on the workspace status bar.

7. On the workspace status bar, click **Split** if it is not already selected.

8. On the **Style** tab, click **Attach Style Sheet** in the **Create** group.

Attach Style
Sheet

The Attach Style Sheet dialog box opens.

9. Click the **Browse** button to the right of the **URL** box.

The Select Style Sheet dialog box opens, displaying the folders, libraries, and files in the root of your site.

Troubleshooting If your site's contents are not displayed, expand Microsoft SharePoint Designer at the top of the left pane, and navigate to your site.

10. In the **Select Style Sheet** dialog box, double-click **SiteAssets**, and then click **MyStyles.css**.

11. Click **Open** to close the **Select Style Sheet** dialog box.

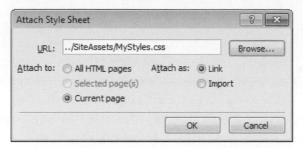

12. Select the **Link** option to the right of **Attach as**, if it is not already selected, and then click **OK** to close the **Attach Style Sheet** dialog box.

The page refreshes. An asterisk appears on the MyPage.aspx label. In the Code view portion of the workspace, a new line containing a <link> tag appears. No styles appear in the CSS Properties task pane; however, MyStyles.css is listed in the Manage Styles task pane.

13. Right-click the **MyPage.aspx** tab, and then click **Save**.

Both MyPage.aspx and MyStyles.css are now saved, and the Save Embedded Files dialog box closes.

CLEAN UP Close all open task panes. Leave SharePoint Designer open if you are continuing to the next exercise.

Creating a Functioning HTML Page

After you have agreement on the branding for your site, you need to convert the visual presentation of your user interface design (known as a *wireframe*) to a functioning HTML page. You might first prototype your design by creating one page that contains the components for both the master page and the content page. Create your CSS styles using that page, and then when you have sign-off, create the master page and templates for the content pages. Creating a prototype page first means that you can fine-tune the HTML for the master page and the CSS styles without having to wait to see the result of merging two files. The prototype should reflect the design decisions about usability and accessibility that you considered as part of the planning process, as well as whether you will use tables or <div> tags for the page layout. SharePoint Designer can be used to create the prototype, the actual master pages, and content pages.

In this exercise, you create one **<div>** region that contains two other **<div>** regions.

 SET UP Using SharePoint Designer, open the team site you used in the previous exercise if it is not already open. Open MyPage.aspx and display MyPage.aspx in Split view.

HTML

<div>

1. In the Design view portion of the page, click in the **form#form1** rectangle. On the **Insert** tab, click the **HTML** down arrow in the **Controls** group, and then under **Tags**, click **<div>**.

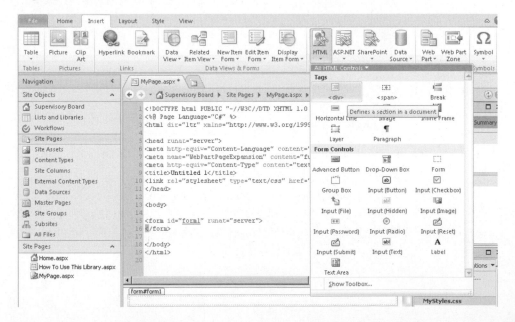

In Code view, the tags <div> and </div> are added on separate lines between the opening and closing <form> tags. In Design view, a rectangle with blue lines appears with the label *div*. On the Quick Tag Selector area in the workspace status bar, <div> is highlighted in orange.

2. On the Quick Tag Selector area, click **<div>**, and then click **Tag Properties**.

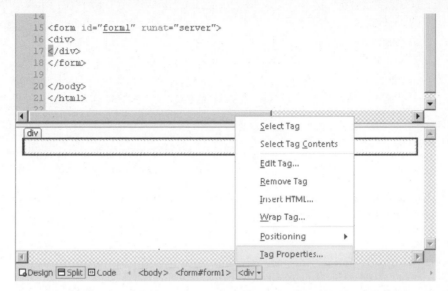

The Tag Properties task pane opens and displays the properties for the <div> tag.

3. In the **Tag Properties** task pane, under **Attributes**, click the cell to the right of **id**, type **container**, and then press **Enter**.

4. Place the insertion point in the rectangle under **div#container**, and press **Enter**.

The div#container consists of two lines, and in Code view, a <br /> tag appears.

5. Place the insertion point on the first line under **div#container**. On the **Insert** tab, click the **HTML** down arrow, and click **<div>**. In the **Tag Properties** task pane, under **Attributes**, click the cell to the right of **id**, type **page_content**, and then press **Enter**.

6. Place the insertion point on the second line below **div#page_content**. On the **Insert** tab, click the **HTML** down arrow, and then click **<div>**. In the **Tag Properties** task pane, under **Attributes**, click the cell to the right of **id**, type **right_col**, and then press **Enter**.

7. Place the insertion point on the third line in **div#container**, and press **Delete**.

The div#container should contain two <div> tags, which in Design view are displayed on separate lines.

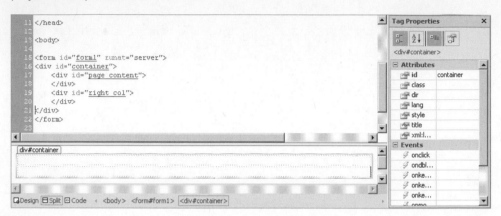

![X] **CLEAN UP** Save your changes. Leave SharePoint Designer open if you are continuing to the next exercise.

Creating Styles

In a previous section I showed how to identify content that is styled using cascading style sheet (CSS) style rules and declarations. To make a change to style rules and declarations, you can use the visual tools that SharePoint Designer provides, or you can edit the styles directly. Both methods produce the same results. If you are new to CSS and learning how to work with style sheets, use the tools in SharePoint Designer and examine Code view to see the CSS that SharePoint Designer generates. This will help you learn style declarations. Start with a simple page, and as your understanding improves, you can move to more complicated pages.

Tip Don't forget to use the Preview In Multiple Browsers option. You should keep checking your design in a variety of different browsers and screen sizes to be sure it will be displayed correctly to visitors to your site. If your latest changes are not quite what you expect, use the Undo button on the Quick Access Toolbar or the shortcut keystroke CTRL+Z, as you would in Microsoft Word or Microsoft Excel when the latest edits are not to your liking.

SharePoint Designer adds new styles to the end of a style sheet. Some CSS authors organize styles within style sheets by separating them into groups according to where the styles are located on the Web page. Others organize styles in the order in which they were created. Your company might have naming standards and best practices for the development of a CSS. If you are creating a style sheet that will be maintained by other users, you might have to adhere to those standards. Microsoft has a naming standard for styles they create for use in SharePoint. For example, most of the SharePoint classes begin with .ms- and include WP in the name if the style applies to components related to Web Parts.

Tip Selectors using the same declarations can be grouped in a shorthand format. This reduces the size of your style sheet and the need for adding declarations for each selector.

In this exercise, you will create two nested regions that appear side by side.

 SET UP Using SharePoint Designer, open the team site you used in the previous exercise if it is not already open. Open MyPage.aspx and display MyPage.aspx in Split view.

New Style

1. On the **Style** tab, click **New Style** in the **Create** group.

    The New Style dialog box opens.

2. In the **Selector** box, delete **.newStyle1**, and then type **#page_content**. In the **Define in** list, select **Existing style sheet**, and then click the **Browse** button to the right of the **URL** box.

    The Select Style Sheet dialog box opens.

3. Click **MyStyle.css**, and then click **Open**.

    Troubleshooting If the MyStyles.css file does not appear in the Select Style Sheet dialog box, click Microsoft SharePoint Designer in the left pane and navigate to the style sheet.

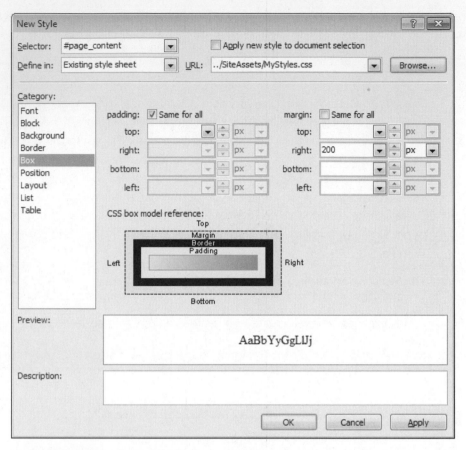

4. In the **New Style** dialog box, under **Category**, click **Box**, clear the check box to the right of **margin**, and then in the **right** list, type **200**.

   The Description box contains the CSS declarations that will be created as the result of filling in the boxes in this dialog box.

5. Click **OK** to close the **New Style** dialog box.

   The MyStyles.css file opens as a tab to the right of the MyPage.aspx tab.

6. On the **Style** tab, click **New Style** to open the **New Style** dialog box.

7. In the **Selector** box, delete **.newStyle1**, and then type **#right_col**.

8. If **Existing style sheet** is not selected in the **Define** list, and the **URL** box does not contain **MyStyle.css**, repeat steps 2 and 3.

9. In the **New Style** dialog box, under **Category**, click **Position**. In the **position** list, click **absolute**. In the box to the right of **width**, type **200**. In the box to the right of **top**, type **0**, and in the box to the right of **right**, type **0**.

10. Click **OK** to close the **Select Style Sheet** dialog box.

11. Using steps 6 through 10, create the new style **#container** with the following declarations: **position**: **relative** and **width**:**100%**.

    Tip To select %, click px in the drop-down list to the right of Width and then select %.

    The positioning style elements created are applied to MyPage.aspx, and in Design view, div#container contains div#page_content and div#right_col, side by side on one line. In Code view, there are no changes to the definitions of the <div> tags.

12. Click the **MyStyles.css** tab. The following CSS declarations were created:

```css
#page_content {
    margin-right: 200px;
}
#right_col {
    position: absolute;
    width: 200px;
    top: 0px;
    right: 0px;
}
#container {
    position: relative;
    width: 100%;
}
```

 CLEAN UP Save your changes. Leave SharePoint Designer open if you are continuing to the next exercise.

Modifying and Deleting Styles

After you create and test your styles, you might need to manually edit the styles that SharePoint Designer automatically generated. You might also want to include comments to document your branding decisions—for example, /* This is the Home page header style */.

In this exercise, you modify and delete styles.

SET UP Using SharePoint Designer, open the team site you used in the previous exercise if it is not already open. Open MyPage.aspx, and display MyPage.aspx in Split view.

Apply Styles

1. On the **Styles** tab, click **CSS Properties** in the **Properties** group, and click **Apply Styles** in the **Create** group.

   The CSS Properties and Apply Styles task panes open.

2. In Design view, place the insertion point in the **div#page_content** region, and then type **Wide World Importers**.

   In the Apply Styles task pane, the three style elements are listed below MyStyles.css. Each red icon to the left of a style element is surrounded with a gray circle, indicating that each element is used in MyPage.aspx. The style element #page_content is surrounded with a blue rectangle, indicating that this style is applied to the area of the page where the insertion point is.

B

Bold

3. Select **Wide World Importers**, and then on the **Home** tab, click **Bold**.

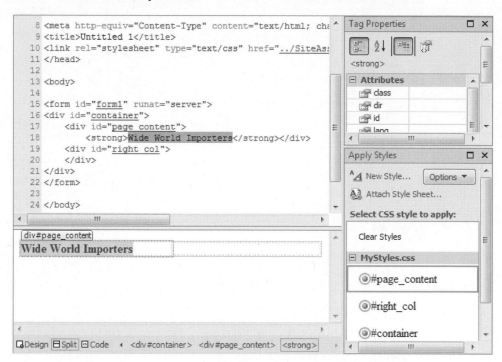

CSS Properties

4. In the **CSS Properties** task pane, click the cell to the right of the background-color property, and then click the arrow that appears.

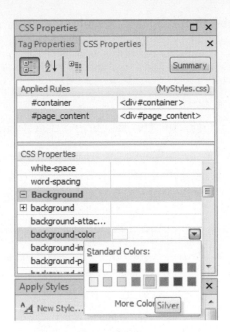

5. In the list, select **Silver**.

In the CSS Properties task pane, the background-color property is set to the hex code (a combination of six numbers and/or letters to define a color) #C0C0C0. In the document window, the text *Wide World Importers* has the background color silver, and in the Apply Styles task pane, the #page_content style has the background color silver.

6. Place the insertion point on the line below **Wide World Importers** (outside the <div> tags), and then type **Oak Furniture**.

The text is placed inside a <p> (paragraph) tag. In Code view, you can see that the <p> tag is created after the </form> tag.

Center

7. Select **Oak Furniture**, and on the **Home** tab, click **Center**.

SharePoint Designer creates a new class-based style in the current page, named .style1, and associates it with the <p> tag. This new tag appears in the Apply Styles and CSS Properties task panes. The Current Page heading is lower in the Apply Styles task pane, indicating that the styles defined on the current page are applied after styles in the MyStyles.css file.

Tip If a class style is not created, verify that the CSS tab of the Page Editor Options dialog box is set to Auto Style Application.

8. Place the insertion point on the line below **Oak Furniture** (outside the <p> tag), and then type **Office Furniture**.

   The text is placed inside a <p> tag, and the tag is associated with the style1 class.

   Tip You can remove styles from an element by selecting the element and then clicking Clear Styles on the Apply Styles task pane.

Align Text Right

9. Select **Office Furniture**, and then on the **Home** tab, and click **Align Text Right**.

   SharePoint Designer creates a new class-based style, .style2.

   Tip You can create a new style by using an existing style as its basis. In the Apply Styles task pane, right-click the style you want to use as the basis of the new style, and then click New Style Copy.

10. Click **Office Furniture**, and then in the **Apply Styles** task pane, click **.style1** to revert the <p> tag to .style1.

    The class-based style .style2 is deleted from the current page.

11. In the **Apply Styles** task pane, point to **.style1**, click the arrow that appears, and then click **Modify Style**.

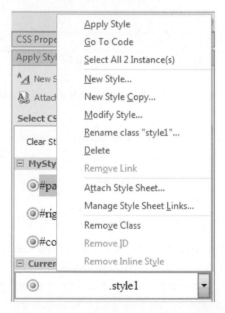

The Modify Style dialog box opens.

Tip Notice that the Block category is bold. Click that category, and you will see that text alignment is set to Center.

12. Under **Category**, click **Border**. Under **border-style**, in the **top** list, click **double**. Click **OK** to apply the style and close the **Modify Style** dialog box.

The two <p> tags are now surrounded by a double-line border.

13. In Code view, hold down the **CTRL** key and click **style1**.

Code view displays the .style1 rule enclosed in a <style> tag in the <head> portion of the page.

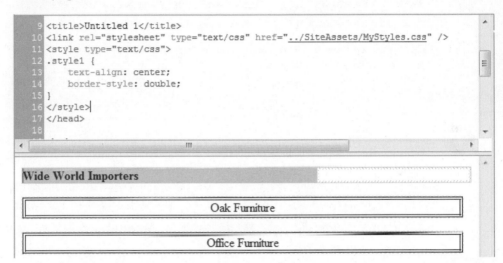

```
 9 <title>Untitled 1</title>
10 <link rel="stylesheet" type="text/css" href="../SiteAssets/MyStyles.css" />
11 <style type="text/css">
12 .style1 {
13     text-align: center;
14     border-style: double;
15 }
16 </style>
17 </head>
18
```

Wide World Importers

Oak Furniture

Office Furniture

14. Right-click the **MyPage.aspx** tab, and then click **Save**. If the **Save Embedded Files** dialog box opens, click **OK**.

 CLEAN UP Leave SharePoint Designer open if you are continuing to the next exercise.

Using the Style Application Group Commands

On the Style tab, the Style Application group of commands provides quick access to components you often use. By using the Page Editor Options dialog box, you can configure SharePoint Designer to automatically create styles on your behalf (auto mode), or you can configure SharePoint Designer to allow you to manually create styles (manual mode). If you are comfortable working with CSS, you might find that staying in auto mode or manual mode all the time does not suit you. In this situation, commands in the Style Application group can come in handy.

Use the Mode list to switch between auto and manual mode, which provides you with control over how styles are generated. When you are in manual mode, the other commands in the Style Application group become active.

The Target Rule list allows you to quickly apply styles you have already created. By default, the style that has the highest precedence is targeted. The Target Rule list can also be used to modify a particular style or create a style for the selected element. You can choose to create CSS properties on the style attribute of the selected element (*Inline Style*) or allow SharePoint Designer to generate a new style class (*New Auto Class*).

Tip The SharePoint Designer status bar indicates whether you are editing a page in Style Application auto or manual mode. You can change modes or open the CSS tab in the Page Editor Options dialog box by right-clicking Style Application in the status bar.

In this exercise, you use the Style Application group of commands**.**

 SET UP Using SharePoint Designer, open the team site you used in the previous exercise if it is not already open, and display MyPage.aspx in Split view.

1. In the Design view portion of the workspace, place the insertion point on the line below **Office Furniture** (outside the <p> tag), and then type **Garden Furniture**.

2. On the **Style** tab, in the **Mode** list, select **Manual**, and in the **Target Rule** list select **New Inline Style**.

In the Style Application group, the Show Overlay button, the Target Rule list, and the Reuse Properties button are active. The SharePoint Designer status bar displays Manual.

Font Color

3. On the **Home** tab, click the arrow to the right of **Font Color**, and click **Red**.

In Code view, the color property, with a value of #FF0000, is added to the style attribute on the <p> tag.

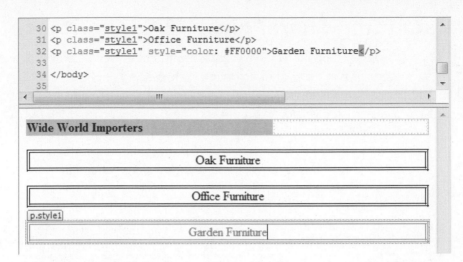

```
30 <p class="style1">Oak Furniture</p>
31 <p class="style1">Office Furniture</p>
32 <p class="style1" style="color: #FF0000">Garden Furniture</p>
33
34 </body>
35
```

Wide World Importers

Oak Furniture

Office Furniture

p.style1

Garden Furniture

4. Press **CTRL+Z** to undo the last edit. On the **Style** tab, in the **Target Rule** list, select **New Auto Class**. On the **Home** tab, click the arrow to the right of **Font Color**, and click **Red**.

In Design view, the label for the <p> tag is p.style1 style2. In Code view, you can see a new class, .style2, applied to the <p> tag that surrounds the text *Garden Furniture*.

5. Press **CTRL+Z** to undo the last edit. On the **Style** tab, in the **Target Rule** list, select **Apply New Style**.

The New Style dialog box opens with Font selected under Category.

6. Delete **.newStyle1**, and then type **.red**. With **Font** selected under **Category**, select **Red** in the **color** list.

7. Click **Apply**, and then click **OK** to close the **New Style** dialog box.

The text *Garden Furniture* is colored red and justified to the left with no border. The classes .style1 and .style 2 are no longer applied to the text. The label for the <p> tag is *p.red*, and in Code view, the class value is now set to red.

8. Right-click the **MyPage.aspx** tab, and then click **Save**.

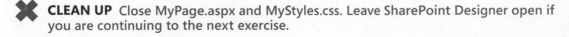 **CLEAN UP** Close MyPage.aspx and MyStyles.css. Leave SharePoint Designer open if you are continuing to the next exercise.

Understanding SharePoint's CSS Inheritance

As with many other files you have worked with in this book, corev4.css and the other style sheets live in the root directory on each Web server. If you modify and save them with SharePoint Designer, you create customized pages. Child sites do not inherit styles from a customized version of corev4.css. They will still point to the uncustomized page in the root directory. If you customize corev4.css on a number of sites, each site will have its own copy of the file. If the version of corev4.css in the root directory is changed and distributed to the Web server(s), those changes do not affect your sites.

See Also For more information about the root directory, see Chapter 1.

When you need all the sites in a site collection to have the same branding, breaking the link to the uncustomized corev4.css file can be a major problem. It's a best practice to not change corev4.css or any of the other built-in style sheets by using SharePoint Designer or any other product. To use SharePoint Designer to customize one site, you should make a copy of the styles in corev4.css that you want to amend. Then place those styles in a master page surrounded by <style> tags, or place them in your own style sheet. You might need to consult with a developer to obtain a greater understanding of the inheritance structure of all the styles in all the style sheets that both SharePoint Foundation and SharePoint Server use.

If your aim is to brand more than one site, SharePoint has a mechanism for attaching an alternative style sheet that can be used on multiple sites. Styles defined in this file are always applied after the styles in corev4.css, whether or not you customize corev4.css. SharePoint Server exposes a method of assigning alternate style sheets by using the browser. SharePoint Foundation does not. There are also other methods of applying your custom styles. Add themes to this discussion and the ability to define additional cascading style sheets in site definitions and features, and you can understand why you might need the skills of a developer.

In this exercise, you review the relationship that corev4.css has with the default master page. You will also edit a style within corev4.css, resulting in a customized page that you then revert to a file on the Web server.

 SET UP Using SharePoint Designer, open the team site you used in the previous exercise.

1.   In **Navigation** pane, click **Master Page** to display the gallery page in the workspace, and then double-click the icon to the left of v4.master.

The v4.master page opens in the workspace.

2. In the **Apply Styles** task pane, click **corev4.css**, and then continue to point to it until a ScreenTip appears.

Troubleshooting If the Apply Styles task pane is not open, on the Style tab, click Apply Styles in the Create group.

The ScreenTip points to a location in the _layouts directory, which is a folder in the root directory on the Web servers.

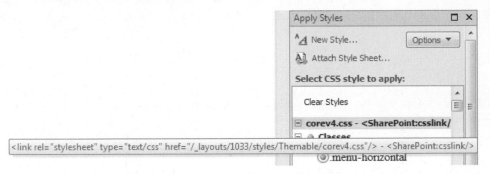

3. In the Design view of **v4.master**, on the Quick Launch, click **Libraries**, and then in the **CSS Properties** task pane, click **Summary**.

Troubleshooting If the CSS Properties task pane is not open, on the Style tab, click CSS Properties in the Properties group.

The Quick Launch Navigation control is selected, and only styles that are applied to that control are listed in the CSS Properties task pane.

4. In the **CSS Properties** task pane, click the arrow to the right of **font-size**, and select **medium**.

The corev4.css file opens as a tab. Both v4.master and corev4.css have an asterisk on their tab labels, indicating that you have changed both files.

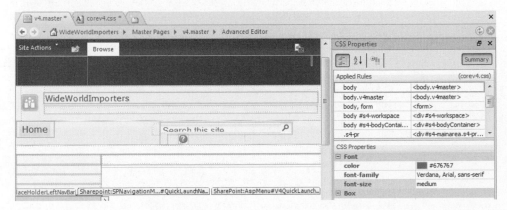

> **Tip** If the corev4.css file does not open in the workspace, you might have another SharePoint Designer window open. Look in this window for the corev4.css file. When working with styles, you should have only one site open in SharePoint Designer.

5. Right-click the **corev4.css** tab, and then click **Save**.

   A Warning dialog box opens.

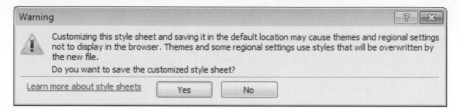

6. Click **Yes** to close the Warning dialog box.

   The All File mini-gallery opens below the Navigation pane, and a folder is created named _styles. You might need to scroll down to see this folder.

7. In the **All Files** mini-gallery, expand **_styles**.

   The file corev4.css is listed with a blue information circle to its left.

8. In the workspace, click the **v4.master** tab. Then, in the **Apply Styles** task pane, click **corev4.css**, leaving your pointer over it so that a ScreenTip appears.

   The ScreenTip indicates that corev4.css is now stored in /_styles.

9. Click the **corev4.css** tab, and then in the **All Files** mini-gallery, right-click **corev4.css**, and click **Reset to Site Definition**. When the **Site Definition Page Warning** dialog box opens, click **Yes**.

   The _styles folder contains core.css and corev4_copy(1).css.

10. Click the **v4.master** tab, and in the **Apply Styles** task pane, click **corev4.css**, leaving your pointer over it so that a ScreenTip appears.

    The ScreenTip states that corev4.css is still located in /_styles.

11. Click the **corev4.css** tab, and in the **All Files** mini-gallery, right-click **corev4.css** and click **Delete**.

    The Customized Stylesheet Warning dialog box opens, stating that this action will cause you to use a default version of the style sheet.

12. Click **OK** to close the **Customized Stylesheet Warning** dialog box. When the **Confirm Delete** dialog box opens, click **Yes**.

The _style folder now contains only the corev4_copy(1).css file.

13. Close **v4.master** and **corev4.css**. Click **No** when prompted to save the file.

 **CLEAN UP** Leave SharePoint Designer open if you are continuing to the next exercise.

Using IntelliSense to add CSS

Like many of Microsoft's Web editing programs and development environments, SharePoint Designer provides IntelliSense to help you write code quickly. When you type in Code view, a list appears suggesting possible tags, declaration names, properties, and values. Selecting items from the list reduces the amount of code you need to type, and the list also acts as a reference source and learning aid.

In this exercise you add CSS rules to Code view for a master page file by using IntelliSense. The CSS rules will change the title, also known as the banner area, of the master page.

 SET UP Using SharePoint Designer, open the team site you used in the previous exercise. To complete this exercise you need the practice file bg.jpg in the Chapter10 practice file folder.

1. In the **Navigation** pane, click **Site Assets**, and then click **Import Files** in the **New** group. The Import dialog box opens.

2. Click **Add File**. In the **Add File to Import List** dialog box, click the practice file, **bg.jpg**.

3. Click **Open**, and then click **OK**.

The Add File To Import List and Import dialog boxes close.

4. In the **Navigation** pane, click Master Pages. Right-click **v4.master**, and click **Copy**, and then right-click in the workspace, and click **Paste**.

A file named v4_copy(1).master appears.

5. With **v4_copy(1).master** selected, on the **Master Pages** tab, click **Rename** in the **Edit** group. Type **SPDSBSprototype.master**, and press **Enter**.

6. On the **Master Pages** tab, click **Edit File**.

The SPDSBSprototype.master page is displayed.

Note It is common practice when developing a prototype to insert CSS code into a master page to confirm that you have identified the CSS declarations and properties you want to amend. After you have developed the code, you can move it to a CSS file.

7. On the **View** tab, click **Split**, and then in the Code view portion of the page, find the closing **</head>** tag; it should appear at about line number 35. Place the insertion point to the left of **</head>**, and press **Enter** to create a new line before the tag.

8. On the new line, type **<st**, and then press **Tab** to select **style**.

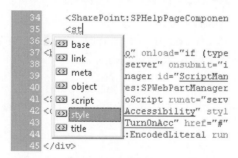

9. Press the Spacebar, type **ty**, and then press **Tab** to select **type=""**. Press the **Down Arrow** key, press **Tab** to select **text/css**, and then type >. The closing tag **</style>** is automatically appended to the line. Press **Enter** twice to insert two new lines.

10. On the new line between the two **style** tags, press Tab, and then type **.s4-t**. Press **Tab** to select **.s4-title**.

11. Type **{b**, and then press the **Down Arrow** key twice to select **background-color**. Type **#336699;** and then press **Enter** to place the insertion point on a new line.

12. Continue to use IntelliSense where possible, and add the following code to your master page:

```
background-image: url('/SiteAssets/bg.jpg');
background-repeat: repeat-x;
background-position: left top;
min-height: 80px;}
/* Recolor header text */
.s4-titletext h1 a, .s4-title h2, .ms-socialNotif-text {color: #fff;}
```

Note If your site is not the root site of a site collection, replace the URL value in the CSS property background-image code with '<site>/SiteAssets/bg.jpg', where site is the relative address of your site. For example, if your team site name is http://wideworldimporters/sites/human_resources, the CSS property should be background-image: url('/sites/human_resources/SiteAssets/bg.jpg');.

The code on the master page should look like the following:

```
<SharePoint:SPHelpPageComponent Visible="false" runat="server"/>
<style type="text/css">
 .s4-title {
    background-color: #336699;
    background-image: url('/SiteAssets/bg.jpg ');
    background-repeat: repeat-x;
    background-position: left top;
    min-height: 80px;}
 /* Recolor header text */
 .s4-titletext h1 a, .s4-title h2, .ms-socialNotif-text {color: #fff};
 }
 </style>
</head>
```

13. Click in the Design view portion of the master page for the CSS coding to take effect.

```
34    <SharePoint:SPHelpPageComponent visible="false" runat="server" />
35    <style type="text/css">
36        .s4-title {
37            background-color: #ff0000;
38            background-image: url('/SiteAssets/bg.jpg');
39            background-repeat: repeat-x;
40            background-position: left top;
41            min-height: 80px;
42        }
43        /* Recolor header text */
44        .s4-titletext h1 a, .s4-title h2, .ms-socialNotif-text {color: #fff;}
45    </style>
46 </head>
47 <body scroll="no" onload="if (typeof(_spBodyOnLoadWrapper) != 'undefined') _spBodyOn
48    <form runat="server" onsubmit="if (typeof(_spFormOnSubmitWrapper) != 'undefined')
```

Site Actions   Browse

Wide World Importers

14. Right-click the **SPDSBSprototype.master** tab, and then click **Save**.

A Site Definition Warning dialog box opens.

Note Because the original master page is a site definition page, when you made a copy of the master page, you also created a template page. Customizing master pages is not best practice, but because this master page was created for prototyping purposes, customizing this copy is a fast method of developing a branding solution.

15. Click **Yes**.

Tip You can change the site's logo in the browser by using the Site Settings, Title, Description And Icon page.

CLEAN UP Close SPDSBSprototype.master. Leave SharePoint Designer open if you are continuing to the next exercise.

Using CSS Reports

As you can with any other customization technique, you can easily make mistakes when developing styles or produce a solution that is hard to maintain. This is where SharePoint Designer CSS reports can help you. CSS reports check one or more pages within your site and produce a usage report showing you where class, ID, and HTML tag selectors are used and on what lines. These reports can help you find errors and identify styles that are defined but not used.

In this exercise, you use CSS Reports to determine the usage of CSS styles in the Home. aspx page.

 SET UP Using SharePoint Designer, open the team site you used in the previous exercise. The site settings page should be displayed.

1. In the **Customization** area of the workspace, click **Edit file**, and then on the **Home** tab, click **Advanced Mode** in the **Editing** group.

   The Home.aspx page opens in the workspace in advanced edit mode.

2. On the **View** tab, click **Task Panes**, and then click **CSS Reports** to open the **CSS Reports** task pane.

Play

3. On the **View** tab, click **Code**, and then in the **CSS Reports** task pane, click the **Play** button to open the **CSS Reports** dialog box.

   Troubleshooting If the commands on the View tab are inactive, click in Code view in the workspace.

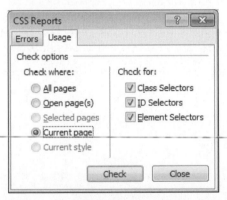

4. Click the **Usage** tab, and verify that **Current page** is selected as well as the three check boxes under **Check for**. Click **Check**.

   The Check Reports task pane lists the CSS selectors that have been applied to the current page and indicates the line on which the selector is used and the location where the selector is defined.

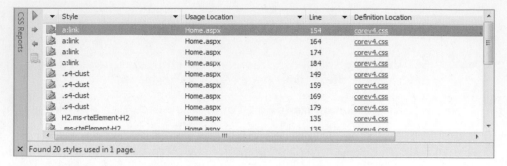

5. In the **CSS Reports** task pane, double-click the first line.

In the Code view portion of the workspace, the line where the style is used is highlighted.

6. In the **CSS Reports** task pane, on the first line, click the **corev4.css** link in the **Definition Location** column.

Corev4.css opens at the line where the style is defined.

CLEAN UP Close Home.aspx, corev4.css, and the CSS Reports task pane. Leave SharePoint Designer open if you are continuing to the next chapter.

Key Points

- SharePoint Designer provides you with a range of tools to help you manipulate cascading style sheet styles and files.

- SharePoint Designer uses a set of configuration options to decide how it should add the cascading style sheet tags to your page.

- The main cascading style sheet for both SharePoint Foundation and SharePoint Service is corev4.css.

- The Manage Styles and CSS Properties task panes provide useful tools to identify where styles are used and the cascade order of those styles. With the Style Application group commands, you can switch between automatic and manual CSS modes and quickly apply styles.

- You can save your styles in files that you can attach to pages.

- IntelliSense is Microsoft's implementation of auto-completion and acts as a reference source and learning aid.

- Use CSS reports to check your styles and to produce CSS usage reports.

Chapter at a Glance

Understand master pages, **page 368**

Customize a master page, **page 379**

Manage content placeholders, **page 387**

Create a Web page from a master page, **page 391**

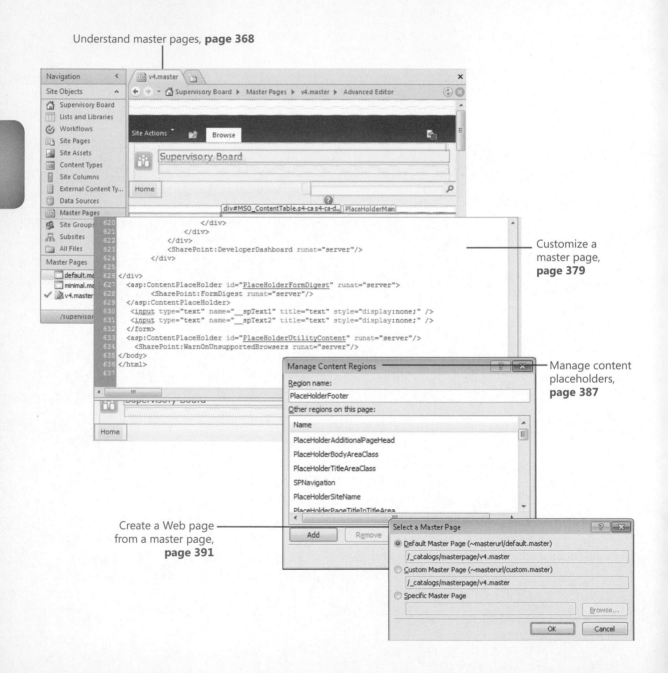

11 Working with Master Pages

In this chapter, you will learn how to

- ✔ Understand master pages.
- ✔ Copy and save a master page.
- ✔ Customize a master page.
- ✔ Change the default master page.
- ✔ Manage content placeholders.
- ✔ Create a Web page from a master page.
- ✔ Export a master page.
- ✔ Reset a master page to the site definition.

You have already worked with master pages earlier in this book. For example, in Chapter 4, "Creating and Modifying Web Pages," you saw that when you use a browser to request a page from a site, it combines two Microsoft ASP.NET pages: a master page and a content page. You discovered that when you open a content page in Microsoft SharePoint Designer 2010, Design view displays the merged page (not only the content page). You also attached a master page to a newly created page.

Microsoft SharePoint Foundation 2010 and Microsoft SharePoint Server 2010 make heavy use of master pages to control the general layout of pages within a SharePoint site. The *default master* page, usually a file named v4.master, is the master page that is applied to all pages in your site when you first create the site. When you install SharePoint 2010, the default master page and other master pages are located on the Web server. Each master page contains multiple core controls, called ContentPlaceHolder controls that must be included to display site pages correctly. SharePoint Designer is an excellent tool to use to customize master pages and manipulate content placeholders.

In this chapter, you will explore the master pages provided with SharePoint 2010 and learn about some of the new items on those master pages as well as the differences between them. You will modify a master page, manage ContentPlaceHolder controls, and reset a master page to its site definition. You will also create a content page from a master page. If you worked with SharePoint Designer 2007, some of this will not be new to you. However, if you are just starting out in SharePoint and want to change the layout of your site, it is important to understand master pages and how they are used in SharePoint.

Important To complete the exercises in this chapter, you must have permission to modify master pages. By default, site owners and designers are not allowed to modify master pages; you must be a site collection administrator. A site collection administrator or Web application administrator can give site owners and designers permission to modify master pages. For more information, see "Controlling the Use of SharePoint Designer" in Chapter 1, "Exploring SharePoint Designer 2010."

> **Practice Files** Before you can complete the exercises in this chapter; you need to copy the book's practice files to your computer. A complete list of practice files is provided in "Using the Practice Files" at the beginning of this book.

Understanding Master Pages

Master pages were included as part of ASP.NET. SharePoint Foundation 2010 is built on top of ASP.NET and supports master pages, which help to provide a common look and feel across entire sites. Because SharePoint Server 2010 is built using SharePoint Foundation, it too uses ASP.NET.

The best way to plan the structure of a master page is to follow the same steps you take to structure a regular Web site page. Create a diagram of the layout of the master page, and indicate where you want to locate components that will remain consistent across all pages on the site—for example, a header area, a left or right navigation area, or a footer area. Also indicate where you want to locate components from the content pages. The parts that contain unique content—on a page-by-page basis—are usually located in the center of the page.

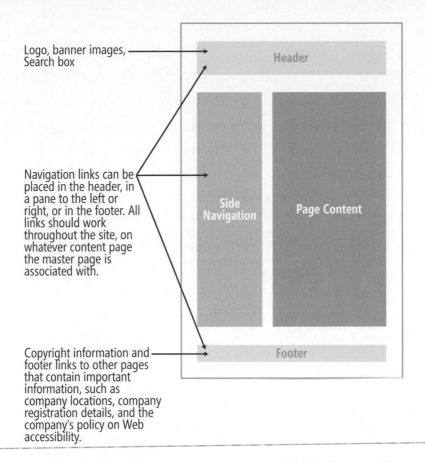

Logo, banner images, Search box

Navigation links can be placed in the header, in a pane to the left or right, or in the footer. All links should work throughout the site, on whatever content page the master page is associated with.

Copyright information and footer links to other pages that contain important information, such as company locations, company registration details, and the company's policy on Web accessibility.

Master pages have the same structure as typical Web pages. They contain the same tags, such as <html>, <head>, and <body>. Their file names have the extension .master instead of .aspx or .html. They also contain most of the content and functionality of normal pages, including JavaScript , Web Parts (including Data Views and XLV Web Parts), and components such as the Search box and the Site Actions button. Master pages cannot contain Web Part zones, however.

You can include style information in a master page, but it's good practice to use a style sheet that is linked to the master page. The key benefit of using a master page is that any global design changes to your site can be made in one place. By using a master page, you can design your site efficiently and quickly and avoid having to make changes on every page in the site.

See Also Information about using SharePoint Designer with cascading style sheets is detailed in Chapter 10, "Branding SharePoint Sites."

Default Master Pages

As with other pages, site definitions play a key role with master pages. Each site definition can contain a number of master pages, one of which can be set as the default master page for the site. However, most site definitions do not contain master pages and use a global default master page instead. When a site is first created, a site property, referred to by the token *~masterurl/default.master*, is used to save the default master page's location. After a site is created, you can change the value stored in this token.

Each page in a site is initially configured to use the site's default master page. However, you can modify which master page a content page uses. For example, you can specify whether you want to use the default master page or a different master page. Theoretically, each page within a site collection could use a different master page. Such a scenario would defeat the purpose of using master pages, however, because, as stated earlier, master pages were introduced to support a common look and feel across entire sites.

So how many master pages does a SharePoint installation have? In a default installation of SharePoint Foundation, only the following master pages are used:

- *Global master pages*   There are three default master pages:
  - **default.master**   Provides the look and feel and controls included in a Windows SharePoint Services 3.0 or Microsoft Office SharePoint Server 2007 installation. This means that the ribbon is not included.
  - **v4.master**   The primary master page for a SharePoint 2010 installation.
  - **minimal.master**   This is not the same minimal master page you might have used with a Windows SharePoint Services 3.0 or SharePoint Server 2007 installation. The minimal master in SharePoint 2010 is applied to pages that use the Office Web Applications as well as the Search Center.
- *Global meeting workspace master pages*   All meeting workspaces use one of the global meeting workspace master pages: mwsdefaultv4.master or mwsdefault.master.

By using global master pages, all your team sites will look the same and all your meeting workspace sites will look the same. SharePoint Server has additional master pages, such as mysite.master, which is used on My Sites, and DynamicView.master, which is used with the PerformancePoint Web Parts. Other master pages can be found in the _layouts folder on each Web server, such as application.master, applicationv4.master, simple. master, simplev4.master, and pickerdialog.master. These master pages and a number of content pages that also usually live in the _layouts folder cannot be modified by SharePoint Designer. These content pages (including Login.aspx, SignOut.aspx, Error.aspx, ReqAcc.aspx, Confirmation.aspx, WebDeleted.aspx, and AccessDenied.aspx) do not use the same master pages you use for your SharePoint sites, and if you corrupt your site's master pages, these pages will still display. You can find instructions for how to modify these pages at *msdn.microsoft.com/en-us/library/ee537576(v=office.14).aspx*, however, you should carefully consider any customizations, and developer skills will often be required.

Note In a default SharePoint Server installation, team and meeting workspace master pages work as they do in SharePoint Foundation. Publishing sites also use the default master page mechanism described earlier—that is, each site is configured to use a default master page. Publishing sites, however, can use an alternate type of master pages, called *custom master pages*. The site property that contains the location of a custom master page is referred to by the token *~masterurl/custom.master*.

On publishing sites, when you are working in the browser, if you click Master Page under Look And Feel on the site settings page, the Site Master Page Settings page is displayed. Use this page to choose a custom master page in the Site Master Page section or a default master page in the System Master Page section. The default master page section is named System Master Page because it is used for nonpublishing pages and for system pages, such as those used to display the contents of lists and libraries.

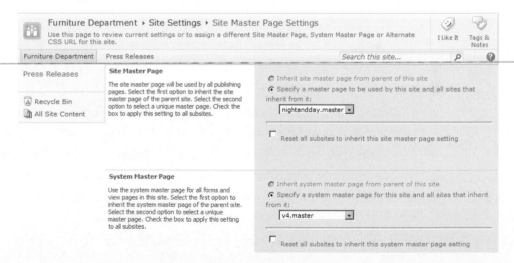

If a master page is selected in both the Site Master Page and System Master Page sections, publishing sites will use the master page selected in the Site Master Page section. In other words, when custom master pages are set, they are used in preference to default master pages on publishing sites.

Controls Used on the Master Page

Much of the functionality of a master page is provided by components that comprise application logic and user interface declarations in the form of ASP.NET or SharePoint Server controls.

See Also More information on controls can be found in Chapter 14, "Using Controls in Web Pages."

Several controls are required for a master page. These requirements can be different if you are creating a master page for a SharePoint Foundation installation or a SharePoint Server installation, and they also depend on the type of functionality you want to use on your SharePoint site. For example, when you create or modify a master page, the following controls should be placed on your page within the <head> tag (<head>...</head>):

```
<SharePoint:SPPageManager runat="server" />
<SharePoint:ScriptLink defer= "true" runat="server"/>
```

Similarly, the following ASP.NET server control should be placed in the <form> tag but before the ribbon:

```
<asp:ScriptManager id="ScriptManager" runat="server" EnablePageMethods="false"
 EnablePartialRendering="true" EnableScriptGlobalization="false"
 EnableScriptLocalization="true" />
```

See Also You can find more information about upgrading an existing master page to the SharePoint Foundation master page at *msdn.microsoft.com/en-us/library/ ee539981(v=office.14).aspx.*

The controls added to a master page can be divided into four types:

- Controls for links, menus, icons, and navigation components, such as the SiteMapPath control that populates the *global navigation breadcrumb*.
- Content placeholders, such as the PlaceHolderMain control, that match areas on the content page where you can enter information.
- Delegate controls, which define a region on the page in which content can be substituted for by another control driven by feature activation.
- Controls for scripts. These manage the communication of the page and assist with the ribbon, toolbars, and other controls.

See Also For more information, refer to Chapter 5, "Pages and Navigation," in *Inside Microsoft SharePoint 2010*, by Ted Pattison, Andrew Connell, and Scot Hillier (Microsoft Press, 2011).

As you have seen with other types of SharePoint pages, SharePoint Designer provides full design support for master pages. In Design view, you can manipulate the controls on a master page in a WYSIWYG manner. In addition, you can modify any part of the page that is displayed and selectable. However, master pages contain many controls and tags, and it can be a challenge to accurately modify the page in Design view. In this situation, Code view is particularly useful.

Note In a browser, you can see only the effect of a master page merged with a content page; you cannot view a master page itself.

SharePoint Designer displays a program window for each site you open, which allows you to modify only one site at a time. There is no mechanism by which you can publish your changes from one site to another. Therefore, in SharePoint Designer, master pages are always modified at the site level.

In this exercise, you locate the default master page and explore the ASP.NET and SharePoint controls used by that master page.

 SET UP Using SharePoint Designer, open the site you created from the SBSSPDPracticeSite_Starter.wsp practice file.

1. In the **Navigation** pane, click **Master Pages**.

   The workspace contains the gallery page that displays the master pages for your site. This page is similar to page-settings pages you saw in Chapter 4. For example, you can edit the master page name, change permissions, and view the version history of the master page.

   Note In a top-level team site on a SharePoint Server installation or on a publishing site, the Master Page gallery also contains other files.

2. Click **v4.master**.

   The settings page for v4.master is displayed.

Check Out

3. On the **Page** tab, click **Check Out** in the Manage group, and then click **Edit File** in the **Edit** group.

   The master page opens in the workspace, and on the breadcrumb the text *Advanced Editor* indicates that the page is open in advanced edit mode.

   Tip Using the Edit File command in the Customization area in the workspace is equivalent to clicking the Edit File command on the ribbon.

4. Look in the status bar for the SharePoint Designer window. If **Visual Aids** is not specified as **On**, click **Visual Aids** on the **View** tab, and then select **Show**.

   The controls on the page are displayed and surrounded by a purple line. The label for the active control, PlaceHolderMain, appears above a purple box. In the workspace status bar, <asp:ContentPlaceH...#PlaceHolderMain> is highlighted in orange to identify it as the active tag. In the mini-gallery below the Navigation pane, a green check mark appears to the left of v4.master, indicating that the file is checked out.

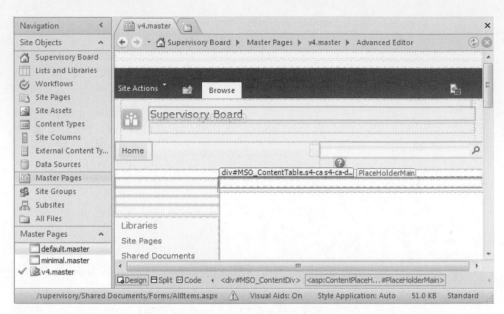

Tip If control names do not appear, verify that Template Region Labels is selected on the Visual Aids menu. Using visual aids can help as you build your master page, but if you find them distracting, simply clear the options you do not want to show.

Visual Aids

5. On the **View** tab, click the down arrow on the **Visual Aids** command, and then select **ASP.NET Non-visual Controls** if no orange box appears to the left of it.

   The master page refreshes, and hidden controls, such as ScriptManager, SPWebPartMaster, DelegateControl, and DeveloperDashboard, appear.

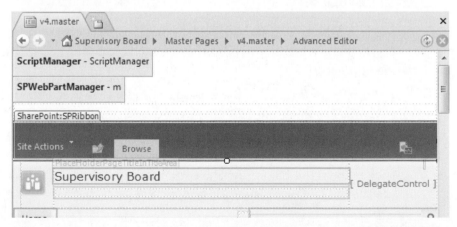

Split

6. On the workspace status bar, click **Split** to display the page in both Code view and Design view.

Find

7. Click in Code view, and then on the Home tab, click Find in the Editing group.

The Find And Replace dialog box opens.

8. In the **Find what** box, type **<asp:**. Under **Find where**, select Current page (if this option is not already selected), and clear all other check boxes.

Note Under Advanced, you will see that the Find In Source Code check box is selected, but the option is dimmed.

9. Click **Find All**.

The Find And Replace dialog box closes, and the Find 1 task pane opens, docking below the workspace. The lines returned in the results window refer to ASP.NET controls.

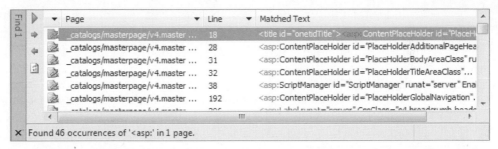

10. Press **CTRL+F** to open the **Find and Replace** dialog box. Type **<SharePoint:**, and then click **Find All**.

The Find And Replace dialog box closes, and the search results appear in the Find 1 task pane.

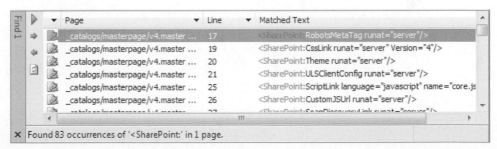

 CLEAN UP Close the Find 1 task pane and the v4.master page, leaving v4.master checked out. Leave SharePoint Designer open if you are continuing to the next exercise.

Creating a Master Page

Depending on your requirements, creating a master page can be easy or so difficult that you need developer assistance. You need to decide whether you need to change just one site or a number of sites, because this requirement also affects the decision about which tool to use.

If you want to change the master page for all the sites on a SharePoint installation, you cannot use SharePoint Designer because SharePoint Designer lets you alter master pages only at the site level. For typical SharePoint master pages, however, SharePoint Designer is the perfect tool.

When you have a site that requires some heavy design customizations, take time to understand the components of the master page and become comfortable working in Code view or Split view. You do not have to be a developer to create a master page, but you might need the assistance of a developer to help with particular functional requirements.

It's fairly simple to move components around on a master page, and you might think that removing one will not cause harm. However, if your master page does not contain all the necessary content placeholders, content pages based on that master page will fail to render, and users will see an error message.

In SharePoint Designer, on the *Master Pages* tab, you can create a blank master page, which will contain one content placeholder. This master page is suited to team sites and system pages.

On the *Master Pages* tab on publishing sites, you can create a custom master page by using the *From Content Type, Publishing Master Page* command. The new master page includes the minimum number of content placeholders and other components required by the Publishing Framework, but the page contains no styling or layout.

You can use the v4.master as the basis of your master page, but it's a complicated master page and not the easiest page to learn from. I recommend using one of the starter master pages that come with SharePoint Server, like the Night And Day master, or the community-created master page under Starter Master Pages for SharePoint 2010 on the CodePlex Web site, *startermasterpages.codeplex.com/.*

Other people in the SharePoint community have produced sample master pages that you can use as the basis for your own. When searching for these pages, use search keywords such as *SharePoint2010 minimal master page* or *starter master page.*

Copying and Saving a Master Page

In SharePoint Designer, master pages can be located by using the Master Page option on the Navigation pane. Their actual location in a site is in the _catalogs folder in the masterpage (Master Page Gallery) library, which you can navigate to by using the All Files gallery or the mini-gallery. This master page library is hidden from the browser's All Site Content page, but you can display it by using the Master Page link on the site settings page.

On publishing sites, two master page content types, *Master Page* and *Publishing Master Page*, are added to the Master Page Gallery library so that it can contain both default master pages and custom master pages. On nonpublishing sites, such as a team site, only the *Master Page* content type is included.

On SharePoint Foundation, versioning is enabled on the Master Page Gallery library, and all visitors to the site have read access to allow the combined master page and content page to be displayed in the browser. On SharePoint Server sites, the master page library has major and minor versioning enabled, content approval is enabled, and check out is required. These settings mean that you can modify master pages and restore a previous version if you find errors in your modifications. On a SharePoint Server site, you can make modifications to your master page and publish the master page as a major version only when those modifications are correct.

Changes to the master page that is set as the default master page cascade down to all pages that are associated with the site's default master page. If you do not have your own site and are working on a team site that other members of your team have access to, making modifications to a site's default master page might not be acceptable, especially if your modifications contain so many errors that no content page will render in the browser.

The preferred method for modifying a default master page is to create a customized master page and set it as the master page for one content page. When you have tested your modifications by displaying that content page, you can then set your customized master page as the site's default page.

A customized master page can be created in several ways. You can create a new master page by using the Blank Master Page or From Content Type command on the Master Page tab, or you can copy a master page and customize it to meet your needs. If modifying the existing default master page seems overwhelming, you can use a starter master page. Starting with the site's default master page (v4.master) or using a starter master page is the best option because these pages will already meet most of your needs.

See Also For more information about creating a master page, see the sidebar "Creating a Master Page" earlier in this chapter.

Like site definition files, master pages that are created when you install SharePoint are stored in the root directory on the Web server. In SharePoint Designer, you can edit master pages only in advance edit mode. When you save changes, you do not alter the file on the Web server. SharePoint takes a copy of the file, including your amendments, and saves it in the Microsoft SQL Server content database—that is, the page becomes a customized page. If a developer subsequently changes the master page on the Web server, your site will not reflect those changes.

See Also For more information about site definitions and the root directory, see Chapter 1.

In this exercise, you create and save a copy of the v4.master page.

SET UP Using SharePoint Designer, open the team site you used in the previous exercise if it is not already open. The settings page for the site should be displayed.

1. In the **Navigation** pane, click Master Page to display the gallery page in the workspace.

2. Click the icon to the left of **v4.master**. On the **Master Pages** tab, click **Copy** in the **Clipboard** group, and then click **Paste**.

   On the gallery page and in the mini-gallery below the Navigation pane, the file v4_copy(1).master appears

   Note You could complete this task by using the All Files mini-gallery and navigating to the master page (Master Page Gallery) library in the _catalogs folder. You could then save your master page anywhere in your site. However, the best practice is to save the master page in the site's Master Page Gallery library.

3. Click the icon to the left of **v4_copy(1).master**, and then on the **Master Pages** tab, click **Check Out** in the **Manage** group.

Check Out

4. Click **Rename** in the **Edit** group. Type **v4-test.master**, and press **Enter**.

   Important Be sure to name the file with the .master extension.

   A dialog box briefly appears stating that your file is being renamed.

Rename

5. On the **Master Pages** tab, click **Edit File** in the **Edit** group.

   The v4-test.master page opens in Split view.

Edit File

   Troubleshooting If your page does not open in Split view, click the Split button in the workspace status bar.

Save

6. On the Quick Access Toolbar, click **Save**. In the **Site Definition Page Warning** message box that opens, click Yes.

7. In mini-gallery below the **Navigation** pane, right-click **v4-test.master**, and then click **Check In**.

8. Click **OK** to close the **Check In** dialog box that opens.

    The green check mark to the left of v4.master is replaced with a blue information circle, indicating that the page is customized and now saved in the SQL Server content database.

 CLEAN UP Leave SharePoint Designer open if you are continuing to the next exercise.

Customizing a Master Page

Eventually you might find that you want to alter all the pages in your site to display a certain piece of information or image. You could navigate through the site and modify all the pages and add this information to any new pages. But just imagine the daunting task of updating a typical corporate intranet site that has hundreds of pages. The most efficient way to repeat items consistently across the site is to create or modify the master page.

Important When you customize the current default master page (v4.master or any page that is set as the default master), changes are immediately visible on any associated content page. In light of this, the best practice is to customize a copy of the default master page. Never customize a master page associated with a production site.

In this exercise, you add a Data View Web Part (DVWP) at the bottom of the master page. The DVWP will display links to pages stored in the Site Pages library that are classified as footer pages. You then add an existing CSS class to the DVWP so that the extra code you add to the master page will not be displayed in any pop-up dialog boxes.

 SET UP Using SharePoint Designer, open the team site you used in the previous exercise if it is not already open. Check out and open v4-test.master so that it appears in the workspace in Split view in advanced edit mode.

1. In the Code view portion of the workspace, scroll down. To the left of the last closing **<div>** tag, press **Enter** to add a new line.

    Tip The last closing <div> tag will appear on or about line 625 or 654, depending on whether you are using SharePoint Foundation or SharePoint Server. The line number might be different if your organization modified the master page or you used a different or modified site template to create your site.

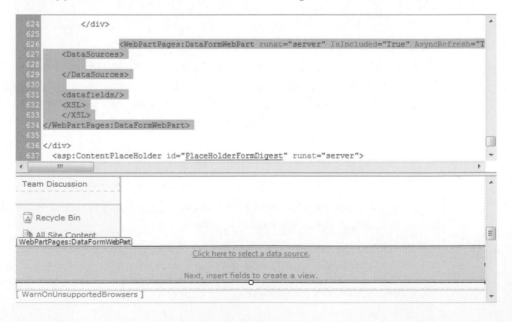

Data View

2. In Design view, click where the cursor is flashing. On the **Insert** tab, click Data View in the **Data Views & Forms** group, and then click **Empty Data View**.

Troubleshooting If the Data View tab is not active and appears dimmed, click once anywhere in Design view, and then click to the left of the last closing <div> tag in Code view.

A WebPartPages:DataFormWebPart control is added to the master page, and an asterisk appears on the v4-test.master tab, indicating that it contains unsaved content.

3.   In the Design view portion of the workspace, click **Click here to select a data source** to open the **Data Sources Picker** dialog box. Click **Site Pages** under **Document Library**, and then click **OK**.

The Data Sources Picker dialog box closes, and the Data Source Details task pane appears.

4.   In the **Data Source Details** task pane, scroll down, click URL Path, click **Insert Selected Field as**, and then click Multiple Item View.

The page view refreshes, and in Design view, the DataFormWebPart control shows the URL for all the files stored in the Site Pages document library.

Tip On a master page on which you use Web Parts or a Data View, verify that users have permission to view the information displayed. Test your modifications by using a variety of permissions levels.

5.   In Design view, click the **WebPartPages:DataFormWebPart** control to display the **Data View Tools** tabs on the ribbon. On the **Design** tab, click the **More** down arrow in the **View Style** group.

An expanded drop-down list appears.

6. Under **Out of Box**, point to each of the styles, and click the layout that displays the ScreenTip **Horizontal list of titles**.

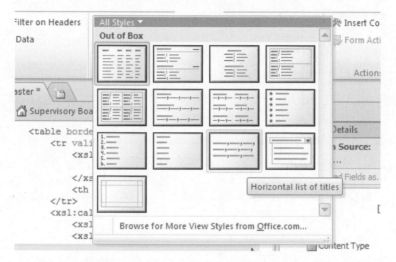

A Microsoft SharePoint Designer message box appears, warning you that any custom formatting and provider Web Part connections will be removed.

7. Click **Yes** to close the message box.

The master page refreshes, showing horizontally the page names from the Site Pages document library.

8. Click inside the **WebPartPages:DataFormWebPart** control, right-click any of the page names, point to **Format item as**, and then click **Hyperlink**.

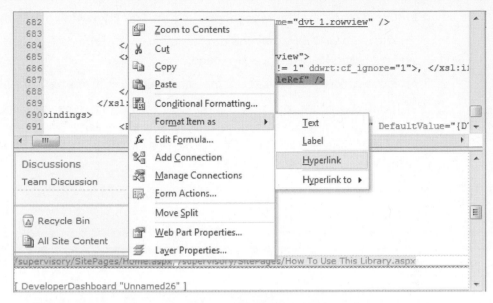

9. Click **Yes** to confirm the change. The **Edit Hyperlink** dialog box opens.

Function

10. In the **Text to display** box, delete **{@FileRef}**, and click the function button to the right of the **Text to display** box. In the **More Fields** dialog box, under **Click to se-lect a field**, scroll down and click **FileLeafRef.Name**.

11. Click **OK** to close the **More Fields** and the **Edit Hyperlink** dialog boxes.

The page view refreshes and displays the names of the pages. The page names are now linked to their respective pages.

12. Right-click one of the page names, and then click **Zoom to Contents**.

The Design view portion of the workspace displays page names, and in the Code view portion, <xsl:value-of select="@FileLeafRef.Name" /> is highlighted. Directly above this text is the comma used in the layout to separate the page names: approximately line 691.

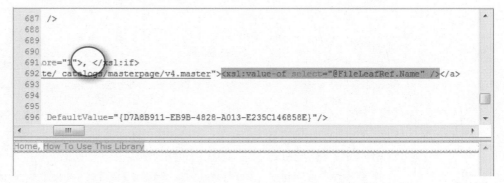

13. In Code view, delete the comma, press **SPACE**, and then type |. (Press Shift+Backslash to type this character, which is known as the *pipe character.*) Click in the Design view portion of the workspace to refresh the page and display the page names separated by the pipe character.

Filter

14. Click any of the page names, and then on the **Options** tab, click **Filter** in the **Filter, Sort & Group** group. In the **Filter Criteria** dialog box, click the **Field Name** arrow. In the list, click **PageType**, and under **Value**, select **Footer** (if it is not already selected). Click **OK**.

Troubleshooting If the column name PageType does not appear in the Field Name list, you might not have created the team site from the solutions .wsp practice file. See "Using the Practice Files" at the beginning of this book.

The page view refreshes and shows only those pages that are classified as footer pages. You should still be in Zoom To Content view

15. In Design view, click one of the page names. In Code view, visually search for **<p class="ms-vb">**, which should be just above the **dvt_1.body xsl:call-template** tag. Delete **ms-vb**, and type **s4-notdlg**.

```
664           </table>
665       </xsl:template>
666                     <xsl:template name="dvt_1">
667                         <xsl:variable name="dvt_StyleName">HorzTitl</xsl:vari
668                         <xsl:variable name="Rows" select="/dsQueryResponse/Ro
669                         <xsl:variable name="dvt_RowCount" select="count($Rows
670                         <xsl:variable name="dvt_IsEmpty" select="$dvt_RowCour
671                         <xsl:choose>
672                             <xsl:when test="$dvt_IsEmpty">
673                                 <xsl:call-template name="dvt_1.empty" />
674                             </xsl:when>
675                                 <xsl:otherwise>
676                 <p class="s4-notdlg">
677                 <xsl:call-template name="dvt_1.body">
678                     <xsl:with-param name="Rows" select="$Rows" />
679                 </xsl:call-template>
680                                 </p>
681             </xsl:otherwise>
682                             </xsl:choose>
683                         </xsl:template>
684                     <xsl:template name="dvt_1.body">
685                         <xsl:param name="Rows" />
```

Tip Use this CSS class when you want to hide the footer in dialog boxes that appear, for example, when you click Edit List Item in the browser.

 CLEAN UP Save, check in, and close the v4-test.master page. Leave SharePoint Designer open if you are continuing to the next exercise.

Changing the Default Master Page

When you first create a SharePoint Foundation or SharePoint Server site, all pages but a select few use the site's default master page. By using SharePoint Designer, you can set a new master page as the site's default master page.

Note In a SharePoint Server 2010 installation, you can alter the master page associated with a site by using the browser. To access the master page, click Master Page in the Look And Feel list on the site settings page. On SharePoint Foundation, you have to set the default master page through SharePoint Designer.

In this exercise, you set the default master page to use the master page you created in the previous exercise.

 SET UP Using SharePoint Designer, open the team site you used in the previous exercise if it is not already open. The settings page for the site should be displayed.

Set as Default

1.   In the **Navigation** pane, click **Master Pages**. In the workspace, click the icon to the left of **v4-test.master.** On the **Master Pages** tab, click **Set as Default** in the **Actions** group.

> **Tip** If the Set As Default command is not available, then the master page v4-test.master is already set as the site's default master page.

2. In the **Navigation** pane, click **Site Pages**. In the workspace, double-click the icon to the left of **Home.aspx** to open the page in edit mode.

> **Note** In the Site Pages mini-gallery, no blue information circle appears to the left of Home.aspx. The master page v4-test.master is a customized page, but the content page, Home.aspx, is an uncustomized page.

3. In the lower-left area of the Home.aspx page, point to one of the page names listed from the Site Pages library.

> **Tip** You might need to scroll down Home.aspx to see the page names.

A no-entry symbol appears over the page name.

4. Press **F12** to open the home page in the browser.

5. At the bottom of the page, click one of the page names.

The page that opens should be associated with the link you select.

6. On the Quick Launch bar, under **Libraries**, click **Site Pages**.

The All Pages view of the Site Pages library is displayed. At the bottom of the page you should still see footer links to the page names.

7. On the **Documents** tab, click New Document in the **New** group.

The New dialog box opens. At the bottom of the dialog box no pages from the Site Pages library are displayed. This occurs because the s4-notdlg CSS class was used in the previous exercise.

8. In the **New page name** box, type **Test-Page**, and then click **Create** to close the **New** dialog box.

The Test-Page opens, and a link to the new page appears at the bottom of the page.

> **Troubleshooting** If a link to Test-Page is not displayed at the bottom of the page, you might have set the default value of the PageType column to a value other than Footer.

> **Note** On a Windows SharePoint Services 3.0 or SharePoint Server 2007 installation, if you click the Documents or List link in the Quick Launch bar, you are taken to a page in the _layouts folder. This page does not have your customized version of the master page applied. This is not the case in SharePoint Foundation 2010. Your _layouts page has the footer links at the bottom of the page. The difference is that in SharePoint 2010, the default master page is also used by the _layouts pages.

✖ **CLEAN UP** Close the v4.master page and the browser. Leave SharePoint Designer open if you are continuing to the next exercise.

Tip You can attach a master page to a single page when you have a page open in advanced edit mode by using the Attach command in the Master Page group on the Style tab. This is very useful when you want to test a new or a modified copy of an existing master page. Once you have completed your tests, you can use the exercise in this section to set the site's default master page as your new or modified master page.

Managing Content Placeholders

As I previously described, master pages are used to keep a consistent look and feel across your site pages. However, master pages have other special features, such as ContentPlaceHolder controls. The ContentPlaceHolder control is a key component of a master page. These controls define the areas of the master page where unique content on a content page appears when the content page is merged with the master page. Master pages must contain content place holders. If they don't, some if not all the pages on your site might not work correctly and error pages will be displayed.

In SharePoint 2010, application pages (those pages with _layouts in their URL) and content pages use the same content placeholders. Application pages also contain a new attribute, DynamicMasterPageFile—in the @Page directive. These two improvements mean that both sets of pages can use the same master page. This gives a consistent look and feel across a site, which was not the case in Windows SharePoint Services 3.0 and SharePoint Server 2007. Simply put, if you modify a site's master page, your application pages will share those modifications.

A master page typically has a number of content placeholders, the most important of them being PlaceHolderMain. This is the name of the *content placeholder* that maps to the region on the master page where the majority of the unique content from the content page should be placed. It usually appears in the center of the page.

See Also For a description of the default content placeholders, refer to *office.microsoft.com/ en-us/sharepointdesigner/HA101651201033.aspx*.

You might remember from Chapter 4 that when you attached a master page to OfficeFurniture.aspx, SharePoint Designer opened the Match Content Regions dialog box so that you could match the content on OfficeFurniture.aspx with a content placeholder on the master page. In this case, defining a match was easy, and you accepted SharePoint Designer's suggestion of mapping the data in the <body> tag on OfficeFurniture.aspx with the PlaceHolderMain control. SharePoint Designer replaced the <body> tag in OfficeFurniture.aspx with an <asp:Content> tag with the attribute *contentplaceholderid* set to *PlaceHolderMain*. Therefore, to plug content from a content page into a master page, the content page must have at least one content control that matches an ID of a content placeholder on the master page.

Tip In SharePoint Designer, content placeholders are also known as *content regions*. If you developed a common look and feel for a site on Windows SharePoint Services 3.0 or SharePoint Server 2007 by using Dynamic Web Templates (DWT), the concept of content regions will not be new to you.

When you create a new content page from a master page, all content placeholders cannot contain any unique content—that is, all content placeholders are placed in a noneditable state. In SharePoint Designer, the text in the label above the content placeholder will look similar to *PlaceHolderNAME (Master)*. When you open an existing content page, such as Home.aspx, you see *Custom* in the placeholder name, such as *PlaceHolderNAME (Custom)*. This indicates that unique content can be placed within the region defined by the content placeholder. You worked with this aspect of a content placeholder in Chapter 4 if you completed the exercise to create a new page from a master page. All the content placeholders on that page were marked with *Master*. You enabled the PlaceHolderMain content region as editable, and as a result, *Custom* replaced *Master*. You were then able to add content to your content page. Adding content to a content placeholder on the master page allows you to specify content that is visible on every content page associated with that master page, but it also allows you to customize that content for each particular content page.

While working with master pages in SharePoint Designer, you manage content placeholders by using the Manage Content Regions command on the ribbon's Style tab. Content placeholders cannot be managed from a content page. When the Manage Content Regions command is clicked on a content page, a warning dialog box appears, asking if you want to save the content page as a master page.

In this exercise, you will place the DVWP you created in the previous exercise in a content placeholder on the master page. Then, on a content page, you will override a content placeholder and revert to a content placeholder on the master page.

 SET UP Using SharePoint Designer, open the team site you used in the previous exercise if it is not already open. Check out and open v4-test.master so that it appears in the workspace in Split view in advanced edit mode.

1. In the Design view portion of the workspace, scroll down if necessary and click the DVWP you created in the previous exercise in this chapter. Select the label **(WebPartPages: DataFormWebPart)** when it appears.

The DVWP code is highlighted in the Code view portion of the workspace.

2. On the **Style** tab, click **Manage Content Regions** in the **Master Page** group.

The Manage Content Regions dialog box opens.

Manage Content
Regions

3.   In the **Region name** box, type **PlaceHolderFooter**, and then click **Add**.

Tip When you add a new content region, it must have a unique name.

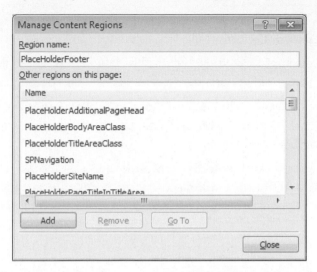

PlaceHolderFooter appears (in alphabetic order) in the Manage Content Regions dialog box. The Add button changes to the Rename button, and the v4-test.master page is refreshed. The new region, PlaceHolderFooter, appears, and your DVWP is now contained in that content region.

Save

4.   Click **Close** to close the **Manage Content Regions** dialog box, and then click **Save** on the Quick Access Toolbar. If a dialog box opens stating that there are pending updates, click **Continue**.

5.   **In the Navigation pane, click Site Pages, and then click the icon to the left of Test-Page.aspx. On the Pages tab, click Check Out in the Manage group, and then click Edit File in the Edit group.**

The page opens. In the Code view portion of the workspace, the code has a yellow background color.

Tip The yellow background indicates that the page is open in safe mode.

6.   On the **Home tab, click Advanced Mode in the Editing group.**

The page refreshes, and the code no longer has a yellow background.

7.   In the Design view portion of the workspace, scroll to the bottom of the page and point to the DVWP that you created previously. Click **On Object User Interface (OOUI)**, which is represented by a small arrow floating just outside the control.

The Common Content Task list opens.

8. Click **Create Custom Content**.

   The Common Content Tasks list closes, and the label on the content placeholder changes from PlaceHolderFooter (Master) to PlaceHolderFooter (Custom).

9. Click one of the page names in the DVWP so the **WebPartPages:DataFormWebPart** label appears. Click the **WebPartPages:DataFormWebPart** label, and then press **Delete** to delete the DVWP.

10. In the Quick Launch bar, click **Recently Modified** so that the **PlaceHolderLeftActions (Custom)** content placeholder label appears. Click the OOUI arrow floating just outside the control to open the Common Content Tasks list.

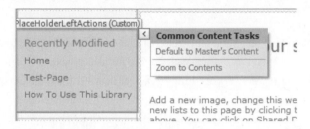

11. Click **Default to Master's Content**.

    The Confirm dialog box opens, stating that by defaulting to the master page content, everything in this region will be removed from this page.

12. Click **Yes** to close the **Confirm** dialog box.

    The content page refreshes, and the PlaceHolderLeftActions content placeholder contains no content.

Save

13. On the Quick Access Toolbar, click **Save**. When the **Site Definition Page Warning** dialog box appears, click **Yes**.

14. If a Microsoft SharePoint Designer dialog box appears, asking if you want to reload the page because the content in the EmbeddedFormField may be changed by the server to remove unsafe content, click **No**.

15. In the breadcrumb, click **Test-Page.aspx** to display the page's settings page. On the **Page** tab, click **Check In** in the **Manage** group. Click **OK** to close the **Check In** dialog box that appears.

In the Site Pages mini-gallery, a blue information circle appears to the left of Test-Page.aspx.

16. Press **F12** to open the page in a browser.

Test-Page.aspx opens in the browser with a message that the page has been customized from its template. The Recently Modified region in the Quick Launch bar is not displayed, nor does the list of footer pages appear at the bottom of the page.

17. In the Quick Launch bar, click **Site Pages**.

The All Pages view of the Site Pages library is displayed. The Recently Modified region and the list of footer pages appear on the page.

✖ **CLEAN UP** Check in v4-test.master. Close your browser and all pages open in the document windows. If you are continuing to the next exercise, be sure to leave SharePoint Designer open.

Creating a Web Page from a Master Page

You can use several different methods to create an ASP.NET page within SharePoint Designer. However, because the page will be part of a SharePoint site, you will most likely want to keep the same navigation elements and the look and feel of other pages. You achieve this by linking the content page with a master page. Earlier in this chapter, you created an ASP.NET page by copying an existing page (Home.aspx). This page was associated with a master page.

When you create your own master page and want to test the master page in the browser, you must attach it to a content page and display the content page in the browser. However, you do not want to associate all content pages within your site to your new master page until you have completed your modifications. Creating a new content page is a quick way of creating a content page and associating it with a master page in one step. When you complete your new master page, you can then assign it as the site's master page, and all pages associated with the site's master page will inherit the same structure and look and feel.

In an exercise in Chapter 4, you attached a master page to an ASP.NET page. You then added your own customizations, such as Web Part zones and Web Parts. When you attached a master page, this customization was stored in a content region, PlaceHolderMain. When you create a content page from a master page, you can't make any changes to the content regions. To make changes to the content, you must make the content regions editable.

In this exercise, you create a content page from a master page and then make the PlaceHolderMain content region editable.

 SET UP Using SharePoint Designer, open the team site you used in the previous exercise if it is not already open.

1. In the **Navigation** pane, click **Master Pages**.

   The Master Page gallery is displayed.

Pages from Master

2. On the **Master Pages** tab, click **Page from Master**.

   The Select A Master Page dialog box opens.

3. Select **Specific Master Page**, and then click **Browse**.

   A second Select A Master Page dialog box opens and displays the contents of the _catalogs/masterpage library.

4. Click **v4.master**, click **Open**, and then click **OK**.

   The two dialog boxes close, and the New Web Part Page dialog box opens.

5. In the **Enter a name for this new Web Part Page** box, type **MyContent**, and then click **OK**.

The New Web Part Page dialog box closes, and a dialog box opens warning that the page does not contain any regions that are editable in safe mode.

6. Click **Yes** to confirm opening the page in advanced edit mode.

The MyContent.aspx page opens in workspace as a new tab.

 CLEAN UP Leave SharePoint Designer and the MyContents.aspx page open if you are continuing to the next exercise.

Upgrading Your Master Pages

If you have a Windows SharePoint Services 3.0 or a SharePoint Server 2007 installation and you created your own master pages, you have a couple of options to move those master pages to SharePoint 2010. You can use your master pages unchanged on a SharePoint 2010 installation, and they will have the same functionality as they had before. However, if you want to upgrade your master pages to incorporate SharePoint 2010 functionality, you can do the following:

- Create a SharePoint 2010 master page and amend it to incorporate any elements from the master page you created with the previous version of SharePoint.

- Modify your existing master page by adding SharePoint 2010 elements.

Change is for the better, and there are some substantial changes from the default master pages provided with Windows SharePoint Services 3.0 and Office SharePoint Server. For example, the use of tables has diminished substantially, the HTML <DOCTYPE> tag is now included, and navigation uses unordered lists.

Another key change that you should be aware of when upgrading your master pages is that the following controls have to be completely removed. The functionality they provide has been replaced by the functionally provided by the ribbon.

● Publishing Console <PublishingConsole:Console>

● Site Actions Menu <PublishingSiteAction:SiteActionMenu>

● Sign-in and Log-in Control; if you use a custom sign-in control, you can move it outside the ribbon.

As in the previous version of SharePoint, when you create your own master pages, all content placeholder controls must be included for your master pages to function correctly. Customized master pages created for publishing sites, especially Internet sites, usually have a small number of content placeholders, but the majority of those placeholders are unique to an organization, and the content placeholder used on those sites should be carefully assessed by developers.

Briefly, when you upgrade a master page that you used on a Windows SharePoint Services installation or a master page that was created for team sites, you must add the two new content placeholders: PlaceHolderQuickLaunchTop and PlaceHolderQuickLaunchBottom. The remaining placeholders that you included on your Windows SharePoint Services master page should be included on your new SharePoint Foundation master page, as shown in the following list.

PlaceHolderQuickLauchTop (new)	PlaceHolderCalendarNavigator
PlaceHolderQuickLaunchBottom (new)	PlaceHolderLeftNavBarTop
PlaceHolderPageTitle	PlaceHolderLeftNavBar
PlaceHolderAdditionalPageHead	PlaceHolderLeftActions
PlaceHolderBodyAreaClass	PlaceHolderMain
SPNavigation	PlaceHolderFormDigest
PlaceHolderSiteName	PlaceHolderUtilityContent
PlaceHolderTitleInTitleArea	PlaceHolderTitleAreaClass
PlaceHolderPageDescription	PlaceHolderPageImage
PlaceHolderSearchArea	PlaceHolderTitleLeftBorder
PlaceHolderGlobalNavigation	PlaceHolderMiniConsole
PlaceHolderTitleBreadcrumb	PlaceHolderTitleRightMargin
PlaceHolderGlobalNavigationSiteMap	PlaceHolderTitleAreaSeparator
PlaceHolderTopNavBar	PlaceHolderNavSpacer
PlaceHolderHorizontalNav	PlaceHolderLeftNavBarBorder
PlaceHolderLeftNavBarDataSource	PlaceHolderBodyRightMargin

Two of these placeholders need to be in the <head> tag—that is, between <head> and </head>. The PlaceHolderBodyAreaClass should already be present in the header. The PlaceHolderTitleAreaClass needs to be moved to the header.

Note Now when the PlaceHolderTitleAreaClass tag is used on a page, the page will render an error if a Content tag is used within a Web Part zone.

Another key element to be aware of is the addition of the ribbon, which is the main toolbar you use to interact with SharePoint Foundation. The ribbon also offers new functionality in the SharePoint Foundation user interface. The ribbon in SharePoint 2010 can be extended to include your own custom commands. SharePoint Designer can be used to add new custom actions on pages related to lists and libraries. (See Chapter 3, "Working with Lists and Libraries," for more information.) To add custom commands to the ribbon on other pages or generically on every page on a number of sites, use the information on customizing the server ribbon at *msdn.microsoft.com/en-us/library/ee539395(v=office.14).aspx*.

Tip As you customize a master page, you should identify page elements that are not relevant when a modal dialog box is displayed. For example, a modal dialog box might appear above a list view page to display the properties of a list item, and in a situation such as this, you might not want the left navigation area to appear. To handle this, you can add the class s4-notdlg to the <div> container for the left navigation area so that the elements in the <div> container on the master page no longer load in the modal dialog box.

This sidebar only briefly describes what you should consider when you upgrade an existing master page to a SharePoint Foundation master page. Use the steps outlined in the Microsoft article at *msdn.microsoft.com/en-us/library/ ee539981(office.14).aspx*. If you find this task overwhelming, use the starter master pages from the CodePlex Web site referred to earlier in this chapter.

See Also More information on upgrading to SharePoint 2010 can be found on the Upgrade Resource Center at *msdn.microsoft.com/en-gb/sharepoint/ee514557.aspx*.

Exporting Master Pages

After you have created and tested a master page by using SharePoint Designer, you need to work with a developer if you want to use that master page throughout the SharePoint farm or if you need to move it from a development environment to a systems integration and test environment and then to a production environment. The developer can import the master page and any associated image, JavaScript, and CSS files into a Microsoft Visual Studio 2010 SharePoint project to create a solution package that can be deployed to the other environments. SharePoint Designer allows you to export a master page for such a scenario.

In this exercise, you export a master page.

 SET UP Using SharePoint Designer; open the team site you used in the previous exercise if it is not already open.

1. In the **Navigation** pane, click **Master Pages**. In the workspace, click the icon to the left of the master page you want to export, such as **v4-test.master**.

Export File

2. On the **Master Pages** tab, click **Export File** in the **Manage** group.

   The Export Select As dialog box opens.

3. Navigate to **Documents**, and then click **Save**.

   A Microsoft SharePoint Designer dialog box opens and indicates that the file was successfully exported.

> Microsoft SharePoint Designer
>
> (i) _catalogs/masterpage/v4-test.master has been successfully exported to the file: C:\Users\peter\Documents\v4-test.master
>
> OK

4. Click **OK** to close the dialog box.

   Tip You can use similar steps to export pages from the Site Pages library. To export an image, JavaScript, CSS, or other related files from other libraries, including the Site Assets library, use the browser or the All Files site object in the Navigation pane to display the contents of the library. You can then use the Export File command on the All Files tab.

CLEAN UP Leave SharePoint Designer open if you are continuing to the next exercise.

Resetting a Master Page to the Site Definition

In Chapter 1, you reset a content page to its site definition. Resetting a master page to its site definition is not any different. You lose any customizations you made to the page, including any static text, images, controls, or Web Parts you placed on the page. SharePoint Designer creates a copy of the page before it resets it to the site definition, so you can recover your customizations if needed. If you choose to reset a content page to the site definition, the any Web Parts or Data Views you added to Web Part zones on the content page remain as long as the Web Part zones are defined in the site definition file and have the same Web Part zone label as the customized content page.

In this exercise, you reset a customized master page to the site definition and see that your modifications are lost.

 SET UP Using SharePoint Designer; open the team site you used in the previous exercise if it is not already open.

1. In the **Navigation** pane, click **Master Pages**. In the workspace, right-click **v4-test. master**, and then click **Reset to Site Definition**.

   Troubleshooting If the Reset To Site Definition command is not active, be sure that v4-test.master is checked in.

2. When the **Site Definition Page Warning** dialog box opens, click **Yes**.

   In the gallery page in the workspace, the blue information circle to the left of v4-test. master disappears, and v4-test_copy(1).master appears with a blue information circle.

3. Double-click the icon to the left of **v4-test.master** to open the master page in the workspace.

4. Scroll to the bottom of the page, and notice that the Data View you added in an earlier exercise has disappeared.

5. In the **Navigation** pane, click **Site Pages**, and then double-click **Test-Page.aspx** to open it in the workspace. Click **Yes** to confirm that you want to open the page in advanced edit mode.

   A master page error message appears because the content placeholder, PlaceHolderFooter, whose contents you customized in an earlier exercise, no longer exists on the master page.

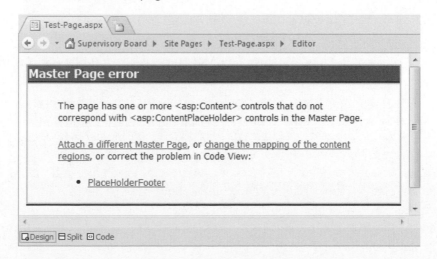

 CLEAN UP Close all the open pages and document windows. If you are not continuing to the next chapter, close SharePoint Designer.

Key Points

- Master pages maintain a consistent look and feel for all the pages on your site. They combine the layout of a master page with the content from a content page, allowing common features to be shared among many pages on a site.

- Master pages have the same basic structure as normal pages, but their file names use the extension .master instead of .aspx.

- Use master pages to control the general layout of pages, and use cascading style sheets to apply common styles to elements on each page on a site.

- SharePoint Foundation provides a global default master page called v4.master. This master page defines the base look and feel for site pages and _layouts pages, which was formerly controlled by the separate application.master.

- SharePoint 2010 includes an out-of-the-box master page called minimal.master. This page is used for Office Web Application interaction with SharePoint and for pages created on a site based on the Search Center site template.

- SharePoint 2010 includes a version of default.master that is based on the default master page used on Windows SharePoint Services 3.0 and SharePoint Server 2007 installations. This page makes for an easy upgrade because the content can be up-graded separately from the new SharePoint user interface.

- Meeting workspaces have their own special master pages.

- SharePoint Server provides the same master pages as SharePoint Foundation plus a number of custom master pages for publishing sites.

- When you save any of the built-in master pages by using SharePoint Designer, you create customized pages.

- Much of the functionality of a master page is provided by ASP.NET or SharePoint controls.

- Content placeholders, also known in SharePoint Designer as *content regions*, specify where content from content pages should be placed on the master page. They also define content on the master page that can be modified or deleted on content pages.

- Modify the v4.master page if it already meets most of your needs.

Chapter at a Glance

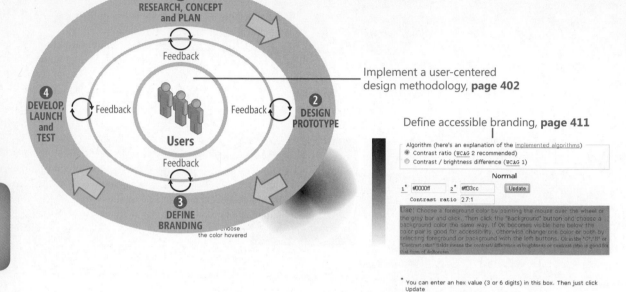

①
RESEARCH, CONCEPT
and PLAN

Feedback

④
DEVELOP,
LAUNCH
and
TEST

Feedback

Users

Feedback

②
DESIGN
PROTOTYPE

Feedback

③
DEFINE
BRANDING

Implement a user-centered
design methodology, **page 402**

Define accessible branding, **page 411**

Test for usability, **page 414**

Maintain accessibility and
other legislation compliance,
pages 418 and 423

Accessibility Report Template

Use the checkboxes for tracking; mark off problems as you review and repair your pages.

Summary

Pages Checked: 2
Found 1 problems in 1 pages

Page SitePages/Index.aspx

Found 1 Problem

Priority 1

WCAG 1.1

1. Error: Image is missing a text equivalent (either an alt="X" or longdesc="X"). Consider brief alternative text that describes the information that the image conveys. You can use the picture properties dialog to add alternative text.
☐ Line 102

12 Understanding Usability and Accessibility

In this chapter, you will learn how to

- ✔ Implement a user-centered design methodology.
- ✔ Establish user and compatibility requirements.
- ✔ Design a prototype.
- ✔ Define accessible branding.
- ✔ Test for usability.
- ✔ Understand accessibility legislation and testing.
- ✔ Maintain legislation compliance.

Most companies today consider usability and accessibility to be essential ingredients in a successful SharePoint project. Of course, a chapter of this size cannot go into great depth about either of these subject areas, but it will provide you with information about what you need to consider. Each project and SharePoint site is different, and you will need to research and decide on policies that suit your situation.

In this chapter, you first explore how to implement a user-centered design methodology and learn about the benefits of implementing usability and accessibility best practices. The rest of the chapter demonstrates how you can apply a user-centered design life cycle to your project. You will learn how to translate and apply usability and accessibility methods to the Microsoft SharePoint environment and how Microsoft SharePoint Designer 2010 can help you. You will learn how to establish user and compatibility requirements, design a prototype, define accessible branding, and test for usability. You will then learn about accessibility legislation and how to test for accessibility, and finally, you will learn how to maintain your compliance with legislation.

You should apply the methods described in this chapter throughout the lifetime of any customizations or modifications you make to your site. Usability and accessibility are very important to the success of your customizations, and conforming to accessibility legislation could save you or the company owners from being sued.

> **Practice Files** Before you can use the practice file in this chapter, you need to copy the book's practice files to your computer. The practice file you will use to complete the exercises in this chapter is in the Chapter12 practice file folder. A complete list of practice files is provided in "Using the Practice Files" at the beginning of this book.

Implementing a User-Centered Design Methodology

At the center of usability and accessibility considerations are people, the prospective users. A growing number of companies now implement a user-centered design (UCD) methodology within a SharePoint project's life cycle to ensure that the site's design and development are focused on the end users throughout.

UCD methodology ensures that a site meets all user requirements by engaging users at every stage in its life cycle. The four stages of the life cycle are:

- Researching, conceptualizing, and planning (establishing user and compatibility requirements)
- Designing a prototype
- Defining the branding (with accessibility in mind)
- Developing, launching, and testing (testing for usability and accessibility)

The figure below shows that feedback from users should be gathered at all four stages. The more often you obtain and integrate user feedback into your project life cycle, the better.

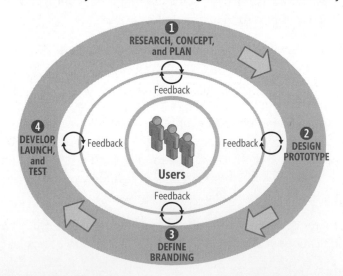

There is a strong overlap between usability and accessibility, and while many of the issues that users might encounter in using and accessing your Web site efficiently and effectively can be addressed by implementing a user-centered design methodology, legislation related to the accessibility of Web sites needs to be met and taken seriously.

In a number of court cases worldwide, companies and organizations have been sued for producing inaccessible Web sites. One of the most prominent cases involved the Web site for the 2000 Summer Olympics in Sydney, Australia. A site's conformance to relevant accessibility guidelines is commonly deemed to be a measure of the site's accessibility. The message from governments worldwide, however, is that ultimately, disability legislation is in place to protect the individual. Therefore, best practice dictates that a site should not only conform to accessibility guidelines, but also that disabled users should be included in the site's development life cycle and, at the very least, in the testing processes.

Implementing usability and accessibility best practices primarily ensures that any member of your audience—regardless of disability, age, software, and device—can efficiently and effectively use your Web site. However, provisioning usable and accessible solutions has a wealth of additional benefits as well.

If you do not have any internal policies with regard to usability and accessibility, a number of online resources are available that can help you develop them. At a minimum, you should start to document any procedures you carry out and then further develop your policies over time.

Tip Two useful resources detailing the wide range of benefits to both business and society of investing in usable and accessible technology solutions are the online report "Accessible Information and Communication Technologies, Benefits to Business and Society," from the U.K.'s OneVoice for Accessible ICT Coalition (published in 2010 and available at *www.onevoiceict.org*) and "Developing a Web Accessibility Business Case for Your Organization," from the World Wide Web Consortium (W3C), at *www.w3.org/WAI/bcase/*.

The rest of this chapter demonstrates how SharePoint Designer 2010 can help you apply a UCD methodology and usability and accessibility methods to your SharePoint project.

Establishing User and Compatibility Requirements

The first stage in the user-centered design life cycle is researching, conceptualizing, and planning. In essence, this means establishing the requirements for your Web site and all its prospective users. *User requirements* is a broad term, and it should initially include research to determine any accessibility requirements and the platforms, browsers, and devices that you want your Web site to be compatible with.

User requirements should then be established in line with business requirements so that you can conceptualize and plan your Web site and determine the scope of its usage and the functionality required. User-requirement documents generally involve the use of *personas*, usage scenarios, or use cases.

To take one example, personas can be as detailed as you like, but generally, when creating a persona, you should look to include the following information about a user:

- Name, age, and role within a company (if applicable); for example, team leader
- Level of IT competence; for example, ten years of experience with IT/Web sites
- IT requirements; for example, uses a PC with the Internet Explorer 8 browser
- Specific requirements; for example, visually impaired and uses browser zoom functionality
- Usage scenario(s) for the system; for example, a team site contributor who produces content on a weekly basis

Tip A number of useful resources about creating personas are available on the Internet. Two good articles can be found at *www.nytimes.com/2009/07/19/automobiles/19design.html?_r=2* and *www.themonitor.eu/content/?p=33*.

The step of producing a persona can be carried out on paper or in relevant modeling tools, such as Microsoft Word, Microsoft Visio, or Microsoft PowerPoint. You can create one or numerous personas. An example is shown in the following illustration.

SharePoint Designer can assist you in determining which browsers your Web site should be compatible with. It provides several tools that can give you a better understanding of browser compatibility and the potential work involved in making your site accessible to users on a wide range of browsers.

On the *Home* tab, you can click the Preview In Browser down arrow in the Preview group at any stage in your development. SharePoint Designer provides you with a number of options for browsers and screen resolutions in which you can preview your Web site. This list of browsers can be expanded by clicking *Edit Browser List*. You can then add browsers and screen resolutions of your choice. Ideally, throughout the life cycle of development, you should test the compatibility of your Web site with the browsers and screen resolutions used by your target users.

The preview functionality in SharePoint Designer is a great mechanism for checking how your Web site will look in different browsers. However, SharePoint Designer also provides a mechanism by which you can check the compatibility of your code and/or your *cascading style sheets* (CSS) with the browsers, <!DOCTYPE>, or CSS standard of your choice.

Like any browser, SharePoint Designer by default uses the HTML/XHTML and cascading style sheet (CSS) schemas defined in the <!DOCTYPE> tag on the first line of the *master page* when deciding how to render a page. When you edit or modify a page, SharePoint Designer flags code that is invalid or incompatible, depending on the schemas defined in the <!DOCTYPE> tag. If a page doesn't contain a <!DOCTYPE> declaration, it uses the default schemas configured in the Page Editor Options dialog box.

When you use the compatibility checker, you can specify the same or a different schema to produce the compatibility reports.

In this exercise, you use the SharePoint Designer Compatibility task pane to help test the compatibility of your Web site.

SET UP Using SharePoint Designer, open the team site you created and modified in earlier chapters. If you did not yet create a team site, follow the steps in Chapter 1.

Edit File

1. In the **Navigation** pane, click **Site Pages**. Verify that **Home.aspx** is selected, and then on the **Pages** tab, click **Edit File** in the **Edit** group.

The home page opens in edit mode.

Task Panes

2. Click the **View** tab, click the **Task Panes** down arrow in the **Workspace** group, and then click **Compatibility**.

The Compatibility task pane opens at the bottom of the page.

Run Compatibility Checker

3. In the **Compatibility** task pane, click the **Run Compatibility Checker** button.

The Compatibility Checker dialog box opens.

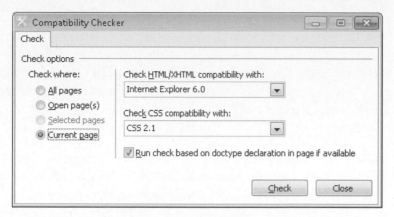

Tip The SharePoint Designer status bar displays the HTML/XHTML and cascading style sheet schemas it uses to flag code as invalid or incompatible for a page.

4. Under **Check where**, click **Open page(s)**, and then click **Check**.

The Compatibility Checker dialog box closes. The Compatibility task pane displays the results of the compatibility check.

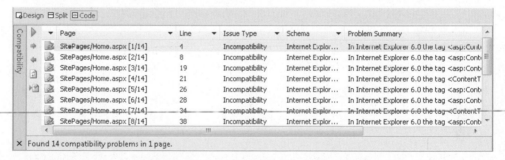

5. In the workspace, click **Code** to display the Home.aspx page in Code view.

In the SharePoint Designer status bar, an "incompatibility code" icon appears.

Tip The incompatibility code icon appears only if you have the page open in Split view or Code view. If the page also contains code errors, you will see the code error icon in the SharePoint Designer window.

✖ CLEAN UP Close the Compatibility task pane. Leave SharePoint Designer open if you are continuing with the other exercises in this chapter.

Designing a Prototype

Designing a prototype is the second stage in the user-centered design life cycle and involves defining a site's information architecture (IA). The IA defines the relationships between individual pages—the navigation—and the relationships between internal page elements—the user interface (UI). At this stage, you should also start to consider which SharePoint templates to use for your content, such as a team site or a wiki page.

When organizing and structuring your Web site, consider carefully how to group the information in a logical fashion for your users. This helps you define the navigation structure, the page structures (UI), and the metadata taxonomy you need to create so that users can tag information. This step also assists in defining guidelines about where information should be stored and how your search center should be structured.

See Also A detailed blog about organizing your information with SharePoint can be found at *sharepoint.mindsharpblogs.com/Bill/archive/2010/04/02/Organizing-Information-in-SharePoint-Server-2010.aspx*.

The step of defining the relationships between individual pages (or navigation) can be carried out on paper or by using a modeling tool such as Microsoft Visio or Microsoft PowerPoint. You can create a navigation structure similar to the following.

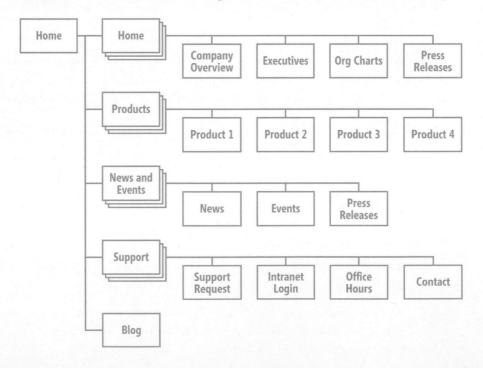

Tip Card sorting is a powerful technique for assessing how people group related concepts. Card-sorting workshops are a great way to involve end users in designing the navigation for a site. There are numerous resources on card sorting on the Internet. These sessions are also a great way to perform housekeeping on content if your development involves migrating from another application.

When you are defining the relationship between internal page elements (the UI), establish those elements that will appear sitewide and be contained on a master page—such as the banner and navigation menus—and those that will occur within content areas and be contained in the layout, such as *Web Parts*. This step helps determine whether you need to customize or build any new master pages or layouts for your Web site.

You can carry out this step on paper or in tools such as Microsoft Visio or Microsoft PowerPoint. You can create a number of screen designs, such as the wireframe example shown here.

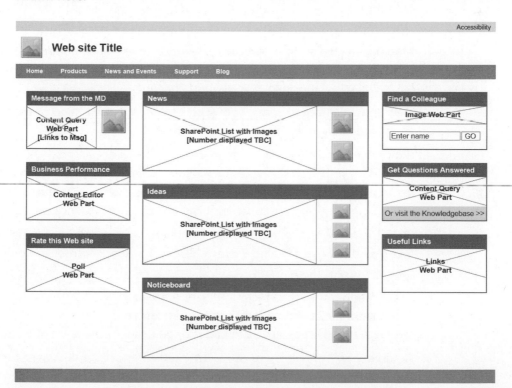

After the IA is established and designed, you can easily build a concept prototype. The concept prototype might be as simple as a low-fidelity paper-based version, or you can create a more advanced interactive version using wireframe production software or develop a version in SharePoint.

Tip Ideally, user testing should be carried out at all stages of production. You can test using early paper-based prototypes and early developed prototypes, with feedback influencing further design and development. It is much easier to rectify problems with the design early on than after the site is well along in development.

Ten-Point Usability Checklist

It is a good idea to keep a ten-point usability checklist handy when you develop early prototype designs. SharePoint inherently considers standard usability heuristics such as the following, which were defined by Jakob Nielsen. However, it is also a good idea to bear these in mind when you are customizing your development.

1. **Visibility of system status**   On every page, inform users of what is happening at any given point within a reasonable time. For example, include a breadcrumb to show where a user is on the site, or show a progress bar to indicate what action is taking place.

2. **Match between system and the real world**   Use words, phrases, and concepts that are familiar to users. For example, the terms *home* and *sitemap* have a direct relationship to real-world concepts.

3. **User control and freedom**   Allow users to change their mind or easily exit any functionality they have accessed by mistake.

4. **Consistency and standards**   Use master pages, layouts, and CSS correctly to ensure that your Web site has a consistent look and feel and a consistent placement of elements. Be sure that words and actions always mean the same thing, and that the site conforms to accessibility and other compliance standards.

5. **Error prevention**   Design carefully to prevent an error from occurring in the first place. Early user testing can establish any potential errors and point to how to prevent them.

6. **Recognition rather than recall**   Minimize the user's memory load by making as many elements, actions, and options as possible visible without cluttering the screen. Make sure that any instructions or guidelines for use are obvious.

7. **Flexibility and efficiency of use**   Cater to both novice and experienced users. Give experienced users the option to complete tasks more efficiently; for example, provide them with keyboard shortcuts.

8. **Aesthetic and minimalist design**   Keep page design clean and content uncluttered. Users tend to scan online material, and certain users (such as people with dyslexia) require paragraphs to be kept to a minimum length, with plentiful space between lines and paragraphs.

9. **Help users recognize, diagnose, and recover from errors**   Express error messages in plain language, precisely indicate the problem, and constructively propose a solution.

10. **Help and documentation**   Make sure any Help system and documentation are easily available, focus on user tasks, offer steps as a solution, and are not too lengthy. In addition to the standard SharePoint Help text and documentation, you might consider providing more contextual help on your Web site screens.

Defining Accessible Branding

The third stage in the user-centered design life cycle is defining your branding, ensuring that it is accessible. As mentioned in Chapter 10, "Branding SharePoint Sites," the extent to which you brand your SharePoint development will vary depending on the size of your project. A simple branding exercise can take as little as two days; extensive branding to comply with accessibility and company guidelines can take months and lead to alternative Web site versions branded specifically for dyslexics and/or for high contrast.

Regardless of the extent of your branding, there are some basic exercises you can carry out to ensure that your branding is accessible. Primarily you need to make certain that your branding is accessible to those with a visual impairment—be that poor vision or color blindness. Most countries have laws similar to the U.K.'s Disability Discrimination Act (DDA) 1995, that state that companies that provide services must make a reasonable adjustment for people with disabilities. Companies are used to meeting these obligations by providing correspondence in Braille, large print, or other formats. However, many forget about their Web sites. Although SharePoint Designer does not provide a mechanism that lets you check whether branding is accessible to those with a visual impairment, the Internet can assist with sites such as Vischeck (*www.vischeck.com/vischeck/*).

When you brand your Web site, you'll find that certain color schemes work better together than others. Just as you would take care to color-coordinate the rooms in your house, so you should choose colors for your Web site carefully. SharePoint Designer provides you with a color wheel similar to the one that you might have used in home decoration. Colors opposite each other on the wheel work better together than those that are next to each other. This is known as the *complementary color scheme*. Similarly, colors from points of an equilateral triangle—the *triadic color scheme*—are also a good choice.

However, the computer color wheel is different from the home decoration color wheel. Web colors viewed on monitors and flat screens are defined in hexadecimal notation combining red, green, and blue (RGB) color values. The World Wide Web Consortium (W3C) provides 16 standard color names to refer to certain hexadecimal values.

In the past, not all browsers or screen devices produced the same color when rendering these hexadecimal values or color names. Therefore, a cross-browser color palette with 216 colors was produced, known as the *Web-safe color palette*. The color wheel you see in SharePoint Designer is based on this color palette. When you click the color wheel in SharePoint Designer, look at the hexadecimal values it produces. You will see hexadecimal values of only 00, 33, 66, 99, CC, and FF. In other words, you will see values of #CCFF00, #669900, and #00FFFF—not #887722, #FD3798, and #4400FF. Technology has improved, however, and now you can choose colors that are not from the Web-safe color palette, which means that SharePoint Designer provides you with an alternative method of choosing colors from the whole hexadecimal range.

In this exercise, you identify colors on the SharePoint Designer Web-safe color palette and check the suitability of a color scheme.

SET UP Using SharePoint Designer, open the site you used previously in this chapter if it is not already open. The Home.aspx page should be shown in edit mode in Design view.

Task Panes

1. On the **View** tab, click **Task Panes**, and then click **CSS Properties**.

   The CSS Properties task pane opens.

2. In the workspace, click some text within the **PlaceHolderMain** region, and in the **CSS Properties** task pane, under **CSS Properties**, click the cell to the right of **background-color**. Then click the arrow that appears, and click **More Colors**.

   The More Colors dialog box opens, displaying a Web-safe color wheel. The color selected for the background color is bordered in white on the wheel, and the Value text box contains Automatic or the hex values of the background color's red, green, and blue color coordinates.

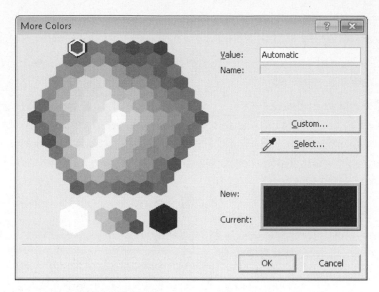

3. In the **More Colors** dialog box, click **Custom**.

The Color dialog box opens. The hue, saturation, and luminance color coordinates are displayed, together with the red, green, and blue coordinates.

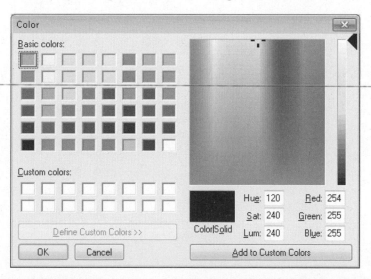

4. Click **Cancel** twice to close the **Color** and **More Colors** dialog boxes.

5. Open a browser, and in the **Address** bar, type **http://gmazzocato.altervista.org/colorwheel/wheel.php** to open the **Accessibility Color Wheel** page.

6. Under the **Normal** section, in the **1*** box, type #0000ff, and in the **2*** box, type **#ff33cc**. Click **Update**.

   The text and background colors of the Normal, Deuteranope, Protanope, and Tritanope text areas change to reflect how the color scheme looks to people who have visual impairments. The contrast ratio in each area is updated, which you can check to see whether it meets relevant accessibility guidelines.

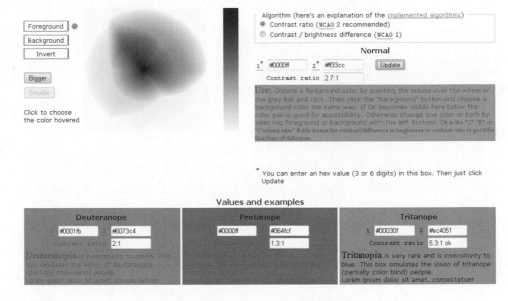

CLEAN UP Close the browser. Close the CSS Properties task pane. Leave SharePoint Designer open if you are continuing to the next exercise.

Testing for Usability

Developing, launching, and testing is the fourth and final stage in the user-centered design life cycle. At this stage you might already have a fully functioning prototype developed using SharePoint. If your prototype is a low-fidelity paper-based version or a more advanced interactive version using wireframe production software, you will need to translate your information architecture and branding into the SharePoint environment of master pages, layouts, CSS files, and imagery.

At this stage, this conversion should be relatively easy because you have already established the IA, including the navigation structure and the UI design for the elements to be used (their placement within master pages and layouts). You will, however, need to decide whether the out-of-the-box master pages, *page layouts*, and CSS files meet your requirements or whether you need to customize these elements or build your own.

See Also Information on how to customize or change a master page is described in Chapter 11, "Working with Master Pages," and information on how to brand your SharePoint site is described in Chapter 10, "Branding SharePoint Sites."

Once your Web site is developed and launched, it needs to be tested for usability and accessibility. Usability testing is a key step in ensuring that your users can successfully use your SharePoint Web site. Accessibility testing should be taken seriously given that your company could be sued for presenting an inaccessible Web site. More information and methods for addressing these processes are covered in detail in the next sections.

Depending on the size of your project, you can carry out usability testing in a number of ways:

- Study users who perform tasks based on usage scenarios or use cases developed in stage 1 of the UCD life cycle, and then document any issues the users have using the Web site.

- Use in-house/expert testers who test sample parts of the system and document any issues. Normally these parts are the most frequently used or are critical to the success of a project. Distribute your budget for user testing across as many small tests as you can afford, with no more than five users per test.

- Test a representative page from each SharePoint template.

Usability testing will highlight any usability problems with your site, such as broken links; poor navigation design; problems with rendering in different browsers, at different screen resolutions, or with devices such as smart phones; and forced scrolling (the user should never be forced to scroll right). Ideally, usability testing should be carried out during the life cycle of your development.

In this exercise, you use the SharePoint Designer Hyperlinks task pane to help test the usability of your Web site. In particular, you'll test whether the information architecture has any broken links.

SET UP Using SharePoint Designer, open the site you used in the previous exercise if it is not already open. To complete this exercise, you need the practice file Index.aspx in the Chapter12 practice file folder.

Import Files

1. In the **Navigation** pane, click **Site Pages**, and then on the **Pages** tab, click **Import Files** in the **Manage** group.

    The Import dialog box opens.

2. Click **Add File**. In the **Add File to Import List** dialog box, select the practice file **Index.aspx**, and click **Open**.

    The Add File To Import List dialog box closes, and Index.aspx is listed in the Import dialog box, with a URL of SitePages/Index.aspx.

3. Click **OK**. The Import dialog box closes.

Edit File

4. With **Index.aspx** selected, on the **Pages** tab, click **Edit File**. On the **View** tab, click **Task Panes**, and then click **Hyperlinks.**

    The Hyperlinks task pane opens at the bottom of the page. A list of any broken links appears in the task pane.

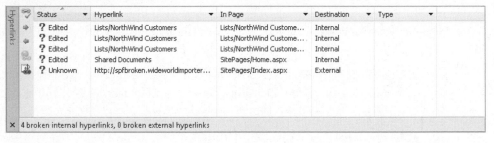

Tip At the bottom of the task pane you can see how many of these broken links are internal links and how many are external links.

5. Double-click (or right-click and click Edit Hyperlink) any of the broken links listed within the task pane, such as **http://spfbroken.wideworldimporters.com** in the page **SitePages/Index.aspx**.

    The Edit Hyperlink dialog box opens.

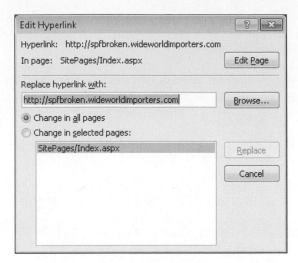

6. In the **Replace hyperlink with** box, type **http://www.microsoft.com**. If you do not have Internet access, type a valid internal URL for your organization.

Tip You can change the location of the hyperlink in all pages or just selected pages.

7. Click **Replace**. The Edit Hyperlink dialog box closes.

Verify
Hyperlinks

8. Click the red tick and link symbol in the left pane with the ScreenTip **Verifies hyperlinks in the current web**.

The Verify Hyperlinks dialog box opens.

9. With **Verify only unknown hyperlinks** selected, click **Start.**

The Verify Hyperlinks dialog box closes. A green check mark appears to the left of the hyperlink *http://www.microsoft.com.*

Tip The hyperlinks do not have to be broken for you to use the Hyperlinks task pane to replace hyperlinks. This can be a very useful method of completing a global change of one URL address with another.

 CLEAN UP Close the Hyperlinks task pane. Close Index.aspx, and leave SharePoint Designer open if you are continuing to the next exercise.

Understanding Accessibility Legislation and Testing

Most of the world's countries have accessibility legislation, which you need to meet if you publish public Web sites and/or internal Web sites, especially for government departments and educational institutions. Two examples of such legislation are the U.K.'s Disability Discrimination Act (DDA) 1995 and Section 508 of the United State's Rehabilitation Act.

In many situations, should a court case take place, the level of conformance to relevant accessibility guidelines will be taken into consideration. Two of the most prominent guideline documents are the *Web Content Accessibility Guidelines (WCAG)* from the W3C (now *version 2.0*) and the U.S. government's *Section 508, Voluntary Product Accessibility Templates* (VPATs).

Microsoft is active in producing VPATs to show how its software products meet key regulations of Section 508 and also encourages harmonization of Section 508 with WCAG 2.0. Microsoft joins the European Commission in the view that only common accessibility standards will ensure compatibility and interoperability of technologies.

Most importantly, SharePoint 2010 now has a prime focus on meeting European guidelines and makes it far easier than previous versions of SharePoint for you to meet WCAG version 2.0 A, AA, and even AAA guidelines. The improvements in SharePoint 2010 include:

● A W3C XHTML <!DOCTYPE> reference.

● Use of <div> tags for page construction rather than tables.

● Correct heading hierarchy—that is, H1, H2, H3.

● The UseSimpleRendering property for the <SharePoint:AspMenu> control, which is used in SharePoint to dynamically create the navigational elements on a page, such as the top navigation tabs. When UseSimpleRendering is set to True, the SharePoint navigation menu is rendered in the browser using a cleaner, unordered XHTML list.

See Also   Microsoft's conformance statement to WCAG 2.0 for SharePoint Server 2010 can be found at *technet.microsoft.com/en-us/library/ff852108.aspx*.

Conformance to accessibility guidelines, in turn, helps ensure that your Web site will be compatible and interoperable with any assistive technologies that your prospective audience might use. Still, when testing for accessibility, you should ideally test against accessibility guidelines and with the assistance of disabled users.

See Also   The W3C's Web Accessibility Initiative (WAI) provides a great resource for all applicable laws and policies regarding Web accessibility for 20 or so countries. See *www.w3.org/WAI/Policy/*. The W3C also provides a free online markup validation service, currently residing at *validator.w3.org*.

From stage 1 of the UCD life cycle, any accessibility requirements for users should be known. Testing against guidelines and these requirements alone is ample provided that you are confident you have covered your target audience. For example, if your Web site is on an intranet, you should have recognized any accessibility requirements for users in your company. Ideally, it is individuals like these, with specific accessibility requirements, that should be included in the user group that tests your Web site.

However, in addition to conforming to accessibility guidelines, any public Web site needs to take into consideration the wide range of potential accessibility requirements from its prospective audience. The real test of the accessibility of your Web site will always be to have as many people as possible test the site—those with different platforms, browsers, and devices, and those with varying disabilities using assistive technologies such as the following:

- Mouth sticks
- Specialist keyboards or the keyboard only
- Screen readers
- Voice recognition software

To better understand the experience of users making use of these assistive technologies, you can carry out the following steps:

- Utilize SharePoint's *more-accessible mode* by pressing the **Tab** key immediately after placing focus on the page in a browser. More-accessible mode is particularly beneficial for users of mouth sticks. Dynamic menus are converted to static menus that make the links much easier to locate with the end of the stick.
- Use your Web site with the keyboard only. This highlights for you any areas that are inaccessible, problematic, or create a keyboard trap where the user is unable to proceed.

● Download a trial version of screen-reader software and use it with your Web site. Freedom Scientific always offers a download of the widely utilized screen reader JAWS in a 40-minute demo mode, and many modern platforms have screen reader software incorporated. Turn off your monitor while using it to truly understand how a user who is blind would use your Web site.

● Download a trial version of voice recognition software, and use it with your Web site. One of the most popular is Dragon voice recognition software.

There are many ways you can assist disabled users in using your Web site with assistive technologies. Good practice is to start by creating a prominent accessibility statement on your Web site (you'll find many examples on the Internet) that explains to users the accessibility considerations you have made. Include the advantages of more-accessible mode, and describe any issues you are aware of. Always provide users with contact information in case they have any problems accessing or using your site in any way.

Ten-Point Accessibility Checklist

It is a good idea to keep a ten-point accessibility checklist handy when you are developing your Web site. The ten points below are based on W3C Web Content Accessibility Guidelines version 2 and will go a long way in making your Web site accessible to as many people as possible. Ideally, all checkpoints within W3C WCAG version 2 should be met during development.

When developing your Web site be sure of the following:

1. **Font sizes are set to ems in the CSS**   Users who need to can change the text size in a browser. Fixed pixels and points will not allow this, but many modern browsers allow users to take advantage of zoom functionality.

2. **All images have alt text**   Users who have images turned off or users of screen readers will be able to understand the image purpose and description.

3. **Font size/spacing is easy to read**   Users want to digest information quickly and easily. Keep sentences, line length, and paragraphs short and well spaced.

4. **Adequate text to background contrast**   Users with different vision levels, including color blindness, and users with different monitors with varying graphics cards will be able to read your Web site easily.

5. **Pages are well structured**   Users who turn off CSS or who use screen readers or mobile devices will have content presented in the correct sequence.

6. **A sensible tab index and access keys**   Users using only the keyboard will be able to access all functionality through a keyboard efficiently. Custom-built access keys (such as those recommended by governments worldwide) will greatly assist keyboard users with shortcuts to information on a page.

7. **An ability to bypass blocks**   Out of the box, SharePoint provides users with the ability to use Skip To Main Content, allowing keyboard or screen reader users to bypass any navigation elements.

8. **Link purpose is clearly defined**   Screen-reader users especially will find the site easier to use if the purpose of each link can be determined from the link text alone. Also, keep the number of links on the page to a minimum to further assist users working with voice recognition software.

9. **Clear titles, headings, and labels**   All users will better understand the content structure.

10. **Valid code**   All users will find the site more usable and accessible if the HTML/XHTML is valid against W3C standards.

In this exercise, you use the SharePoint Designer Accessibility task pane to help test the accessibility of your Web site.

 SET UP Using SharePoint Designer, open the site you used in the previous exercise if it is not already open. Open Index.aspx in edit mode. (You imported Index.aspx into Site Pages in the previous exercise.)

1. On the **View** tab, click **Task Panes**, and then click **Accessibility.**

    The Accessibility task pane opens at the bottom of the workspace.

Run Accessibility
Checker

2. Click the green arrow at the top of the left pane, which reads **Run Accessibility Checker**.

    The Accessibility Checker dialog box opens.

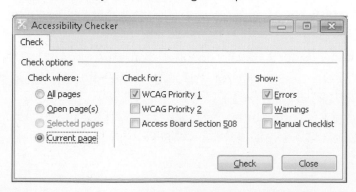

3. Under **Check where**, click All pages. Under **Check for**, ensure that WCAG Priority 1 is selected, and clear the **WCAG Priority 2** check box. Under **Show**, leave the **Errors** check box selected.

    Tip You can carry out the accessibility check for all pages, open pages, or the current page and check against WCAG Priority 1 or 2 or Access Board Section 508. You can also choose to show errors, a warning, or a manual checklist.

4. **Click Check.**

    The Accessibility task pane displays the results of the accessibility check.

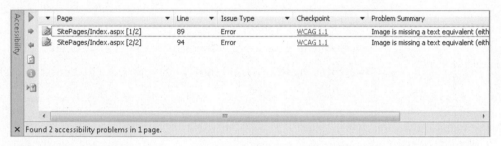

5. In the **Accessibility** task pane, right-click the first line if it is not already selected, and then click the blue circle icon in the left bar with the ScreenTip **Show Problem Details**.

    Show Problem
    Details

    The Problem Details dialog box opens, stating that the image is missing a text equivalent, with details on how to correct this error.

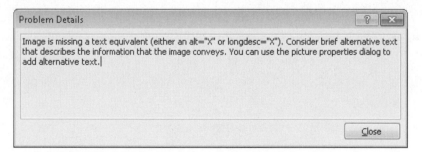

6. Click **Close**. The Problem Details dialog box closes.

7. In the **Accessibility** task pane, double-click the first line.

8. If Index.aspx is not displayed in Split view, press **CTRL**+**Page Up** to display the page in both Code view and Design view.

    In Design view, the offending image is selected.

9. Right-click the offending image, and then click **Picture Properties**.

The Picture Properties dialog box opens.

10. Under **Accessibility**, select the check box, and in the **Alternate Text** box, type **Microsoft SharePoint Foundation logo**, and then click **OK**.

The Picture Properties dialog box closes.

Refresh Changed
Results

11. In the **Accessibility** task pane, right-click the first line, and then click **Refresh Changed Results**.

Tip You can refresh the changed results by clicking the Refresh icon on the vertical pane to the left of the results.

The Accessibility task pane contains one fewer error.

Warning Any usability or accessibility checker will not find all errors. For example, in the Index.aspx page there is white text displayed on a white background. This was not highlighted in any of the reports run in this chapter.

Maintaining Legislation Compliance

Creating a usable and accessible Web site is a great start, but it will only remain so if it is well maintained. You must always remember that the accessibility improvements in SharePoint 2010 are focused on out-of-the-box SharePoint components. If you customize your environment, the changes you make create the possibility of accessibility errors. Furthermore, any content that goes into SharePoint has the ability to create accessibility errors—for example, a blog could have images missing alternative text.

You should take the following actions to maintain the accessibility of your Web site:

● Carry out periodic checks against accessibility guidelines such as WCAG version 2 or Section 508 VPATs.

● Carry out periodic disabled-user testing or use an expert who tests with a wide range of assistive technologies.

● Provide your company's content editors with guidelines and training about producing accessible Web content for blogs and wikis and especially with the Content Editor Web Part and rich text editors.

● Update your accessibility statement as the accessibility of your site improves.

In addition to complying with accessibility legislation, you may need to ensure that your Web site always conforms to other legislation and regulations. Here are some examples:

- **Copyright** Most Web sites include a copyright notice to prove, if necessary, when the material was produced. Web sites might also contain guidelines about the use and reproduction of material exposed on their pages.

- **Privacy** Different countries have their own privacy laws, such as the U.K. Data Protection Act, the European Commission Directive on Data Protection, and Canada's Personal Information Protection and Electronic Documents Act (PIPEDA). Many of these laws can be divided into two types of privacy policies: those concerning data that is readable by humans and those that pertain to machine-readable data. The W3C has produced some guidelines in this area as part of the Platform for Privacy Preferences (P3P) Project.

- **Licensing** Both SharePoint Foundation and SharePoint Server have licensing implications, which are different if you create intranet, extranet, and Internet Web sites. And even though you do not need to purchase SharePoint Foundation, you still need to verify that you have the correct licenses in place for Microsoft SQL Server, Windows Server, FAST Search Server for SharePoint 2010 (if necessary), and Office client software.

   See Also More information on SharePoint 2010 licensing can be found at *sharepoint.microsoft.com/en-us/buy/Pages/Licensing-Details.aspx*.

- **Other** You may need to consider other legislation and regulations. For example, companies based in the U.K. must include certain regulatory information on their Web sites and in their e-mail footers or they breach the Companies Act and risk a fine.

See Also Microsoft InfoPath 2010 browser forms are now compliant with Web Content Accessibility Guidelines (WCAG) 2.0 AA and Web Accessibility Initiative—Accessible Rich Internet Applications (WAI-ARIA). In addition, InfoPath 2010 browser forms are now fully XHTML 1.0 compliant. See *office.microsoft.com/en-us/infopath-help/design-an-accessible-form-template-HA010381869.aspx* for more information on designing an accessible form template.

Third-Party Accessibility and Compliance Tools

A number of organizations provide tools to assist with creating and maintaining an accessible SharePoint Web site. For example, to assist content editors in creating accessible content, HiSoftware and Telerik provide accessible rich-text editors to replace the out-of-the-box editor.

See Also A useful resource for maintenance is the Web Accessibility Toolbar (WAT) found at *www.visionaustralia.org.au/ais/toolbar/*.

HiSoftware is a Microsoft Gold partner that provides Compliance Sheriff, a product that includes a workflow integrated into SharePoint, which you can use to verify content as it goes in the system. Business decisions can be made with this workflow, such as rejecting noncompliant content or passing the content to a person in the organization who is focused on remediating content so that compliant content can be posted.

Compliance Sheriff also allows organizations to develop, implement, and monitor a proactive strategy for compliance with accessibility guidelines and for preventing, detecting, and/or managing inappropriate content, such as personally identifiable information (PII), personal health information (PHI), and secure sensitive information (SSI or OPSEC), that flows through the system.

In addition, the company provides the Accessibility Foundation Module (AFM) to assist with the creation and maintenance of an accessible Web site infrastructure (including Web Parts and custom code). The most significant advantage of AFM is the enterprise-friendly installation method that allows a SharePoint server administrator to easily apply a master configuration to multiple SharePoint applications. AFM allows you to build a SharePoint environment that meets WCAG version 2.0 guidelines and can also be used to address Section 508 VPATs.

AFM uses techniques that are part of the Accessible Rich Internet Applications (ARIA) specification to make SharePoint even easier to use for users of assistive technologies. It can be integrated with Compliance Sheriff for SharePoint to allow users to create reports before and after its application to demonstrate that content has actually improved in compliance.

By using Compliance Sheriff in combination with AFM to evaluate SharePoint Web sites with custom code or custom Web Parts, you have a way to assess and remediate your SharePoint infrastructure no matter what configurations have been applied.

Creating periodic accessibility reports is a great way to keep a record of how the accessibility of your Web site has improved. SharePoint Designer can assist with monitoring and recording the accessibility of your Web site.

In this exercise, you use the SharePoint Designer Accessibility task pane to create an accessibility report.

 SET UP Using SharePoint Designer, open the site you used in the previous exercise if it is not already open. Open Index.aspx in edit mode (You imported index.aspx into Site Pages in a previous exercise.) Open the Accessibility task pane.

Generate HTML
Report

1. In the **Accessibility** task pane, click the **Generate HTML Report** button.

   The Accessibility Report.htm file opens in the document window.

Accessibility Report Template

Use the checkboxes for tracking; mark off problems as you review and repair your pages.

Summary

Pages Checked: 2
Found 1 problems in 1 pages

Page SitePages/Index.aspx

Found 1 Problem

Priority 1

WCAG 1.1

1. Error: Image is missing a text equivalent (either an alt="X" or longdesc="X"). Consider brief alternative text that describes the information that the image conveys. You can use the picture properties dialog to add alternative text.
   ☐ Line 102

---

2. Close the **Accessibility** task pane, and then click **Design** so that the accessibility report is displayed the full length of the document window.

3. Close **Accessibility Report.htm**, and if prompted to save changes, click **No**.

4. Right-click the **index.aspx** tab, and then click **Save**.

Key Points

- Be sure that your Web site is both usable and accessible. This not only ensures that as many people as possible can use and access your Web site, but also may stop your company from being sued. It also offers a wealth of other business benefits.

- Follow a user-centered design methodology for the design and development of your Web site to best ensure that your site is usable and accessible.

- Keep handy the ten-point usability and accessibility checklists when you are designing and developing your Web site.

- Generate or enhance in-house policies with regard to usability and accessibility of any Web site you produce.

- Ensure that there is an accessibility statement on your Web site that highlights the considerations you have made and provides tips and contact information so that anyone who has problems accessing or using the site can get in touch with you.

- Make use of the tools available to assist you in making your site more usable and accessible, from those that assist you with an accessible framework to those that assist you with accessible content.

- Be sure that all your content editors have guidelines and training with regard to creating usable and accessible content.

- Maintain the usability and accessibility of your Web site by carrying out periodic usability and accessibility tests.

Chapter at a Glance

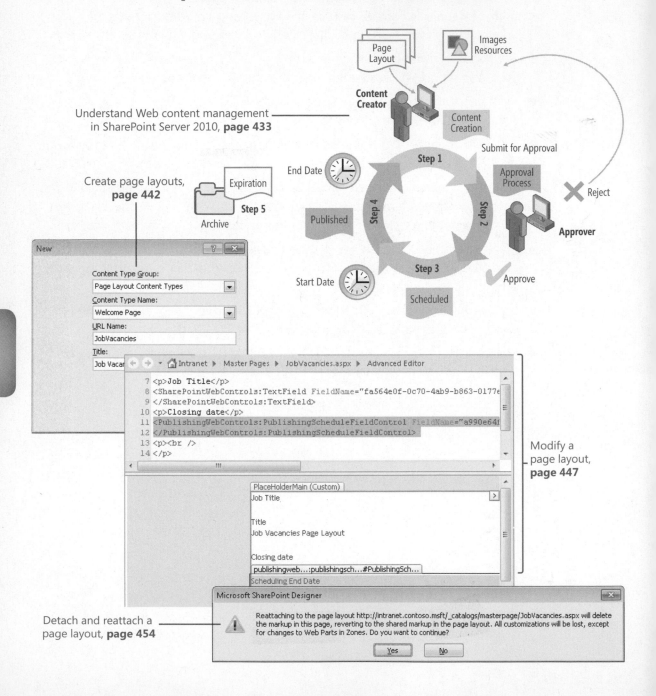

Understand Web content management
in SharePoint Server 2010, **page 433**

Create page layouts,
page 442

Modify a
page layout,
page 447

Detach and reattach a
page layout, **page 454**

13 Managing Web Content in the SharePoint Server Environment

In this chapter, you will learn how to

- ✔ Create a publishing site.
- ✔ Understand Web content management in SharePoint Server 2010.
- ✔ Understand the page model.
- ✔ Create and modify a page layout.
- ✔ Allow users to rate Web content.
- ✔ Approve a page layout.
- ✔ Restore an earlier version of a page layout.
- ✔ Detach and reattach a page layout.

Web Content Management (WCM) is just one of the features included in the SharePoint Server Enterprise Content Management (ECM) area. The WCM feature uses document-management capabilities to manage pages. This places *content pages* in a source control system so that you can check pages in and out, as well as use the Approval workflow. WCM pages are known as *publishing pages*, which are created from publishing templates, known as *page layouts*. SharePoint Server provides a number of publishing templates.

In Microsoft Office SharePoint Server 2007, WCM was used to create public-facing Web sites and to host companies' internal sites, also known as *portals*. However, WCM comes in many shapes, from a very structured Web site with strict governance rules to sites whose contributors define the structure as the content grows. In SharePoint Server

2010, a new publishing site template is available: the Enterprise Wiki site. This template is aimed at sites that do not require an approval mechanism, contain many authors, and are lightweight publishing sites that are lightly branded.

SharePoint Server's WCM feature provides mechanisms for authoring, branding, and controlled publishing. These mechanisms are linked to the SharePoint Server Publishing features, which provide a number of additional capabilities not available on team sites, such as the use of *variations* to support the creation and management of multilingual sites and additional Web Parts—for example, the Content Query Web Part (CQWP)—that you can use to aggregate data from multiple data sources. The Content Query Web Part is greatly improved in SharePoint Server 2010 when compared with the version of that Web Part in SharePoint Server 2007.

One of the key constructs of publishing sites is the ability to control the strict layout of content on a page, known as the *page layout*. Each Web content management page, also known as a *publishing page*, is based on a page layout. Each page layout is associated with a master page so that the branding and navigation are the same on Web content management pages as on ordinary content pages. However, on a publishing page, you are not modifying a live page, where your changes are immediately visible to visitors. You can restrict the content shown in different areas of the page to be only text or to not include images. These features are available because a publishing page is associated with a page control, and it is the page control that dictates the content rules and the look and feel in the content portion of the page.

Important In this chapter, you concentrate on how to use SharePoint Designer with the Web Content Management feature of SharePoint Server, in particular the page layouts. If you do not have SharePoint Server installed on your computer, you will not be able to complete the exercises in this chapter.

In this chapter, you will explore the Web content management functionality in SharePoint Server and the publishing page model. You will create a publishing site and a new page layout, which you will modify and then restore to a previous version. You will add new field controls to an existing page layout and approve a page layout. Finally, you will detach a page from its page layout and then reattach the page layout to the page.

Practice Files You do not need any practice files to complete the exercises in this chapter. For more information about practice file requirements, see "Using the Practice Files" at the beginning of this book.

Creating a Publishing Site

A *publishing site* is a site that uses the SharePoint Server Web content management functionality; that is, pages require content approval before they are generally available.

Publishing functionality is enabled on SharePoint Server sites when the SharePoint Server Publishing feature is activated. A *feature* allows you to activate or deactivate functionality at the level of a site, *site collection*, *Web application*, or SharePoint farm. The SharePoint Server Publishing feature depends on the activation of the SharePoint Server Publishing Infrastructure feature at the site-collection level. Microsoft developed both these features, which are installed when SharePoint Server is installed on each Web front end. Site owners can activate features to extend the functionality of their sites. Therefore, it is possible to turn a SharePoint site based on the team site definition into a publishing site by activating the SharePoint Server Publishing feature.

Note The SharePoint Server Publishing Infrastructure feature adds a number of objects to the top-level site of your site collections. These objects include the SharePoint groups Approvers, Designers, Hierarchy Managers, Restricted Readers, and Style Resource Readers; and several new libraries: Pages, Site Collection Documents, Style Library, and Site Collection Images. They also include the Content And Structure Reports and Reusable Content lists. In addition, the Publishing Infrastructure feature adds new Web Parts, site columns, content pages, and the NightandDay.master publishing master page; replaces the top link bar with a global navigation menu; and adds a number of new links to the site settings page.

Typically, publishing sites are created as subsites (or *child sites*) in a site collection in which the site collection was created, for example, by using the *Publishing Portal* or Enterprise Search Center site template. Typically, you use the Publishing Portal site template to create intranet or public-facing sites. These templates can only be used to create the root site of a site collection and have the SharePoint Server Publishing Infrastructure feature automatically activated. When you create a site based on the site definitions Publishing Portal, Enterprise Wiki, Publishing Site, Publishing Site With Workflow, Enterprise Search Center, FAST Search Center, or Business Intelligence Center, you can create publishing pages.

Note The following publishing sites are deprecated in SharePoint Server 2010: Report Center, Site Directory, Collaboration Portal, and Search Center With Tabs. If you want functionality provided by the Site Directory template in SharePoint Server 2007, you can use a community-created Site Directory template for SharePoint 2010 on the CodePlex Web site (*spsitedirectory2010.codeplex.com/*), with a write-up on the U.K. SharePoint team blog site at *blogs.msdn.com/b/uksharepoint/archive/2010/04/05/introducing-site-directory-for-sharepoint-2010.aspx*.

In this exercise, you create a subsite by using the Publishing site template.

Important This exercise requires SharePoint Server 2010 functionality. You will not be able to complete this exercise if you are using a SharePoint Foundation installation.

SET UP You need the URL of a SharePoint site on which you can create the new publishing site as a subsite. Open SharePoint Designer, and display Backstage view.

1. On Backstage view, with the **Sites** tab selected, under **Site Templates**, click **More Templates**.

The Site To Load Templates From dialog box opens.

2. In the **Site name** text box, type the URL of the SharePoint site on which you want to create the subsite.

3. Click **Open**.

SharePoint Designer communicates with the SharePoint site and retrieves a list of SharePoint site templates that can be used as a basis for the new SharePoint subsite. These are displayed on Backstage view. The SharePoint templates listed depend on the configuration or your site collection or whether your organization has created any new site definitions. When you connect to another SharePoint site, different SharePoint templates might be displayed.

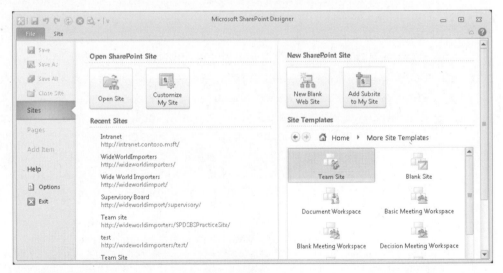

4. Click **Publishing Site** under **Site Templates**.

Tip You might need to scroll down to find the template.

The New Publishing Site dialog box appears.

5. In the **Specify the location of the New Web site** text box, delete **subsite**, and type **JobVacancies**. Click **OK**.

The Please Wait dialog box opens.

The dialog box closes, and the publishing site settings page is displayed.

✖ CLEAN UP Close SharePoint Designer.

Understanding Web Content Management in SharePoint Server 2010

As with any other Web content management program, with SharePoint Server you can create and manage Web content from its creation to live publication. The process is iterative to account for periodic modifications. Using the Web content management functionality in SharePoint Server, a content approval process could look similar to the following:

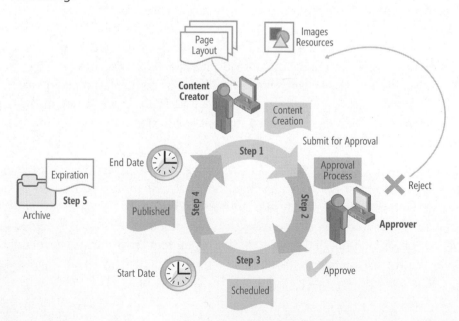

- **Step 1, Content creation** The content creator creates a page from a page layout, which is the blueprint for how a page looks without any content. Pages created from page layouts are known as *publishing pages*. On a live Internet site, each page layout might have dozens or hundreds of publishing pages associated with it. Each page layout contains a number of *field controls* that the content creator can use to enter data, and the page layout can optionally contain one or more Web Part zones. Each field control can provide a number of tools that the content creator can use to choose fonts, links, images, and other resources to make content creation as simple as possible, including a spelling checker. Each site collection contains a Site Collection Images library that the content creator can use to store images that are used through the site collection. Page layouts are stored in the Master Page gallery.

- **Step 2, Approval process** After a publishing page is formatted, including with any scheduling properties, the content creator submits it for approval. The approver can edit, reject, or approve the page.

- **Step 3, Scheduled** After approval, the publishing page is either published or scheduled for publication.

- **Step 4, Published** The publishing page is visible to all visitors to the site.

- **Step 5, Expiration** When the publishing page reaches the end of its life, the content is no longer visible on the site and can be archived.

When you use the Publishing Site template or the Enterprise Wiki template, the default content approval process contains only steps 1 and 4. The Publishing Site template does not have content approval enabled, but the template is enabled for major and minor versioning. As the content creator amends the page, draft copies of the page are stored as a minor version. Only when a content creator has completed the page to his or her liking and then clicked Publish will the page move from step 1 to step 4. The page is then converted to a major version. The page moves from step 4 to step 1 whenever a content creator decides to amend it.

On a site based on the Publishing Site With Workflow template, both content approval and the Approval workflow are enabled so that a page moves from step 1 to step 2 before moving to either step 3 or step 4. Also, by configuring the page's schedule settings, the content creator can place the page in a scheduled state (step 3), whereby the page will not be visible until the specified date. The content creator can also configure an end date with the option to automatically send the page's contact an e-mail message when the page expires.

To maintain a large Internet or intranet site, you need a number of people who have the following roles:

- **Site owners** For a large site that contains many child sites, this might be a team of people who determine the site structure and governance and also manage centrally stored resources such as images. For each child site, another person or team might decide on the list and libraries the site contains or specify the pages required. Such a team would produce wireframe diagrams that represent how each component on the page should be laid out.

- **Page layout designer** This person uses SharePoint Designer to create and maintain page layouts. You might need a developer if the requirements are complex.

- **Content creator** These users create and modify publishing pages based on page layouts. Users who are placed in the Members SharePoint group can amend items, documents, and publishing pages. On most installations, administrators will create an additional SharePoint group so that they can differentiate between users who can edit and modify publishing pages and those, for example, who can upload and approve files in other document libraries.

- **Approver** These users moderate, edit, and approve publishing pages. This special SharePoint group is created automatically and, on a site created from the Publishing Site With Workflow template, is linked to the Page Approval workflow on the Pages library. Users in this group can approve any item or document in any list or library that has content approval enabled.

- **Visitor** These users have read-only access to pages.

In this exercise, you create and explore a publishing page.

 SET UP Using the browser, open the publishing site you created in the previous exercise.

1.   Click **Site Actions**, and then click **New Page**.

The New Page dialog box opens.

2.   In the **New page name** box, type **Welcome**.

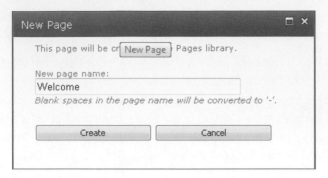

3. Click **Create**.

   The page is displayed in edit mode with the Editing Tools tabs visible on the ribbon. The status is Checked Out And Editable. Within the content portion of the page, three controls are displayed: Title, Page Content, and Rollup Image, which is used in conjunction with the Content Query Web Part.

Page Layout

4. On the **Page** tab, click **Page Layout** in the **Page Actions** group.

   Under Article Page, an orange rectangle surrounds the Body Only page layout.

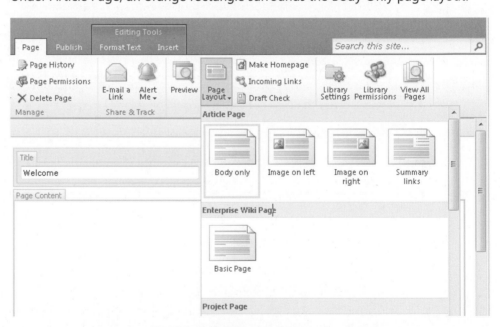

5. Scroll down, and under **Welcome Page**, click **Summary Links**.

   A dialog box is briefly displayed and indicates that the page layout is changing. The page refreshes, and within the content portion of the page, five controls are displayed—Title, Page Image, Page Content, Summary Links, and Summary Links 2—as well as three Web Part zones—Top, Left Column, and Right Column.

6. Place the insertion point in the **Page Content** field control, and type **Welcome to the Wide World Importers internal Job Vacancies site**.

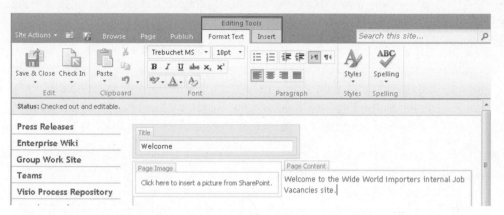

7. Scroll down the page, and in the **Summary Links** field control, click **New Link**.

The New Link—Webpage Dialog dialog box opens.

8. In the **Title** box, type **Wide World Importers Internet Site**, and in the **Link URL** box, type **http://www.wideworldimporters.com**. Click **OK**.

The New Link—Webpage Dialog dialog box closes, and Wide World Wide Internet Site appears in the Summary Links field control.

Tip The Summary Links field control offers similar features to the Summary Links Web Part and allows content creators to create a list of hyperlinks grouped as required.

9. In the **Top** Web Part zone, click **Add a Web Part** to open the Web Parts panel.

10. Under **Categories**, verify that **Lists and Libraries** is selected, and then under **Web Parts**, click **Pages**. Click **Add**.

The Web Parts panel disappears, and the ribbon is displayed. The Pages XLV Web part appears in the Top Web Part zone.

11. On the **Editing Tools**, **Format Text** tab, click **Save & Close**.

The page is taken out of editing mode but is still checked out to you. The field controls and Web Part zones that do not contain information are not displayed.

✖ CLEAN UP Leave the browser open if you are continuing to the next exercise.

Understanding the Page Model

When you create a publishing site, an ASP.NET page is created in the Pages library. On a publishing site, even the home page, Default.aspx, is stored in this library. If you look at the Address box in a browser when you have this page open, you will see that the URL ends with Pages/default.aspx.

The field controls on a page map to columns within the Pages library. When a content creator enters data in a field control—for example, in the Page Content field control on the Welcome.aspx page—the creator is actually entering data in the Page Content column in the Pages library. Using terminology from earlier in this book, by entering data into field controls, you associate metadata with the Welcome.aspx file.

When you look at the column types used within the Pages library, they do not look different from the column types you use to create columns on a team site. However, there is a difference; the Pages library is associated with the Page content type, which uses column types that are associated with field controls. Only if a column is associated with a field control can the column data be displayed on a publishing page. When you delete a column from the Pages library, you delete the data held in that column for all publishing pages; therefore, if page layouts reference that column, no pages display that data. When you remove a field control from a page layout, any pages based on that page layout do not display information from that column. However, you have not deleted any information by removing field controls. When you place the field control back on the page layout, the data is again displayed.

The benefit of this method is that you have all the power of saving information in a library, yet you can display the data as you would on a traditional site. You can create page layouts to display and edit a subset of column values. Content creators then know that by creating a page based on that page layout, the page will contain all the fields needed and that it's laid out for a particular purpose.

Say, for example, that you need to create a solution for maintaining job vacancy details in one location. You create one *content type* for job vacancies, from which you create multiple page layouts. Job vacancies that need to specify security levels use one page layout, those that have no security clearance use another page layout, and both page layouts have the job title, job description, and date posted fields. Similarly, a vehicle manufacturer can store all of its publishing pages in one Pages library. It can use different layouts for cars and for trucks, but both layouts have the same field controls to display information such as the model name; a picture; and the vehicle's top speed, fuel consumption, and carbon dioxide (CO_2) emissions.

Each page layout is based on a content type, which in turn specifies the field controls (columns) the layout can use. Field controls not only have the responsibility of displaying the contents of a column, but when they are used for data entry purposes, they also have the responsibility of writing content back to the column. Because field controls represent the data that is held in columns in the Pages library, if you place the same field control twice on a page, you will show the same data twice. If a user then uses both field controls to enter data, the data is saved to the same column, and the field control that saved its data last overrides the data of the other field control. Placing multiple copies of a field control on a page layout is not similar to placing multiple copies of an XLV Web Part or the Content Editor Web Part on a page. The Web Parts in the Web Part panel are templates that you can use repeatedly, whereas field controls in the Toolbox task pane represent a specific column in the Pages library and should be placed only once on the page layout.

See Also For detail about content types, see Chapter 3, "Working with Lists and Libraries."

In Chapter 4, "Customizing and Modifying Web Pages," I detailed what happens when a user requests the home page of a team site. When you request a publishing page, such as Welcome.aspx, the following events occur:

- The master page, the Welcome.aspx page, and the site properties are retrieved. The properties include the site title, permissions, and the links that should be shown on the Quick Launch bar.

- The Welcome.aspx page properties are retrieved, including its title and the page layout it is using.

- The page layout file and its properties are retrieved, including the field controls and Web Part zones it contains.

- The Welcome.aspx properties associated with the page layout are retrieved, such as the values from the columns that map to the field controls and whether the Web Part zones contain any Web Parts.

- The Web Parts data that populates the Web Part zones is retrieved.

- The master page, the page layout, the Welcome.aspx page, the information from the field control about how the column data should be displayed, and all the data retrieved (taking into account the security settings of the user) are merged to form one HTML page that is sent to the browser to be rendered.

In this exercise, you explore page layouts and the Pages library.

 SET UP Open the Welcome.aspx page in the browser if it is not already open.

Page Layout

1. On the **Page** tab, click **Edit** in the **Edit** group, and then click **Page Layout** in the **Page Actions** group.

2. Scroll down, and under **Welcome Page**, an orange rectangle surrounds **Summary Links**. Click **Splash**.

   Tip In the Page Layout list, the page layouts are grouped by content type. In the Create Page Web page, the content type is displayed in brackets, and the names of the page layouts are to the right of the bracket.

   The Welcome page is displayed, with no Page Content field and the Pages XLV Web Part in the Bottom Right Web Part zone. Web Parts are placed in the Web Part zone that was last added to the page layout. When there are no Web Part zones on a page layout, the Web Parts are saved in the Closed Web Part gallery.

3. On the **Page** tab, click **Page Layout**, and then under **Welcome**, click **Summary Links**.

   The Welcome page is redisplayed. The Page Content field appears with the text you entered in the previous exercise.

View All Pages

4. On the **Page** tab, click **View All Pages** in the **Page Library** group.

   The All Documents view of the Pages library is displayed. Two files are listed, Default and Welcome. The Welcome page is checked out to you.

Type	Name	Modified	Modified By	Checked Out To	Contact	Page Layout
	default	8/12/2010 3:26 PM	Peter Connelly			Summary links
	Welcome ☐ NEW	8/17/2010 11:36 PM	Peter Connelly	Peter Connelly	Peter Connelly	Summary links
➕ Add new item						

5. Click **Site Actions**, and then click **Edit in SharePoint Designer**.

   The site opens in SharePoint Designer.

6. On the **Navigation** pane, click **Lists and Libraries**, and then under **Document Libraries**, click **Pages**.

   The list settings page is displayed in the workspace. In the Content Types area the Article Page, Folder, Page, and Welcome Page content types are displayed.

Edit Columns

7. In the **Content Types** area, click **Page**, and then on the **Content Type Settings** tab, click **Edit content type columns**.

   The Columns editor page is displayed with the following columns listed: Name, Title, Comments, Scheduling Start Date, Scheduling End Date, Contact, Contact E-mail Address, Contact Name, Contact Picture, Variation Group ID, Variation Relationship Link, Rollup Image, and Target Audiences.

8.   On the workspace breadcrumb, click the arrow to the right of **Content Types**, and click **Welcome Page**.

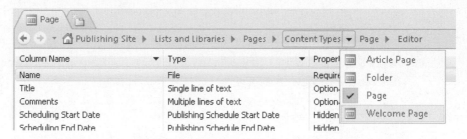

9.   On the **Content Type Settings** tab, click **Edit content type columns**.

The Columns editor page is displayed, and the same columns from the Page content type are listed in addition to the following columns: Page Image, Page Content, Summary Links, and Summary Links 2.

Edit Properties

10.   Return to the browser, where the **All Documents** view of the **Pages** library is displayed. Rest the mouse pointer over **Welcome**, and click the check box that appears. On the **Documents** tab, click **Edit Properties** in the **Manage** group.

The Pages - Welcome.aspx page is displayed. Toward the bottom of the page, the Page Image, Page Content, and Summary Links fields are displayed. The contents of Web Part zones are not displayed.

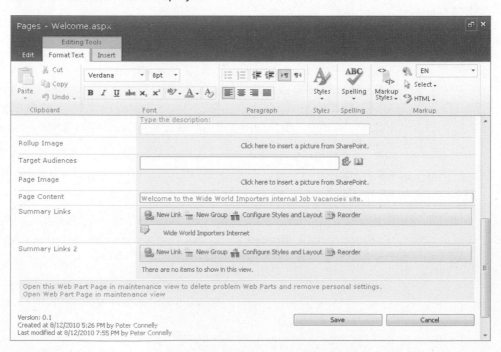

11. In the **Page Content** field, place the insertion point at the end of the sentence, after **site**, and type **On this site, you will find information on job vacancies**.

   Note You cannot edit a publishing page in SharePoint Designer or modify the properties of a publishing page. You can, however, create and modify content types and page layouts in SharePoint Designer.

12. Click **Save**, and then in the **All Documents** view of the **Pages** library, click **Welcome** to view the page.

✖ CLEAN UP Close the browser. Leave SharePoint Designer open if you are continuing to the next exercise.

Creating a Page Layout

You can create a page layout by using a browser and SharePoint Designer. To create a page layout, you need to specify a page layout content type, which in turn specifies which field controls (columns) you can place on your page layout.

SharePoint comes with a set of default content types that are installed when you create a site collection (from the Publishing Portal site template, for example). Root-level content types are used to create all the default lists, libraries, and page layouts. SharePoint Server comes with the following built-in page layout content types:

- **Page** Use this content type when you want to create your own page layout.

- **Article Page** This content type is based on the Page content type and is used to create the Article Page page layouts. SharePoint Server provides four Article Page page layouts For example, Image On The Right is used for presenting an article (as in a magazine article) on a Web site. It contains a Page Image field control and a Page Content field control to capture data, as well as a few other simple field controls.

- **Enterprise Wiki Page** This is the default content type for the Enterprise Wiki site template. It provides a basic content area as well as ratings and categories.

- **Project Page** This is a content type included with the Enterprise Wiki site. It provides some basic information to describe a project by using Project Status and Contact Name field controls.

- **Redirect Page** This content type is used to create a variations page layout to direct users to the variations home page when the variations settings are configured.

● **Welcome Page** This content type is based on the Page content type and is used to create Welcome Page page layouts. A site created from the Publishing Portal site template contains 13 Welcome Page page layouts.

All page layouts are stored in the Master Page gallery for the top-level site of a site collection. Although the Master Page gallery has all the features of a normal document library, because of its importance for the whole site collection, it is secured to limit the rights of most users. As a page layout designer, you must have at least the Design permission levels or higher to work with the files in this library. Such permission levels are automatically assigned to you if you are a member of the Designers SharePoint group. To protect the contents of the Master Page gallery further, content approval and minor and major versioning are enabled by default. For users to see pages based on your page layouts, the page layouts must be published as a major version and approved. To facilitate this process, you might consider enabling the Approval workflow for the Master Page gallery.

By using a browser, you can configure each site within a site collection to display all or some of the page layouts. Therefore, if you create page layouts that are specifically for the Human Resources department, you can limit the Human Resources site to use only the Human Resources page layouts, and any child site of the Human Resources site can be configured to inherit the preferred layouts from its parent site.

To display new data on a page layout, you must first add a site column to the content type used to create the page layout. The site column then exposes a new field control for you to use on your page layout. Microsoft has provided a number of column types specifically for publishing sites—that is, those that have the Formatting And Constraints For Publishing capability and the Summary Links data field controls.

In this exercise, you create a page layout and then create a publishing page from your page layout.

 SET UP Using SharePoint Designer, open the publishing site you created earlier in this chapter if not already open.

New Page Layout

1. In the **Navigation** pane, click **Page Layouts**, and then on the **Page Layouts** tab, click **New Page Layout** in the **New** group.

   The New dialog box opens.

2. In the **Content Type Name** list, select **Welcome Page**. Then, in the **URL Name** box, type **JobVacancies**, and in the **Title** box, type **Job Vacancies Page Layout**.

3. Click **OK** to close the **New** dialog box.

   If you were working on a subsite of a site collection, a new SharePoint Designer window opens at the site-collection level. The JobVacancies.aspx page opens as a new workspace tab at the site-collection level.

   Troubleshooting When you open a subsite of a site collection in SharePoint Designer, the Page Layouts gallery page might look empty. The Page Layout gallery page shows page layouts only when you open the top-level site in a site collection. You can use the New Page Layout command on a subsite; however, the name of your page layout must be unique at the site-collection level. Therefore, when you save your page layout, a Microsoft SharePoint Designer dialog box might open and indicate that the file might already exist, even though your view of the Page Layout gallery looks empty on your subsite.

4. On the workspace status bar, click **Split**. In Design view, scroll up and place the insertion point in **PlaceHolderMain**, if necessary.

   Code view contains two content placeholders, PlaceHolderPageTitle and PlaceHolderMain.

Zoom to
Contents

5. On the **View** tab, click **Zoom to Contents**, and then press **Enter** four times.

SharePoint

6. On the **Insert** tab, click **SharePoint** in the **Controls** group, and then click **Show Toolbox**. In the **Toolbox** task pane that opens, scroll down to view the **SharePoint Controls**.

The Page Fields section lists field types (columns) from the content type(s) inherited by the associated content type, which although not shown in the task pane, is in this case the Page content type. The Content Fields section lists field types from the associated content type, which is the Welcome Page content type.

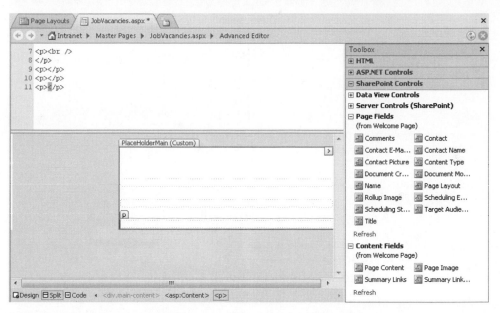

7. Place the insertion point on the first line inside the **PlaceHolderMain** control. Type **Job Title**, and then in the **Toolbox** task pane, under **Page Fields**, double-click **Title**.

In the Advanced Editor window, the publishing Title field control appears with the text Title, and the Job Vacancies page layout appears.

8. Place the insertion point below the **Title** field control. Type **Closing date:**, and then in the **Toolbox** task pane, under **Page Fields**, double-click **Scheduling End Date**.

In the Advanced Editor window, the publishing Schedule End Date field control appears.

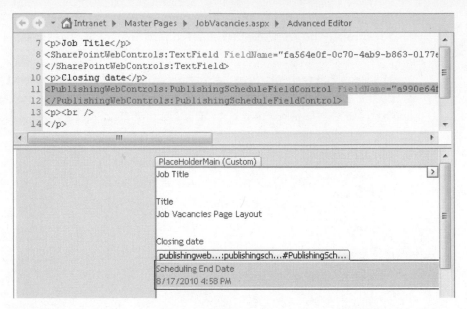

9. On the Quick Access Toolbar, click **Save**, and then click the **Page Layouts** work-space tab.

   A green check mark is displayed to the left of JobVacancies.aspx.

Check In

10. Click the icon to the left of **JobVacancies.aspx**, and then on the **Page Layouts** tab, click **Check In**. When the **Check In** dialog box opens, click **OK**.

   The file JobVacancies.aspx is checked in as a minor (draft) version and will be visible only to other page layout designers.

11. In the browser, click **Site Actions**, **All Site Content**, and then on the **All Site Content** page, under **Document Libraries**, click **Pages**.

12. On the **Documents** tab, click **New Document** to display the **Create Page** page. In the **Title** box, type **HR Manager EMEA**, and then press **TAB**.

   HR-Manager-EMEA appears in the URL Name box.

13. In the **Page Layout** section, scroll down the list, and click **(Welcome Page) Job Vacancies Page Layout**. Click **Create** to display the All Documents view of the Pages library.

14. Click **HR-Manager-EMEA**, to display the page in the browser, and then on the **Page** tab, click **Edit**.

   Two field controls are listed: Title and Scheduling End Date. The Title box does not provide you with the ability to modify the look and feel of the text, such as the font, font size, or color.

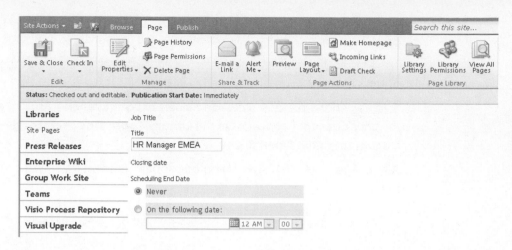

 CLEAN UP Leave the browser open if you are continuing to the next exercise. Close all SharePoint Designer windows.

Modifying a Page Layout

As with any other component you use to develop your solution, you need to modify page layouts by adding, removing, and configuring field controls, Web Part zones, and Web Parts. Field controls, like Web Parts, can have a number of properties. Field controls that are created from some of the basic column types might not have any properties. Others, like the Full HTML Content With Formatting And Constraint For Publishing column type, has nearly 50 properties, as well as its own cascading style sheet. Because a field control is an ASP.NET control, its properties can be configured by using the Tag Properties task pane. A developer can also create additional field controls.

Tip You cannot delete a page layout if you have created publishing pages based on that page layout.

In this exercise, you add and delete field controls for a page layout and configure the properties of a field control.

SET UP In the browser, open the site you used in the previous exercise if it is not already open.

1. Click **Site Actions**, and then click **Site Settings**.

2. When the site settings page is displayed, under **Galleries**, click **Master pages and page layouts**.

   The Master Page gallery page is displayed. Notice that you are at the top-level site of the site collection.

3. Scroll down the page, and click to the left of **JobVacancies.aspx** to select the check box that appears. On the **Library Tools**, **Documents** tab, click **Edit Document** in the **Open & Check Out** group.

   A Message From Webpage dialog box appears, asking if you want to check out the item.

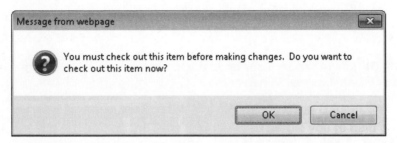

4. Click **OK** to check out the page layout, and then click **OK** in the **Open Document** dialog box that appears, warning you that some files can harm your computer.

   SharePoint Designer opens, and then a Microsoft SharePoint Designer dialog box opens, stating that the page does not contain any regions that are editable in safe mode.

5. Click **Yes** to open the page in advanced edit mode.

   The JobVacancies.aspx page opens in the workspace.

6. On the **View** tab, click **Design**, and then click **Zoom to Contents**.

Zoom to Contents

7. Within **JobVacancies.aspx**, click **Scheduling End Date**, and then press **Delete**.

   The Scheduling End Date field control is deleted.

8. In the **Toolbox** task pane, scroll down in the **SharePoint Controls** header section. Under **Content Fields**, double-click **Page Content**.

   The Page Content field control is added to the JobVacancies.aspx page.

Task Panes

9. On the **View** tab, click **Task Panes**, and then click **Tag Properties**.

   The Tag Properties task pane opens.

10. In the **Tag Properties** task pane, under **Misc**, click in the cell to the right of **AllowImages**, click the arrow that appears, and then click **False**.

11. Press **CTRL+S** to save the page layout.

12. In the browser, open the publishing page you created at the start of this chapter. On the Quick Launch bar, click **Libraries**, and then on the **All Site Content** page, under **Document Libraries**, click **Pages**.

The All Documents view of the Pages library is displayed.

13. Click **HR-Manager-EMEA**, and then on the **Page** tab, click **Edit**.

The Scheduling End Date field control is no longer on the page. The Editing Tools tabs (Format Text and Insert) are visible.

Tip If the Editing Tools tabs are not visible, place the insertion point under Page Content.

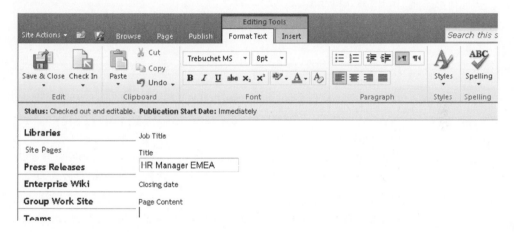

 CLEAN UP Close the browser. Close the Tag Properties task pane. Leave SharePoint Designer open if you are continuing to the next exercise.

Allowing Users to Rate Web Content

In SharePoint Server 2010, rating functionality has been introduced for all lists. This functionality can be used on publishing pages to allow users to rate the content on the page by using a 0-to-5-star rating scale. To add this functionality to publishing pages, you must enable the rating settings in the Pages library. With these settings enabled, you can add the Rating site column to the content type that the page layout for the publishing pages use.

In this exercise, you add a new site column to a page layout content type and then add the corresponding field control to a page layout.

 SET UP Open the top-level site of your site collection in SharePoint Designer.

1. In the **Navigation** pane, click **Content Types**, and then under **Page Layout Content Types**, click **Welcome Page**.

    The Welcome Page settings page is displayed.

Add Existing
Site Column

2. On the **Content Type Settings** tab, click **Edit Columns**, and then on the **Columns** tab, click **Add Existing Site Column**.

    The Site Columns Picker dialog box opens, with Enter Search Keywords highlighted.

3. Type **rat**.

    The Site Columns Picker dialog box displays two Ratings site columns: Number Of Ratings and Rating (0-5).

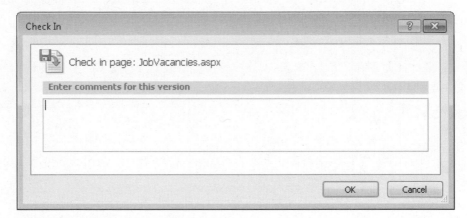

4. Click **Rating (0-5)**, and then click **OK**.

    The Site Columns Picker dialog box closes, and the Rating (0-5) site column appears at the bottom of the Welcome Page settings page.

Save

5. On the Quick Access Toolbar, click **Save**.

Edit File

6. In the **Navigation** pane, click **Page Layouts**. Click the icon to the left of **JobVacancies.aspx**, and then on the **Page Layouts** tab, click **Edit File**.

    In the Toolbox task pane, under Content Fields, Rating (0-5) is displayed.

7. In the **Advanced Editor** window, place the insertion point below the **Page Content** field control. In the **Toolbox** task pane, under **Content Fields**, double-click **Rating (0-5)**.

    The Rating field control is added to the page layout.

Save

8. On the Quick Access Toolbar, click **Save**.

9. In the browser, open the publishing page you created at the start of this chapter. On the Quick Launch bar, click **Libraries**, and then on the **All Site Content** page, under **Document Libraries**, click **Pages**.

    The All Documents view of the Pages library is displayed.

10. Click **HR-Manager-EMEA**.

    Five rating stars appear on the page.

    Troubleshooting If you hover the mouse pointer over the rating stars and they do not change color, you need to enable rating settings on the Pages library. Navigate to the Administration Web Page for the Pages library, and then under General Settings, click Rating Settings. On the Rating Settings page, select Yes to allow items in this list to be rated, and then click OK.

 CLEAN UP Close the browser and SharePoint Designer.

Approving a Page Layout

For visitors to your publishing site to view pages, the page layout and the pages must be checked in as a major version and approved. This is particularly true for the home page, Default.aspx, which in a newly created publishing site is checked in only as a draft version. If page layouts and pages are not checked in and approved, the Error: Access Denied page is displayed to visitors to your site. Also, any components you use on your page layout or page must be checked in and approved as a major version. These components include images in the Site Collection Images library or reusable content stored in the Reusable Content list at the top-level site of a site collection.

Tip When a publishing page is approved, its content is automatically checked for spelling and components that are not approved are surrounded with a red border.

You can check in a page layout as a major version by using SharePoint Designer. However, you must use the browser to approve the page layout.

In this exercise, you check in a page layout as a major version and then approve it.

 SET UP Open the top-level site of your site collection in SharePoint Designer.

1. In the **Navigation** pane, click **Page Layouts**, and then click **JobVacancies.aspx**.

    The page settings page for JobVacancies.aspx opens.

Check In

2. On the **Page** tab, click **Check In.**

    The Check In dialog box opens.

3. Click **OK**.

    The Check In dialog box closes.

4. In the **Customization** area, click **Manage all file properties in the browser**.

    The browser opens and displays the properties of the page layout. It has an approval status of Pending.

5. On the **View** tab, click **Approve/Reject**.

    The Approve page is displayed.

6. In the **Approval Status** section, select **Approved**, and then click **OK**.

    The All Master Pages view of the Master Page gallery is displayed.

✖ **CLEAN UP** Close the browser and SharePoint Designer.

Restoring an Earlier Version of a Page Layout

All page layouts are stored in the Master Page gallery at the top-level site of a site collection. This library has versioning enabled, which means you can restore a previous version of a page layout if you decide that your current modifications do not meet your business needs or you want to start modifying your page layout by using a previous version.

In this exercise, you restore an earlier version of a page layout.

 SET UP In SharePoint Designer, open the publishing site you created at the start of this chapter if it is not already open.

1. On the **Navigation** pane, click **All Files**, and then click **Pages**.

   The All Files gallery page for the Pages library is displayed in the workspace.

Open

2. Click the icon to the left of **HR-Manager-EMEA.aspx**, and on the **All Files** tab, click **Open** in the **Edit** group.

   A Microsoft SharePoint Designer dialog box opens, stating that you cannot edit the page in SharePoint Designer but that you can edit the corresponding page layout.

3. Click **Edit Page Layout**.

4. If your page layout is checked in, a **Microsoft SharePoint Designer** dialog box opens stating that the file is under source control. Click **Yes** to check it out.

   The Microsoft SharePoint Designer dialog box closes. A Microsoft SharePoint Designer dialog box opens, stating that the page does not contain any regions that are editable in safe mode.

5. Click **Yes** to open the page in advanced edit mode.

   If you are working on a subsite of a site collection, a new SharePoint Designer window opens at the site-collection level. The JobVacancies.aspx page opens in a separate workspace tab.

6. In the workspace breadcrumb, click the arrow to the right of **JobVacancies.aspx**, and click **Version History**.

   The version history for JobVacancies.aspx is displayed.

Restore
Previous
Version

7. Click the icon to the left of **0.1**. On the **Version History** tab in the **Manage** group, click **Restore Previous Version**.

   Tip The page layout must be checked out before you can restore a previous version. If your page layout is checked in, a Microsoft SharePoint Designer dialog box opens, stating that the file must be checked out before a previous version of the file can be restored. Clicking OK in the dialog box does not check the file out. You need to navigate back to the page layout settings page or to the Advanced Editor window to check it out.

   The workspace refreshes.

8. On the workspace breadcrumb, click the arrow to the right of **JobVacancies.aspx**, and then click **Editor**.

   A Microsoft SharePoint Designer dialog box opens, stating that the page does not contain any regions that are editable in safe mode.

9. Click **Yes** to open the page in advanced edit mode.

   The page layout does not contain any field controls.

   Tip If you restore version 0.1, you have not gained anything more than you would by re-creating a page layout—that is, restoring version 0.1 results in page layout with no field controls.

 CLEAN UP Close the browser and all SharePoint Designer windows.

Detaching and Reattaching a Page Layout

If you do want to edit a page associated with a page layout, you can use SharePoint Designer to detach the page from the page layout. This turns the page into an ordinary content page, similar to the Home.aspx page of a team site. The page is associated with a master page and contains a PlaceHolderMain (Custom) control. With SharePoint Designer, you can reattach the page to its original page layout. However, when you reattach the page to the original page layout, you lose any customizations you completed on the page.

Tip You cannot attach a page layout to a page that was not originally associated with the page layout.

The detach and reattach methods for page layouts are the reverse of one another, unlike detaching and attaching master pages. When you detach a page from its master page, all the controls and tags are copied from the master page to the content page. When you then attach a master page back to the content page, the original controls from the master page remain on the content page, with the effect that controls are applied twice—once from the original master page that was detached and also by attaching the master page again. You will have two Site Actions menus, two Navigation panes, two

Quick Launch bars, and other duplicates. Detaching and reattaching page layouts does not suffer from this effect, but you should think carefully about what you are trying to achieve, because an undo mechanism might not be readily available to you.

In this exercise, you detach and reattach a page layout.

SET UP In SharePoint Designer, open the publishing site you created at the start of this chapter.

1. On the **Navigation** pane, click **All Files**, and then click **Pages**.

   The All Files gallery page for the Pages library is displayed in the workspace.

Detach from
Page Layout

2. Click the icon to the left of **HR-Manager-EMEA.aspx**, and then on the **All Files** tab, click **Detach from Page Layout** in the **Actions** group.

   A Microsoft SharePoint Designer dialog box opens, warning you that detaching the page from the page layout will copy the page layout's markup to the page, and any changes to the page layout will not affect the page.

3. Click **Yes** to close the Microsoft SharePoint Designer dialog box.

   Another Microsoft SharePoint Designer dialog box opens, stating that the detachment was successful.

4. Click **OK** to close the Microsoft SharePoint Designer dialog box.

Open

5. On the **All Files** tab, click **Open** in the **Edit** group.

   A Microsoft SharePoint Designer dialog box opens, stating that the page does not contain any regions that are editable in safe mode.

6. Click **Yes** to open the page in advanced edit mode.

   The HR-Manager-EMEA.aspx page opens in the workspace in advanced edit mode.

7. On the workspace breadcrumb, click **Pages**.

8. Right-click the icon to the left of **HR-Manager-EMEA.aspx**, and then click **Reattach to Page Layout**.

   A Microsoft SharePoint Designer dialog box opens, warning you that by reattaching the page, any customizations will be lost, except for changes to Web Parts in Web Part zones.

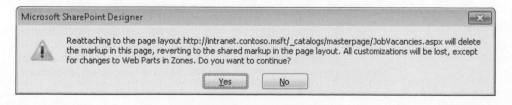

9. Click **Yes** to close the dialog box.

   The dialog box closes, and a Microsoft SharePoint Designer dialog box opens stating that the reattachment was successful.

10. Click **OK** to close the dialog box.

✖ **CLEAN UP** Close SharePoint Designer.

Key Points

● Web content management is just one of the functions included in the ECM feature of SharePoint Server.

● Both the Publishing Site and the Publishing Site With Workflow site definitions enable the SharePoint Server Publishing feature, which provides a number of features not available on team sites.

● The key concept of publishing sites is page layouts. A master page controls the look and feel of the branding and navigation, whereas the page layout controls the look and feel of the content portion of the page.

● Page layouts are stored in the Master Page gallery in the top-level site of a site collection. Content approval, minor versioning, and major versioning are enabled on this library, which means that you must publish a page layout as a major version and approve it before pages based on it can be viewed by visitors to your site.

● Page layouts are created from page layout content types and publishing pages are created from a page layout.

● Page layouts use field controls and Web Part zones to control where content can be placed on a publishing page.

● Content creators using a browser manage publishing pages, which are stored at the site level in the Pages library.

● Field controls map to columns in the Pages library and are responsible for displaying and modifying column values.

● Microsoft has provided a number of new column types specifically for publishing sites, such as those that have Formatting And Constraints For Publishing features.

Chapter at a Glance

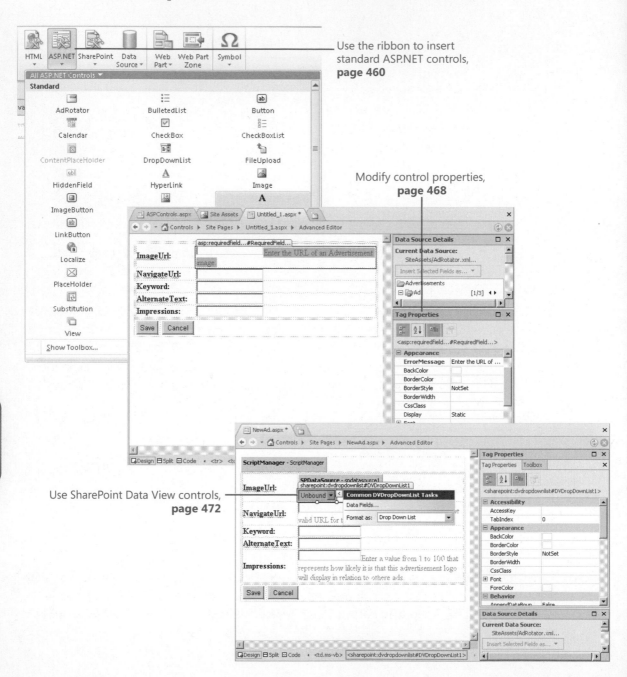

Use the ribbon to insert standard ASP.NET controls, **page 460**

Modify control properties, **page 468**

Use SharePoint Data View controls, **page 472**

14 Using Controls in Web Pages

In this chapter, you will learn how to

✔ Work with the ribbon and Tag Properties task pane.

✔ Use a standard ASP.NET server control.

✔ Validate user data entry.

✔ Use ASP.NET validation and SharePoint Data View controls.

✔ Test an ASP.NET form.

✔ Use SharePoint server controls.

Microsoft SharePoint Foundation 2010 and Microsoft SharePoint Server 2010 are installed on top of Microsoft .NET Framework 3.5. ASP.NET is part of the .NET Framework and enables you to separate user interface declarations from application logic. User interface declarations are typically HTML and include other client-side scripting mechanisms, such as JavaScript, AJAX, and Silverlight. Application logic is precompiled into *dynamic-link libraries (DLLs)* that reside on Web servers and are fast to load when a Web server needs to respond to a Web page request. These DLLs contain code for common tasks, such as displaying a calendar, and are exposed in the user interface as *controls*.

Microsoft SharePoint Designer 2010 categorizes controls into four groups: HTML, ASP.NET, SharePoint, and data source. Controls are very similar to *Web Parts;* you place them on a Web page and customize their properties to meet your needs.

See Also For more information about controls, read the article at *msdn.microsoft.com/en-us/ library/bb386416(VS.90).aspx* and visit *www.w3schools.com/aspnet/*.

In this chapter, you will first insert ASP.NET and HTML controls on a Web page. You then create Web pages that use standard ASP.NET controls, ASP.NET validation controls, a SharePoint Data View, and data source controls. You will also review SharePoint server controls.

> **Practice Files** Before you can use the practice files for this chapter, you need to copy the book's practice files to your computer. The practice files you'll use to complete the exercises in this chapter are in the Chapter14 practice file folder. A complete list of practice files is provided in "Using the Practice Files" at the beginning of this book.

Working with the Ribbon and Tag Properties Task Pane

The Controls group on the ribbon's Insert tab and the Tag Properties task pane allow easy access to a large number of controls and their properties. In SharePoint Designer 2007, you insert controls by using the Toolbox task pane. This method is still available in SharePoint Designer 2010, however, the Controls group provides a quick way to insert on a page any of the following types of controls:

- **HTML** This type is further categorized into Tags (such as <div>, <br>, and <hr>) for static display and Form controls for user input.

- **ASP.NET server controls** SharePoint Designer 2010 includes ASP.NET controls similar to those exposed by the Microsoft Visual Studio Toolbox task pane. In both products, the controls are classified into the groups Standard, Data, Validation, Navigation, and Login. The big difference is that when you use ASP.NET controls in Visual Studio, you can write and compile code into an assembly that can be deployed on each Web server, which you cannot do with SharePoint Designer.

- **SharePoint controls** These controls are ASP.NET server controls specific to SharePoint Foundation 2010 and SharePoint Server 2010 installations.

- **Data source controls** These controls include the connection information for data sources such as lists, libraries, SQL Server databases, and XML files. Almost any ASP.NET control can be bound to a data source control, thereby allowing you to create pages to access data without needing to write code.

With SharePoint Designer, you create the presentation layer of a page. On the page, you place HTML tags, XSLT, client-side scripts, and controls that can be interpreted by SharePoint or the browser. You do not specify any server-side code that needs to be compiled, such as code written in a programming language like C# (pronounced C sharp), Visual Basic (commonly abbreviated as VB), or Visual J# (pronounced J sharp). However, each page does have a language associated with it.

SharePoint and ASP.NET controls are server-side controls—that is, they execute code on the Web servers. SharePoint controls are prefixed by a set of characters that point to DLLs, also known as assemblies. The entry points within an assembly are known as *namespaces*. All similar controls are placed in the same namespace. The prefix characters are used throughout the Web page to reference the controls in the assembly so that using the full name of the namespace is not necessary. The controls contain a number of attributes (such as the *runat="server"* attribute) that identify them as server controls. They contain an *id* attribute that allows you to identify controls by name and also allows the code on the Web servers to manipulate the controls so that the correct tags and data are sent back to render a page correctly in the browser.

A control's attributes are known as *properties*. You can alter the behavior and appearance of a control by modifying its properties in the Tag Properties task pane or in Code view (in which case, SharePoint Designer provides Microsoft IntelliSense to help you).

In this exercise, you insert controls using the ribbon and set control properties in the Tag Properties task pane.

SET UP Using SharePoint Designer, open the team site you created and modified in earlier chapters. If you did not yet create a team site, follow the steps in Chapter 1.

Page

1. In the **Navigation** pane, click **Site Pages**. On the **Site Pages** tab, click **Page** in the **New** group, and then click **ASPX**.

   A file named Untitled_1.aspx is displayed in the Site Pages gallery page.

2. Select **Untitled_1**, type **ASPControls**, and then press **Enter**.

   A Windows dialog box is displayed, stating that the file is being renamed.

Edit File

3. On the **Pages** tab, click the **Edit File** down arrow in the **Edit** group, and then click **Edit File in Advanced Mode**.

4. On the **View** tab, click **Split** in the **Page Views** group.

Split

   The workspace divides horizontally and displays Code view in the upper pane and Design view in the lower pane. Code view reveals an *@Page* directive that sets the language for the page and one *<form>* element containing a *runat* attribute with a value of *server*.

ASP.NET

5. On the **Insert** tab, click **ASP.NET** in the **Controls** group, and then under **Standard**, click **Label**.

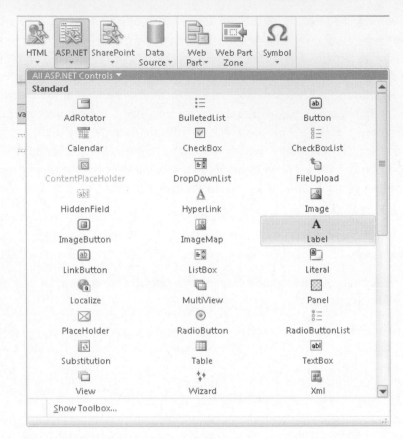

SharePoint Designer adds the Label control inside the *<form>* element. The <asp:label#Label1> tag is active on the Quick Tag Selector at the bottom of the workspace.

6. On the **View** tab, click the **Task Panes** down arrow in the **Workspace** group, and then click **Tag Properties**.

Task Panes

The Tag Properties task pane opens.

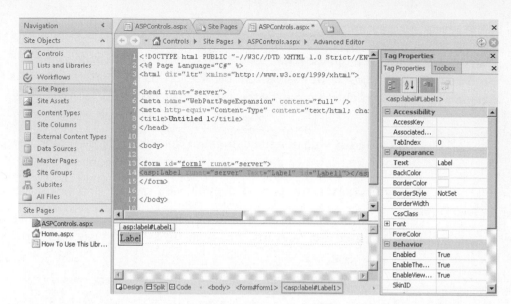

7.   In the **Misc** section of the **Tag Properties** task pane, click the cell to the right of **ID**, and type **lblWelcome**. Press **Enter**.

     In the Design portion of the workspace, the tag control is named *asp:label#lblWelcome*, where *lblWelcome* is the ID of the ASP.NET label control. This tag is active on the Quick Tag Selector. In the Code view portion of the window, the ID of the label control is set to *lblWelcome*.

8.   In the **Appearance** section of the **Tag Properties** task pane, click the cell to the right of **Text**, type **Welcome to the Wide World Importers Web site**, and then press **ENTER**.

     In Code view, the *Text* attribute is set to *Welcome to the Wild World Importers* Web site, and in Design view, the text appears within the asp:label control.

9.   In the workspace, place the insertion point to the right of the word **site**. On the **Insert** tab, click **HTML** in the **Controls** group, and then under **Tags**, click **Break** to insert a line break.

Design

10. On the **View** tab, click **Design** in the **Page Views** group, and then on the Quick Access Toolbar, click **Save**.

 CLEAN UP Leave SharePoint Designer open if you are continuing to the next exercise.

Using a Standard ASP.NET Server Control

Although you can use HTML controls on all types of Web pages, the real power comes when you use ASP.NET server controls. ASP.NET server controls appear as ASP.NET options in the Controls group on the Insert tab and in the Toolbox task pane in the following groups:

- **Standard** Contains a standard set of controls, such as buttons, check boxes, drop-down lists, image maps, and calendar and wizard controls.

- **Data** Contains two types of controls: view controls and data source controls.

  - View controls allow you to view the content from data sources in sophisticated grids and lists, very similar to XSLT List View Web Parts (XLVs) and Data Views.

  - Data source controls allow you to define a data source.

  Before you use a view control, you must insert a data source control on the page. You then bind the data source control to the view control. You can create a data source control from a data source in the Data Sources library or use one of the data source controls in the Data group.

- **Validation** Controls that allow you to validate data entered in a Web form.

- **Navigation** The Menu, SiteMapPath, and TreeView controls in this group allow you to navigate between pages in a Web site.

- **Login** Controls that support form authentication and allow you to create a membership system.

In this exercise, you add one of the standard ASP.NET controls, the AdRotator control, to a Web page. The AdRotator control displays a sequence of images chosen randomly from a set of images specified in an XML file known as the *advertisement file*.

 SET UP Use the site you modified in the previous exercise. Copy the practice files in the Chapter14 practice file folder—ADRotator.xml, LucernePublishing.png, WideWorldImporter.png, and ConsolidatedMessenger.png—to the Site Assets library. Open the Toolbox and Tag Properties task panes and the ASPControls.aspx page in the workspace.

Edit File

1. In the **Navigation** pane, click **Site Assets**. Click the icon to the left of **AdRotator. xml**, and then on the **Assets** tab, click **Edit File** in the **Edit** group.

    The AdRotator.xml file opens in the workspace, displaying the XML data needed by the AdRotator ASP.NET control.

Close

2. Click the **Close** button, and then click the **ASPControls.aspx** page tab if the page is not the active file in the workspace.

3. In the workspace, click the line of text under **Welcome to the Wide World Importers Web site**.

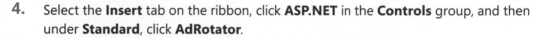

ASP.NET

4. Select the **Insert** tab on the ribbon, click **ASP.NET** in the **Controls** group, and then under **Standard**, click **AdRotator**.

    The AdRotator control is added to the page inside the <form> tags. The *On Object User Interface* (OOUI), which is represented by a small arrow, floats just outside the control, and the Common AdRotator Tasks panel appears.

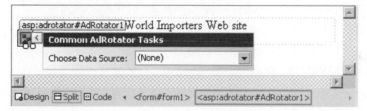

    Note ASP.NET controls must be placed inside a form. SharePoint Designer will automatically insert ASP.NET controls within <form> tags.

Ellipsis

5. In the **Tag Properties** task pane, scroll to the **Behavior** section, and click the plus sign (**+**) to expand it if necessary. Click the cell to the right of **AdvertisementFile**, and then click the ellipsis button.

6. In the **Select XML File** dialog box, within your team site, navigate to the **Site Assets** library, click **AdRotator.xml**, and then click **Open**.

    Note If the Select XML File dialog box does not automatically open showing the contents of your team site, under Microsoft SharePoint Designer, click your team site.

7. In the **Tag Properties** task pane, click the cell to the right of **AlternateTextField**, and type **Welcome Advertisements**.

8. In the **Tag Properties** task pane, click the cell to the right of **KeywordFilter**, type **Shipping**, and then press **Enter**.

    Only advertisement images associated with that keyword are displayed.

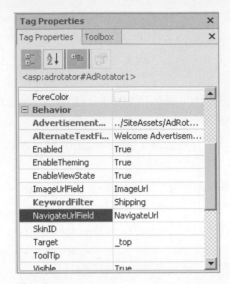

Save

9. On the Quick Access Toolbar, click **Save**, and then press the F12 key to preview **ASPControls.aspx** in your default browser.

Refresh

10. Click the **Refresh** button several times to see the advertisement image change from **Consolidated Messenger** to **Wide World Importers**.

The third image specified in AdRotator.xml is not associated with the keyword *shipping* and should not appear.

 CLEAN UP Leave SharePoint Designer open if you are continuing to the next exercise. Close any open pages and browser windows.

Validating User Data Entry

You can validate the data that users type into controls by using a validation control. The input controls can be HTML input tags or standard ASP.NET controls.

In this exercise, you create a data entry form and use the RequiredFieldValidator control to identify to the user that input is mandatory.

SET UP Use the site you modified in the previous exercise.

Page

1. On the **Navigation** pane, click **Site Pages**. On the **Pages** tab, click **Page** in the **New** group, and then click **ASPX**.

A file named Untitled_1.aspx is displayed in the Site Pages gallery page.

Edit File

2. On the **Pages** tab, click **Edit File**, and then click **Edit File in Advanced Mode**.

A Microsoft SharePoint Designer dialog box opens.

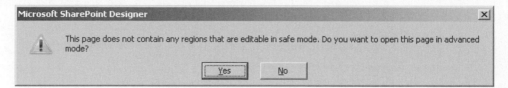

3. Click **Yes** to open the new page in advanced edit mode.

New Item Form

4. On the **Insert** tab, click the **New Item Form** down arrow in the **Data Views & Forms** group, and then under **XML Files**, click **ADRotator.xml**.

A DataFormWebPart control is added to the new page, and the Data Source Details task pane opens.

5. Click the box to the right of **ImageUrl**, and then click the arrow (OOUI) that appears.

The Common TextBox Tasks panel opens, showing that the text box is bound to the ImageUrl data field and that the Data View XSLT will format the field as a text box. Similarly, all the text boxes on this page are bound to elements within the XML file.

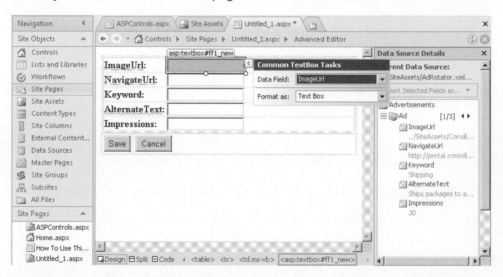

The tag name of the ImageUrl text box is <asp:textbox#ff1_new>, which means that the ID of this control must be set to ff1_new.

Warning If you change the IDs of these ASP.NET controls, the data bindings to the XML fields in the AdRotator.xml file will be lost, and your new form will not function correctly.

ASP.NET

6. On the **Insert** tab, click **ASP.NET** in the **Controls** group, and then under **Validation**, click **RequiredFieldValidator**.

The RequiredFieldValidator control appears to the right of the ImageUrl text box.

7. In the **Tag Properties** task pane, under **Appearance**, type **Enter the URL of an Advertisement image** in the cell to the right of **ErrorMessage**.

Note If the Tag Properties task pane is not open, select the View tab on the ribbon, click the Task Panes down arrow in the Workspace group, and then click Tag Properties.

8. In the **Tag Properties** task pane, under **Behavior**, click the cell to the right of **ControlToValidate**, click the arrow that appears, and then click **ff1_new**.

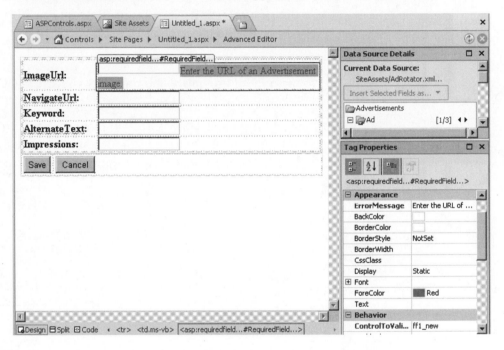

✖ **CLEAN UP** Save Untitled_1.aspx. Leave SharePoint Designer open if you are continuing to the next exercise. Close any open browser windows.

Using ASP.NET Validation Controls

ASP.NET includes six validation controls that solve the common validation scenarios encountered in many Web development projects:

- **CompareValidator** Compares the data entered in one field with the data entered in another field to see whether the data matches.

- **CustomValidator** Allows you to write your own validation code. This code could be server-side code or client-side code, such as code written in JavaScript or Microsoft Visual Basic Scripting Edition (VBScript). If server-side code is required, you need to involve a developer.

- **RangeValidator** Ensures that the value entered by a user falls within a certain range.

- **RegularExpressionValidator** Validates the data against a specific pattern.

- **RequiredFieldValidator** Checks that a user enters data in a field.

- **ValidationSummary** Displays a summary of validation errors for a page.

These server-side controls can be configured by using the EnableClientScript property to complete the validation process on either the client or the server. The controls generating JavaScript are run on a user's computer when the user browses to the page. The ASP.NET controls link to a JavaScript file, WebUIValidation.js, which is sent down to the browser when the user requests the page. By supporting client-side validation, there is no round trip to the server to validate the user's input: As the user tabs between input fields, the error message is displayed. After the page is validated, it is posted back to the server, where the validation process is repeated to guard against a security breach at the network level.

Tip SharePoint includes validation controls based on these ASP.NET controls. They are not visible either on the ribbon or on the Toolbox task pane, but you can use them by editing the page in Code view. More information can be found at *karinebosch.wordpress.com/ sharepoint-controls/sharepoint-validation-controls/*.

In this exercise, you create a data entry form and use the validation controls to verify data input. You then configure the validation controls to associate them with input controls and to define error messages.

 SET UP Use the site you modified in the previous exercise. Open the page Untitled_1. aspx that you created in the previous exercise.

1. On the **View** tab, click the **Task Panes** down arrow in the **Workspace** group, and then click **Toolbox**.

    The Toolbox task pane opens.

2. In the workspace, click the text box to the right of **NavigateUrl**.

    The tag <asp:textbox#ff2_new> appears above the text box.

3. In the **Toolbox** task pane, under **Validation**, double-click **RequiredFieldValidator**, and then double-click **RegularExpressionValidator**.

The two ASP.NET validation controls appear to the right of the NavigateUrl text box.

4. To the right of the **NavigateUrl** text box, click **RequiredFieldValidator**. In the **Toolbox** task pane, click the **Tag Properties** tab to bring the **Tag Properties** task pane to the front. Under **Behavior**, click the cell to the right of **ControlToValidate**, click the arrow that appears, and then click **ff2_new**.

5. To the right of the **NavigateUrl** text box, click **RegularExpressionValidator** to show the control's properties in the **Tag Properties** task pane. In the **Tag Properties** task pane, under **Appearance**, in the cell to the right of **ErrorMessage**, type **Enter the valid URL for the Advertiser's Web site**.

6. Under **Behavior**, click the cell to the right of **ControlToValidate**, click the arrow that appears, and then click **ff2_new**.

Ellipsis

7. Under **Behavior**, click the cell to the right of **ValidationExpression**, and then click the ellipsis button that appears. In the **Regular Expression Editor** dialog box, under **Standard expressions**, click **Internet URL**.

A regular expression appears in the Validation Expression text box.

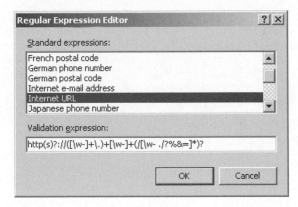

Tip If the standard expressions do not meet your needs, you can enter a custom regular expression, such as for U.S. phone numbers, as described at *msdn.microsoft.com/en-us/library/ms998267.aspx* and *blog.shkedy.com/2007/01/improving-on-aspnet-regular-expression.html*.

8. Click **OK** to close the **Regular Expression Editor** dialog box.

9. In the workspace, click the text box to the right of **Impressions**.

The tag <asp:textbox#ff5_new> appears above the text box.

10. In the **Toolbox** task pane, double-click **RangeValidator**.

    The ASP.NET validation control appears to the right of the Impressions text box.

11. Click **RangeValidator** to show the control's properties in the **Tag Properties** task pane. In the **Tag Properties** task pane, under **Appearance**, in the cell to the right of **ErrorMessage**, type **Enter a value from 1 to 100 that represents how likely it is that this advertisement logo will display in relation to other ads**.

12. Under **Behavior**, in the **ControlToValidate** list, click **ff5_new**. Enter **100** in the **MaximumValue** cell, enter **1** in the **MinimumValue** cell, and then select **Integer** from the **Type** list.

Save

13. On the Quick Access Toolbar, click **Save**. In the **Navigation** pane, under **Site Pages**, right-click **Untitled_1.aspx**, click **Rename**, type **NewAd.aspx**, and then press **Enter**.

14. Press **F12** to preview **NewAd.aspx** in the browser.

15. In the **NavigateUrl** text box, type **www.nosite**, and then click **TAB**.

    The insertion point moves to the Keyword text box, and the message *Enter the valid URL for the Advertiser's Web site* appears.

16. In the **Impressions** text box, type **none**, and then click **Save**.

    Two other error messages appear.

Tip The space to the left of the *Enter the valid URL* error message is for the error message associated with the NavigateUrl RequiredFieldValidator control. You can hide the space by setting the Display property of the RequiredFieldValidator control to Dynamic.

✖ **CLEAN UP** Leave SharePoint Designer open if you are continuing to the next exercise. Close any open pages and browser windows.

Using SharePoint Data View Controls

The Toolbox task pane categorizes SharePoint controls in four groups: Data View, Server Controls, Page Fields, and Content Fields. The first two control groups can also be chosen from the SharePoint button in the Controls group on the Insert tab and require only SharePoint Foundation or SharePoint Server. The other two control groups list controls only if you have a SharePoint Server publishing page layout page open. In this chapter, you will use the Data View controls and server controls.

See Also   For information about Page Field and Content Field controls, see Chapter 13, "Managing Web Content in the SharePoint Server Environment." SharePoint controls and their properties are described in the SharePoint Foundation and SharePoint Server Software Development Kits.

By using SharePoint Data View controls, you can expose data from one of the data sources you have defined. One of the best methods of data entry validation is to allow users to choose from a set of options. In lists and libraries, when one list contains data that you want to use in another list, you can use a lookup column. For data that is not stored in lists or libraries, the Data View controls enable you to bind to one data source and expose the data using check boxes, radio buttons, or drop-down lists from which the user can choose. The selected input is then used in a different data source.

In this exercise, you insert a Data View control so that a user can choose data from one data source as input to another data source.

SET UP   Use the site you modified in the previous exercise. Open the NewAd.aspx page in the workspace.

1. In the workspace, click the text box to the right of **ImageUrl**, and then press **Delete**. Click **Enter the URL of an Advertisement image**, and then press **Delete**.

   The td.ms-vb HTML cell should now be empty.

Data Source

2. On the **Insert** tab, click **Data Source** in the **Controls** group, and then click **Site Assets**.

   A SPDataSource control appears to the right of ImageUrl.

   Tip   If the SPDataSource control is not visible on the page, click the View tab on the ribbon, click Visual Aids, and then click ASP.NET Non-Visual Controls.

3. Click the **SPDataSource** control to show the control's properties in the **Tag Properties** task pane.

Note   If the Tag Properties task pane is not open, click the View tab on the ribbon, click the Task Panes down arrow in the Workspace group, and then click Tag Properties.

4.   In the **Tag Properties** task pane, under **Misc**, click the cell to the right of **ID**, type **SPSiteAssets**, and then press **ENTER**.

The tag above the SPDataSource control changes to <SharePoint:SPDataSource#SP SiteAssets>.

5.   On the **Insert** tab, click **SharePoint** in the **Controls** group, and then click **Data View DropDownList**.

In the workspace, a drop-down list control appears on the page, displaying the OOUI, the Common DVDropDownList Tasks panel, and the tag name <sharepoint:d vdropdownlist#DVDropDownList1> above it. The text *Unbound* appears within the control.

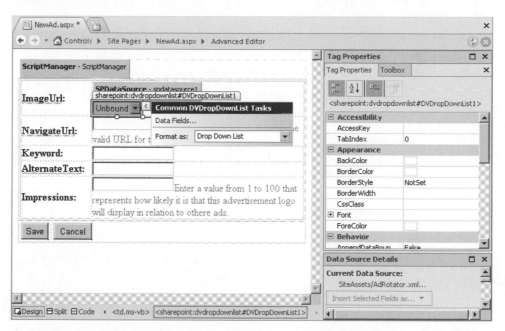

6.   In the **Common DVDropDownList Tasks** panel, click **Data Fields**.

The Change Data Bindings dialog box opens. In the Select A Data Source list, SPSiteAssets is already selected because the page has only one data source control.

7.   In the **Select a data field to save values to** list, click **ImageUrl**. In the **Select a data field for the display text** list, click **Title**. In the **Select a data field for the value** list, click **URL Path**.

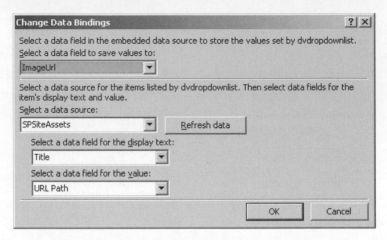

8. In the **Change Data Bindings** dialog box, click **OK**.

   The sharepoint:dvdropdownlist#DVDropDownList1 control contains the word *Databound*.

9. Right-click the **Save** button, and then click **Form Actions**.

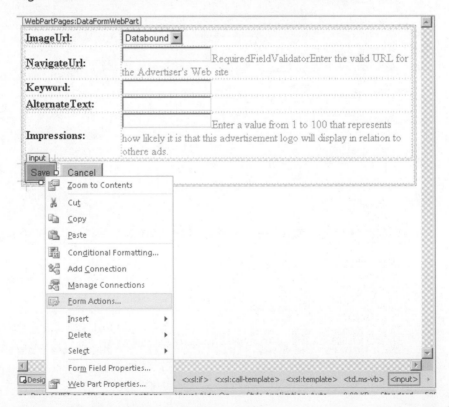

The Form Actions dialog box opens.

10. Under **Actions List**, select **Navigate to page**, and then click **Add**.

   The Navigate To Page action is moved under Current Actions (Run In Order Shown).

11. With **Navigate to page** selected, click **Settings**.

   The Form Actions Settings dialog box opens.

12. Click **Browse**, and in the **Edit Hyperlink** dialog box, click **default.aspx**. Click **OK** to close the **Edit Hyperlink** dialog box, and then click **OK** twice to close the **Form Action Settings** and **Form Actions** dialog boxes.

Save

13. On the Quick Access Toolbar, click **Save**.

 CLEAN UP Leave SharePoint Designer open if you are continuing to the next exercise.

Testing an ASP.NET Form

After you create your ASP.NET form and before you allow other users to enter data using the form, you should test that it meets your business needs.

In this exercise, you test the form you created in the previous exercises.

→ **SET UP** Open SharePoint Designer if it is not already open. Open the site you modified in the previous exercise.

Administration
Web Page

1. In the **Navigation** pane, click **Site Assets**. Click the icon to the left of **ConsolidatedMessenger.png**, and then on the **Assets** tab, click **Administration Web Page** in the **Manage** group.

   The Item view of the file is opened in the browser.

2. On the **View** tab, click **Edit Item** in the **Manage** group.

   The Edit Item form opens.

3. In the **Title** box, type **Consolidated Messenger logo**, and then click **Save**.

   The All Items view of the Site Assets library is displayed.

4. Edit the properties of the image files **LucernePublishing** and **WideWorldImports**, and set their **Title** properties to **Lucerne Publishing logo** and **Wide World Importers logo**, respectively.

5. In the Quick Launch bar, click **Site Pages** to display the All Pages view, and then click **NewAd.aspx** to open the page in the browser.

6. In the **ImageUrl** list, click **Wide World Importers logo**.

7. Press **TAB** to move to the **NavigateUrl** text box, and type **http://intranet. wideworldimporters.com**.

8. Click **TAB** three times to move to the **Impressions** text box, and type **30**.

9. Click **Save**.

   The page refreshes and displays the home page of your site.

10. In SharePoint Designer, in the **Navigation** pane, click **Site Assets**.

    The Site Assets gallery page is displayed.

11. Click the icon to the left of **AdRotator.xml**, and then click **Edit File** in the **Edit** group to display the file in the workspace.

    The last *Ad* element in the file should contain the URL for the image file WideWorldImporters.png, the Wide World Importers portal URL, and an Impressions value of 30.

```
<Ad>
    <ImageUrl>/Teams/Controls/SiteAssets/WideWorldImporters.png</ImageUrl>
    <NavigateUrl>http://intranet.wideworldimporters.com</NavigateUrl>
    <Keyword>
    </Keyword>
    <AlternateText>
    </AlternateText>
    <Impressions>30</Impressions>
</Ad>
</Advertisements>
```

 CLEAN UP Leave SharePoint Designer open if you are continuing to the next exercise. Turn ASP.NET Non-Visual Controls off, and close any open pages and browser windows.

Using SharePoint Server Controls

All controls prefixed with *SharePoint* or *WebPartPages* are part of the SharePoint framework and can be found on the Web server in the assembly Microsoft.SharePoint.dll. All SharePoint pages contain SharePoint Server controls, some of which are shown in the SharePoint option in the Controls group on the Insert tab and in the Toolbox task pane as follows:

- **CssLink** Links to CSS files. By default, this control is placed on master pages and is linked to a file stored on each Web server so that all pages associated with a master page have the same look and feel. When the control is used with no file specified, it defaults to corev4.css.

- **Theme** Adds a reference to the site's current theme CSS file, if one is configured.

- **ScriptLink** Links to JavaScript files. This control is placed on master pages and is linked to a file (core.js) stored on the Web server so that all pages associated with a master page have access to the same set of JavaScript functions.

- **AspMenu** An ASP.NET navigation control to display sites and pages within a site collection. By default, the control is placed on master pages so that all pages associated with the master page share the same navigation.

- **RSSLink** On lists and libraries that are enabled as RSS feeds, this control exposes the URL that RSS aggregators can use to view list items.

- **SPCalendarNavigation** On list views, displays a calendar control that is used to navigate to specific list items. You can find examples of pages with this control in the All Items views of the Announcements and Calendar lists.

In this exercise, you review the SharePoint controls in the Toolbox task pane and investigate their use on pages within a site.

 SET UP Use the site you modified in the previous exercise. Open the NewAd.aspx page in the workspace.

1. On the **View** tab, click **Task Panes** in the Workspace group, and then click **Toolbox**.

   The Toolbox task pane opens.

2. Scroll down to **SharePoint Controls**, expand it if necessary, and under **Server Controls (SharePoint)**, point to **CSSLink**.

   The ScreenTip that appears references the SharePoint namespace, Microsoft.SharePoint.WebControl.CssLink, in which the code-behind logic for this control can be found.

Note The controls visible on the Toolbox task pane will be different if your site was created on a Microsoft SharePoint Foundation installation.

3. In the **Toolbox** task pane, expand the **Page Fields** and **Content Fields** control groups.

   No controls are displayed in these two groups.

Split

4. On the workspace status bar, click **Split**, and then in the **Navigation** pane, click **Master Pages**.

   The Master Page gallery opens.

Edit File

5. Click the icon to the left of **v4.master**, and on the **Master Pages** tab, click **Edit File** in the **Edit** group.

   The page opens in the workspace. In the <head> tag are a number of SharePoint controls, such as CssLink, Theme, ScriptLink, and CustomJSUrl.

6. Click the **NewAd.aspx** page tab to display the page, and in the Code view portion of the workspace, scroll to the top of the page.

   Immediately after the opening <form> tag is a WebPartPages:DataFormWebPart control.

Attach

7. On the **Style** tab, click **Attach** in the **Master Page** group, and under **Default Master Page**, click **v4.master**.

   The Match Content Regions dialog box opens.

8. Click **OK** to close the **Match Content Regions** dialog box.

   The NewAd.aspx page is redisplayed in the Design view portion of the workspace and has the same look and feel and navigation as other pages on the site. In the Code view portion of the workspace, there are no <head>, <body>, or <form> tags because these are now provided by the master page.

9. In the Code view portion of **NewAd.aspx**, scroll to the top of the page so that you see the **@Page** directive, and then scroll to the right until you see the **masterpage-file** attribute on the first line of the page.

✖ **CLEAN UP** Close any open browser windows and exit SharePoint Designer.

Key Points

- With ASP.NET, you can separate user interface declarations from application logic.
- Application logic is precompiled into DLLs that reside on the Web servers.
- There are four groups of controls: HTML controls, ASP.NET controls, SharePoint controls, and data source controls.
- Controls are similar to Web Parts. You place them on a Web page and customize their properties to meet your needs.
- ASP.NET Data controls allow you to define data sources and view the contents of data sources. View controls must be bound to a data source.
- ASP.NET validation controls use JavaScript by default to validate data entry on the client, thereby reducing network traffic when an input form is processed. They can be configured so that only server-side logic is used to validate data entry.
- SharePoint Data View controls expose data as check boxes, radio buttons, or drop-down lists from which the user can choose. Data View controls are inserted into a Data View Web Part and must be bound to a data source.
- All built-in SharePoint pages contain SharePoint Server controls.

A SharePoint Designer Workflow Conditions and Actions

SharePoint Designer 2010 includes workflow conditions and workflow actions. Actions occur as part of a workflow step and are associated with a condition. The actions and conditions listed in this appendix are those you see if you are working on sites in a SharePoint Server 2010 installation. For sites created with SharePoint Foundation 2010, you see only a subset of these actions.

Conditions

A condition is a filter that can be used to determine which actions run. The following table provides an overview of the default conditions you can use in SharePoint Designer. Although actions are divided into a number of groups, there are only two relatively small groups of conditions. Table A-1 provides an overview of the default conditions you can use in SharePoint Designer.

Table A-1 Conditions

Condition Group	Description
Common Conditions	
If Any Value Equals Value*	Creates a filter that lets you compare two values from any data source. This condition replaces the Compare Any Data Source condition available in SharePoint 2007.
If Current Item Field Equals Value*	Creates a filter that lets you compare the current item's field value with a value from any data source. This condition replaces the Compare [List or Library] Field condition available in SharePoint 2007.

Other Conditions

Created By a Specific Person	Creates a filter that lets you specify the user who created the list item.
Created in a Specific Date Span	Creates a filter that lets you specify the start and end dates between which the list item must be created. These dates can also be lookup values that are retrieved from a data source such as another list on the same SharePoint site or from a previously created workflow variable.
If Task Outcome Equals Value**	Allows you to undertake actions based on the number or percentage of task approvals and rejections. The value in this condition can also be a lookup value that is retrieved from a data source such as another list on the same SharePoint site or from a previously created workflow variable.
Modified by a Specific Person	Creates a filter that lets you specify the user who last modified the list item.
Modified in a Specific Date Span	Creates a filter that lets you specify the start and end dates between which the list item must be modified. These dates can also be lookup values that are retrieved from a data source such as another list on the same SharePoint site or from a previously created workflow variable.
Person Is a Valid SharePoint User*	Creates a filter that lets you check whether or not the user is anonymous.
The File Size in a Specific Range Kilobytes	Creates a filter that lets you specify the minimum and maximum file size of a list item. These file sizes can also be lookup values that are retrieved from a data source such as another list on the same SharePoint site or from a previously created workflow variable. This condition is available only for libraries.
The File Type Is a Specific Type	Creates a filter that lets you specify the file type of the list item. This value can also be a lookup value that is retrieved from a data source such as another list on the same SharePoint site or from a previously created workflow variable. This condition is available only for libraries.
Title Field Contains Keywords	Creates a filter that lets you specify a value for the Title column of the list or library the workflow is attached to.

* New in SharePoint 2010.

** New in SharePoint 2010 and available only within Approval workflow tasks by specifying the behavior of a single task. See Appendix B, "Creating a New Approval Process," for more information.

Core Actions

The core actions are 11 common activities that you use in many of your workflows. They allow you to manipulate dates and times, to build a form to collect information from users, and to write information to the history list. The default core actions are listed in Table A-2.

Table A-2 **Core Actions**

Action	Description
Add a Comment*	Allows you to write a string value as an informative comment. This value can also be a lookup value that is retrieved from a data source such as another list on the same SharePoint site or from a previously created workflow variable (defined by you). Comments can be viewed in Microsoft Visio Premium 2010.
	Every well-designed workflow should provide a generous number of comments and logging information. This facilitates the maintenance of custom workflows.
Add Time to Date	Allows you to add or subtract minutes, hours, days, months, or years in a date value. The date is commonly a lookup value that is retrieved from a data source such as another list on the same SharePoint site or from a previously created workflow variable.
	The output of this action can be saved to a new or existing workflow variable. This allows you to reuse the outcome at a later stage of the workflow's life cycle.
Do Calculation	Allows you to add, subtract, multiply, divide, or calculate the modulus of two numeric values. These values can also be lookup values that are retrieved from a data source such as another list on the same SharePoint site or from a previously created workflow variable.
	The output of this action can be saved to a new or existing workflow variable.
Log to History List	Allows you to write a string value to the workflow history list. This value can be a lookup value that is retrieved from a data source such as another list on the same SharePoint site or from a previously created workflow variable. Use this action to write a summary of the workflow or information concerning a significant event or for troubleshooting purposes.

Pause for Duration	Allows you to specify in days, hours, and minutes the amount of time you want to pause the execution of the workflow. These time values can also be lookup values that are retrieved from a data source such as another list on the same SharePoint site or from a previously created workflow variable.
Pause Until Date	Allows you to pause the execution of the workflow and specify the date when the workflow needs to be continued. This date can also be a lookup value that is retrieved from a data source such as another list on the same SharePoint site or from a previously created workflow variable.
Send an Email	Allows you to create an e-mail message containing string values, lookup values, formulas, and workflow variables. The action also allows you to specify the To, CC, and Subject fields of the e-mail message.
Send Document to Repository**	Allows you to copy, move, or move and leave a link referring to a document in a record repository.
Set Time Portion of Date/Time Field	Allows you to set a specific time in hours and minutes and add this to a date. This date can also be a lookup value that is retrieved from a data source such as another list on the same SharePoint site or from a previously created workflow variable. The output of this action can be saved to a new or existing workflow variable.
Set Workflow Status*	Allows you to set a custom workflow status to a value other than In Progress or Complete. The addition of this action might seem like only a minor enhancement of the workflow framework, but this action is extremely valuable because your customers probably don't think in terms of In Progress and Complete, and you will find that you use this action many times when you create workflows.
Set Workflow Variable	Allows you to set the value of a new or existing workflow variable. This value can also be a lookup value that is retrieved from a data source such as another list on the same SharePoint site or from a previously created workflow variable.
Stop Workflow	Allows you to stop the workflow. Also allows you to write a string value to the workflow history list that is retrieved from a data source such as another list on the same SharePoint site or from a previously created workflow variable.

* New in SharePoint 2010.
** New in SharePoint 2010 and available only on document libraries.

Document Set Actions

The actions listed in the Document Set category are completely new. They work on sites created on SharePoint Server 2010, which introduced the concept of document sets. Document sets are groups of documents that have a specific meaning as a group and share a specific life cycle. For instance, all documents related to a certain legal matter can be grouped as a document set. You will not find these actions on a SharePoint Foundation installation. The default document set actions are listed in Table A-3.

Table A-3 Document Set Actions

Action	Description
Capture a Version of the Document Set*	Allows you to capture the last major or the latest minor version of a document set.
Send Document Set to Repository*	Allows you to copy, move, or move and leave a link referring to a document set in a repository. The output of this action can be saved to a new or existing workflow variable.
Set Content Approval Status for the Document Set*	Allows you to set the current status of the document set. You can also add comments to the document set in the form of a string value or a lookup value that is retrieved from a data source such as another list on the same SharePoint site or from a previously created workflow variable.
Start Document Set Approval Process*	Allows you to start a custom approval process for an entire document set at once.

* New in SharePoint 2010.

List Actions

This category contains a number of new actions as well as an extensive set of actions you might have worked with in SharePoint Designer 2007. List actions allow you to manipulate list items, including creating, copying, and deleting list items. These actions can be applied to documents within libraries as well as to list items because libraries are just special lists. This group also includes specific document-related actions, such as undoing a check out. The default list actions are shown in Table A-4.

Table A-4 **List Actions**

Action	Description
Add List Item Permissions**	Allows you to grant additional list item permissions to a selection of SharePoint users.
Check In Item	Allows you to check in the current item or specify a column name and value that indicate the item that must be checked in. This action requires you to specify a check-in comment that is either a string value or a lookup value that is retrieved from a data source such as another list on the same SharePoint site or from a previously created workflow variable. This action can be used only with libraries.
Check Out Item	Complements the Check In Item action. This action allows you to check out the current item or specify a column name and value that indicate which item must be checked out.
Copy List Item	Allows you to copy an existing list item to another list on the SharePoint site. The list item can be the current list item or you can select a column and value to indicate which list item you want to copy. There must be at least one column that is common to both lists.
Create List Item	Allows you to create a new list item in a list on the SharePoint site. You can choose any list you want, but you must specify values for all required fields. These values can also be lookup values that are retrieved from a data source such as another list on the same SharePoint site or from a previously created workflow variable.
	The list item ID of this action can be saved to a new or existing workflow variable.
Declare Record*	Allows you to declare an item as a record for records management. SharePoint records management functionality allows organizations, using some advanced tools, to manage records from the time the records are created up to their eventual disposal. Usually, records are managed to adhere to specific compliance regulations.
Delete Drafts*	Allows you to delete a draft version of an item. Major and minor versioning need to be enabled to use this action.
Delete Item	Allows you to delete the current item or specify a column name and value that indicate which item must be deleted.
Delete Previous Versions	Allows you to delete all but the current version of an item. Versioning needs to be enabled to use this action.
Discard Check Out Item	Allows you to discard the check out of the current item or specify a column name and value that indicate for which item the check out must be discarded.

Inherit List Item Parent Permissions**	Allows you to specify a list item from which the current list item will inherit permissions. Please note that you cannot use this action to inherit from list permissions. If you want a list item to inherit list permissions, you should not use a workflow action; you can configure this via the SharePoint list management pages instead.
Remove List Item Permissions**	Allows you to select the list item permissions that will be removed from the current set of permissions for a selection of SharePoint users.
Replace List Item Permissions**	Allows you to select a set of list item permissions that will replace the current permission settings for a selection of SharePoint users.
Set Content Approval Status*	Allows you to set the current status of the list item. You can also add comments in the form of a string value or a lookup value that is retrieved from a data source such as another list on the same SharePoint site or from a previously created workflow variable.
Set Field in Current Item	Allows you to specify the value of a selected column of a list item. This value can also be a lookup value that is retrieved from a data source such as another list on the same SharePoint site or from a previously created workflow variable.
Undeclare Record*	Complements the Declare Record action. This action allows you to roll back the declaration of an item as a record for record management.
Update List Item	Allows you to update a list item in a list on the SharePoint site. You can choose any list you want and specify the values for the required fields. This value can also be a lookup value that is retrieved from a data source such as another list on the same SharePoint site or from a previously created workflow variable.
Wait for Change in Document Check-Out Status*	Allows you to pause the execution of the workflow until the current document check-out status is changed.
Wait for Field Change in Current Item	Allows you to pause the execution of the workflow until the value of a column in the list or library the workflow is attached to is equal or not equal to the value specified in this action. This specified value can also be a lookup value that is retrieved from a data source such as another list on the same SharePoint site or from a previously created workflow variable. In SharePoint Designer 2007, this action was listed in the Core Actions category.

* New in SharePoint Designer 2010.
** New in SharePoint 2010 and available only within an impersonation operation.

Relational Actions

A new category that is available on SharePoint Server 2010 installations. This group contains a single action that helps gather information about the social surroundings of a SharePoint user. The default relational action is listed in Table A-5.

Table A-5 Relational Action

Action	Description
Lookup Manager of a User*	Allows you to look at a SharePoint user's profile and return the user's manager specified in the profile. The output of this action can be saved to a new or existing workflow variable.

* New in SharePoint 2010.

Task Actions

The task actions manipulate task items. The default task actions are listed in Table A-6.

Table A-6 Task Actions

Action	Description
Assign a Form to a Group	Allows you to build a custom survey to collect information from one or more users. The workflow is paused until all users have completed the survey.
Assign a To-do Item	Allows you to assign a to-do item in the tasks list to one or more users. The workflow is paused until all users have completed the to-do item.
Collect Data from a User	Allows you to create and assign a task to a specified user or group. This task can contain custom form fields. The output of this action can be saved to a new or existing workflow variable.
Start Approval Process*	Allows you to start a custom approval process.
Start Custom Task Process*	Allows you to start a custom task process.
Start Feedback Process*	Allows you to start a custom feedback process.

* New in SharePoint 2010.

Task Behavior Actions

This is a special group of actions that are available only within approval workflows, such as Start Approval Process and Start Feedback Process, described in Appendix B. In such workflows, you can add task actions that let you modify the behavior of the task or task process.

When the task action is added, a new category, called Task Behavior Actions, is visible. The task behavior actions are listed in Table A-7. Depending on the context in a workflow, only a subset may be available at any one time.

Table A-7 Task Behavior Actions

Action	Description
Append Task**	Appends a new task and assigns it to a user.
Delegate Task**	Rescinds a task assigned to the current user and then assigns the task to a new user, which could be a single user or a group.
End Task Process*	Allows you to end the task process from within the workflow.
Escalate Task**	Allows you to assign a task to the manager of the user who is currently assigned the task.
Forward Task**	Similar to the Delegate Task. If the new user is a group, a task is created for each member in the group.
Insert Task**	Allows you to insert a new stage where the user specified in the action is the only participant.
Reassign Task**	Reassigns the task to another user.
Request a Change**	Allows you to request a change and assign a new task to the current user when the change is completed.
Rescind Task**	Completes the task without an outcome.
Send a Task Notification Email**	Allows you to include the Edit Task button in the e-mail message that is sent to specific users.
Set Content Approval Status (as author)*	Allows you to set the approval status to Approved, Rejected, or Pending. This action runs under the identity of the workflow author. Use this action if the person who starts the workflow instance does not have permissions to approve a document.
Set Task Field**	Allows you to set a field within a task item to a value. This value can also be a lookup value that is retrieved from a data source such as another list on the same SharePoint site or from a previously created workflow variable.
Wait for Change in Task Process Item*	Waits for any change in the item the task process is running on.
Wait for Deletion in Task Process Item*	Waits for the deletion of the item the task process is running on.

* New in SharePoint 2010.

** New in SharePoint 2010 and available only when customizing the Start Approval Process.

Utility Actions

A new category in SharePoint 2010. It is available on sites created using SharePoint Server and SharePoint Foundation. The extract substring actions replace the SharePoint Designer 2007 Build Dynamic String core action. The default utility actions are listed in Table A-8.

Table A-8 Utility Actions

Action	Description
Extract Substring from End of String*	Allows you to retrieve a part of a string, starting at the end.
Extract Substring from Index of String*	Allows you to retrieve a part of a string, starting at a specific position.
Extract Substring from Start of String*	Allows you to retrieve a part of a string, starting at the beginning.
Extract Substring of String from Index with Length*	Allows you to retrieve a part of a string of limited length, starting at a specific position.
Find Interval Between Dates*	Allows you to find an interval consisting of minutes, hours, or days between two dates.

* New in SharePoint 2010.

B Creating a New Approval Process

Thanks to the new Start Approval Process and Start Document Set Approval Process actions provided with Microsoft SharePoint Server 2010, you can now create your own approval process. These two actions are similar to the Approval workflow template that is available out of the box with SharePoint Server 2010, and they represent generic approval workflows that can be incorporated into your own custom workflow or amended to meet your needs. Prior to using these actions, you must be familiar with how to use the Approval workflow template in the browser. Additionally, it is important that you understand what these actions do and how you can modify them. I'll cover these topics in this appendix.

These actions are subworkflows—that is, workflow logic is already defined in the actions, and they use task items that are assigned to one or more users, known as *task participants*. The approval task item contains the fields Status, Due Date, Requested By, and Consolidated Comments and also a number of task buttons that depend on the configuration of the approval action. The form Approval.xsn is automatically created as a Microsoft InfoPath form with four views—Main, ChangeRequest, ChangeView, and ReassignTask.

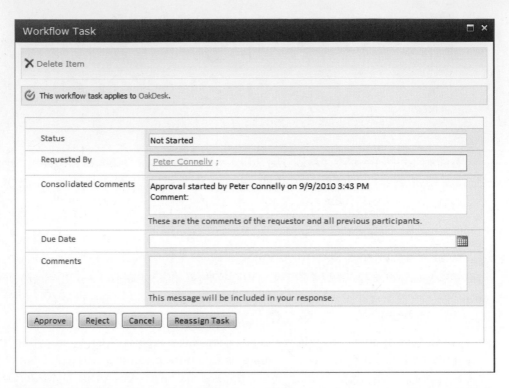

See Also For more information about customizing InfoPath forms, see Chapter 9, "Using Reusable Workflows and Workflow Forms."

To explore these actions in SharePoint Designer, create a new workflow (for example, a list workflow), and then add either of the aforementioned actions, such as the Start Approval Process action, to a step in the workflow, as described in Chapter 8, "Understanding Workflows."

The Start Approval Process action presents three links that you can use to customize the workflow: Approval, Current Item, and These Users. The Current Item link opens the Choose List Item dialog box, which you use to assign an object to the approval action.

No initiation form variables are created for these actions. You need to provide the information you find on the initiation form for the Approval workflow templates you use in the browser as configuration settings on the approval actions. Use the These Users link to open the Select Task Process Participants dialog box. The dialog box allows you to configure task participants, assignment stages, the task title, the duration per task, and the due date for the task process.

Tip If you want to mimic the Approval workflow templates in the browser, you need to create your own initiation form variables and pass them to the approval action.

The approval actions create a number of local variables, such as NotificationMessage, DueDateforAllTasks, Approvers, and CancelonChange to pass information between the different steps. These variables can then be used by subsequent conditions or actions that you add to the workflow.

Tip You can find a list of the local variables by clicking Local Variables on the Workflow tab.

Local Variables

The Approval link is quite different from other workflow action and condition links you have seen in this book. This link does not display a dialog box, but instead displays a page—the Approval page—that details the approval subworkflow. You can use the links on the Approval page to customize the subworkflow. The Start Feedback Process action can be similarly configured.

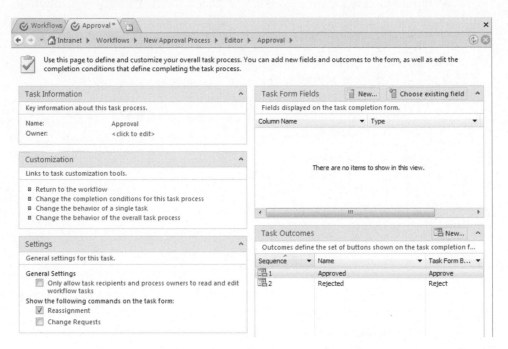

- **The Approval page contains the following areas: Task Information** Use to specify the name of the new approval process, which should be descriptive of the type of approval process you are creating and meaningful to users of this workflow. The Task Information area also allows you to specify the owner of the task process, which can be a user or a SharePoint group. Additional information about owners is described in the section about the Settings area of the page later in this appendix.

- **Task Form Fields** Use to collect information via a task form. You can add more custom data fields by clicking **New** in the title bar of the Task Form Fields area or by using the Form Fields tab and clicking New Site Column in the New group. The Add Field dialog box opens. You use this dialog box to create a site column.

  Tip Before you create a site column, check whether that site column already exists. By avoiding duplication, you prevent confusion about having a large number of similar site columns. When you create a site column, use a meaningful name so that other users who are creating solutions can easily identify the purpose and use of the site column.

Add Field	? X

  Field name:

  | |

  Description:

  | |
  | |
  | |

  Information type:

  | Single line of text | ▾ |

  ☑ Add to default view

  | < Back | Next > | Cancel |

Add Existing
Site Column

You can also create custom data fields from an existing site column by clicking **Choose Existing Field** in the title bar of the Task Form Fields area or by using the Form Fields tab and clicking Add Existing Site Column in the New group. The Site Columns Picker dialog box opens.

Outcome

New Site Column

Tip To activate the Form Fields tab on the ribbon, click Column Name in the Task Form Fields area.

● **Task Outcomes** Use to define the various outcomes for the approval process. By default, the outcomes **Approved** and **Rejected** are created. Outcomes are displayed as separate buttons on the task completion form in sequence order. You can add more outcomes by clicking **New** in the title bar of the Task Outcomes area or by using the Outcomes tab and clicking Outcome in the New group. The Outcomes tab also allows you to rename or delete an outcome or to move an outcome up or down to change the sequence order.

Tip To activate the Outcomes tab on the ribbon, click one of the outcomes in the Task Outcomes area.

● **Settings** Contains the following three options:

   ○ **Only Allow Task Recipients And Process Owners To Read And Edit Workflow Tasks** Select this option if you want only the task recipients and the process owner specified in the Task Information area to have read and edit access to workflow tasks.

○ **Reassignment**   Select this option to display an extra button on the task form that allows the task recipient to reassign the task to somebody else.

○ **Change Request**   Select this option to display an extra button on the task form that allows the task recipient to change the request itself.

● **Customization area**   Contains four links:

○ **Return To The Workflow**   Use this link to display the workflow editor.

○ **Change The Completion Conditions For This Task Process**   Select this link to display the Completion Conditions page. This page shows the actions that run every time a task is completed. You can add more conditions, actions, and steps and modify the completion conditions as needed.

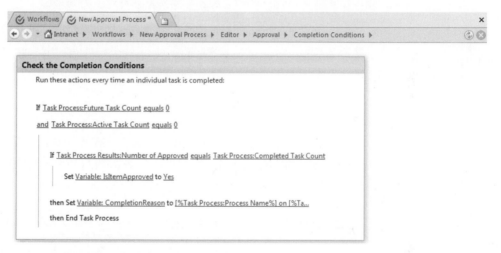

○ **Change The Behavior Of A Single Task**   Select this link to display the Task Behaviors page. This page contains five steps that are triggered by the following events:

The On Task Assigning event triggers the Before A Task Is Assigned step. This step is executed before individual task items are created.

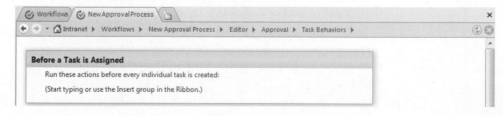

The On Task Pending event triggers the When A Task Is Pending step. This step is executed after an individual task item is created. The default configuration of this step adds history items to the workflow history list and sends task notifications via e-mail.

When a Task is Pending

Run these actions after every individual task has been created:

If Current Task:External Participant is empty

    Log Task created for [%Current Task:Assig... to the workflow history list

    then Email task notification to Current Task:Assigned To

Else

    Log Task created for [%Current Task:Assig... to the workflow history list

    then Email task notification to Workflow Context:Initiator

---

The On Task Expired event triggers the When A Task Expires step. This step runs when a task item does not have a Completed status after the task's due date has expired. It sends an e-mail task notification to the participant(s) the task is assigned to.

When a Task Expires

Run these actions every time an individual task is still incomplete past its due date:

Email task notification to Current Task:Assigned To

The On Task Deleted event triggers the When A Task Is Deleted step. This step runs when a task item is deleted. Two history log items are created, noting who deleted the task item and that the task item was automatically rejected because it was deleted. An e-mail notification is then sent to the participant(s) the task is assigned to.

When a Task is Deleted

Run these actions every time an individual task is deleted before it is completed:

Log Task assigned to [%Current Task:Assig... to the workflow history list

then Log Task assigned to [%Current Task:Assig... to the workflow history list

then Email Current Task:Assigned To

The On Task Completed event triggers the When A Task Completes step. This step is run every time a task is completed. It adds history workflow items and sets a local variable, CompletionReason, if the task item was rejected and the approval process is configured to cancel the workflow instance if a task item is rejected.

When a Task Completes

Run these actions every time an individual task is completed:

If Current Task:Outcome equals Approved

    Log Task assigned to [%Current Task:Assig... to the workflow history list

Else if Current Task:Outcome equals Rejected

    Log Task assigned to [%Current Task:Assig... to the workflow history list

    If Variable: CancelonRejection equals Yes

        Set Variable: CompletionReason to [%Task Process:Process Name%] on [%Ta...

        then End Task Process

○ **Change The Behavior Of The Overall Task Process**   Select this link to display the Task Process Behaviors page. Most of the steps on this page set values to many of the local variables, depending on the event that is triggered. This page contains four steps that are triggered by the following events:

On Approval Started   This event runs when an approval workflow instance starts.

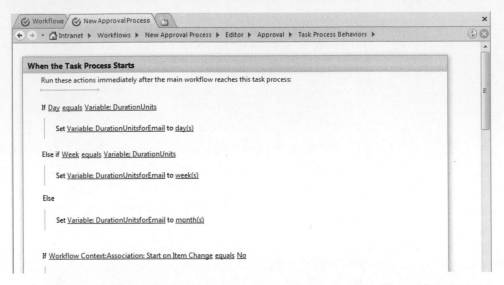

On Approval Running This event runs before an approval workflow instance assigns its first task item. It consists of two nested steps that run in parallel.

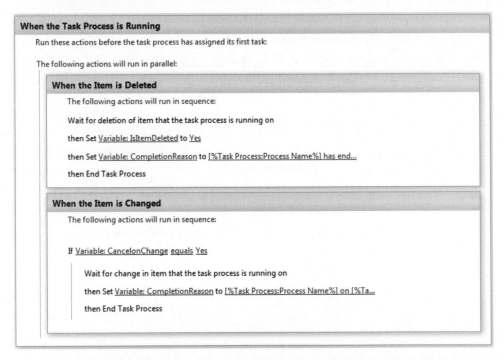

On Approval Canceled This event runs when a task process is canceled.

When the Task Process is Canceled

Run these actions if the task process is canceled:

If <u>Workflow Context:Association: Start on Item Change</u> <u>equals</u> <u>No</u>

    If <u>Workflow Context:Association: Start to Approve Major Version</u> <u>equals</u> <u>Yes</u>

    <u>or</u> <u>Variable: EnableContentApproval</u> <u>equals</u> <u>Yes</u>

        Set content approval of item that the task process is running on to <u>Rejected</u> (run as the workflow author)

then Email <u>Workflow Context:Initiator</u>

then Log <u>[%Task Process:Process Name%] on [%Ta...</u> to the workflow history list

then Set workflow status to <u>Canceled</u>

On Approval Completed   This event runs when the last individual task is completed or when the End Task Process action is run.

When the Task Process Completes

Run these actions either when the last individual task is complete, or when the End Task Process action is run:

If <u>Variable: IsItemApproved</u> <u>equals</u> <u>Yes</u>

    Set workflow status to <u>Approved</u>

    If <u>Workflow Context:Association: Start on Item Change</u> <u>equals</u> <u>No</u>

        If <u>Workflow Context:Association: Start to Approve Major Version</u> <u>equals</u> <u>Yes</u>

        <u>or</u> <u>Variable: EnableContentApproval</u> <u>equals</u> <u>Yes</u>

            Set content approval of item that the task process is running on to <u>Approved</u> (run as the workflow author)

Else

    Set workflow status to <u>Rejected</u>

    If <u>Workflow Context:Association: Start on Item Change</u> <u>equals</u> <u>No</u>

        If <u>Workflow Context:Association: Start to Approve Major Version</u> <u>equals</u> <u>Yes</u>

        <u>or</u> <u>Variable: EnableContentApproval</u> <u>equals</u> <u>Yes</u>

            Set content approval of item that the task process is running on to <u>Rejected</u> (run as the workflow author)

C Administrative Tasks Using SharePoint 2010

This appendix details tasks that you might find you need to complete. Explanations of these tasks are outside the scope of this book, but they can be found in the following resources:

- *Microsoft SharePoint Foundation 2010 Step by Step*, by Olga Londer and Penelope Coventry (Microsoft Press, 2011). Print ISBN: 978-0-7356-2726-0, ISBN 10: 0-7356-2726-6.

- *Microsoft SharePoint 2010 Administrator's Companion*, by Bill English, Brian Alderman, and Mark Ferraz (Microsoft Press, 2011). Print ISBN: 978-0-7356-2720-8, ISBN 10: 0-7356-2720-7.

- *Microsoft SharePoint 2010 Administrator's Pocket Consultant*, by Ben Curry (Microsoft Press, 2010). Print ISBN: 978-0-7356-2722-2, ISBN 10: 0-7356-2722-3.

SharePoint 2010 products on Microsoft's TechNet site, at *technet.microsoft.com/en-us/library/ee428287(office.14).aspx*.

This appendix describes the following administrative tasks:

- Downloading, installing, and configuring SharePoint Foundation 2010 on a single server with a built-in database.

- Creating a site collection.

- Enabling all site templates on a SharePoint Server site.

- Restricting the use of SharePoint Designer 2010 at the Web-application level.

- Configuring permissions on external content types.

- Configuring the external content type profile page host.

- Enabling or disabling user-defined workflows.

Installing SharePoint Foundation 2010

This section details how to download, install, and configure SharePoint Foundation 2010 on a single server with a built-in database. This server can be used as a temporary SharePoint environment. More information about server computer requirements can be found in "Using the Practice Files" at the beginning of this book.

See Also For more information on deploying a single server with a built-in database, see *technet.microsoft.com/en-us/library/cc288005(office.14).aspx*.

Important You need to follow these steps only if you do not already have access to a SharePoint environment.

 SET UP Open your browser on the computer where you want to install SharePoint Foundation 2010 before beginning this exercise.

1. Browse to **www.microsoft.com/downloads/** and search for **SharePoint Foundation 2010**.

2. In the list of results, click the most recent copy of SharePoint Foundation 2010—that is, the download with the title **Microsoft SharePoint Foundation 2010 with SPx**, where *x* is the number of the latest service pack. If no service pack has been released, click **Microsoft SharePoint Foundation 2010**.

   Tip At the time of writing, the link that points to the most recent copy of SharePoint Foundation 2010 is *www.microsoft.com/downloads/en/details. aspx?FamilyID=49c79a8a-4612-4e7d-a0b4-3bb429b46595*.

3. Click **Download**. Click **Save**, and save the file to your computer's Desktop.

4. Double-click the file you downloaded.

5. On the **Microsoft SharePoint Foundation 2010** start page, below **Install**, click **Install software prerequisites**.

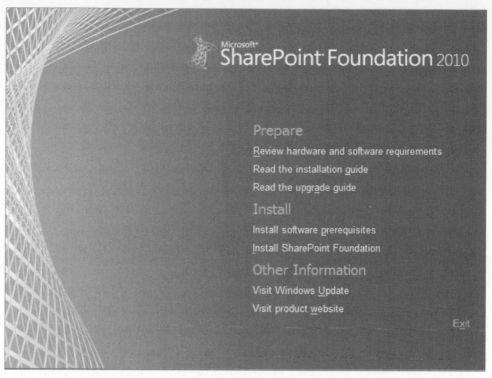

6. On the **Welcome to the Microsoft SharePoint 2010 Products Preparation Tool page**, click **Next**.

7. If you agree with the **Microsoft Software License Terms**, select the **I accept the terms of the License Agreement(s)** check box, and click **Next**.

    The prerequisites are downloaded from the Internet and installed. This step can take some time; please be patient.

8. On the **Your system needs to restart to continue. Press Finish to restart your system** page, click **Finish**.

9. After the computer has rebooted, log on as an administrator to complete the installation of the software prerequisites, and then on the **Installation Complete** page, click **Finish**.

10. Double-click the file that you saved on your computer's **Desktop**.

11. On the **Microsoft SharePoint Foundation 2010** start page, below **Install**, click **Install SharePoint Foundation**. If you agree with the **Microsoft Software License Terms**, select the **I accept the terms of this agreement** check box, and click **Continue**.

12. Click **Standalone** to begin the installation.

    Important You should use a stand-alone installation only for a developer or evaluation SharePoint installation.

13. On the **Run Configuration Wizard** page, leave the **Run the SharePoint Products Configuration Wizard now** check box selected, and click **Close**.

    The SharePoint Products Configuration Wizard launches automatically.

14. On the **Welcome to SharePoint Products** page, click **Next**. In the warning box that appears, click **Yes** to acknowledge that some services need to be stopped during configuration.

    SharePoint Foundation is installed and configured. This step can take some time; please be patient.

15. On the **Configuration Successful** page, click **Finish**.

    The browser will open the home page of the top level of a site collection. This top-level site is created using the Team Site template.

    Troublshooting Depending on how your server is configured, you might be prompted to log on. Enter the administrator's user name and password.

 CLEAN UP Close the browser.

Creating a Site Collection

If you have been given total control of a SharePoint environment for the purpose of completing the exercises in this book and need to create a site collection, complete the following steps.

 SET UP Log on with sufficient rights to use the SharePoint 2010 Central Administration Web site.

1. On the Windows taskbar, click the **Start**, point to **All Programs**, click **Microsoft SharePoint 2010 Products**, and then click **SharePoint 2010 Central Administration**.

2. If the **User Account Control** dialog box appears, click **Yes**, or if prompted, type your user name and password, and then click **OK**.

3. In the **Application Management** section, click **Create site collections**.

   The Create Site Collection page is displayed.

   Tip In the Web Application section, if the Web application in which you want to create the site collection is not selected, click the arrow to the right of the Web application name, and then click Change Web Application. On the Select Web Application page, click the Web application in which you want to create the site collection.

4. In the **Title and Description** section, type the title and description for the site collection.

5. In the **Web Site Address** section, under **URL**, select the path to use for your URL (for example, an included path such as /sites/, or the root directory, /).

6. In the **Template Selection** section, in the **Select a template** list, select the template that you want to use for the top-level site in the site collection. For the purposes of this book, choose **Team Site** from the **Collaboration** tab if you are working with SharePoint Foundation. Choose **Publishing Portal** from the **Publishing** tab if you are using SharePoint Server.

7. In the **Primary Site Collection Administrator** section, enter the user name (in the form DOMAIN\username) for the user who will be the site collection administrator.

8. Click **OK**.

 **CLEAN UP** Close the browser.

Enabling All Site Templates on a SharePoint Server Site

In a SharePoint Server environment, when you want to create a new site, you might find that the site template you want to use in the browser is not listed on the Create page.

Troubleshooting If you want to base the new site on one of the practice solution .wsp files, be sure you have first uploaded the file to the Solutions gallery. See "Using the Practice Files" section at the start of the book.

To make the site template visible in the site template list, complete the following steps. These steps can be completed only on publishing sites or on sites on which the SharePoint Server Publishing Infrastructure site-collection feature and the SharePoint Server Publishing site feature are enabled.

 **SET UP** In your browser, display the home page of the SharePoint site where you want to create the new site as a subsite. You must be logged on as a member of the Site Owners group.

1. On the **Site Actions** menu, click **Site Settings**.

   The site settings page is displayed.

2. In the **Look and Feel** section, click **Page layouts and site templates**.

   The Page Layout And Site Template Settings page is displayed.

3. In the **Subsite Templates** section, select **Subsites can use any site template**, and then click **OK**.

   The site settings page is displayed.

CLEAN UP Close the browser.

Note These steps affect the visiblity of site templates when you are using the browser. This procedure does not restrict the site templates available when you use SharePoint Designer.

Restricting the Use of SharePoint Designer 2010 at the Web-Application Level

SharePoint Designer 2010 is a powerful tool that you can use to create robust, business-focused solutions that require little if any knowledge of the code that is needed to make them work. This does not mean that SharePoint Designer should be used by everyone in an organization. The use of SharePoint Designer can be restricted in many ways. Perhaps the easiest is for the site owner to give users of the site only the minimum permission rights they need to complete their tasks. However, a SharePoint server administrator can restrict at the Web-application level what site collection administrators can and cannot do with SharePoint Designer.

Note The SharePoint Designer settings at the Web-application level are the same as those available at the site-collection level, which are detailed in Chapter 1, "Exploring SharePoint Designer." However, when configured at the Web-application level, these settings affect all site collection administrators, site collections, and sites within the Web application. When they are configured at the site-collection level, they apply only to site owners and designers and sites within that site collection.

To apply restrictions at the Web-application level, complete the following steps.

 SET UP Log on with sufficient rights to use the SharePoint 2010 Central Administration Web site.

1. On the Windows taskbar, click **Start**, point to **All Programs**, click **Microsoft SharePoint 2010 Products**, and then click **SharePoint 2010 Central Administration**.

2. If the **User Account Control** dialog box appears, click **Yes**. If prompted, type your user name and password, and then click **OK**.

3. In the **Application Management** section, click **Manage web applications**.

    The Web Applications page is displayed.

4. Click the Web application for which you want to restrict the use of SharePoint Designer. On the ribbon, in the Manage group on the **Web Applications** tab, click General Settings, and then click SharePoint Designer.

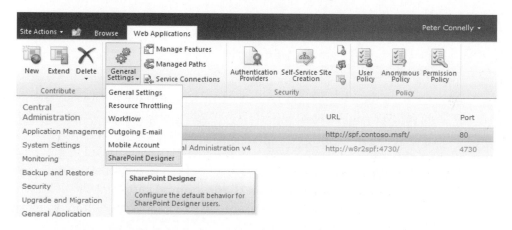

    The SharePoint Designer Settings dialog box is displayed.

5. Clear or select the check boxes as needed, and then click OK.

 CLEAN UP Close the browser.

Configuring Permissions on External Content Types

When an external content type (ECT) is created by SharePoint Designer, by default no permissions are configured to allow users to see the data in external lists created from the ECT.

To set permissions on an ECT, your SharePoint server administration needs to take the following steps on the SharePoint 2010 Central Administration Web site.

 SET UP Log on with sufficient rights to use the SharePoint 2010 Central Administration Web site.

1. On the Windows taskbar, click **Start**, point to **All Programs**, click **Microsoft SharePoint 2010 Products**, and then click **SharePoint 2010 Central Administration**.

2. If the **User Account Control** dialog box appears, click **Yes**, or if prompted, type your user name and password, and then click **OK**.

3. In the **Application Management** section, click **Manage service applications**.

   The Service Applications page is displayed.

4. Click the name of the Business Data Connectivity service for which you want to manage permissions.

5. On the **Service Application Information** page, on the **Edit** tab, check that **External Content Types** is selected in the **View** group, and then select the check box to the left of the ECT for which you want to configure permissions, such as **SPD SBS Customers**.

6. On the **Edit** tab, click **Set Object Permissions** in the **Permissions** group.

7. In the **Set Object Permissions** dialog box, enter the appropriate users or groups and assign the appropriate permissions.

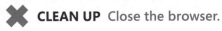 **CLEAN UP** Close the browser.

Configuring the External Content Type Profile Page Host

The Business Data Connectivity service profile pages are used to display the details of an instance of an ECT. In SharePoint Foundation, you must build these profile pages yourself and place controls or Web Parts to display the data. In SharePoint Server, once the profile page hosted location is configured, you can create profile pages with one click of a button by using the Central Administration Web site or SharePoint Designer.

To configure the profile page host use the following steps.

1. Open a browser, and go to the **SharePoint 2010 Central Administration** Web site.
2. Under **Application Management**, click **Manage Service Applications**.
3. On the **Service Applications** page, click the name of the Business Data Connectivity service that you want to configure.
4. On the **Edit** tab, click **Configure** in the **Profile Pages** group.

   The Configure External Content Type Profile Page Host dialog box is displayed.
5. Select the **Enable Profile Page Creation** option, and type the URL of the site where the profile page will be hosted.
6. Click **OK**. The Configure External Content Type Profile Page Host dialog box closes.

 **CLEAN UP** Close the browser.

Enabling or Disabling User-Defined Workflows

At the Web-application level, SharePoint server administrators can control the ability of users to use, create, modify, and publish SharePoint 2010 declarative workflows, such as those created using SharePoint Designer and some of the out-of-the-box workflows, such as *Collect Feedback—SharePoint 2010*, *Approval—SharePoint 2010*, *Collect Signatures—SharePoint 2010*, and *Publishing Approval*. By default, user-defined workflows are enabled whenever a Web application is created.

Tip The Disposition Approval, Three-State, Schedule Web Analytics Alert, and Schedule Web Analytics Reports workflow templates are not user-defined workflows. When user-defined workflows are disabled at the Web-application level, you can still create, modify, and use workflows that have been created from these workflow templates.

When you disable user-defined workflows and then try to create a workflow in SharePoint Designer, a dialog box opens explaining that user-defined workflows have been disabled by the SharePoint administrator, and you will not be able to create any new workflows.

When user-defined workflows are disabled, existing user-defined workflows are not deleted. You can modify existing user-defined workflows and save them. However, when you try to publish a modified workflow, a Workflow Error dialog box appears, stating that the workflow files were saved but cannot be run.

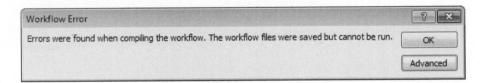

To enable or disable user-defined workflows, complete the following steps.

 SET UP Log on with sufficient rights to use the SharePoint 2010 Central Administration Web site.

1. On the Windows taskbar, click **Start**, point to **All Programs**, click **Microsoft SharePoint 2010 Products**, and then click **SharePoint 2010 Central Administration**.

2. If the **User Account Control** dialog box appears, click **Yes**, or if prompted, type your user name and password, and then click **OK**.

3.   In the **Application Management** section, click **Manage web applications**.

The Web Applications page is displayed.

4.   Click the Web application for which you want to restrict the use of SharePoint Designer. On the ribbon, in the Manage group, click General Settings, and then click Workflow.

The Workflow Settings dialog box is displayed.

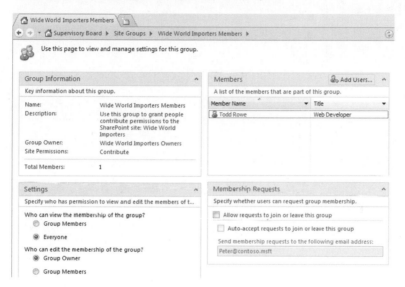

5.   In the User-Defined Workflows section, select the **Yes** or **No** option as needed, and then click OK.

✖   **CLEAN UP**   Close the browser.

Glossary

association A relationship between two external content types (ECTs).

BCS See *Business Connectivity Services (BCS)*.

BDC See *Business Data Connectivity (BDC)*.

breadcrumb A sequence of links that allows users to navigate or keep track of their location. See *global navigation breadcrumb* and *local breadcrumb*.

Business Connectivity Services (BCS) Enables users to read and write data from external systems through Web services, databases, and Microsoft .NET Framework assemblies.

Business Data Catalog A SharePoint Server 2007 feature that provides connectivity to back-end business systems and data sources. Renamed Business Connectivity Services (BCS) in SharePoint 2010.

Business Data Connectivity (BDC) The BDC provides the BCS connectivity component. It uses the declarative model that you can create using SharePoint Designer.

cascading style sheet (CSS) A style sheet language interpreted by a browser that describes the presentation of a Web page.

child site A site within a site collection, where there is a hierarchy of a top-level site and one or more child sites, also called subsites.

Code view Displays the code that a page contains, showing the HTML tags, client-side script (such as JavaScript), and controls. The code elements are color-coded to make it easier to distinguish the text that users see in their browser from the code surrounding the text. Each line of code is numbered so that error messages can reference them, and you can quickly identify problems.

column A SharePoint list or library contains columns or fields that define the kind of data that is collected for each list item or document. The values that each column contains are referred to as metadata.

composite key A primary key that is made from multiple columns.

content page An ASP.NET page that is combined with a master page on the Web server to produce an HTML page that is sent to the client to be rendered in the browser. An example of a content page is the home page of a SharePoint site, Home.aspx

content placeholder Placed on a ASP.NET master page; it defines a region for content and renders all text, markup, and server controls from the related content control found on a content page.

content region An alternative name for a content placeholder.

content types Content types define a reusable collection of settings that can include columns, workflows, and other attributes.

contributor settings Settings that control how SharePoint Designer 2007 can be used to modify a SharePoint site. This feature was removed in SharePoint Designer 2010 and replaced with advanced edit mode and restrictions that can be placed on SharePoint Designer 2010 at the Web-application and site-collection levels.

controls Components that are commonly used on Web sites. Controls are defined to display a calendar, change a password, or validate entry in an input form, for example.

CSS specificity Determines which CSS style is applied by a browser.

custom actions Define an extension to the user interface, such as a command on the server ribbon, a link on the site settings page, or a command on the list item menu.

customized Web page A Web page that is stored in the SQL Server content database. Previously known as an unghosted Web page in Windows SharePoint Services 2.0, where they caused significant performance implications. These performance implications have mostly been removed from Windows SharePoint Services 3.0 and Microsoft SharePoint Foundation 2010 with the use of ASP.NET 2.0, master pages, and SharePoint features. Web pages cannot be customized using the browser, but they can be customized by using SharePoint Designer.

custom master page This is a site property, represented by the token ~masterurl/customer. master, that is used by publishing pages in a publishing site.

Data Form Web Part (DFWP) A Web Part that reads data from and writes data to a data source in the form of XML and applies XSLT to it. SharePoint Designer allows you to add Data Form Web Parts to a Web Part page and has a WYSIWYG XSLT editor, so you don't need to know XSLT to customize a Data Form Web Part.

Data View Web Part (DVWP) A Web Part that allows you to view and manage data coming from different data sources. See *Data Form Web Part (DFWP)*.

default master This is a site property, represented by the token ~masterurl/default.master, that points to a master page that is used by all pages in your site.

Design view Displays the page in the SharePoint Designer workspace as it would appear in a browser and provides a WYSIWYG editing environment.

dirty page A page that you have changed using SharePoint Designer but have not saved. Denoted by an asterisk on the page tab.

dynamic-link library (DLL) A shared program library, also known as an assembly. For example, when you create a solution for SharePoint in Visual Studio 2010 that includes several class or program files and then build that solution, Visual Studio generates a file name with the extension .dll.

ECT See *external content type*.

Extensible Application Markup Language (XAML) A language used by the Windows Workflow Foundation (WF) to describe workflows.

eXtensible Markup Language (XML) A defined markup language for documents that describes document content and structure rather than appearance. An XML document has to be formatted before it can be read, and the formatting is usually accomplished by using an XSL template file.

eXtensible Stylesheet Language (XSL) A language used to create stylesheets for XML, similar to CSS (cascading style sheets) used for HTML. XSL Transformations (XSLT) can be used to transform XML to HTML or to another type of XML.

eXtensible Stylesheet Language Transformation (XSLT) A language for transforming XML documents into other XML documents.

external content type (ECT) Represents data that is stored in an external data source, such as a SQL Server or other relational database, SharePoint, and Web services. ECTs are created using SharePoint Designer 2010 or Visual Studio 2010.

external data column A column in a list or library that stores data that originally existed outside SharePoint.

external list Used to present data that is stored outside SharePoint.

feature Allows you to activate/deactivate functionality in a site, site collection, Web application, or farm.

field controls Used on page layouts to define the strict layout and data entry constraints of content. They bind to columns in the Pages publishing library.

File Transfer Protocol (FTP) Protocol used for copying files to and from remote computer systems on a network using TCP/IP. The mechanism cannot be used on SharePoint sites, and the FTP client was removed from SharePoint Designer 2010.

foreign key A column that points to the primary key of another list or database table. This establishes a relationship between the two lists or between two database tables.

formula column Additional columns that can be created using the XPath Expression Builder.

ghosted Web pages The same as uncustomized Web pages.

globally reusable workflow A workflow that can be used as a workflow template that is reusable for all sites within a site collection. SharePoint Server 2010 is shipped with three globally reusable workflows. Additional globally reusable workflows can be created using SharePoint Designer.

global master pages Master pages defined centrally and used by most sites, no matter which site definition the site is created from.

global meeting workspace master page A Master page defined centrally and used by all sites created from a meeting workspace site definition.

global navigation breadcrumb A navigation icon next to Site Actions that displays the ScreenTip "Navigate Up" and shows the path from the top-level site to the current site. See also *local breadcrumb*. Users can use a combination of the two breadcrumbs to navigate or keep track of their location.

HTTP GET method Used to communicate with the Web server. The information is appended to the end of the URL. Usually used to retrieve data from the Web server.

HTTP POST method Used to communicate with the Web server. The information is provided in the body of the request. Used to transmit data to the Web server, where the data is stored, updated, or deleted. The data could also involve ordering a product or sending an e-mail message.

inline editing A configured page that can be used to display, edit, insert, or delete list items, where links are added to every row so that in the browser you can edit items directly in place.

layer An absolute positioned HTML division <div> tag. You use the <div> tag to group elements so that you can format them with styles or create animations or flyout menus.

library A specialized list that contains files and metadata properties associated with those files. Microsoft SharePoint Foundation 2010 has four types of libraries: Document, Form, Wiki Page, and Picture. SharePoint Server 2010 contains additional libraries, such as Report, Translation Management, Data Connection, and Slide. See *list*.

list A container that stores structured tabular data items that are related to one another through similar values, metadata, or security settings. Lists provide columns for storing metadata and a user interface for viewing and managing the items.

list template A definition of a list that you can use as a blueprint to create a new list or library in the browser. List templates are stored in the SQL Server database and include information about the columns, list views, and forms to be created, plus general settings such as whether versioning or content approval is enabled when the list is created. Optionally, list templates can contain content—that is, list items or, if the list template is for a library, documents together with their metadata.

local breadcrumb A sequence of links that shows the path from the home page of a site to the current page. See also *global navigation breadcrumb*. Users can use a combination of the two breadcrumbs to navigate or keep track of their location.

master page A special ASP.NET 2.0 Web page that allows you to share code between pages. There primary use is to provide a Web site with a consistent look and feel and navigation for each page within a site

metadata Data about data. For example, the metadata for a file can include the title, subject, author, and size of the file. In a document library, the metadata for a file is stored in the columns of the document library.

namespace Defines an entry point within an assembly. All controls that are similar are placed in the same namespace.

NaN Not a Number; a label displayed when you use a presentation column in an XPath expression to complete mathematical computations.

node An XPath reference to XML elements, attributes, and content

On Object User Interface (OOUI) A small arrow floating just outside a control that can be used to toggle the visibility of a task panel.

page layout A page template that strictly controls the layout of content on a page. Publishing pages are based on a page layout.

personas Characters created to represent different user types within a targeted demographic or with a specific attitude and/or behavior set that might use a site, brand, or product in a similar way.

PlaceHolderMain A SharePoint content placeholder control that defines a region of a page that contains unique content on a per page basis.

primary key A unique identifier for each row in a database table or for each list item in a list.

Publishing Portal A site hierarchy for an Internet-facing and intranet-facing Web site. It includes a home page and subsites. Most of these Web sites are based on the Publishing Site With Workflow template that uses SharePoint Server Web content management functionality. Typically, these Web sites have more readers than contributors.

Publishing site A Web site that uses SharePoint Server Web content management functionality. Contributors can work on draft versions of a publishing page, which, once it is approved, is made visible to readers. The approval process is also known as publishing.

Recycle Bin You can use the Recycle Bin to restore items that have been deleted from the Web site. It provides two-stage protection against accidental deletions. When you delete a document or other item from the SharePoint site, it is deleted from the Web site and moved to the Web site's Recycle Bin, where it can be restored if needed. If you then delete this item from the Web site's Recycle Bin, it is moved to the site collection's Recycle Bin. From there, the document can be restored to its original location or permanently deleted.

Representational State Transfer (REST) Similar to a SOAP service in that it allows the transport of XML data between computer systems. However, unlike a SOAP service, REST supports only the four basic application methods: GET, POST, PUT, and DELETE.

REST See *Representational State Transfer (REST)*.

Section 508 U.S. government accessibility guidelines.

SharePoint farm One or more servers that are used in a SharePoint installation and share one SharePoint configuration database.

Simple Object Access Protocol (SOAP) A protocol for transporting XML data between computer systems, normally using HTTP or HTTPS.

site collection A set of Web sites in a Web application that has the same owner and that share administrative settings. Each Web site collection contains a top-level Web site and can contain one or more subsites, also known as child sites. You can have multiple site collections within each Web application.

site column A reusable column that is created at the site collection or site level and can be used across multiple sites, lists, and libraries.

site definition A set of files that define the capabilities of a SharePoint site. Site definition files include .xml, .aspx, .ascx, and .master page files, as well as document template files (for example, .dotx and .htm) and content files (for example, .gif and .docx). The files are located in the \\Program Files\Common Files\Microsoft Shared\web server extensions\14\TEMPLATE subdirectories of Web front-end servers that run SharePoint Foundation or SharePoint Server.

site template A blueprint used to create a SharePoint site, which can automatically generate lists, libraries, Web Parts, and features. This term can refer to a site definition or to a file that captures the configuration and customizations of a Web site at a point in time.

Split view Divides the SharePoint Designer workspace horizontally and displays Code view at the top and Design view at the bottom.

subsite See *child site*.

top-level site A Web site that does not have a parent Web site. The top-level site in a site collection is created from the SharePoint 2010 Central Administration Web site.

uncustomized Web page A Web page that references files on the file system of a SharePoint front-end server. In Windows SharePoint Services 2.0, these were known as ghosted Web pages. From a technical perspective, the SharePoint SQL Server content database contains a row in one of its tables for each Web page on a SharePoint site. For an uncustomized Web page, this row contains a pointer to the file on the file system.

unghosted Web pages The same as customized Web pages.

Universal Data Connection (UDC) An XML file format that contains data connection information; used when creating data sources in SharePoint Designer.

URL An alphanumeric address that is used to locate a Web site.

variations Part of the SharePoint Web content management functionality. Variations make content available to specific audiences on different sites by copying content from a source site to each target variation site. Often use to build multilingual sites.

view A Web page that displays a subset of the contents of a list or library based on specific criteria defined by the metadata. Views allow you to find information easily.

Web application Previously referred to as a virtual server, a Web application hosts SharePoint site collections that users can access over the HTTP or HTTPS protocol. The clients may be browsers or other servers.

Web Content Accessibility Guidelines (WCAG) Part of a series of Web accessibility guidelines published by the World Wide Web Consortium's Web Accessibility Initiative.

Web Part A modular unit of information that consists of a title bar, a frame, and content. Web Parts are the basic building blocks of a Web Part page.

Web Part zone A rectangular region on a Web page that facilitates working with Web Parts.

Web Service Description Language (WSDL) The description of the methods and parameters that a SOAP service supports. The service definition can be registered in a Universal Description Discovery and Integration (UDDI) registry.

workflow associator The person who associates a workflow template with a list, library, content type, or site.

Workflow Interchange (.vwi) file A Microsoft Visio 2010 zip file that contains workflow files used to import the workflow design into SharePoint Designer.

XML See *eXtensible Markup Language (XML)*.

XML Path Language (XPath) Provides a mechanism to manipulate and navigate through XML data. XPath models XML data as a tree of nodes. See *node*.

XML Web services Computer systems that provide services to other computer systems. The data is transferred between computer systems formatted as XML and is transported using the Simple Object Access Protocol (SOAP). The computer system that requests data is called the XML Web Service Requester or client, and the computer system that provides XML data is called the XML Web Service Provider.

XPath See *XML Path Language (XPath)*.

XSL See *eXtensible Stylesheet Language (XSL)*.

XSLT See *eXtensible Stylesheet Language Transformation (XSLT)*.

Index

V

About the Author

Penelope Coventry is a Microsoft Most Valuable Professional (MVP) for Microsoft SharePoint Server and an independent consultant based in the United Kingdom, with more than 30 years of industry experience. She currently focuses on the design, implementation, and development of SharePoint technology–based solutions. She has worked with SharePoint since 2001. Most recently, she has worked for the international financial services group Aviva PLC, the U.K. Parliament, and the ATLAS U.K. defense consortium, as well as provided consultancy services to Microsoft Gold partners ICS Solutions and Combined Knowledge. She has produced SharePoint-related courseware for Mindsharp since 2002.

Penny has authored and coauthored a number of books. They include both editions of *Microsoft Office SharePoint Designer 2007 Step by Step, Microsoft SharePoint 2010 Administrator's Companion, Microsoft Office SharePoint Server 2007 Administrator's Companion, Microsoft SharePoint Products and Technologies Resources Kit, Microsoft SharePoint Foundation 2010 Step by Step*, and both editions of *Microsoft Windows SharePoint Services Step by Step*. Penny is frequently seen at TechEd and IT Forum, either as a technical learning guide or on the SharePoint Ask-the-Experts panels. She also speaks at the SharePoint Best Practices conferences, the European SharePoint Evolution Conference, Swedish SharePoint and Exchange Forums, SharePoint User Group U.K. meetings, and U.K. SharePoint Saturdays.

Penny lives in Hinckley, Leicestershire, England, with her husband, Peter, and dog, Poppy.

What do you think of this book?

We want to hear from you!

To participate in a brief online survey, please visit:

microsoft.com/learning/booksurvey

Tell us how well this book meets your needs—what works effectively, and what we can do better. Your feedback will help us continually improve our books and learning resources for you.

Thank you in advance for your input!

Stay in touch!

To subscribe to the *Microsoft Press® Book Connection Newsletter*—for news on upcoming books, events, and special offers—please visit:

microsoft.com/learning/books/newsletter